Number Two

The Elma Dill Russell Spencer Foundation Series

Silhouette of Mary Austin Holley about 1827. It is one of a trio of silhouettes made for William A. Leavy, the others being of President Holley and of Leavy himself. The three silhouettes were bequeathed by Miss Elsie Leavy, of Austin, Texas, granddaughter of William A. Leavy, to Transylvania College. Courtesy Transylvania College Library.

MARY AUSTIN HOLLEY

A Biography

by

Rebecca Smith Lee

UNIVERSITY OF TEXAS PRESS : AUSTIN

Library of Congress Catalog Card No. 62-9787
Copyright © 1962 by Rebecca Smith Lee
All Rights Reserved

Printed in the United States of America by
the Printing Division of the University of Texas

For
MARION
and
OWEN

CONTENTS

ILLUSTRATIONS

MAPS

MARY AUSTIN HOLLEY

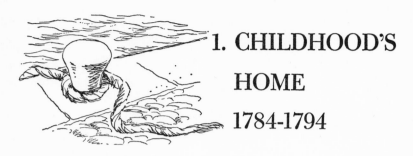

1. CHILDHOOD'S HOME
1784-1794

The small girl held tightly to her father's hand and matched his long strides with short, quick steps as they walked toward the Harbour. Fortunately for her they slowed down whenever passersby said, "Good day to you, Mr. Austin," and he in turn touched his tricorn hat and bowed respectfully. If one of them happened to be Captain Trowbridge, her father bade her brothers, who were older and livelier than Mary, to run along down to the Wharf while he passed the time of day with his neighbor. Usually it was only the weather they discussed, but, being maritime men, they sounded each other out for news of the whereabouts of the New Haven seagoing vessels. Staying close by her father's side, she listened attentively to what they said, and tucked her head demurely when the old captain lifted her chin and remarked, "'Tis a pretty child, Elijah, and she takes after your wife."

Besides being pretty, Mary was bright and knowing for a girl of eight. Already she understood that gentlemen who owned ships were very important people, much more so than the sunburnt men who sailed on them, and more important even than Uncle Nathan Beers, who had fought against the British. Her father had fought in the War, too, but when people greeted him with great respect they were thinking of his tall-masted ships tied up alongside his dock on the Long Wharf.

Her father's world was very large and exciting. On special days like this, when he took his older children with him down to his store on the Wharf, she was transported as if by magic out of the four walls of home, away from proper tasks of sewing fine seams or minding her little sister and brothers, into a more fascinating realm. As they turned out of their own lane into the top of Meadow Street, the broad thoroughfare leading down to the waterside, they passed the hammered stone house where their doctor lived. He was the richest physician in town, and drove four good horses just for his practice. Beyond were other solid homes owned by the men her father paused to greet. Then they stepped onto Long Wharf, and it was like walking on the windy deck of a long, long ship. Small whitecaps flecked the smooth, misty gray of the water, and her father showed them a sailing vessel tacking out toward the Lighthouse and the Sound beyond, going maybe to New York, maybe to the West Indies, or maybe to the Orient.[1]

Inside the storehouse was a warm smell of spice and tar, of sandalwood and pepper; and the dim light revealed a clutter of quarter-chests and crates as yet unpacked. She knew what was in some of them, because she had spelled out for herself the advertisement in the town's newspaper that "Elijah Austin has for sale at his store on the Union Wharf Bohea Tea, of a superior quality, in whole, half-, or quarter-chests, as low as it is sold in New York—Bristol & Queensware in Crate, assorted, very cheap." When Mr. Austin and his children entered, the clerks rose respectfully and fetched bills of lading and other papers for his inspection. No news yet about his great venture, the sealing vessel he had sent out to the Falkland Islands under Daniel Greene, with a letter of instruction authorizing him to take the skins on to Canton, trade them for a cargo of China goods, and come back around the world. Three years was a long time to wait for tidings, but Elijah was not at all discouraged. The store rang with brisk orders and scurrying feet.

Elijah was, indeed, a brisk man. The oldest of the four sons of Elias Austin, a prosperous tailor of the nearby town of Durham, he had made an early marriage and settled in New Haven along with his brother Archibald. They engaged in maritime trading, and, during the War, were involved for hundreds of pounds in fitting out privateers to prey on English craft. The brothers enlisted with their New Haven neighbors in the Governor's Foot Guards Company, which was called out for the Lexington alarm and other services.[2] The Austins were energetic and enterprising men, and in the strongest of them there was always an adventurous strain. For example, the youngest of the four brothers, Moses, had moved his wife and household out to the mountains of southwest Virginia to try his fortune in lead mines, a speculation that seemed unaccountably strange to his seafaring Connecticut kinsmen. But there was never any use warning an Austin not to be venturesome, as Elijah well knew when he felt his own pulse quickening at the thought of the profit to be made from that cargo on its way back from Canton. His ship would come in. He had only to watch the almanac a while longer. And now it was time to take the children home and join his wife in a cup of tea. It would be a very special bohea, kept in a mahogany caddy, and served in transparent chinaware cups.

The square, two-story white house in which Elijah Austin lived was just a jog eastward from the head of Meadow Street, on a short lane only recently christened Whiting Street.[3] It was a good residential neighborhood, built up by prosperous families mostly connected with ships and shipping. They were substantial citizens, who liked to live where they could smell the salt water and tell the time of day by the ships' bells. The Austin home was elm-shaded, with a lawn and flowers on one side and fruit trees on the other, and, of course, a kitchen garden. Although the town had nearly four thousand souls and boasted a fine market, every householder took pride in raising at least his own asparagus and love-apples. At the back of the house were the stable and carriage house. The Austins kept a carriage, and a sleigh for the hard winter months. The picket fence around the house was designed not so much to keep anyone out as to keep the numerous children of the household in. There were three sons older than Mary, and two more boys and a girl who were younger. The cradle up in Elijah's and Esther's large bedroom was empty this spring, but, God willing, by midsummer it would not be so.

Esther Phelps Austin, a handsome, buxom woman four or five years younger than her husband, was absorbed in Elijah and their children, and her many relatives.[4] She was deeply attached to this place, which had been their home for fifteen years. Elijah had bought it for her when they first settled in New Haven, and all her children except the oldest son had been born here. Year by year, as the business prospered, they had bought good furnishings, like the Windsor chairs and the desk and bookcase and bureau, all of deep-toned cherrywood. She now had two sideboards, more than fifty good plates besides the everyday ones, and both a silver service and a copper tea urn. She could entertain all her numerous relatives in New Haven at one time, at least with a cold collation, without borrowing a single thing from her two sisters who lived in the town.

They, too, possessed excellent silver and china, both Sister Mary, married to Deacon Nathan Beers, a thriving merchant, and Sister Abigail, whose husband, Judge Isaac Mills, had recently moved over from Long Island. As for being prosperous, however, no one in the whole connection was as well off as the bachelor brother, Timothy Phelps, a maritime merchant and dealer in iron. He was the one who had elegant taste in furnishings, and knew the value offhand of the pair of gilt looking glasses in Esther's parlor.

Esther had been born to solid comfort. Her father, Judge John Phelps, of Stafford Springs, an upstate Connecticut village, was a gentleman of the old school in his wig and ruffles and buckled shoes, who looked like George Washington and was, indeed, well acquainted with the General. The Judge had sent his daughters to be educated at a fashionable Boston boarding school for young ladies, where they had been given piano lessons in a manner so thorough as to require the accompaniment of a flute and a bass viol to preserve the time, thus necessitating the services of three music teachers. Esther was pretty, like all the Phelps women, and attractive, as well. At twenty she was sought in marriage by Elijah Austin, whose Continental uniform jibed with her father's politics. The Judge was a staunch member of the Hartford Convention that ratified the constitution of the new Confederation, and his iron foundries furnished cannon balls for Washington's armies.

Although Esther grew up in wartime as the daughter and wife of active patriots, she had no interest in politics or battles, and no restlessness of spirit. She was happy as the mistress of her comfortable home and bountiful garden, and her dearest wish was to live so the rest of her life. Her household and her children's upbringing revealed her privileged background—the Phelps sons had gone to Yale while their sisters attended Boston finishing schools. She saw to it that all her children grew up to respect book learning. The big boys, Horace and Elijah Phelps and Henry, showed small inclination as yet for college, but they were being taught to do their sums and read well and write a good, clear hand. Mary was the cleverest one at books, and was a natural musician as well. She must have learned to read notes along with her letters. Fortunately, all the young Austins were musically inclined, and no matter what befell them through the years, Esther's children sang whenever they were together. This love of song and their social graces were a heritage from her.

The year 1793 was a lucky one for Elijah Austin. Several of his cargoes from the West Indies and Europe proved profitable; but these were forgotten when at last word came that his sealing vessel from Canton was standing off the Lighthouse. History was made the day it sailed slowly into the Harbour. Every able-bodied man, woman, and child in the town was crowded at the water's edge to watch it glide toward the Wharf. The hull was blackened and the sails were patched, but bright flags fluttered in the breeze—the American flag with the same thirteen stars and thirteen stripes it bore when they sailed away, and beneath it Elijah's own house pennant.

Small Mary saw her father being rowed out to meet the vessel, and watched him step aboard to greet the crew, a memory of him that she was never to forget. Being a child, she could not know why every other merchant on the Wharf eyed with envy the fabulous cargo of tea and chinaware and silk and spices tied up at the Austin pier. They knew, with Yankee shrewdness, that Elijah had been right. This voyage of experiment in sending a sealing vessel direct to Canton had opened up a new era in American trade with China, and given New Haven a chance to get ahead of other ports.

The great good fortune of the venture was brought home to the Austin family a few days later when a drayload of strange smelling bales and boxes was unloaded and lugged into the house on Whiting Street. One bale turned out to be an enormous straw floor covering for the big parlor. This was for use in summer instead of the cherished Wilton carpet with flowery bouquets that had come from England. The Canton matting was wonderfully and beautifully made, with a colored border and the moon and stars in the center, and it became the wonder and admiration of the town. In Esther's opinion, the greatest prize from Canton was an elaborate set of china her husband had ordered for her, with the family initials on each of the hundreds of pieces, from a huge punch bowl to the tiny cups with "waiters." In the boxes were bolts of a lovely soft silk material called Canton crepe, blue like the sky or silvery white or a strange clear green. There were shining lacquered trays, and all sorts of intricate small boxes, and tiny figures carved of ivory or black wood.[5]

A few days later all the uncles and aunts and their families who lived in New Haven came visiting to look over what the Elijah Austins had got from China. The downstairs at Whiting Street was crowded. In the dining room the ladies carefully lifted the transparent cups to test their lightness, and in the parlor the gentlemen were being told in an undertone to stop by the store soon for a glimpse of some heathen paintings on glass that Captain Dan'l Greene had fetched back, which were not for female inspection. Esther's young ones and their many little cousins, all dressed in their company clothes and manners, stood back out of the way, ogling the strange treasures and listening to their fathers talk about fitting out another ship at once for the China trade.

In July, on the thirtieth day, Esther had her baby. It was her eighth child, and her sixth son. By now the excitement and bustle of a new baby's arrival was a familiar experience for Mary, who could clearly recall the birth of five-year-old Henrietta and of John Phelps, now two. This time she was big enough to help take care of a baby brother, and she felt a special responsibility for this smallest one. In due season there was another gathering of all the relatives in Whiting Street when the Reverend Bela Hubbard, rector of Trinity Church and their neighbor, christened him Charles, according to the rites of the recently established Protestant Episcopal Church of the United States of America, reading from a prayerbook so new it was scarcely well thumbed as yet.

Elijah Austin and his brother-in-law, Timothy Phelps,[6] and many of their kinsmen were staunch members of Trinity, which was supported mainly by the merchants and maritime families. These men were venturesome enough in business, but they preferred an orderly and tolerant religion. They left the mighty spiritual wrestlings about damnation or predestination and foreordination to sterner-minded congregations in the meetinghouses on the Green while they continued to worship in the traditional and comfortable Anglican manner. The old Church of England, transformed into the Episcopal denomination, had a better hold here in Connecticut than elsewhere in the New England states.

As New Haven congregations went, Trinity was not particularly old or large. The church was located off the Green, on a thoroughfare leading south toward the water front to which its modest spire gave the name of Church Street. Mr. Hubbard, the rector from its founding some forty years earlier, was a Connecticut man who had made the pilgrimage to England which was necessary for ordination shortly before the Colonies declared their independence. He remained a discreet and inoffensive Tory during the hostilities. The Austin children grew up hearing tales about the kindly little clergyman; how when the British occupied New Haven he had saved the property of some of his patriotic neighbors from destruction. Especially they recalled the story of the night he donned his clerical vestments and went out to rescue a poor, crazed girl from the redcoats who were chasing her along Whiting Street. Few people in the town harbored a grudge against the elderly rector for having remained loyal to his religion's country, and certainly no one in his own parish held it against him.

Soon after the War, the Trinity building was enlarged, and new pews added. Elijah Austin paid ten pounds fifteen shillings for Slip No. 11 on the southwest side of the church;[7] and here on Sundays he and Esther, with a row of sober-faced children, sat under the sound of the Reverend Bela's mild voice while he read the sonorous phrases of the traditional service and delivered his unexciting sermons from neatly written manuscripts.

Mary liked going to church. She gazed quietly around at the ladies' Sunday bonnets or stared up at the black wooden altar with the golden letters painted on it; and always she enjoyed the singing. Mr. Hubbard was devoted to good music, and accorded it a place in congregational worship that the psalm-singing folk in the meetinghouses deemed ungodly. Under his guidance the Trinity vestry had some years since bought an excellent organ and just recently engaged an organist from England at a salary of twenty guineas a year. They had also installed a notably fine bell, so big and loud that on more than one Saturday evening certain mischievous persons had roused the whole town by ringing it. The vestry, well manned with retired sea captains, had taken the matter in hand and put a stop to such rowdyism; but the recollection of the irreverent clamor lingered in the community until the youngest ear that heard it was old.

To small Mary and her brothers and sisters religion was a wholly natural part of a child's life, like visiting their grandparents or going to school or being proud of their new country. They heard so little about hell fire that Mary was never in her life really afraid of it. She cheerfully believed that the Austins and the Phelpses and all other good people were going to heaven when they died.

There was a great deal to keep the child busy the year she was going on eleven. She attended an excellent school, where she learned to write a neat, ladylike hand, and to spell very correctly, according to *Webster's New Spelling Book*. Mr. Noah Webster lived in New Haven, and scholars who saw him daily knew for a fact that he was as ugly as the picture of him that frowned at them in their books. For all that, they were proud to learn from a speller that praised George Washington and even mentioned the East Rock and the West Rock of their own New Haven.

In addition to reading and writing, little girls learned plain sewing and knitting and embroidery and drawing. Mary was very good at all these branches. She was clever at anything she did with her tiny hands. Unfortunately, numbers were not considered important for females, and whatever instruction in arithmetic she received made small impression on her mind. She never displayed any aptitude for figuring, then or later.

She liked the out-of-doors. In her mother's garden she knew the different kinds of flowers, trees, birds, and insects, and remembered their names. She was taken for walks in the well-farmed countryside near New Haven, and along the shore of the Harbour. From childhood she gave evidence of a quick mind and a retentive memory, and she was nicely educated in the polite fashion of the century into which she was born, which esteemed a well-stored mind, even in a lady.

Elijah Austin had an active part during this winter and spring in organizing a company to build a much larger sealing ship for the Chinese trade. Since the successful Canton experiment had been his idea, he plunged to the limit of his resources in the new project, borrowing from his father-in-law and from Timothy Phelps, from his Mills and Beers relatives, and wherever else he could. The keel of the new vessel was laid at Hartford under the direction of Daniel Greene, who was to command her. The project would cost upwards of forty-eight thousand dollars, all of it coming out of Connecticut pockets. Great hopes filled the air, and to clinch the profits of the new trade for their own port, a score or more of the town's prominent men established the New Haven Chamber of Commerce. Elijah, naturally, was one of the founders, as were some of his relatives.

The tardy New England spring of 1794 burst suddenly into the heat of summer, and the ships from foreign ports that docked at the Wharf reeked of bilge water and pitch. One of Elijah's returning West India vessels stood out in the Harbour, and, as was his custom, he went aboard with his clerk, the Reverend Mr. Hubbard's young nephew, to check the arrival. In the course of the inspection they opened a chest of clothes. All seemed in order, and both men went their ways, the owner to New York City on business, and his clerk to Derby.[8] It was a routine occurrence, and there seemed nothing in the events of that nineteenth day of June to make it memorable.

Three days later Elijah Austin died in New York of yellow fever, or, as it was written in the church records, of "ye putred fever." On the same day the clerk died also, of the same disease, which they had contracted from the West India vessel. Elijah must have been attended by kind and influential friends in New York City as he lay dying; for, in disregard of the panic that usually followed any death from the fever, his body was brought back to New Haven for burial.

A quick interment was required, with no decent interval for the remains to lie in state on Whiting Street or for sending out proper funeral notices and procuring mourning clothes for the family. The dreadful news spread like wildfire, and at once a crowd of brothers and cousins

MARY AUSTIN HOLLEY'S FAMILY RELATIONSHIPS

The following charts are designed to show the family relationships most important in the life of Mary Austin Holley. The information is derived from sources cited in the Bibliography, and no attempt has been made to verify or complete all the genealogical data.

I   THE ELIJAH AUSTIN-HORACE HOLLEY-WILLIAM BRAND FAMILY

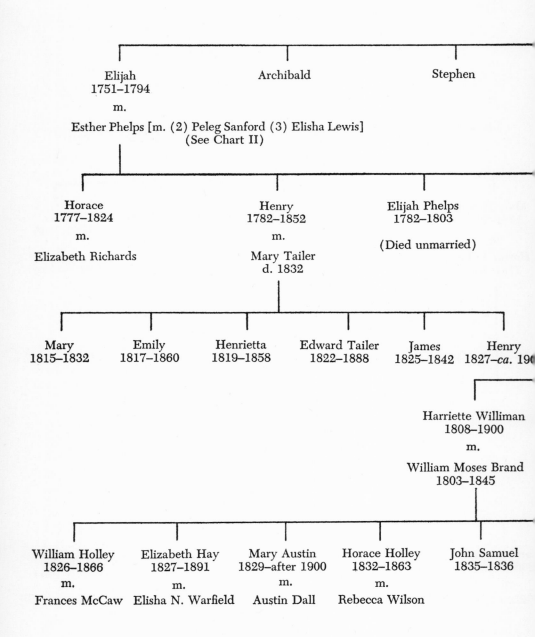

Elijah
1751–1794
m.
Esther Phelps [m. (2) Peleg Sanford (3) Elisha Lewis]
(See Chart II)

Archibald

Stephen

Horace
1777–1824
m.
Elizabeth Richards

Henry
1782–1852
m.
Mary Tailer
d. 1832

Elijah Phelps
1782–1803

(Died unmarried)

Mary
1815–1832

Emily
1817–1860

Henrietta
1819–1858

Edward Tailer
1822–1888

James
1825–1842

Henry
1827–ca. 190

Harriette Williman
1808–1900
m.
William Moses Brand
1803–1845

William Holley
1826–1866
m.
Frances McCaw

Elizabeth Hay
1827–1891
m.
Elisha N. Warfield

Mary Austin
1829–after 1900
m.
Austin Dall

Horace Holley
1832–1863
m.
Rebecca Wilson

John Samuel
1835–1836

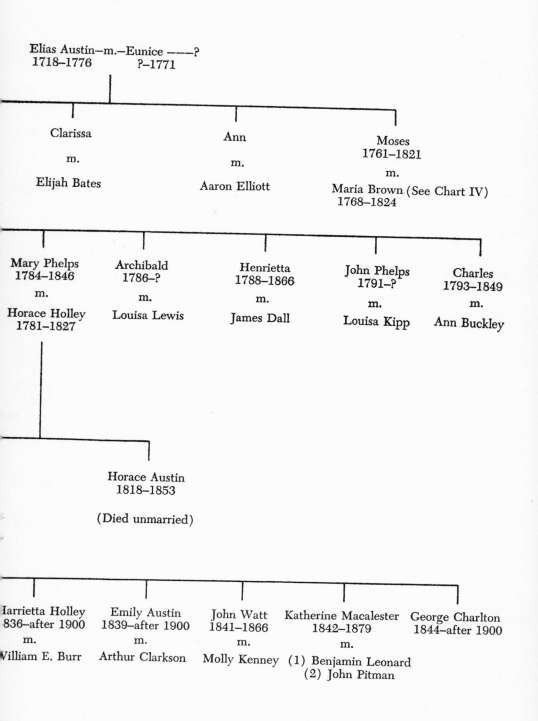

Elias Austin—m.—Eunice ———?
1718–1776   ?–1771

Clarissa
m.
Elijah Bates

Ann
m.
Aaron Elliott

Moses
1761–1821
m.
Maria Brown (See Chart IV)
1768–1824

Mary Phelps
1784–1846
m.
Horace Holley
1781–1827

Archibald
1786–?
m.
Louisa Lewis

Henrietta
1788–1866
m.
James Dall

John Phelps
1791–?
m.
Louisa Kipp

Charles
1793–1849
m.
Ann Buckley

Horace Austin
1818–1853

(Died unmarried)

Harrietta Holley
1836–after 1900
m.
William E. Burr

Emily Austin
1839–after 1900
m.
Arthur Clarkson

John Watt
1841–1866
m.
Molly Kenney

Katherine Macalester
1842–1879
m.
(1) Benjamin Leonard
(2) John Pitman

George Charlton
1844–after 1900

II THE JUDGE JOHN PHELPS-TIMOTHY PHELPS FAMILY

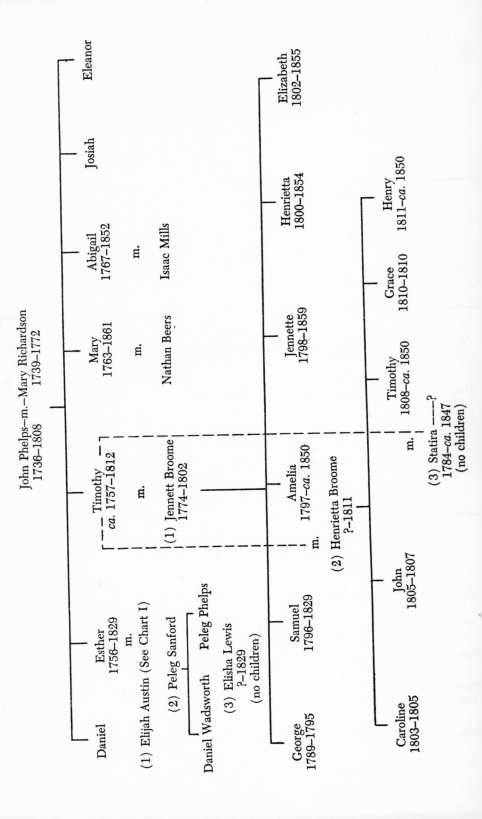

III THE LUTHER HOLLEY FAMILY

Luther Holley–m.–Sarah Dakin
ca. 1755–1826   1755–1830

Milton
1776–1777

John Milton
1777–1836

Myron
1779–1841

Horace
1781–1827

m.

Mary Phelps Austin
1784–1846

(See Chart I)

Edward
1783–1848

Newman
1785–1857

Orville Luther
1791–1861

Caroline
1800–1841

IV THE MOSES AUSTIN FAMILY

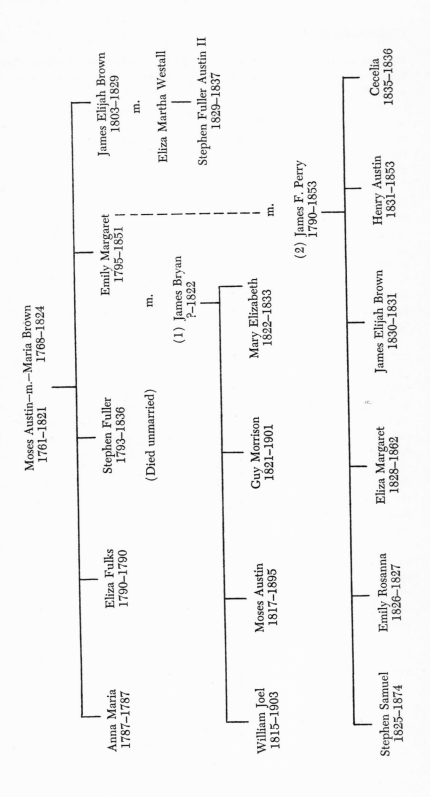

Moses Austin—m.—Maria Brown
1761–1821   1768–1824

Anna Maria
1787–1787

Eliza Fulks
1790–1790

Stephen Fuller
1793–1836
(Died unmarried)

Emily Margaret
1795–1851

m.

(1) James Bryan
?–1822

m.

(2) James F. Perry
1790–1853

James Elijah Brown
1803–1829

m.

Eliza Martha Westall

Stephen Fuller Austin II
1829–1837

William Joel
1815–1903

Moses Austin
1817–1895

Guy Morrison
1821–1901

Mary Elizabeth
1822–1833

Stephen Samuel
1825–1874

Emily Rosanna
1826–1827

Eliza Margaret
1828–1862

James Elijah Brown
1830–1831

Henry Austin
1831–1853

Cecelia
1835–1836

and associates rallied to support the stricken widow and orphans. Grief was mingled with apprehension, because many of the mourners were involved in Elijah's enterprises.

The coffin was borne at once to the Old Burying Ground on the Green near the State House, and everybody stood in the little fenced enclosure under the open sky while Mr. Hubbard read the burial lines: "In the midst of life we are in death . . . Lord, Thou hast been our refuge from one generation to another . . ."

The Reverend Bela was to prove himself a hero that summer as he labored unafraid in the fever-ravaged town and pronounced his words of consolation beside scores of open graves.

Elijah Austin's sudden death was the beginning of a terrible season as the fever, scourge of the coastal cities of all the world, raged on for months along the Atlantic seaboard. None of the rest of the immediate family were smitten although in New Haven alone sixty-four persons died before the autumn frost put an end to the epidemic. Almost the last victim was the old physician in his big house at the head of Meadow Street, who drove his four horses and himself to exhaustion.

It was necessary that Austin's estate should be settled promptly. When administration was begun, it was clear that the situation was complicated.[9] Esther declined to be named administratrix because of her total ignorance of financial matters, and so a sort of committee was appointed, consisting of her brother Timothy, her brothers-in-law Isaac Mills and Nathan Beers, and another Beers kinsman, the postmaster, as surety on the bond. The estate proved to be insolvent. With all sails set for the freshening wind and headed out to sea, Elijah's ship had crashed on the rocks. If he had only lived to see the new vessel that he was building come home from Canton, he would have been as famous as his neighbors. His sons would have gone to Yale, and his daughters would have been married from under his own roof into establishments of their own.

As it was, the Widow Austin could expect only a modest dower of one-third of the real estate, and his children nothing at all. In one respect, however, they were fortunate. The creditors, who included not only relatives but numerous friends in New Haven and Hartford, were uniformly kind and patient, allowing the family of the deceased a long period of grace to settle the estate.

Word of Elijah Austin's death and financial ruin slowly reached all of the scattered members of the family connection, for they were inveterate letter writers. When the news finally got to Moses out in the

Virginia mountains, he was himself in debt and growing restless with his lack of success there. His regard for his oldest brother was evidenced years later when he named his second son Elijah. The first boy had been called Stephen for another of the brothers.

Making out the inventory of all the goods and chattels of the estate was a slow and mournful task, and the list was not ready until the February session of the court for the following year. Elijah's children saw their patrimony dwindle into a sheaf of foolscap sheets filled with items and evaluations.

> 1 coat of arms gilt frame, 40/
> 1 large carpet, £ 11.10
> 1 pr. gilt looking-glasses, £ 11
> 1 pr. card tables, 48/
> 1 saddle, 21/
> 1 gold watch, £ 7

So it went, as even their father's watch must be listed along with all the rest. As it turned out, the sale was not held for another year and a half, but things never seemed really to belong to them once they had been promised to the court. The pew in Trinity Church was on the inventory list, too.

Mary was old enough when her father died to understand dimly that the world she had known was suddenly changed. Their home, made secure by his firm presence, was suddenly swept out from under them, like the sands of the shore in an ebbing tide. Her older brothers were striking out on their own, trying to find jobs to earn a living. Horace was in his uncle's store, and Henry and E. Phelps wanted to go to sea as cabin boys. The smaller children would cling to their mother's skirts, and grow up somewhere without remembering too much about their father. With Mary it was different. The pattern of her life was set, young as she was. All her life she would think of herself as Elijah Austin's daughter.

While the house on Whiting Street was still their home, with the polished cherry and bright andirons reflecting cheerful flames from the great fireplace, she fixed the memory of it in her impressionable young mind. Oftentimes she slipped off by herself in the big parlor to pore over the tooled leather books displayed among the bric-a-brac on the center table, or to explore in the big bookcase. She would plant her small feet before the fireplace to stand and gaze up at the Austin crest suspended in a gilt frame above the mantel. A gold cross between silver cherubs' wings, it had been embroidered neatly on black silk by one of her aunts. It made a deeper imprint on her than anything in the house.

Instinctively she loved this home, not so much the house itself, but the security and elegance of it. She knew that it stood for something that she needed and wanted. In March after her father's death Uncle Timothy married a wealthy, charming young lady, and when they had got settled in their comfortable establishment, they asked Mary to come and live with them. She went. And so, when the dreaded day finally came that the auctioneer stood by the door of the Austin home and knocked down the house and then the contents, item by item, to the highest bidder, she had already found a haven from homelessness.

It was high time that the property be sold in order to make at least a token payment to the creditors, whose claims amounted to more than twenty thousand pounds. The passing of the home place into the possession of strangers was not so shocking as it had seemed when Elijah died, that is, not to anyone but Esther. At the auction she managed to buy back a few things for herself; and Timothy prudently acquired nearly five hundred pounds worth of admirable furnishings for his new place. Other relatives, like the sisters, and prosperous creditors like a Mr. Sanford of Hartford, picked up pieces of furniture and chattels of one sort or another. By the time Mary was twelve, her childhood's home was a thing of the past.

In the autumn after the auction Henry Austin sailed with Captain Daniel Greene on the new ship for the voyage round the world.[10] The *Neptune* was beautiful, just as Elijah Austin had planned; and after being fitted out in New York, she finally set sail from New Haven Harbour in November of 1796, with forty-five men of the town as her crew. Amid all the fanfare, with the *Neptune's* twenty guns booming and her flags flying, Mary had eyes only for her brother as he lugged his gear aboard and disappeared down into the crowded hold where the cabin boys' hammocks would hang.

He looked big for fourteen in his new long trousers and round jacket. He dutifully promised to study the schoolbooks in his sea bag, and to write home from every port of call. He wanted letters waiting for him in Canton, addressed in care of Captain Greene. His mother and brothers and sisters wept as the sails were sheeted home and with anchors aweigh the vessel moved out of the Harbour.

Henry was Mary's favorite brother, the one most akin to her in temperament and energy, and she would miss him sorely. He would be gone for years, if, with luck, he got back at all. Her weeping mother and aunts felt sure he would never return, but in her own heart she believed that Henry would come home. Something inside her simply refused to accept for long the idea of a sad and dismal future. Life with Uncle Timothy was very pleasant, and Aunt Jennett had arranged for her to have lessons on the new rosewood piano.

2. SENTIMENTAL COURTSHIP
1795-1805

Mary's Uncle Timothy Phelps was a lively, sociable man, who liked to be openhanded and free with his money whether he was helping out his less fortunate relatives or signing his name to a public subscription. Not quite forty, he was already a leading drygoods merchant and ironmonger, and he had his eye on some new ventures in the shipping line. He was, moreover, as free with his advice as with his cash, and when Elijah Austin's widow was left in sore straits, he promptly took the lead in assisting her. He put the older boys to work in his store for as long as they wanted to stay, and he offered to take complete responsibility for rearing Mary, just as if she were his own child.

She was his own mother's namesake, and was believed to be the old lady's favorite grandchild, partly, no doubt, because she took after the Phelpses in looks. The child's small features, wide hazel eyes, and smooth brown hair, together with her slender build, came from that side of the house rather than from the more rugged Austins. She was like her mother's people, too, in her lively, sociable ways. Timothy had looked over the Austin offspring, and in doing his duty by his sister, he undoubtedly picked out the one of her children that would give him the most satisfaction and pleasure.

His young wife was fond of the little girl, too, and that was a stroke of good luck for Mary. Jennett was only twenty-one when she was married, so much younger than her husband that it was company for her to have a niece in the household. She had lived in New York City until a few years previous, when her father, the very wealthy Mr. Samuel Broome, had moved up to New Haven, partly for business reasons but also to enroll his son in Yale.[1] His firm became the leading mercantile house in the town for cloth and imported stuffs. The Broomes were related to Sir William Pitt in England and connected with prominent families such as the Long Island Platts and the Hartford Wadsworths, who all came to seem like her own kin to Mary as she grew up in the Phelps home.

Timothy and his wife lived in style, with several servants, and they entertained lavishly. Soon after the marriage he built an excellent brick establishment on Chapel Street near the corner of Church, facing the Green just across from the town pump. It cost him upwards of eighteen thousand dollars, figured in the new American money, by the time the house and stables and the adjacent store were completed. He had waited late to marry, but when he did settle down his home was in keeping with his solid position as a director in the New Haven Bank and in the New Haven Insurance Company. His relatives were proud of his manner of living; indeed, the whole town was impressed by it.

It was in this home that Mary spent her girlhood and young ladyhood in the role of an adopted daughter, much indulged. The tone of the ménage was very different from the easygoing neighborliness of Whiting Street, and its interests did not look toward the Harbour. Instead, from Timothy's front windows the view gave across to the liberty pole and the meeting houses, and beyond the State House to the row of college buildings on the far side of the Green. This was the aristocratic New Haven of Calvinist theology and Federalist politics, supported by hereditary social distinctions.

As a matter of fact, Timothy Phelps did not completely fit into this sedate world of the New Haven Green, although he had been graduated from Yale in the Class of 1780 as a Phi Beta Kappa, and prided himself on being a patron of culture.[2] He patronized Mr. Isaac Beers' bookshop down the street liberally, and lined his library shelves with leather-bound volumes of the classics and de luxe copies of the poems of Connecticut's own Hartford Wits. He was personally acquainted with these witty gentlemen, especially Yale's new president, Doctor Timothy Dwight. But Timothy Phelps had independent notions about both religion and politics, and he often opposed the powerful combination of conservatives who combined to rule the state and the town, the "Standing Order," as it was called, of which the dedicated leader was President Dwight himself. Timothy belonged to the minority party of Connecticut moderates who tried to steer between the ultraconservatism of the Standing Order and the liberal, but dangerous, ideas of Thomas Jefferson's Republicans. A middle-of-the-road man was Uncle Phelps, as the family began to call him now that he was its head, a middle-of-the-road man who saw no reason for being either an antiquary or a fanatic.

Mary saw much of her Phelps relatives after she moved to Timothy's house. Many of them lived close at hand, and only a day's ride up in the hills at Stafford Springs resided her Phelps grandparents in a house big enough to welcome back all nine of their children and their numerous offspring. The grandmother entertained them with tales of her mother, Lady Abigail Richardson, born in Scotland, who sat erect in her great square pew each Sunday, holding her long staff topped with a bunch of flowers and a sprig of fennel, tied with a blue ribbon, the reward which she bestowed upon the best behaved grandchild.[3]

Grandmother Mary, a fine lady herself, presided over a famous board, noted for joints done just to a turn, and succulent green vegetables, and crusty loaves that were kneaded and set to rise under her supervision. Surrounded by ample proof of the Judge's financial position, she delighted to relate how her penniless lover had wooed her in the long ago. She was only fifteen, the story went, and stern Lady Abigail refused to let her be wed to John Phelps, who was nineteen and had nothing as yet; but on a moonlight night just after the town bell tolled nine, she eloped with him. For a while they lived mostly on hasty pudding and were very poor until he read law and got to be a justice of the peace; but she had never regretted her rashness, never. Her descendants always remembered to add this happy touch to the tale as they repeated it down through the years, and Grandmother Phelps joined Lady Abigail in the family gallery of romantic portraits.

A family story that belonged in New Haven was Uncle Nathan Beers' account of how he had stood guard over poor young Major Andre during his last night on earth. Nathan was a loyal captain-lieutenant in the Continental Army; but he had felt very sorry for the British spy, who, as the dawn came, seemed to be only just another brave young man. All Mary's people had been on the side of the Colonists, but they treasured these romantic links with the Old World. The well-to-do Phelpses, who had important connections abroad, counted themselves aristocrats in the American manner.

About two years after her husband's death, Esther Phelps Austin married again. It was no romantic affair, but certainly it was an excellent match, which met with the approval of her family and friends. Her new husband was Mr. Peleg Sanford, a much respected and prosperous grain merchant of Hartford, who had known Elijah in a business way, and who had himself been recently bereaved of his estimable wife.[4] The fact that such an eligible suitor sought Esther's hand in spite of her being poor and forty and encumbered with several small children bespeaks her good looks and charm. At that, she may have had a little help in directing the course of Peleg's affection. As a partner of General

Wadsworth in Hartford, Mr. Sanford was a friend of Timothy Phelps, whose home was a likely place for him to have seen something of the Widow Austin. Whatever the details of the courtship, Peleg and Esther were married and took her younger children to Hartford to grow up in his substantial home. The settlement of her first husband's estate dragged on for years, finally paying off at the rate of only twenty-seven cents on the dollar. Ere long the name of Elijah Austin, who had dreamed the great dream of the direct sealing trade with Canton and brought it to pass, was all but forgotten save in the long memories of his descendants.

Mary did not go to live with the Sanfords in Hartford, although she liked her stepfather and bore no grudge against her mother for marrying again. She made frequent visits there, and it was good to have Mr. Sanford include her with all the little ones, Henrietta and Archibald and John Phelps and Baby Charles, in his generous and affectionate regard. But she felt more at home with the Timothy Phelpses, and she chose to stay with them. Already she was of an independent mind.

Uncle Timothy made up for lost time in founding his family. Jennett's first infant, a son, was born a little more than a year after they were married, and others followed in regular succession.[5] Each was provided with a nurse, and each was duly christened by the Reverend Mr. Hubbard—George and Samuel, Amelia and Jennett, and Frank and Henrietta—as the years went by. The young wife's duties were heavy, for all the luxury of the establishment, and Mary was often needed to help in managing the household. She proved her abilities one spring when her uncle was ill, directing the cooks and maids, planning meals, and entertaining the guests. She was rarely expected to do homely chores, and avoided them when she could. Yet she gladly worked in the flower garden, and sewing was a task she enjoyed. With all the bolts of English challis and crisp lawns and imported silks on the shelves in Timothy's store at her disposal, she learned to design and make suitable garments for herself.

She cared a great deal about the way she looked, as a young lady should. When she grew older, she was still pretty; not beautiful, perhaps, because her features were a trifle sharp, but interesting in a way that people noticed. She had aristocratic hands and feet, and a neat figure to set off the new fashions from France that revealed much more of a lady's charms than the old style flounces and stays. Styles for men were changing, too. Soon nobody but her grandfather and General Washington would be wearing knee breeches and wigs.

She attended school for as long as the female academies had anything to teach her. She read polite French, and studied composition and rhetoric so thoroughly that she wrote as well as if she were a boy. She practiced long hours on the pianoforte, and cultivated her sweet soprano voice. Someone gave her a guitar, a stylish and proper instrument for ladies at the time. On this she modestly accompanied herself and others in sacred and parlor songs. She was taught to dance, and, since it was correct to do so, may have gone to the school at Mrs. Nix's, tuition four dollars a quarter, where cotillions and minuets were demonstrated. She danced easily and well, since time and step came naturally to her.

Her best education, however, was her own reading and the lively talk at the Phelps table. Timothy made it a point to know, or at least to know about, any men of prominence in the community and state. In New Haven lived Jedediah Morse, the geographer; and tall, lean Noah Webster, who was laboring day and night on an American dictionary, so people said; and Eli Whitney, schoolteacher and inventor of a cotton gin for Southern planters, now back in town running an arms factory. Mary learned from her uncle to be interested in important people and what they said or did. Timothy's home almost made up to her for the loss of her father's.

New Haven's chief pride was Yale College, and the town kept its eyes turned in that direction. About the time Mary went to live with her uncle, the noted Dr. Timothy Dwight gave up his small church at nearby Greenfield Hill to accept the presidency of the institution. He was a mighty scholar who had published incredibly long epics, and he had been a chaplain in Washington's army. With his coming, life in the College quickened its pace.[6]

The town felt the change. Everybody kept up even more attentively with the President's boys, who were forever hurrying across the Green to the Commons for their meals or to the butler's to buy soap and quills and cider, then down to the wood stand to saw a few billets of firewood for heating their bedrooms. After all, there was no reason why young scholars should not get exercise fetching in their own wood like everyone else. The chapel where the boys attended two full-length sermons every Sunday was not heated at all, and the President sometimes preached in his brown greatcoat, turning the pages of his manuscript slowly because his thick woollen mittens made his fingers clumsy.

The townspeople knew, especially the shopkeepers, that in spite of President Dwight's regime of strict discipline, hard study, and few worldly pleasures, many of the young gentlemen from the South spent more than four hundred dollars during the college year. Such extravagance was the kind of thing that Dwight set out to stop, and most of the lads were becoming more serious and godly-minded since his arrival. This return to old-fashioned Calvinistic orthodoxy had a sobering effect on the whole town as well. If the young gentlemen who attended Yale were not allowed to participate in dancing or theatrical shows, then of necessity the social affairs arranged by the parents of young ladies must be elevated to the realms of music and poetry and cultured conversation, in which rarefied atmosphere the young people got almost as well acquainted as if they were meeting each other in the ballroom.

This kind of sentimental courting was the fashion in New Haven's best society when Mary began to think seriously about the opposite sex, and fortunately she bloomed into a young woman of refined feeling. She could converse with the more serious students about piety and the soul; but since Uncle Timothy and the other pewholders at Trinity saw no harm in a minuet or a novel, she enjoyed them, too. She was a girl of sense as well as sensibility.

President Dwight's Yale College was an unrealistic world, remote from everyday affairs. While his chosen youths were dedicating their minds to theology inside the sacred walls, the budding women with whom they exchanged fervent glances were getting a far more practical introduction to life than they. Along with the other girls who were her bosom friends of the period, Mary matured early in the midst of a large family with all its complications of birth and death. At frequent intervals she composed romantic, bookish letters to her girl friends, but she did so in the midst of cheerful confusion and noisy distractions.

Within a couple of years after her mother's marriage to Mr. Sanford, he gave up his business in Hartford and removed the family to New Haven.[7] There he formed a partnership with Timothy Phelps, and bought back the Austin home, which he promptly fixed up in style with a new barn and fences and a coat of paint. Thus Peleg gave Esther her home again, and that spring she bore him a son whom they named Daniel Wadsworth, for their good friend back in Hartford. Once more Mary had an opportunity to live with the Sanfords, but Aunt Jennett needed her now more than ever and so she stayed on with the Phelpses.

The academic exercises of the college lads seemed more remote than ever from the world of action when Henry Austin got back that summer from China. The town was agog. In every New Haven diary the date of Thursday, July 14, 1799, was noted as the day the *Neptune* got home. The Austin family hardly recognized Henry when they heard his voice above all the rest as the crew came over the side. He was a man, grown so tall his trousers came halfway to his knees, and his embrace was rough and hearty. Not a day of the two years and eight months of the voyage had been wasted for him, and he fairly exploded with telling them all he had seen and done. He had learned seamanship, and was bound he would be captain of his own ship some day. He had mastered all those schoolbooks by the flickering light of a dim whale-oil lamp in the forecastle—Latin, French, Spanish, and a text on the law that he had learned by heart.

Henry seemed very grown-up when he began to boast of all he had seen on his voyage. Captain Greene had ordered his men to slaughter the seal bloodily on the Falkland Islands, and then the ship had beat her way around the Cape and across the interminable Pacific waters to Canton. Ah, Canton— that was a fairyland of a place, along the bank of a great river where there were ferryboats and sampans, and junks with eyes on the prow, and flower-boats, and great "hongs," as the natives called the warehouses where foreigners lived and traded. Eighty thousand skins the ship had sold there for three dollars and a half apiece; and then brought home three thousand chests of tea, fifty-four thousand pieces of nankeen, and Lord knows how much chinaware and silk and spices.

Elijah Austin's family and friends must have sighed as they heard his stout son tell of the *Neptune's* rich cargo, thinking how they all might have shared in it had things been different. They got nothing at all save the few trinkets the boy brought back, but it was good he was home safe anyway. Mary hung on his words, fascinated by his description of strange luscious fruits and tropical flowers and slant-eyed people. He could hardly wait to be off to sea again, and E. Phelps, too, signed up for a voyage.

That summer Mary, a precocious girl of fifteen, was standing on tiptoe, waiting for something to happen, something exciting like her brothers' setting out to sea. She was uncertain as to precisely what she expected, but she had decided what she did *not* want. She would not be satisfied to be just the mistress of a household, presiding with modest pride over kitchen and fireside. She wanted to be a part of the larger world outside the four walls of a home. In fine, even script she wrote many long, serious letters to her friend, "Dear C——a," who lived in another town, criticizing the books she had read and the plays she had attended, all in a most grown-up manner.[8] Then, at the beginning of the academic year of 1799, an upstate Connecticut youth named Horace Holley enrolled in the freshman class at Yale. He was very handsome, and people soon said he was a bright scholar.

One of the unique advantages enjoyed by the girls of New Haven was the opportunity to meet the young men who enrolled at Yale. In the natural course of events Mary saw young Holley even before she heard him represent his literary society—he joined the Brothers in Unity—in a public debate. She may have met him first at a singing club. She took note of his "bright yet soft and expressive black eyes, and the fine, silky dark hair above his classic forehead."[9] At least, that is the way she pictured him as a collegian when she had occasion long years later to recall his appearance. Like everyone else, she was impressed by his beautiful speaking voice and his commanding presence. The chances are that she secretly fell in love with him the first time she saw him.

Horace Holley was a country boy. He came from Salisbury up in the northwestern corner of the state, and had worked in his father's store before his ambition led him to join an older brother at the nearby academy in Williamstown to prepare for admission to the college there. When he finished his preparatory studies he persuaded his father to send him down to New Haven, where the advantages were superior.

From the day he crossed the Green to enroll as a student at Yale, he made his mark. He studied diligently, was invariably prompt, and never received a reprimand or fine from the tutors. It was soon said that he was a favorite of President Dwight, who had uncanny skill in choosing promising students for his protégés. Horace was more than just a hard student. He was also gay and witty and popular with the other lads, especially those from the South. After he had completed his own assignments, he would dash off a first-rate essay for some less gifted classmate. He was ambitious, without a trace of envy.

When he went home to Salisbury for vacations he read his compositions to his admiring parents and brothers, who were convinced that he was a genius in the making. Horace himself felt that he had talents above those of most of his fellows, and had declared from childhood that he meant to distinguish himself in the theatre of life. His father, Luther Holley, who had been a poor schoolteacher before he became a prosperous merchant-farmer, worried occasionally about his precocious son; but beyond writing him a few mild admonitions about pride and extravagance and intellectual snobbishness, he let the boy have his own way. He even sent another son, Myron, the one who had been at Williamstown with Horace, down to New Haven to study law. He sincerely wanted his sons to have a good start in life.

That fall pretty Mary Austin went back to school again. There was considerable interest in a new Union School, fostered by Noah Webster and patronized by prominent families. Six or eight of the boys and girls from the Beers, Mills, Phelps, and Austin connection were enrolled, and surely it was to this institution that Mary referred when she told "C——a" about her exciting new venture.

"Yes, my dear girl," she wrote along in December, "I have again commenced school girl—and am happy again in assuming that appellation."[10]

Mary was always happy in the classroom or library, and she was following her true bent when she plunged into serious study. She was, as she put it, "something of an enthusiast," and she proceeded energetically to improve her French, pick up a smattering of natural philosophy, and do some solid reading in the English poets and historians that stored her mind with a wide vocabulary and a range of allusions and quotations from which she drew for the rest of her days.

The turn of the century was an exciting time for sensitive young people to grow up. With the death of the great Washington the old era ended, and Mary and her young correspondents thought it proper to exchange fulsome eulogies of the hero in their letters. Then came the struggle between John Adams, the Federalist, and Thomas Jefferson, the Republican, or rather Democrat, as the pro-French liberals were beginning to call themselves. Connecticut politicians were involved, and Timothy Phelps lined up with the more open-minded Federalists, like his good friend, Oliver Wolcott, the former Secretary of the Treasury.[11] To Wolcott he dashed off gossiping messages full of the scandalous goings on of Pierrepont Edwards in his "seraglio at Wallingford," where rumor said the Connecticut Democrats met. Pierrepont was an unbelievably radical grandson of the saintly Calvinist, Jonathan Edwards; and all New England was convinced that he was the actual villain of that sad novel of seduction, *The Coquette*, whose heroine was a lady from Hartford.

In 1802 the Republicans elected Jefferson as President, and that year the French won so many battles under Napoleon that for a while the rest of Europe made peace with him. The revolutionary element seemed to be in the ascendant everywhere. Everywhere, that is, but at Yale. From his post of command Timothy Dwight became the archfoe of all change, religious and political, and especially of French infidelity. He banished these iniquities from his college even if he could not drive them from the town and the state and the nation. There was not much he could do about New Haven merchants and shippers who found some good in Mr. Jefferson's policies. The Austins and the Phelpses, for example, favored the Louisiana Purchase because Moses Austin was out there now operating lead mines near St. Louis on the Mississippi River.

All these matters were discussed at Uncle Timothy's dinner table. Mary listened, but was careful not to express her views openly. It was better if a young lady left politics and theology to the men while she composed French exercises or remodelled her dresses and her figure in accord with the new styles, which required a very short waist and a long, slim skirt. She was glad for any fashion that relieved her from wearing the overwhelming bustles and fichus of her mother's generation.

Meanwhile, Horace Holley became a stout supporter of President Dwight and orthodoxy. Being a born public speaker, his devotion to the cause gave him opportunities to use his talents in the college arena. Like most of the students, he was a loyal member of his literary society, and each Wednesday evening he gathered with the other Brothers in Unity in the room of one of the tutors to read the constitution and elect officers and deliver orations. By his sophomore year he had attained membership on the Standing Committee, and may well have been one of the brothers who on a certain June evening debated the question, "Are the abilities of the sexes equal?"

Horace was a poet, too, and won high praise for a college exercise which he composed at the end of that same sophomore year. It was a violent attack on French equalitarianism, done in creditable couplets:

> When revolution its career began,
> And France commenc'd the cry for "Rights of Man,"
>
> . . . .
>
> We soon discover'd, in this fair disguise,
> Fraud, rapine, lust, and violence and lies.[12]

It sounded like an imitation of Dr. Dwight's well-known poem, *The Triumph of Infidelity*—and that is exactly what it was. The President approved of the poem, and Horace thought well enough of it to keep a copy among his papers.

Mary Austin no doubt heard him declaim these lines at the Exercises that spring. If she paid attention to the substance of his poem, she could hardly have agreed with its extreme orthodoxy in the light of the tolerant ideas she had acquired elsewhere. But because she admired the author, she thought his verses beautiful. Sometimes she herself composed poetry on a memorable New Year's or for some friend's album, although no lady would think of reciting her verses in public. What she was thinking about as she listened to him was not the French Revolution at all! She was thinking that his voice sounded melodious the way it did when he came with the College "Corps" on moonlight nights to serenade before her door.[13] She was remembering how he looked with the silver light shining on his face.

Horace intended to make the law his profession, but ere long he became involved in a religious revival which swept the College. The movement was a complete return to old-fashioned Calvinism. Its doctrine was logical and clear: man is born sinful, and salvation comes only by God's predestined choice of the "elect" who receive it. This was Dr. Dwight's answer to such notions as deism and democratic equality. By the authority of his voice and the magnetism of his personality he convinced most of the students under his tutelage that this harsh creed was the answer to the troubling questions of the new nineteenth century in which they were to live out their young lives. Along with nearly half his class Horace joined the College Church and was admitted to Christian fellowship in August, 1802.[14] He was twenty-one years old, and had not heretofore joined any denomination.

He would hardly have been able to explain clearly, even to himself, why he fell so readily under Dwight's influence, or to perceive that the cause was rooted in his own temperament and background. His nature was intense and eager; his mind was clear and logical; he liked, even as a boy, to settle every problem completely and quickly. In the home of his tolerant parents the children were never put under pressure to declare their belief in creeds. Horace was inexperienced in religion, but when the revival turned his society meetings into theological debates, he plunged into them with ardor. The logic of the great Calvin—and of President Dwight—convinced him. He committed himself wholeheartedly to orthodox views, and found himself more and more interested in the intricacies of dogma.

He sent long letters home to his parents, expounding his new-found beliefs and suggesting that they, too, seek salvation.[15] When his earnest, unschooled mother wrote back in her crabbed hand to say that she was worried because her boy seemed too solemn for his years, he assured her that he was in possession of the "great joys of religion." He was sincere. He was intensely happy because he was discovering himself one of the Elect. Dr. Dwight encouraged him to continue searching his soul to find out God's will.

The young ladies of New Haven could not possibly have escaped the influence of an emotional revival that suddenly transformed their attentive beaus into young men dedicated to the search for salvation. Mary Austin found Horace's solemn considerations somewhat congenial because she was touched at this season by personal sorrows. Word came from some distant port that E. Phelps had perished at sea. He was not so dear to her as Henry, but she had loved him affectionately. Hard upon that loss came the death of the older Sanford baby and then of Mr. Sanford, too. Little Peleg, the second son, was an infant in arms. Esther once more faced a lonely future, although with fewer hardships this time, thanks to Mr. Sanford's generosity. In his will he provided for his wife and son, and even remembered his seven stepchildren by name.

One of Peleg's saddest mourners was Uncle Timothy. The firm of Phelps and Sanford had prospered mightily these past years, and he rightly feared he would not do so well in the future. Misfortune beset him even more sorely within a fortnight when his wife died after giving birth to a daughter who was called Elizabeth.

The responsibility for her uncle's household fell heavily on Mary, however much help she had from servants and aunts. She must have been relieved in mind when a few months later Timothy married Henrietta Broome, his late wife's sister.[16] Mary continued to live in the household, almost as much a foster-daughter to Aunt Henrietta as she had been to Aunt Jennett. She could not have been more welcome, though it was high time for a girl her age to be getting settled in life.

She was probably thinking of just that as she sat sedately among the large audience that attended the graduation exercises of the Yale Class of 1803, and listened with rapt attention to Horace Holley's oration titled "The Slavery of Free-thinking." He looked so ill and wretched that it seemed a wonder that he could even appear on the platform. After completing his senior examinations with honors, among the first in his class, he had gone up to Poughkeepsie to visit in his older brother's family while he prepared his graduation speech. There he came down with fever and ague, and only his ambition got him out of bed and in the stagecoach in time for the ceremonies. He knew there would be a distinguished audience at the commencement, such dignitaries as the Governor and eminent divines from all over New England. He had no idea of missing this chance to deliver his maiden speech before such august hearers.

Mary thought his pallor and emaciation made him seem romantic and deserving of the admiration and sympathy of the audience. She knew that her own heart was beating faster as she twisted her small linen handkerchief nervously and hoped he might be able to finish.

When the formal program was over, the men of the Class of 1803 said farewell to each other. They were, in the phrase of the day, a very "enthusiastic" group; and as they parted they set down in writing a solemn engagement that they would pray for each other at a certain hour every day. Townspeople and visitors watched sympathetically and with curiosity as the young men tearfully embraced and said good-bye. Horace signed the pledge, and regarded it seriously enough to obtain a written release from it later when it proved impracticable.[17]

One of these graduates was the President's son, Sereno Dwight; but it might well have been said that they were all the President's spiritual sons. In this group he saw the fruition of his plan to make Yale a stronghold of orthodoxy, and among those upon whom he was counting to defend it was young Holley from Salisbury. The lad's graduation oration against freethinking met with his approval as thoroughly as had his previous exercise against the French Revolution.

Fortified by their vows and new diplomas, the graduates scattered to Virginia and South Carolina and Georgia as well as throughout New England. Horace was somewhat reluctant to return to his upstate home. He had become attached to New Haven, and his romance with Mary was progressing in genteel fashion. After some deliberation he announced to his father that he desired to read law in New York City in order to have the advantages of great libraries and important connections. He got no encouragement from Luther Holley.

"The advantages of going into New York to study law," Luther wrote after due consideration, "do not strike me as being very great, and the expense will be much more than in some village or small town."[18]

In mid-July he told his son to come on home so that they could talk things over. Horace did so, and shortly began to read law in a little mercantile river town over in New York about thirty miles from Salisbury. His father had overruled him for once.

But not for long. A friend of the family, one Peter William Radcliff, Yale, 1793, had just transferred his successful law practice from Poughkeepsie to New York City. It took only a little maneuvering on Horace's part to secure an invitation to come there and study in the offices of Riggs and Radcliff. He went in the early autumn, with his father's reluctant cooperation.

It was his first adventure in a large city, and there was plenty to amuse and interest him. He might have attended the American Theatre to see Dunlap's *Andre* and other stage shows of distinction. There were numerous taverns and clubs much frequented by lively students of law, some of them already known for clever literary pieces. The old Dutch part of the island was almost like a foreign country. But Horace had taken his religious conversion so seriously that he eschewed amusements. The city around him, filled with crowds intent on money and pleasure, seemed worldly and distracting. He put his excellent mind on mastering the long rows of books in Mr. Radcliff's office to such good purpose that the partners thought him a promising young lawyer.

All the while he was desperately lonely. His thoughts kept turning to religion and philosophy. When he prowled in the city's bookshops, much better than any he had ever seen, he noticed only the volumes of poetry and sermons. By the end of the year his letters home sounded so plaintive that Luther sent him a Christmas message to cheer him up, and bade him go out and buy whatever books he desired.

"Draw on me for money or go where I have credit," he said, and added a word of praise for his son's progress in the law.[19] The letter did not lift the gloom that enveloped Horace, homesick for the plaudits of his friends and professors, and the admiration of his sweetheart.

Mary's letters should have cheered him. She was pleased to have him reading law in New York. She had so many connections there and on Long Island—the Broomes and the Platts and the DeForests—that the idea of living in the city someday was enchanting. In the eyes of a town-bred girl who frankly liked luxuries and formalities, what better goal could a young couple set for themselves than a solid brick home on Broadway near Bowling Green? She was certain that Horace would be a brilliant attorney. Years later she testified to her unchanged belief that he made a wise first choice in studying law because it was "a profession for which the peculiar constitution of his mind, and his uncommon ambition, best qualified him, and in which he undoubtedly would have distinguished himself more than in any other."[20] She surely told him these encouraging things when she wrote to him in the care of Messrs. Riggs and Radcliff.

Horace became unbearably restless. The legal career he had planned, with its unending controversy and struggle for advantage, began to seem a selfish, unworthy way to spend his life. More and more he missed the clear sense of dedication that he had felt during the Revival. It was inevitable that he should ask Dr. Dwight for counsel. There was no other person to whom he might confide his difficulties, not his respected father or even the girl he loved, who was, for all her intelligence, an inexperienced female—no one at all who could understand as well as the President.

The crux of Horace's problem was peculiar to those who believe themselves to be the Elect. He was aware of his gifts as scholar and speaker, yet he earnestly desired to serve God and mankind. How could he follow Divine guidance if he became a lawyer, bound by precedent and process and client's interest? Timothy Dwight did indeed understand the dilemma, having confronted it in his own life. He thought he recognized in Holley a true disciple, and coveted him for the ministry. Now was the chance to point out to him that he could harmonize his convictions and his ambitions in the service of the church. He invited the troubled young man to enroll in the Theological Seminary at Yale.

Horace reached a decision quickly, and almost as quickly severed his connection with the law firm, gathered up his few belongings, and returned to New Haven. On January 7, 1804, Dr. Dwight personally signed a certificate stating that "Horace Holley of the Seminary" was a member in good standing of the Seminary Church. By that time the new student was deep in his studies.

Luther Holley accepted his son's sudden change of profession with judicial calmness, and continued to supply the money for his expenses. He did not agree with Horace's theology, but he respected his earnestness and wistfully admired his scholarly learning.

"Happiness, my son, is the great pursuit of all," wrote this homespun philosopher of the rational era. "If you found it was not to be obtained by the study and practice of law, you were perfectly right to quit it for the study of theology."[21]

Thus encouraged, young Mr. Holley arranged to live pleasantly in the comfortable home of the venerable Dr. Dana and his wife. The neighbors were friendly, and as he went back and forth to the Seminary along the quiet, elm-shaded street, lined with white, piazzaed mansions, he passed the time of day with nearly everyone he met. He felt very much at home in the town now, especially in this inner world of the Green and the Standing Order.

His sudden coming back to New Haven was a joy to Mary. Although she was puzzled to account for his sudden change in plans, she had confidence that he was doing what was right and necessary. What mattered to her was that the two of them would be together again during that springtime of her twentieth year. He was too dignified now to be serenading under her window, but he was a sufficiently ardent suitor, calling upon her as often as was proper.

Many an evening a little before the stroke of seven he lifted the polished knocker of Uncle Timothy's front door and handed his well-brushed hat to the doorman as he proceeded to the back parlor to pay his respects to the old people. Mary could count on him to conduct himself well and to shine in conversation—such a wide range of information he had when he talked with Timothy, and such graceful and suitable compliments for Aunt Henrietta. After a polite interval the young couple would withdraw to the music room for a sacred song and then some gayer tunes with a guitar accompaniment.[22]

Horace had a pleasant singing voice but no proper training in music, and at times he found Mary's renditions a little dull. There was, for example, an evening late in March when he listened as she played some long Italian composition. She was lovely in her flowing French-style gown, with her hair done in fetching curls. He watched the firelight shining on the polished surface of the pianoforte and on her pretty bare arms and nimble fingers moving along the keyboard, and he must have longed to take her in his arms and forget the music. However, he was steeped in a newly discovered suspicion of art, derived from Calvinism, and so, instead, he greeted the end of the rendition by sententiously expressing his doubt about the intellectual powers of those who indulged in that kind of music.

"What good does it do?" demanded the fledgling theologian, rising to stand before the fire, and warming to his subject. "Would not the same time spent in the study of Greek or logic develop the mind more fully?"

Horace Holley liked to reduce every situation to a debate, or at least to a lively conversation; and here was a chance to shine in argument and to make love at the same time. The charming object of his attentions knew, of course, that he meant no disparagement of her playing on the pianoforte. She was pleased that he should consider her an opponent worthy of his argumentative powers, although she knew she was no match for him in debate. He could out-talk her always; but she was still stubbornly unconvinced when the evening came to an end. He flatteringly asked her to set down her thoughts about music in writing, and their parting was all the warmer for the challenging exchange.

Next day she spent hours composing a long formal letter to him defending her sentiments on her favorite art against his poor opinion of it. "I am unused," she began, "to a systematic expression of my opinions and feelings, and may expose to your scrutinizing eye and correct judgement many errors both of thought and style. When you make the request, however, I cannot hesitate to reply."

Admitting herself to be an "enthusiast" about this most delightful of the arts, she declared that she thought life would be intolerable without it. Then she set forth her views of the emotional, moral, and aesthetic value of music for a man as well as for a female, not in excess, of course, but as a balance. "The proper business of music is not to make philosophers and metaphysicians, statesmen and warriors, polemicists and inquisitors. Its appropriate province is to elevate and charm the whole circle of human feelings. . . . With this as with everything else, let the motto be *Usus non abusus.*"

Horace put her letter away with his own treasured compositions. He came later on to agree wholeheartedly with her ideas about music.

Already they were *simpatico* about the delights of reading poetry, and writing it. He sometimes courted her in verse, as was the case when he made amends thus for a social blunder. At some public affair he had been talking rapidly, as always, and had addressed her by the name of another young lady present. She reproved him for it sharply, and got a handsome apology:

> And is it a crime, when thus lost in thy charms,
> When the eye with thy beauty entrances the soul,
> When a smile from thy lips every sympathy warms,
> And bewildering my senses in transport they roll—
> Say, is it a crime, with emotions so sweet,
> If my memory's power for a moment depart,
> If the name of another my tongue should repeat
> While thine should alone lie engrav'd on my heart?[23]

As spring progressed they discovered other pleasures together. There were drives in Uncle Timothy's carriage out to the Cave of the Regicides on West Rock and to the Lighthouse on East Rock. She took him to call upon her mother and her aunts and uncles, who were all pleased with her young man. And surely on moonlight nights that summer, when he was free from his books, they walked all the way down to the Wharf and gazed out on the great sheet of liquid silver, watching the boats pass by with their oars dripping phosphorescent light.

What happy visions of the future they shared, castles in the air, as Horace dubbed them in a little poem. They would not be rich, he prophesied, but they would have an ample competence and "a gay social circle enliven'd by Mind and Love's ardent fire." They were avowed lovers by now, and making their plans.

Mary was not greatly disturbed that fall when her mother was married again, for the third time, to Elisha Lewis, a seafaring man, considerably younger than she. He was, in fact, one of the sailors before the mast whom her son Henry had known on the *Neptune*.[24] It was an undesirable match in the opinion of her relatives, who did not pretend to approve. Elisha was not a sensitive man, however, and he moved his collection of foreign curiosities into the house on Whiting Street and settled down contentedly as an easy-going husband and stepfather. Mary found him rather likable, especially since she did not live there; and the rest of Esther's children accepted him goodnaturedly enough. Henrietta was in the highest grade of the Union School now, and the next two boys were ready to go to work for a living. Henry Austin was the legal guardian for eleven-year-old Charles. Mr. Sanford's son had sufficient means. There was really nothing very wrong with Esther's marriage to Mr. Lewis if she did not mind having around the house a husband whom people called unsuccessful.

It was during that summer that Moses Austin sent his son Stephen all the way back from the Missouri Territory to Connecticut to be educated. He was the same age as Charles, but he seemed older. He had grown up on the frontier, and his odd-looking clothes and different speech made him almost a foreigner to his Eastern cousins. Uncle Moses was ambitious for his boy, and forwarded money to Timothy Phelps to provide suitable clothing for him, and an allowance. He also gave instructions for him to be enrolled in the best school in the area and made a scholar. He had in mind for the lad to enter Yale when he was ready, but not to study divinity. Moses was positive about that.[25]

The solemn-eyed boy went on a round of visits to all the branches of his father's family, according to instructions, and was duly looked over. It was decided to put him under Mr. Bacon at an excellent academy at Colchester, some hours ride away from New Haven. Timothy Phelps and Uncle Beers kept an eye on him and paid his bills whenever his father's drafts were delayed overlong, as was frequently the case. Nobody had time to pay much attention to Stephen, but reports from the academy were good.

Certainly Mary was too busy to give more than a passing glance at the lad, if she saw him at all. She and Horace had decided to be married as soon as he could finish his studies, pass the examinations, and be licensed. He was in his twenty-fourth year and she had turned twenty in October, old enough to be wed—if she was not to be considered a confirmed spinster. It took a deal of time to gather her linens and plan her clothes, even with help from her mother and Aunt Henrietta, and to give some thought to her new career as a minister's wife. Deep as were Horace's religious convictions, he had not tried to make her adopt them, and now she felt the need for a commitment of her own. She had been reared within the teachings and shelter of Trinity Church, but in the laxity and confusion of the newly organized Episcopal denomination she was one of many who had not been confirmed by any bishop. As the time for her marriage drew near, she sought the advice of the Reverend Bela Hubbard. He was Dr. Hubbard now, Yale having forgiven him for his Toryism and made him a D.D. He, in turn, consulted with Bishop Jarvis, a scholarly cleric of New Haven, who looked with kindness upon all mankind, including even opinionated young theological students of other sects who married pretty girls out of his flock. So it came about that Mary was confirmed on the first Sunday in December,[26] and requested of her rector a certificate of membership in Trinity Church, as a sort of passport into the future.

Horace was out of town part of the fall. As he neared the completion of his studies, he made trips over the state and into Massachusetts to visit among the churches and make contacts with the clergy. He was already highly regarded in the Seminary classes, but it was important for him to be more widely known if he expected to receive a call from a good congregation. He kept his mind on the object of his journey, paying his respects to the proper persons, as a prospective applicant should. When his duties were done, however, he made it a point to see the local sights and meet interesting people. At day's end he wrote Mary lively accounts of his adventures.

One evening in Newburyport, Massachusetts, he retired to his room at the inn to share with his fiancée the visit he had just made to the home of the eccentric Timothy Dexter, whose yard was dotted with extraordinary statues of famous men, including one of himself.[27]

He had all but filled the long page with his neat, vertical script when suddenly music struck up in the street below, reminding him of jolly evenings with the "Corps"—and of her. He was tempted to accompany the merrymakers, strangers though they were, but prudently decided not to do so.

"The season is too far advanced," he scribbled, as if talking aloud to her there in the room, "and it is too cold to permit me to join in a serenade where you are not its principal object." He was really a man of feeling, for all his logic.

Horace finished his theological training brilliantly in less than a year's time, and just before Christmas was officially licensed to preach by the New Haven East Association of Ministers.[28] The wedding was set for New Year's, and the Phelps household was thrown into a turmoil of sewing and packing and polishing and baking in order to be ready for the occasion. They were to be married in the home, of course, and all the relatives in the town and countryside would be asked to drink tea on the first or second day. Uncle Timothy's dowry to the niece who lived with him for ten years was a proper wedding that was long remembered in the family and community. He was a generous foster father, and her trunks bulged with stylish dresses and cloaks and pretty gloves, as well as books, sheet music, and her well-worn writing case. The shining guitar was a problem when it came to be packed, but she would manage to take it somehow.

All was in order by the last day of the Old Year. Dr. Hubbard remembered to send a special messenger over to the house with Mary's certificate,[29] which she tucked safely away in the portfolio where she kept letters, especially Horace's, and original verses, and other treasured papers. Unsystematic as she was about her money or keeping account of expenses, she was meticulous about manuscripts and family papers and records. To them she attached great importance because they seemed part of her very self, as money never did.

They were a handsome couple as they stood up to plight their troth in the sight of God and man that New Year's evening.[30] He was tall, erect, vigorous; she was fair and winsome. Their lives stretched out before them as bright and full of promise as the unblemished year. Dr. Hubbard performed the ceremony according to the rites of the bride's church, a truly generous concession on the part of the groom, so newly ordained in another denomination. His yielding this point was proof not only of his consideration for her but of his innate tolerance. He loved Mary with his whole heart, for her intelligence as well as for her beauty. She was the only woman in his life from the moment he slipped the ring on her finger and the minister pronounced them man and wife. It was a plain gold band, incredibly tiny, and inside it was engraved "H.H. & M.A., married Jan. 1, 1805."[31]

3. SALISBURY HONEYMOON 1805

A new year and a new world greeted young Mr. and Mrs. Holley when they bade farewell to Uncle Timothy and departed from his spacious residence, where they had just been married, in order to begin the long journey over icy roads to Horace's family home in Salisbury. It was a hard trip, but they were too much in love to mind either the biting cold or the wretched meals at the coach stops. Bundled up in muffs and shawls and footwarmers, they snuggled under the thick robes, so blissfully happy that the long miles seemed short. They talked the hours away, recalling friends and relatives who came to the wedding festivities, and the marriage gifts, and letters that must be written at once. The joys of first love and youthful passion were merged with the delight of finding how extraordinarily congenial their minds and tastes really were. Travelling together proved far more stimulating than the proper conversations and formal correspondence of their courtship.

The route the coach followed upstate was familiar to Horace, especially as they travelled northward, but it was new to his bride.[1] As the country grew more rugged, he pointed out to her the different peaks that rose beyond the whitened valleys and hills—Prospect Mountain and Canaan Mountain and finally the great east slope of Tarconack Range, dotted with the green points of small firs and the tall black stacks of the iron furnaces tipped with flame like torches in the wind. Rocking along in the coach he discoursed learnedly about the famous Salisbury iron beds that had long supplied the furnaces of the whole Housatonic Valley with brown hematite ore of the best quality, so good that during the war with the British the Governor had caused a foundry to be erected there for the patriot armies. She could have replied that her Grandfather Phelps also supplied the Continentals with cannon balls, but instead, she expressed a polite interest in the furnace that Mr. Luther Holley owned near his farm.

The second afternoon they left the stage at Canaan, a village in the northwest corner of the state, very close to the New York line, where

Mr. Holley had sent a wagon to bring them and their clutter of luggage and boxes six miles farther to the farm. Even with a stout team, the trip over the mountain in winter weather was rough going. The streams had frail bridges or none, and the grades were often so steep that the men got out and walked to lighten the load, leaving Mary perched precariously on the jolting wagon seat. But the grandeur of the scenery more than made up for such inconveniences. As they climbed they could hear the hoarse roar of the cataract mingling with its own echo from across the snow-covered hills; and at last from the very top of the mountain they looked down through the falling dusk at the fierce, crimson blaze of the forges and the tiny faraway lights of the Holley homestead.

The young couple had a serious purpose in spending these first months of their new life under his parents' rooftree. They had got married without waiting for Horace to complete his full ministerial preparation, and it behooved them to live economically until he obtained a settlement. Already he had been asked to preach trial sermons in various communities, but he was determined to accept no invitations until he could be certain of making an auspicious start, one worthy of what was expected of him. He proposed, as he wrote one of his brothers, "to make preparations for preaching during the winter, occasionally speaking, perhaps, in Mr. Crosman's pulpit, and in the spring to itinerate in those places that are vacant, where I should be willing to settle, if called."[2] Mr. Crosman was the pastor of the White Church, a small congregation in Salisbury, which the Holleys attended regularly.

The plan, on the whole, was a good one. The young minister could count on the support and encouragement of his family, all of whom were extremely proud of his record at Yale. He would have the opportunity to work without interruption at his self-appointed studies, and make every day a scholar's day. The only possible flaw in the arrangement was that a city girl like his bride might find it trying to live with her new relatives on a remote farm, snowbound for months, while he pored over his future sermons. The winter was going to be a test of her adaptability and inner resources. Fortunately, she had lived most of her life in the midst of a crowded household. By temperament and long necessity, she got along well with people, and she could be tactful when she chose. Besides, as she told Horace when they made their plans, she was never lonely if there were books to read.

Luther Holley's substantial white house, with its surrounding garden and orchard and pastures, was located on the margin of Lake Wanscopomac, a placid body of water four miles in circumference, set amidst wooded hills. At this season glowing columns of flame and smoke from the furnace were reflected on its icy surface. While the wagon creaked down toward the house, Horace chatted gaily about skating on the lake and coasting on the big bobsled—he would see that they did both very soon.

It seemed to Mary, as the family trooped out to welcome the newly-weds, that there were a great many Holley brothers.[3] John Milton, the oldest, lived with his young wife and baby boy on a farm nearby. Myron, the one she had met in New Haven, was missing because he had settled out in the lake section of western New York. That still left three younger boys and a four-year old sister. It was a big, lively family, like her own in her father's lifetime, and in spite of her weariness she met them eagerly and warmly. At first they were stiff and reserved with Horace's new wife, but before supper was over, everybody was laughing and talking as if she had been in the family always.

Characteristically, Horace plunged at once into his work. He converted their bedroom into a study, arranging a row of Latin and Hebrew books on the handhewn table along with the inkwell and a large supply of quills. Most days he kept steadily at his tasks from early morning to gathering dusk, pausing only to toss fresh billets on the fire or to join in a midday meal at his mother's table, loaded with steaming hasty pudding and spicy sausages and translucent apples.

While her husband wrestled with learned texts behind a closed door, Mary got acquainted with his family around the roaring hearth in the warm, brown country kitchen. Her mother-in-law was a big woman, taller than Luther, who worked from long before sun-up until after dark, looking after her houseful of menfolks and children. A little slow to express herself, she knew her own mind and was capable of being stubborn when she set her head on something. Horace looked like her, with his black hair and eyes; and Mary suspected that he was her favorite. It was no matter, because Sarah Dakin Holley loved all her children with utterly selfless devotion and included their wives and the grandchildren in her affections without question.

Never having had another woman around the house, Sarah probably did not expect her new daughter-in-law to help much with the hard chores. That was just as well, because Mary had never lived before where the mistress of the household cooked and washed and sometimes fetched a stick of wood or a pail of water from outdoors. But she was clever at small tasks like dusting and wiping the dishes and setting the table, and she was thought to be wonderful when she stitched up pretty little dresses for Caroline, adorned with ribbon bows and lace from her own trunks. Thirteen-year-old Orville tagged after her whenever he was in the house, exchanging information about the farm and Salisbury for her tales of the college and of her brother who was at sea. He looked very much like Horace, and seemed to have a quick mind like his.

Of all the Holleys Mary most loved and admired her father-in-law, a short, quick man, with clear blue eyes and a ready smile. Luther had accepted her with open arms when he lifted her down from the wagon and led her into his house, and it was affection at first sight between them. Lean as a rail and as active as his sons, he was young for his years. He was invariably cheerful and hopeful, with a tremendous capacity for work. Mary liked to think that while her husband took after his mother in appearance, he was more like his father in character and temperament.

During some of their long talks before the glowing hearth Luther Holley told Mary that he had never attended a formal school but five days in his whole life, yet she found him well informed and able to converse not only sensibly but elegantly on all general subjects.[4] It was easy to see how he had managed to educate himself. An early riser, he got his day's tasks done promptly, and when he came in from work he would immediately pick up a book and proceed to read with complete concentration in the midst of his bustling household. His memory, too, was prodigious. There had been a time in his younger days, he said, when he could repeat the whole of *Paradise Lost* without looking at the book. As she came to know Luther Holley better, Mary understood why he had named a son John Milton, and why he had always encouraged Horace's scholarly ambitions.

Whenever she saw Luther put aside his book to engage in conversation, she listened with the sympathetic attention that was one of her great charms. One day, in a reminiscent mood, he told her how at sixteen he had taken on the responsibility for his father's little farm south of Salisbury, and cultivated it profitably until an accident to his leg made him less active. Then he qualified himself to teach the neighborhood school, and before long a committee from the Salisbury Furnace Community engaged him. Within a few years he acquired a wife and three children, all on a salary of five pounds a month, figured old style, which was better during the War than Continental money.

The war with the British was still going on, Luther recalled, when Horace was born in 1781; and soon afterward he had gone into the mercantile business across the Hudson in New York State, finally winding up back in Salisbury as both farmer and storekeeper. He had almost got into the West India trade in the nineties, a circumstance that made Mary feel all the more at home with her husband's father.

Luther Holley was descended from sound English stock, who were Anglicans before that church lost its hold in the New England farming communities, and was by nature a religious person. He believed a preacher had to feel what he said, but the preachers of his experience were often hurried too much by the ardor of their own affections to bestow any benefit on their hearers. The "mechanical preachers" he had heard in his youth had never warmed his heart, and, as he explained the matter to Mary, that was probably why he had never joined any sect. His wife, the daughter of an Orthodox Baptist elder who often preached from the pulpit, was a member of that branch but not a very strict believer. She could not, for example, bring herself to believe that anybody she loved would suffer endless torments through eternity on account of a point of faith. All the family attended church regularly. The atmosphere of the home was reverent but there was no stern insistence upon piety.

Mary enjoyed Sundays in Salisbury. Everybody wrapped up in their warmest cloaks and trudged along the country road toward the slim spire rising among the tall, bare trees. As the bell pealed solemnly for forenoon and afternoon preaching, the entire community joined the throng at the meetinghouse door. Soberly they greeted each other and nodded respectfully to young Mr. Holley and his bride in her stylish wrap and bonnet. When her true soprano notes blended with his mellow baritone in the strains of "Old Hundred," the congregation bent an ear to listen, and almost smiled.

As she sat erect hour after hour on the hard bench, Mary Holley's thoughts sometimes strayed from the pastor's propositions to observe how distinguished her husband looked. She had plenty of time to wonder about the quirk of fate that had caused her to be sitting here beside him in an obscure village meetinghouse instead of in their own pew in a New York City church. By now she knew that her husband's own family did not understand any better than she why he had given up the law for the ministry; indeed, Luther had mentioned to her that Horace had first planned to be a merchant. Nor was it clear to any of them why his views had lately taken a still more orthodox and straight-laced turn. During his studies at the Seminary he had espoused the austere doctrine known as "Hopkinsianism," that outdid Calvin himself in depicting God as the stern judge of the Old Testament, and in closing the gates of salvation to all except the Elect. Even President Dwight hardly went so far as to agree that a believer must be willing to be damned and consign his loved ones to torment for the glory of God. It was a case of the pupil exceeding his master in zeal; and, Mary reflected a little wistfully, Horace was very zealous.[5] But she never questioned the necessity of his following his convictions wherever they led him, and even when she disagreed with him she was carried away by his eloquence. Like the Holleys, she was sure that he was destined to be a great and famous man.

There were happy times during that long, cold winter. Whenever Horace shut the door of his study behind him and strode into the kitchen, he was once more his own gay, affectionate self, complimenting his bride with courtly manners and praising his mother's cooking. Then Sarah Holley would relate for the twentieth time what a good, studious boy he had been, never rebellious save when he was kept home from school to do chores. In the evenings Mary sang for them, and they marvelled at her delicate fingering on her guitar. The young ones adored her, not only Orville, but Caroline and Newman, an owlish, quiet lad, who would some day bestow on two of his children the names of Mary and Horace.

The fireside talk frequently got around to Brother Myron and his adventures with the practice of law. He had begun there in Salisbury by defending a penniless wood chopper, reputedly a wizard, against a rough Dutch teamster. The driver had cut gashes on the poor woodsman's forehead for bewitching his horses as they went up the mountain trail. Myron, ever for the underdog, had eloquently proved his client to be no witch, and got damages for him besides. Myron had also practised a while over in the Finger Lake region, where he was now living, but had quit when a client whom he had got acquitted of a serious charge turned out to be guilty. The young lawyer was now a bookseller and gardener.[6]

"Ah, well," said Luther, repeating what he had written his son on hearing of his action, "the height of human felicity is to be able to converse with the wise, to instruct the ignorant, to pity and despise intriguing villains, and to assist the unfortunate." He thought his son did well to live up to his own ideals even if he found it hard to support a growing family by peddling vegetables and books. The advice was comforting to Myron, who had no worldly ambition.

Horace's studies went well. By spring he had done most of the proposed reading and was outlining a series of sermons. When the weather moderated he and Mary got out-of-doors for walks over the well-kept farm and around the neighborhood. He showed her the little district schoolhouse on the hill, now rather shabby, where he had been entered when only a little more than three years old. By the time he was ten he had mastered all the classes that were offered, and his father put him to work in the store rather than have him acquire lazy habits. At twelve the boy was trusted to drive a pair of horses over to the freighting villages on the Hudson, to deliver goods, and even to transact business. Had his father carried out the plan to send him down to New York City as a mercantile apprentice, Horace laughingly teased his young wife, she might never have got to be Mrs. Holley.

When the roads became passable in the late spring, they drove to Redhook and Rhinebeck and Poughkeepsie, little towns on the river. As they drove out of Salisbury, lofty Tarconack Mountain loomed up, a landmark for the whole region. On its top was a rude column of stone, visible for miles around. Once each year all the young people of the vicinity climbed to the summit, each striving to be the first to add a stone. Horace's face beamed as he recalled that he had got there first many times. As Luther Holley's good horses trotted under his skillful handling, he remembered all sorts of small triumphs of his youth.

The Salisbury countryside, rugged in winter, grew lovely and tender as the trees misted with green and the Lake rippled again in the sunlight. Mary filled her sketchbook with views of Wanscopomac, ringed by woods and meadows, with a little skiff upon its placid mirror. Horace thought her drawings pretty, as indeed they were, thanks to excellent teachers. He, too, loved nature. It was only when he was composing sermons about wrath and damnation that he conceived of this lovely region as a vale of tears.

Sometimes during the placid months of their early married life Mary wondered how her ardent young husband could think that the world glistening in the still, white moonlight outside their window could possibly be under the curse of divine displeasure. Could he really believe that they or any other lovers so blessed in the sight of God and man could be in danger of hell-fire? She did not know for sure, but as long as he was happy in his vocation, she was happy, too; and they made the most of this interlude, this scholar's honeymoon. There was very little left of about thirteen hundred dollars that Luther Holley had given his son as his patrimony,[7] and Mary had brought no dowry to the marriage. It was time for Horace to get settled somewhere with a church of his own.

4. GREENFIELD HILL
1805-1808

By summer the young Holleys were back in New Haven visiting with her people until the all-important matter of their first settlement could be determined. Horace let it be known that he was now prepared to preach, and soon invitations pressed upon him from many places. Much was expected of him both by his friends and by the discriminating congregations who listened to a fledgling preacher's sermons as critically as a New York audience to an actor in his first Shakespearean role. There was, naturally, no question as to the theological soundness of any graduate of the Yale Seminary. But did this young man possess the gift of eloquence, that crowning glory of the clerical calling?

Mary accompanied him on his rounds to meetinghouse after meetinghouse, and sat among the members of the congregations, thrilling to the mellow richness of her husband's voice and noting the favorable impression he invariably made. As she herself admitted, she was a "not unconcerned spectator" of his debut in the ministry. Their whole future was at stake. When she bent her head reverently during these long services, she must often have added a silent plea in the familiar words of her own Prayer Book for him and for herself that the desires and petitions of their hearts might be fulfilled as was most expedient for them.

Once again it was President Dwight who influenced the crucial decision. Although Horace had garnered many college laurels, he had no influential relatives, no important connections to secure for him a call to a prosperous church, and he looked to his revered advisor. The President cherished an especial regard for the little congregation at Greenfield Hill in the northwest part of Fairfield County, just westward along the Sound from New Haven. There he himself had served as pastor for more than a decade just before becoming president of Yale; there in its rustic quietude he had composed some of his most famous poems. He had also established a widely recognized academy for boys and girls, had cultivated an extensive garden, and had enjoyed pleasant society and literary ease. It was a small, poorly supported parish, entirely overshadowed by the larger congregations nearby; and since Dwight's day it had been irregularly ministered to by temporary pastors. Mr. Griswold, the last "supply," had departed some months previously after staying only a year. The salary was now less than formerly, and lately three men in succession had declined a call, in spite of the extra money they could hope to make by teaching in the school. Horace Holley could surely have done better than this post if he had broken away from college ties and looked farther afield.[1]

He made up his mind within a short time, however, to begin his chosen career as pastor of the church at Greenfield Hill. On September 3, 1805, he was ordained by the Western Consociation of Fairfield County, and his people voted "to give Mr. Holley five hundred and sixty dollars a year for his services in the ministry so long as said society and Mr. Holley could agree." It was well understood, in the aggressively congregational mode of the time, that either party could dissolve the connection whenever it so desired.[2]

To the romantic young minister and his wife it seemed that their desires and petitions had been granted in their first charge. They deeply wanted a home of their own—they had been married for close on to a year without Mary's ever having had a chance to unpack her linens —and leisure time for books and music and congenial society. Greenfield Hill offered idyllic surroundings and security. Whether it was the course most expedient for them they would have to find out in the coming years.

There was a tang of autumn in the air as Horace conveyed his wife and their increasingly voluminous belongings to the home he had rented near his new church. The Post Road they followed out of New Haven ran westward toward New York, keeping almost always in sight of the Sound. They passed through Milford and across the Housatonic River and into Fairfield, a fine, rich town that was now rebuilt after being partially burned down by the redcoats. There they left the Post Road to wind away from the shore up to Greenfield Hill, the highest elevation in the county. For miles they had caught glimpses of the slender spire of the church, a landmark for men at sea and a vantage point from which General Washington's secret agents had once watched the movements of British ships in the Sound. At the top of the Hill was the Green, a grassy common that served as the village center, where the meetinghouse and school were located, along with the tavern. And, sure enough, halfway up the meetinghouse steeple was the elevated circular walk where the villagers said that Dr. Dwight had paced out the rhyming couplets of his epic, *Greenfield Hill,* walking round and round as he composed its seven long parts. The very sight of it charmed the Holleys.

Dwelling houses, large and small, were dotted along the roads that went winding down the slopes from the Green to "orchards and fields and groves and houses rare," as the famous poem described the scene. They knew some of these residents already, notably Mary's relatives in the Beers connection; and by coincidence, their new home, located on Bronson Road, had at one time been owned by Mr. Samuel Broome, Uncle Timothy's father-in-law. It was a plain, unprepossessing house, built during the War, but it was big and substantial.[3] One of the previous pastors had occupied it in comfort with his family of seventeen children, and young Mr. and Mrs. Holley doubtless took a little kindly teasing when that bit of village lore was related to them. They needed a sizable house already, because they proposed to have the brothers and sisters on both sides to live with them from time to time. They felt responsible for helping the younger ones to get a proper start in life. Horace meant to direct Orville's studies, and was willing to help Charles Austin, too, as they were about of an age. That plan pleased Mary, who knew that her youngest brother must be looked after. Mr. Lewis was no help to Esther, financially or with his stepsons. Charles was a bookish, gentle lad, the one of all Elijah's sons who ought to go to college, and Henry offered to pay his fees if Mr. Holley would prepare the boy for Yale.[4]

Henry was back in the States from one of his voyages, spending most of his time in New York City, on the lookout for ways to make a fortune. Sometimes he and the oldest brother, who was doing only tolerably well at making a living for his young family over in Middletown, thought of emigrating to Missouri to join Uncle Moses. Such restless talk was what Mary had heard all her life from the men in her family. There were always Austins ready to risk danger and failure if a big chance offered. Whenever the wind of change blew, they set their sails to catch it.

Now, however, she listened to her brothers with a serene assurance that no such risks lay ahead of her. At twenty-one she was the wife of an orthodox minister serving in a quiet village, and the proud mistress of a home, the first since childhood that she could call her own. She had to admit that she herself had taken a considerable chance in marrying a man of such strict and puritanical views, but she loved him so devotedly that she joined cheerfully in the tasks to which he dedicated their lives. Their days were filled with hospitable household chores and the planning of sermons and the hum of children's voices spelling simple words. In the evenings they read poetry together and shared the joys of music and love. The Bard of Greenfield Hill had not exaggerated these "pure pleasures of parochial life." As sophisticated literati, they liked their rustic village all the more because it had been celebrated in a noted epic.

The household was put in order before winter set in. Cords of firewood, beech and oak and nutwood, must be provided, and the storeroom filled with flitches of bacon and hams, with jars and barrels and cannikins. They had little furniture of their own at first, but they garnished the rooms with many books and a deal of bric-a-brac she had collected during her girlhood in a wealthy home. She missed her piano —it belonged to Uncle Timothy, of course—but her guitar served to accompany their musical evenings. When neighbors and friends came visiting she sang and played for them, hymns or romantic melodies, as their taste dictated.

Autumn was a glorious time that challenged the artist in Mary. She could not capture in her pencil sketches the red-gold that blazed amid the fading greens and misty blues of the Connecticut countryside, but she caught the spirit of the season. She was more effective with words when she described her favorite view from the church steps:

". . . that beautiful sheet of water, Long Island Sound, with the Island in the distance; while nearer might be seen, reposing among rich fields and lawns, villages with their spires and villas, with their orchards and cultivated grounds."[5]

She and her husband admired nature before it became fashionable to do so in America. As they rounded out a lovers' calendar of the seasons they became enamored of "romantic scenery." With so much of happiness in his heart, the young husband thought less and less often about the essential wickedness of the world and the flesh, or even of the devil.

Of course, when he stood in the pulpit looking down at his neighbors dressed in their Sunday best, he was still stern enough. Shortly after his coming the Greenfield Hill congregation adopted its first confession of faith to replace the simple assent to the old covenant with which they had been getting along since 1776. The new confession was a logical covering of eight articles of Calvinist doctrine, undoubtedly composed by the minister. New members were attracted by Mr. Holley's fresh manner of preaching. He began delivering his sermons without reading from a manuscript—in contrast to the way most clergymen intoned their discourses without lifting their eyes from the paper—always enlivening and enriching his expositions with references to whatever he had read or noticed during his pastoral calls and daily walks. He had so good a memory that he preached from a brief introduction and notes, trusting to the inspiration of the occasion for an effective ending. In its vigor and popular appeal, the result was closely akin to the political eloquence heard in the State House.

This virtually extemporaneous style of preaching proved successful and easy for Horace Holley. The trouble was that it ran counter to an accepted clerical practice of the day. Virtually all scholarly clergymen made a studied point of printing and circulating their more important sermons; and a long list of such publications was the standard measure of a man's prestige and industry. Many of these pamphlets were precisely those "mechanical sermons" that Luther Holley considered cold, and were better suited to the shelves of a library than to the pulpit. Horace's discourses were lively and appealing, but he was not disciplining himself to learn to write effectively. It ought to be said in his behalf that he was an extremely busy young man, not only with his parish people but with the village school.

The Academy of Greenfield Hill occupied a smallish, square building topped by a neat cupola, which had been erected across the Green from the church to accommodate Dr. Dwight's pupils when they overflowed the parlor in the little brown house where Gershon Hubbell, the tanner, dressed leather and where his daughter made gloves. According to village tradition, the Doctor had regularly spent six hours a day in the classroom. Although he never used the rod, he made an indelible impression upon the boys and girls who sat transfixed by the gaze of his piercing black eyes or stood with trembling knees in his presence for the weekly declamations and spelling bees. Since his departure the Academy had been neglected and a rival had sprung up over on Fairfield Green; but the new minister had no doubt that he could revive the local school.

Horace was interested in the training of the young although he had never done any teaching before and knew far less about proper methods than his wife, who had attended good schools in New Haven in her childhood. He saw that the schoolrooms were cleaned and refurbished, and supplied with copy paper and hornbooks and quills and spellers. Before long the hard benches were lined with the neighbors' children, and the Green rang with the chant of rote spelling and reading. Mary guided the grubby fists in forming their letters and crossing the t's and dotting the i's, and taught the girls to sew and draw. He had charge of classes in Latin and geography and mathematics. Whenever Charles or Orville was there, so much the better. Both lads were clever and helpful.

The Holleys enjoyed having bright young people around them, although Mary frankly found routine classes tiresome. Horace, on the other hand, discovered that he liked all kinds of teaching. He was patient with his humbler pupils, and remarkably skillful with the little children, whom he instructed sometimes by a method of his own. He would engage them in dialogue, guiding them to ask serious questions, which he would then answer kindly. He, or somebody, should have guessed that he possessed this gift, but it apparently never occurred to them that while he was experimenting with storekeeping and the law and the ministry, he was essentially a teacher. In Greenfield he thought of his work as the village pedagogue merely as a means of adding the tuition fees to his meager salary.

It was after they were settled at Greenfield Hill that young Stephen Fuller Austin came over from the academy at Colchester to pay them a visit.[6] The boy was in touch with his New Haven relatives, and it may have been that young Charles brought him over during a yuletide vacation. He was a snub-nosed, round-headed boy, nicely dressed now in good broadcloth instead of the unfashionable garments he had worn when he came to the East. He had excellent manners and spoke correctly as he answered their many polite questions.

At Colchester he was living in the headmaster's home, and he liked his studies, especially composition and languages. When he left Missouri his parents were living in a settlement called Potosi, forty miles west of the Mississippi River, near the mines. His father had a store and a furnace and a shot manufactory, too. The Frenchmen who worked for him were dark-eyed and small, and they lived with their families nearby, but the roving Spaniards came and went on the River. The boy could speak a bit of both languages. All the settlers had had to become Spanish citizens when they first went out, and even yet, the only church was a Catholic one in Ste. Genevieve on the Mississippi. His sister Emily was in school in Lexington, Kentucky, but he himself meant to go to Yale and become a lawyer.

Visitors were an everyday matter at the parsonage, and most little boys who came were promptly forgotten. But not so with Stephen, whose visit made an impression upon everybody, especially his Cousin Mary. He, too, remembered the occasion—recalling years afterward that he was shy in the presence of his kinswoman. She was nine years older than he, an impassable barrier to a self-concious boy. More than likely it was not Mary who made him feel ill at ease but her tall, commanding husband, who naturally looked upon the visitor as just another schoolboy being readied for college.

As time passed the Holleys came to know their Greenfield Hill neighbors: the storekeeper Bradleys on the one side and the village physician on the other. Around the corner lived good Mr. Gershon Hubbell, who had sheltered the Academy in its beginnings. His home was a very old pitch-roof house with a buttonball tree in the yard and a well at the rear, where the family pewter and silver were dropped when the British soldiers marched up the road. The whole countryside was full of historic places and interesting tales. In every gathering a tradition was repeated that Dr. Dwight had attended the monthly dances at Mr. Bulkley's Tavern in Fairfield to hear a famous fiddler. Always he had one glass of wine and some cake, told a pleasant story, and left at the end of half an hour.

The Holleys visited oftenest in the Bronson home, a large brick mansion located a short distance down the southern slope of the hill.[7] This was the "Verna" of Dwight's poem, which he had sold to Dr. Isaac Bronson, a banker, on leaving the village. The new owners had greatly improved it by setting out a fine double row of dogwood along the driveway, and enlarging the modest garden of parsnips and golden pumpkins into a spacious estate. The Bronsons did not attend the Greenfield Hill meetinghouse, but they liked the young minister and his wife. The Doctor had been a surgeon's mate in the War, and like Uncle Nathan Beers was a member of the Society of the Cincinnati. He and his hospitable wife adopted their new neighbors as if they had been relatives.

These early years at Greenfield Hill fell into a pleasant pattern of living. Sundays were strictly observed, with no worldly reading or secular songs or even social letter writing, although in the evenings groups of church members sometimes came to the house to talk on appropriate topics. During the week the Holleys enjoyed the society of well-bred friends, and kept their home open to young people. They were eagerly hoping for children of their own.

Most satisfying of all, the two of them found each other's companionship delightful. When *The Lay of the Last Minstrel* by the new Scottish poet came fresh from Isaac Beers' bookshop, they could hardly wait to share it in the evenings by their glowing fire. Horace would begin in eloquent tones—

> Breathes there a man with soul so dead . . .

and Mary would take her turn by waxing sentimental over Scotland—

> O Caledonia! stern and wild,
> Meet nurse for a poetic child!

Mr. Scott's poetry was not the only new verse to stir their imaginations. There were Tom Moore's "Lake of the Dismal Swamp" and his "Canadian Boat Song" with a touch of the American scene in them.

The musical gatherings at the parsonage improved when Horace bought a piano from Uncle Timothy Phelps, who was emigrating to Missouri, and installed it in the parlor. It was the first one in Greenfield Hill, and attracted young and old to admire it.[8] So gay and polite were these gatherings that the circle of the Holleys' friends soon extended far beyond the membership of the congregation.

Horace took up versifying again. He wrote a neat little poem to head the first page of a handsome album that the Bronsons gave Mary, entitling it "Dedication of a Lady's Album: The Book Speaks to its Future Patrons." The point of his verse was to describe an ideal society where people were witty and harmlessly mirthful. He was paying a compliment to the charming society in the Greenfield Hill environs as he penned his approval of

> Whate'er may please the judgment, mend the heart,
> Beguile the anxious, and a joy impart,
> Engage the young, or renovate the old,
> Arrest the gay, or check the rudely bold;
> Whate'er may soothe the matron's ready frown,
>
> .   .   .   .   .   .
>
> Whate'er of use you start for harmless mirth,
> To which the laughter-loving mind gives birth.[9]

Almost without the young minister's being aware of it, a change was taking place in his beliefs and the goals he set for himself. He had come to Greenfield Hill to follow in the steps of Dwight, the stern theologian. As he remained, he discovered other aspects of his mentor's personality: the genial man of letters, the kindly schoolmaster, and the patient gardener, sifting the earth around the roots of his seedlings. If these revelations of his idolized teacher surprised him, so did the discovery of what was happening in his own breast. His Hopkinsian convictions about a stern, implacable Ruler of the Universe were evaporating like mists in the valleys below when he looked down from the steeple walk on a sunshiny morning. He kept no diary of this return to the liberal faith of his youth, and the one person who could have known much about it was his wife. She thought that it was "no sudden change" but "the gradual progress of an inquiring mind." In later years, when many other persons became interested in the evolution of Horace Holley's religious beliefs, she declared that he gave up the harsh dogma he learned at Yale because he learned to "trust to his own powers, look with his own eyes, and think his own thoughts."

She was in love with him, and so dazzled by the evidences of his genius that she saw only part of the picture. She failed to realize how deeply he was influenced in this change by their happy life at Greenfield Hill. The trust and affection of the wide-eyed boys and girls whom he taught so gently and well, his own deep desire for children—these simple experiences nullified the doctrine of infant damnation for him. The constant delight with which he and Mary beheld nature's beauties unfold before their eyes and their shared response to poetry and music seemed good in themselves and in the sight of the Maker. The world and the flesh and the devil, lumped together in the theological texts, did not turn out to be one and the same thing at all. Mary had never thought so, and her love of life had no small part in bringing about his change of mind.

Thus there was nothing sudden in Horace's rediscovery that man and nature are good. As Mary put it, he was "emancipated from views deemed by many as derogatory to God," and there is no doubt that she included herself among the many who deemed them so. She was thankful to see him abandon the orthodoxy with which he had shackled himself when he entered the ministry. His preaching became more optimistic, but very gradually, so that it aroused no doctrinal disputations among his listeners.

The members of the congregation were satisfied with him, and gave him proof of their favor. In the spring of his second year he was granted permission to travel through some of the seaboard states, especially to the southward. He wanted to see for himself what the new nation was like. He planned to try out the fine turnpikes now radiating out from all the bustling towns, and compare the manufactories and churches and statehouses elsewhere with those he knew in Connecticut. He had never been very far from his native Salisbury, and he wanted to widen his horizon.

The good Mr. Isaac Lewis, acting for the congregation, gave him a handsome certificate as a "worthy and respectable clergyman," and recommended him to all ministers and churches on his journey.[10] With such a letter to open the right doors for him, he carried out a good part of his plan, journeying through New York, New Jersey, and Pennsylvania, to his great pleasure and edification. The world he saw was notably larger than Yale College and Fairfield County, and after his return his point of view continued to expand. He acquired new interests, one of which got him into print in a prominent scientific journal.

In mid-December of 1807, at dawn of Monday, the fourteenth, a shower of meteoric stones fell upon Fairfield and the surrounding area. A surprising number of people witnessed the phenomenon, and everybody gossiped excitedly about it. It thereupon occurred to the young minister and his neighbor, Dr. Bronson, that they should devote the following Saturday to ascertaining the exact facts for a report to the proper scientific authorities. They interviewed the farmers in whose dooryards the stones had fallen; they measured distances; they recorded testimony; and they collected specimens.

Within a fortnight the conscientious investigators had compiled a report to send to Dr. Samuel L. Mitchell, eminent physician and the professor of chemistry in the University of New York, as well as editor of *The Medical Repositary*, published in that city. He may well have been a professional friend of Dr. Bronson's. The report appeared shortly as a three-page article titled, "An Investigation of the Facts relative to a descent of Stones from the Atmosphere to the Earth, etc. etc.," by the Rev. Horace Holley and Isaac Bronson, Esq., of Fairfield. This fall of meteoric stones was hardly "one of the most extraordinary, though not unprecedented, events in the history of the world," as the article stated; but young Mr. Holley had reason to be proud of the publication. It was his first published article, and he could think of himself now as a man of letters in a modest way.[11]

Mary was looking beyond Greenfield Hill, too. Henry and Uncle Timothy were in Missouri, trying their fortunes. Thousands of settlers were going west in the excitement roused by the reports of Lewis and Clark's expedition to the Pacific. Another brother, Horace Austin, was setting out to Missouri with his family, taking Aunt Henrietta and the younger Phelps children by carriage to Pittsburgh, from whence they would then go down the Ohio and up the Mississippi by flatboat all the way to Ste. Genevieve, the French village young Stephen had talked about.[12]

These family moves made Mary a little sad. Her uncle's departure left her with only a memory of the gracious home of her girlhood, her courtship and marriage. At Whiting Street, Henrietta and Charles still lived with their mother and Mr. Lewis, but New Haven had no ties for Mary now. The Holleys were ready to leave Greenfield Hill even before the spring of 1808, when she found that she was going to have a child. That happy prospect made it all the more desirable for them to seek a better situation at once. They could not afford to stay longer in a charge that would never offer them more than a modest livelihood. Horace told his congregation plainly that he must leave to obtain a larger salary. Mary, far more diplomatic than he, explained to callers that "though the situation was delightful, the tender charities of life agreeable, still a larger portion of substantial comforts was necessary to the well-being of a family."[13]

It was meet and right now for the young clergyman to be ambitious. As he looked abroad for prospects, he cast his eye eastward toward the older New England settlements. He was ready to sever the ties that bound him to Yale and President Dwight. He could stand upon his own reputation, and this time he meant to make a judicious choice. He desired a charge where his burgeoning mind could obtain a still more extended view of Christianity, and where he and Mary could enlarge their experience of ideal society.

5. HOSTAGES
TO FORTUNE
1808-1809

On a warmish day in early summer Mr. Holley dismissed his Academy classes for the last time, and the boys and girls ran out across the Green calling gaily to each other. Their master, sedate and uncomfortable in black clerical coat and formal neckcloth, might well have run out the door with them and shouted that he, too, felt free. But there were still chores to be done. He had to see that the little white building was swept clean and the doors fastened against the weather. Tuition accounts must be figured up so that the parents who had neglected to pay them could be politely dunned. He would send his brother Orville around the village with the bills.[1]

Very certainly, come next fall, he would not ring the bell to summon these merry scholars back to their books. His apprenticeship in the ministry here at Greenfield Hill was nearly over, and, in all likelihood, his teaching days were done for good. He was in no great hurry to leave. With school closed, he could now take his time about corresponding with people to let them know he was available.

As he went through his papers preparatory to his departure, he carefully laid aside the family letters and his college exercises and all his personal mementoes. He was at heart deeply sentimental. But he ruthlessly burned the stack of discourses written that winter at Salisbury and also his notes and outlines for sermons here. When Mary protested, he declared that old manuscripts were cumbrous and troublesome, and furthermore, he did not need them because they were all treasured in his mind. She felt otherwise about her own belongings. She kept all her papers, even compositions and schoolgirl correspondence, discarding nothing out of her bulging portfolio. She never wanted to discard her past, the way Horace did whenever he turned a corner. Even the prospect of having a child made her treasure her own souvenirs all the more. She would never think of herself simply as the baby's mother.

She was satisfied to spend the summer months in Greenfield reading or knitting for the baby or puttering in her garden. It was always good for her to work with flowers. This old house, where nothing disturbed the quietness but the creaking of cart wheels pulling up the hill or the barking of some neighbor's dog, was a peaceful place to wait for her time. She had never been robust, and sometimes now she had restless nights when she became anxious about what the future might hold for them. Horace enjoyed his usual good health. He was bursting with pride at the prospect of an heir, and was making arrangements for leaving Greenfield as if his new optimistic view of the universe guaranteed a happy outcome of his personal plans.

Mary's sister Henrietta came to be with her while he was away during their last months in Greenfield, and so she was not lonely. She and Horace made the best of their separation by frequent letters, reiterating their affection for each other and coining apt phrases for this new joy they had created.

"I think of you," she wrote to him, "in the enduring relation of the father of my sweet child . . . and the chains of love bind you still closer to my heart."[2]

At the end of one of his letters he filled out the rest of the paper with the wish that he could fall into the arms most dear to his heart. These two were offering each other proud, youthful gifts. She proffered to him the "first pledge of love"; he promised her a settlement worthy of her and their child.

They were not troubled by the fact that they had saved practically no money in well over two years of married life. It was agreed that Horace must travel very frugally on his trips of exploration, and when they gave up their home in Greenfield Hill, she was to go to her mother's in New Haven, but, as a matter of fact, both of them were extravagant in their tastes. Her habits had been formed by Uncle Timothy's lavish ways, and Horace savored the good things of life fully as much as she. He cherished no longing for the plain, country ways of his parents' home, and all the "castles in the air" which he imagined for his sweetheart in the days of their courtship were furnished not only with "a competence ample" but with a genial society and an atmosphere of culture. The Holleys had outgrown the state of being happy on a salary of $560 a year.

By summer's end Horace had completed his plans for a preaching trip extending over into Massachusetts and Maine; he then asked for a release from his duties at Greenfield Hill. His congregation proceeded with resignation and dispatch to appoint the necessary committees and gather the votes to "concur with Mr. Holley in his application for dismission." Through the years the little church had seen many a promising clergyman come and go. It wished the Holleys well as it calmly sent them on their way with its blessing. Mr. Samuel Goodrich, Scribe, set down in a clear hand in the church minutes that on September 13, 1808, the Consociation of the Western District dismissed him with regret and declared "their entire approbation of his ministerial character," recommending him to "the grace of God, and likewise to the church as a gospel minister."[3] Horace Holley could not have wished for a more complimentary dismission. The matter of his leaving was accomplished without the least disaffection between him and his people.

Soon the Holleys' possessions, now grown bulky, were carted to New Haven to be stored. Mary was expecting her child in early December, and if her husband was to get back from his trip in time to "administer the consolations and encouragements of conjugal affection," as she rather primly described his share in the forthcoming event, then he needs must get started right away while the weather was open and the turnpikes passable. Both husband and wife were torn by the necessity for his leaving her at this time; yet she was fully as eager as he for him to make the journey. Perhaps some of his urgency derived from his desire to make another, a fresh start on his career. He was already twenty-seven.

The house in New Haven over which Esther Phelps-Austin-Sanford-Lewis had presided for most of the past thirty years was shabbier than it had ever been, but there was room and welcome for Mary and her husband, and also for Orville, who wanted to continue his schooling in New Haven instead of going back to Salisbury. Mr. Lewis' collections occupied considerable room, and the pigeons he raised were something of a bother, but the heterogeneous family adapted itself admirably to the circumstances. Henrietta entertained her company in the parlor, allowing Charles a corner in which to study his Latin or play softly on his harmonica. Small Peleg was a healthy boy of eight, who seemed more like Esther's grandchild than her son. They called him Phelps now.

The house was even livelier when Henry returned from Missouri. Uncle Moses was prospering, and Timothy Phelps was almost as full of affairs in a small frontier town as he had ever been in New Haven. Besides running his iron and lead business he served as the postmaster and a trustee of the newly founded Ste. Genevieve Academy. Henry talked less enthusiastically about Missouri, however, than about the wonders of New York City, where he now proposed to settle. His friend and roommate, Robert Fulton, had completed a steamboat that could make the trip upstream to Albany and back in five days.[4] If steamboats could be designed for the Western waters, Henry thought, it might be worth while to try it again there.

Henry's vehement conversation—he was always vehement—found two attentive listeners. That inveterate rover, Elisha Lewis, paid such good heed that he began to figure how he could manage to get to see the Mississippi. Mary, fascinated as usual by Henry's projects, put what he said away in the back of her mind with all the other talk about frontier adventure. Along with her husband she was now turning her face toward the cultured centers on the Eastern seaboard where bold new ideas promised to be more challenging to a young minister than faraway places.

In mapping out his preaching tour, Horace accepted a warm invitation from Middletown, a thriving Connecticut community some twenty-five miles to the east, where he was already favorably known. After that he would fill engagements at Portland and Marblehead, and finally go on to Boston in the hope of being invited to preach in that city.[5]

It turned out at the last moment that Henry, too, wished to make a trip in that direction, and the two of them travelled part of the way together, sharing their lodging expenses. The cost made no difference to Henry, who was prosperous at the time, but every dollar mattered to Horace. He had felt obliged to make some contribution to his mother-in-law's household expenses, and then there would be bills to pay to the physician and the *accoucheur*. He was regretful and a trifle embarrassed that his wife, in her delicate condition, could not afford a carriage to take the air and return her relatives' calls.

The sermons he delivered in Middletown were decidedly successful. Prominent members of the church—like Judge Miller and Mr. Hosmer —urged him to stop again on his way home, making no secret of their eagerness to secure him. But Horace was resolved to look beyond the confines of his native state; and in spite of his real liking for Middletown, he went on with the trip as he had planned.

It was nearly ten years since he had come down from Salisbury as an impressionable country boy to commit himself to the shaping guidance of Yale College. He realized that while he had been wrestling with Hebrew and Hopkinsianism, the nation had been growing apace and breaking away from old notions and limits. Connecticut was teeming with manufactories that made guns and clocks and cotton gins, and every tenth person you met was applying for a patent for some new thingumbob. In the larger coast towns, all the way from Maine to South

Carolina, the ministers and scholars were joining with the merchants and lawyers and politicians to build a new country, rich and full of opportunities for bold ways of thinking. He wanted to get a good look at these places, and most especially at Boston.

Mary was more fully in her husband's confidence than most wives, and she understood the mixture of emotions in his heart when he clasped her affectionately and said goodbye. She knew that he was sorry to leave her, and yet eager to be on his way. In her imaginings she followed him through every day of his journey, arranging her life around the schedule of the post that brought his letters to her and bore her prompt replies to him. Charles or Orville or even Mr. Lewis must go rushing to the post office whenever she calculated that a letter was due or when she was seized with a feminine whim that she might have an extra one.

Horace was a faithful correspondent, even when his messages showed his weariness by the way his writing began to turn into a careless scrawl near the end of the sheet. His penmanship was naturally round and neat, but he always thought faster than his quill could move and he was likely to end hastily. She limited herself to sending him two or three long, detailed missives a week unless something came up that he must know sooner, like the visit Dr. Dwight paid her.[6]

It was on a Monday evening, not very long after Horace's departure, that the President came, bringing along a gentleman from Albany, to inquire where Mr. Holley was and when he would be home. Fortunately, Mary was feeling well, all things considered, and the visit turned out to be an extended one. The gentleman from Albany wanted Mr. Holley to supply a pulpit just vacated by the eminent Dr. Romayne, who had accepted a call to New York City. Dr. Dwight had already written to Albany that Horace was "the person best qualified for that place of any he knew." Mary noted his exact words, because they proved that he had not come just out of curiosity. The great man quizzed her about her husband's plan to visit Boston and seemed genuinely surprised to learn that he had been invited to preach in the South End Church there. His interest was flattering, and Mary drew him out diplomatically in order to get all the news for her next letter. When she wrote she did not underestimate the importance of the visit.

"Thus, you see, my dear Husband, that you are considerably in demand," she commented. "I think the great difficulty will be to make a judicious choice among so many offers."

Meanwhile her days were rarely dull or lonely. Esther was patient and helpful, and for the first time in years impressed her daughter by her store of woman's wisdom. Having no household cares, Mary took frequent walks, sometimes going to visit her aunts or cousins. She drank tea with Aunt and Uncle Beers, who were agog with gossip about his middle-aged brother, Isaac the bookseller, who had recently married equally middle-aged Mrs. Townsend. A nice gentleman from Greenfield Hill called at Whiting Street to relieve her of some counterfeit bills that had been passed off on Orville in settlement of a tuition account; and members of the Legislative Assembly, then in session, who came from Salisbury brought letters to Orville.

Sundays were the days when she was most lonely, especially after her condition made it no longer proper or prudent to go to church. Once, when she was unable to keep off the "vapours" by constant employment or walking, she was compelled to break her rule never to write letters on that day. She wrote to her husband, and on serious topics, which seemed to be a sufficient excuse.

"Everything wears a melancholy appearance today," she began. "It is the Sabbath and very stormy. The wind whistles without, the rain beats against the windows, and there is nothing cheerful within."

Her spirits rose as she communed with him, and she ended on a happier note.

"Do not be uneasy about me. I am very comfortable today, except for the temporary inconvenience I feel for want of sleep last night. I shall be in good spirits tomorrow, after receiving a letter informing me that you are so. Adieu! my dearest, best Friend, my tenderest love ever attends you . . . Mary."

She soon had good news from him. In a long letter marked "No. 17," written from Portland, he gave her all the details of his journey from Andover through Haverhill to Exeter, where the principal of the Academy invited him to drink tea at his house and meet a circle of gentlemen and ladies. He had gone on to Durham and Berwick, to Kennebunk and Scarboro, encountering hospitality at every stop, and being invited to preach in the larger places like Portland. A pretty girl or two had cast tender glances at his travelling companion, but to no avail. Henry was getting tired and would start for home soon.

Ere long Horace wrote her from Boston that his sermon at the South End Church had made a good impression, and that he had engaged to supply a pulpit at nearby Marblehead for a few weeks. Not with any idea of settling in that village, he hastened to assure her, but "to employ time to make calculations for the capital."

"For if I do not have an offer there," he went on to say, "I do not intend to accept of any in this region. I had much rather have Middletown than any place about here besides the capital. This, however, is all for yourself."

They were too congenial a married pair for her to take offense at his admonition not to tell anyone about his plans. But she needed no coaching in the art of diplomatic conversation, and she took occasion to tell him so gently in her next letter.

"I am very careful about speaking of your views and plans to any one, & should be, if you had not cautioned me. But I like to find out what I can about others."

She knew by now that he had set his heart on Boston, and would leave no stone unturned to obtain a call there, no matter how long he had to stay in that vicinage to get it. She even encouraged him to remain by pretending that he might break in upon her too suddenly and thereby injure her health. It was sheer pretense, but she was not one to let having a baby stand in the way of her husband's getting the right call.

Horace boarded in Marblehead in the home of a respectable widow and her two daughters, one of whom, he observed to his wife, was also pregnant. He had considerable leisure, during which he read the copy of *Marmion* he had picked up in a Boston bookshop. He promised to read it aloud to Mary at the earliest possible opportunity. The members of the little church liked his sermons so much that they tried to engage him at once, but he stayed only a few weeks, just long enough to make his "calculations."

They proved to be effective. He was invited to the South End Church in Boston for the customary period of probation while he was being considered. Meanwhile he also appeared in the pulpit of the famous Old South congregation, and spoke before the Thursday Lecture Society, both times to crowded audiences. He was becoming known in the whole city, and he could not afford to leave now, if he hoped for a call. His letters to Mary were full of hope that he could get home in time for the birth of their child, and he made elaborate suggestions about having the doctor get a good *accoucheur* and inquiries as to how her money was holding out.

It was the middle of December before he received the formal invitation from the Society in Hollis Street to become pastor of the South End Church, as it was usually called. The call was all he could have hoped for, and he knew that he was going to accept it.

In the meanwhile, Mary bore her child, a little daughter, there in the old home where she herself had been born.[7] She had the services of the good *accoucheur* and of her mother and sister, and the solicitous attentions of aunts and cousins and friends. The baby was healthy and good, and, so Esther said, unusually pretty for a newborn infant. Somebody hastened to notify the father, and his reply, addressed to Mary, sounded as if it was intended to be read aloud to the whole family:

I cannot realize the joy the event has given me. I think of the mother and I think of the daughter; and my soul is filled with gratitude. . . . I am extremely anxious to see you and your first gift. The era of brighter hopes seems to have commenced in our history. We were married before we obtained a settlement. That settlement proved to us a term of severe trial. We now have a daughter before a second settlement, and I trust the favorable omens are not the deception of evil *genii*. I shall write immediately to our friends and lead them to partake in our happiness.[8]

Another wife than Mary might have found his message cold and formal, but she recognized this rhetorical manner as a sign that he was excited and happy. He wrote as a man who had indeed given hostages to fortune.

He delayed in Boston long enough to complete his formal acceptance of the call and to make a few arrangements about where they would live; then he came posthaste to New Haven to see his wife and child. For about a month, during the Christmas and New Year season, they knew an interlude of calm, rest, and happiness. Mary recuperated satisfactorily. They received callers who came to congratulate them on their double good fortune—a new baby and a new charge. Meanwhile, they hovered fondly over the old family cradle in which tiny Harriette lay. She was called "Harriette" after a friend of Mary's, a Miss Williman, whose name somehow caught their fancy.[9] Perhaps the old names like "Mary" and "Abigail" had been too often repeated among the branches of the family.

Horace already had absurdly serious plans for the baby—should they teach her to say "Father" and "Mother," or "Mamma" and "Pappa?" He was more concerned over the responsibilities of being a parent than was his wife, and the miracle of their child confirmed and strengthened his optimism about the universe. Mary, too, was deeply moved by this new experience, which fulfilled and matured her personality; yet she remained more a wife than a mother. Even while she nursed her baby she was asking him about Boston. He had a great deal to tell her.

His charge was a prosperous but not very large congregation in the

South End, which, as they both knew, was an unfashionable part of town.[10] Hollis Street was located only a short walk above the Neck, where the Charles River and the Harbour all but cut off the Boston peninsula from the mainland. Numerous mills and factories were operated in the area. The little white meetinghouse with its twin cupolas—Bulfinch had designed it a generation ago when an earlier one burned—stood midway between Nassau and Orange, busy streets that led down to the Neck, where many of the congregation resided and carried on their business. They were mostly cabinet makers, hatters, chandlers, well-diggers, and so on, with an upper crust of very substantial merchants and lawyers and bankers.

It was a friendly neighborhood church, guided for the past twenty years by an amiable and learned pastor, Dr. Samuel West, who lived just around the corner on Nassau. A mildly liberal Calvinist, as could be seen from his many published sermons, he had been discreet and a trifle dull in the pulpit. His pastorate had been uneventful.

The leaders of the congregation were estimable gentlemen, like Otis Everett, who lived at the head of Orange; Samuel May, a hardware merchant and city leader; the well-to-do Dalls, father and son; Charles Davis; and many others. All who had flocked to hear his probationary sermons had been his friends on sight; and he was sure that Mary would like them and approve of their wives. It was probable that they would reside near the church, either on Nassau near Dr. West and the well-known Mr. John Quincy Adams, or over on Orange, which was lined with the homes of pewholders at Hollis Street. He had heard of a suitable dwelling available there.

Many other influential citizens had been hospitable, too, in addition to the Hollis Street members. Dr. Morse, over in Charlestown, whom Mary recalled as one of Dr. Dwight's sources of information about Horace's prospects in the East, had entertained him; as had the Codmans, and most of the other ministers. He had been treated like a son by venerable Dr. Eckley, of Old South Church, the long-standing friend of the Hollis Street Society; and the reception by Mr. Buckminster of Brattle Street and Mr. Kirkland and Mr. William Emerson, both pastors on the South Side, was flattering, to put it mildly. The town seemed to be full of vigorous clergymen, who welcomed an addition to their ranks without a trace of grudge, especially if he came as an accredited scholar. Horace's Phi Beta Kappa key was not from Harvard, as theirs were, but they had accepted him. That much he could tell the wife of his bosom without seeming to boast.

New Year's was always a special anniversary for them. The turning of the calendar recalled their wedding. His voice had a ring in it as he read to her of Young Lochinvar in the new copy of *Marmion*. He waited only about three weeks for the roads to clear, and then set out for Boston. Just out of town he ran into a heavy snowfall, and at Hartford he left the stage for a call on his good friend, Jeremiah Day, now a professor at Yale and rumored to be Dwight's choice to be his successor.[11] It would have been only human if Horace Holley had been a trifle jealous of the man whose advancement blocked his own prospects there, but, instead, he enjoyed this chance for a cordial visit. Envy had no part in his nature; and he was himself a very happy man. His mind was full of sweet memories of the nursery where his infant daughter lay, and of beautiful theories about the upbringing of children. He felt kindly toward the whole world, including the part of it over which President Dwight still ruled as dictator. Horace Holley was leaving that domain for good and all, without a backward look.

6. BY STAGE
TO BOSTON
1809-1811

The journey from New Haven to Boston in mid-February was hard on Mary with a two-months-old baby, even though Horace had been very considerate and helpful about the move. He had arranged for sending their household goods, and had carefully instructed Orville, who accompanied her, about every detail. It was a short trip, but it seemed an endless time that she huddled in the coach, holding tiny Harriette under her cloak to keep the little thing warm and to shield her as they lurched from side to side on the deeply rutted roads.

At last, in the falling dusk of the second day, they rode through the village of Roxbury and onto Boston Neck. She could hardly peer over the sea wall that protected the narrow cobbled roadway, but she sniffed the salt breeze from the Harbour, laden with the smell of breweries and tanneries. The driver pointed out the ruins of the old Continental fortifications near Roxbury, and slowed down at the Boston boundary to let Orville have a look at the gallows looming up in the shadows, where pirates were sometimes hanged. Grim welcome for a stranger coming into the city, Mary thought. Then, all of a sudden, before she could get herself and the baby ready, they were clattering up to a tavern near the Commons where Horace was waiting for them with a conveyance.

Back down Orange Street they drove to No. 92, which was to be their new home.[1] On one side lived the Knapps; and on the other Mr. Barzillai Homes had a store and also his residence. Both attended the Hollis Street Church. These neighbors and others from the congregation were there to greet the new minister's wife. Some motherly soul took charge of the baby, and already fires were burning in all the fireplaces and supper was laid. The kindly people of Hollis Street received them with open arms.

Mary came to Boston at this early season because her husband's installation to the pastoral care of his charge was set for the eighth of March, and they wanted to be established in their new home before that time. She would not have missed the occasion for all the world.

On the appointed Sabbath day the white meetinghouse was filled to overflowing, and no wonder. The ceremony was conducted by some of Boston's first luminaries, and the pews reserved for visitors were crowded with delegates from the Boston Ecclesiastical Council, including Mr. William Ellery Channing, Mr. Emerson, and Mr. Buckminster, with numerous representatives from Roxbury and Charlestown and other nearby towns.[2] Mary had witnessed scene after scene in the career of her husband, but none so impressive as this.

The sermon was delivered by white-haired Dr. Eckley, patron saint of the Hollis Street Society, who had laid the cornerstone of this building. He was clearly proud to install this "young man with lofty brow and trumpet tongue," as someone called Holley. He took his text from Hebrews XII, 7, preaching a cautious, Trinitarian doctrine, and admonishing the new minister to spend his life "in the service of the Redeemer."[3]

A bolder note was struck when the Reverend Mr. John Lathrop, D.D., of Old North Church, rose to deliver the Charge. He spoke mostly about freedom of thought. His words sank deeply into Mary Holley's memory, and they seemed to her for all future time to be the watchword of Boston: "I can testify from the experience of many years that the people of this metropolis are remarkable for their love of peace, and for their candour towards each other on religious subjects." The Charge that he added was to prove prophetic to Horace Holley:

In your present situation, my brother, you will have an opportunity to exercise all your talents in the investigation of truth, and in communicating that knowledge to others. There is no part of the world, I believe I may say with safety and I hope without boasting,—there is no part of the world where the principles of Christian liberty are better understood, or more fully exercised, than in this vicinity.[4]

After that, the genial Dr. Kirkland, of the New South Church, rose to extend the Right Hand of Fellowship, and what he said did not make a great deal of difference. What mattered was his participation in the ceremonies. It was rumored that he would soon be named president of Harvard College.

As the lengthy installation service drew to a close, the Hollis Street pewholders had every reason to be satisfied with their new minister, while he and his wife, too, could feel that he had made a right choice this time. He would have every opportunity for a brilliant career, one peculiarly suited to his genius and temperament. Mary, who understood him far better than he understood himself, was sure that here in Boston he would find his spiritual home.

Rich and poor, old and young, came to seek counsel of Mr. Holley, and he opened the manse to them at all hours, receiving them himself, save when he was in his study preparing his sermons. Such hospitality in addition to the demands of the nursery, made housekeeping at No. 92 Orange Street more complicated than in placid Greenfield Hill. The baby was unbelievably good, but she required a good deal of her mother's attention. Mary was thankful for her years of tending the small Phelpses for Aunt Jennett and Aunt Henrietta. They kept a manservant, Lucas, to look after the manse and the church building, and his wife became their "female domestic," as the highly respectable white women servants of Boston preferred to be called. Rose was a devout worshipper at Hollis Street, who admired Mr. Holley so much that she was discovered to have hidden the manuscript outline of one of his sermons under the carpet in order to copy it before she put it back in his desk.[5]

In due time all the families of the church called at No. 92 Orange Street, and many other cordial people. Among the outsiders who became warm friends were the Channings, both William Ellery and his younger brother Walter, who was a physician.

Horace was hospitable to the point of extravagance, both in money and time. When Orville went back to New Haven to school word was sent that the young brothers and sisters on both sides were welcome to live at the manse until they got started in life. Mary, on whom the burden of such open-handedness chiefly fell, was a little less recklessly hospitable. She was intelligently selfish enough to keep in mind the important goal of their coming to Boston—her husband's career.

The whole routine of life in the household was arranged to prepare for the climax of the week, Horace's sermons on the Sabbath. With the devotion of a priest and the intensity of an artist he committed himself to the severe exertion of achieving performances on the morning and evening of each Sabbath that were as original and dramatically effective as he could possibly make them. Mary saw to it that nothing ordinary was permitted to interfere with his preparations, neither the baby's wailing nor casual visitors.

Years later when she undertook to recapture the essence of their life in Boston, what she recounted most vividly was the ritual that her husband performed as preacher and pastor of Hollis Street. She remembered every step and detail, because in the exercise of his vocation she was his acolyte.

It was his custom to enter his study on Saturday evening and remain there until a late hour, more for the purpose of reflection than composition, to arrange the plan of a discourse, and to make notes. After a few hours sleep, he was again in his study, when he would suffer no interruption, either for breakfast, or from any other circumstance. He then entered the church with his whole mind fired with his theme, and rivetted all attention for an hour or more, with scarcely a reference to his notes. If the evening service required a similar effort, he ate no dinner. If he dined, he would take a familiar subject and treat it less elaborately, as he could not so soon again excite his mind to the necessary point of ardor when it had once been suffered to cool. He preferred, however, not to be interrupted until the services of the day were finished, when his mind still dwelt with pleasure on the thoughts which had so filled and engrossed it. It was then that he enjoyed a social circle with his family and two or three friends, who loved to discourse upon the strains of eloquence which had not yet died upon the ear, and whose salutary influence still warmed the heart, and excited the understanding.[6]

It exacted a good deal from her to guard his solitude, dutifully to attend the services, listening carefully to every logical point, and in addition to arrange for a Sunday evening repast and a social hour with choice friends. But she likewise enjoyed keenly these Sunday evening gatherings when Horace discussed his sermons with his listeners to get their reactions and "improvements," as he called their criticisms. Their intelligent comments suggested topics for other discourses.

He was always on the lookout for new themes, since he almost never used a sermon more than once or twice. He obtained some of his most fruitful ideas from his parochial visits or his participation in civic duties in the town. Once after attending a political debate at Fanueil Hall, he devoted the forenoon sermon to a political topic, speaking an extra half hour in his enthusiasm. Another time he preached on Marquis de Rochefoucauld's *Maxims*, using no Scriptural text at all. Yet on many another occasion he portrayed the perfections of the Divine Being with such "celestial fire" that his hearers wrote him grateful and touching letters. His reputation as an orator grew along with his popularity as a pastor.

On Monday mornings Mary's household returned to something like normalcy, when her husband set out on his parish calling and the women folk undertook to set things in order again. However, Horace had his ideas about Monday, too, in the schedule of a clergyman. He thought this day a proper time for him to indulge his heart in ease, in poetry, and "in all things to give play to benevolent affections." Sometimes he and Mary read aloud to each other from *The Lady of the Lake*, or *Paradise Lost*, both more popular in Boston, they found, than the doleful graveyard poets. Likely enough, they laughed together over *Knickerbocker's History of New York*, and guessed that it must be the work of that young lawyer, Washington Irving. Now that they were settled in Boston, they had no nostalgic regrets about New York, although it had been the center of their young ambitions.

Tuesday found them caught up once more in the exacting routine of a minister's household. He spent the morning hours in intense study, and the rest of the day in visiting the sick and afflicted or conducting funerals and weddings, and delivering public lectures. His name was on the rotating list of ministers in the city for Thursday morning lectures at Mr. William Emerson's First Church in Chauncey Place. Soon he was an active member of the School Committee, and, in due time, received the appointment dearest to his heart, membership on the Board of Overseers of Harvard.

Mary's life fell into a proper pattern. She went to the nearby Boylston Market, followed by Lucas with a bushel basket on either arm, to shop for the generous table she and Horace set. So many of his classmates and fellow clergymen stopped for a meal with them that she had bought additional silver and china. They were going in debt, in a modest way, but since all their associates lived well, it would have been unseemly for them to be parsimonious.

People were forever doing generous things for them. Mr. Goddard sent a couple of barrels of fine apples when he moved away from the congregation over into Brookline,[7] and thoughtful attentions came from Mr. Joseph Knapp, the merchant-distiller next door, who sent over delicacies and books by the sister who presided over his comfortable establishment. Of all the Hollis Street deacons, Mr. Samuel May took the most personal interest in their welfare, even to the extent of insisting that they save a little money and let him invest it safely for them.[8]

Mary's closest friend came to be Mrs. Charles Davis, wife of an attorney in their congregation. Many an afternoon did Mrs. Holley leave Rose to watch over the baby while she put on her nicest walking dress and bonnet for an afternoon in Summer Street, where the Davises lived as neighbors to the Perrin Mays, Mr. Samuel May's kin, who were in the India trade, and the Otis Everetts. The ladies may often have gone over to Cotton's excellent bookshop, strolling past the famous Cushing house that was surrounded by a wall of Chinese porcelain concealing peacocks and slant-eyed Oriental servants inside it.[9] That was how rich the successful merchants had become in the China trade, Mary thought, with a touch of wistfulness and pride. But she felt no resentment toward these hospitable Boston people who opened their doors to her and her husband.

They were received socially ere long by some of Boston's best families—the fabulously rich Otises on Beacon Street, and Colonel Thomas Handasyd Perkins, who collected *objets d'art*, and James Lloyd, who was said to be more influential in Washington City than old John Adams himself. Such attentions were in sharp contrast to their daily contacts, and added to the unending variety of their new life.

One day Horace would come home to tea and gaily re-enact a droll story about a humble friend. He had just been to the bootmaker's to settle his account, and had offered a fifty-dollar bill in payment. As he waited for the old man to go for change, he sat down and stitched a shoe. Then the bootmaker, coming back with a fistful of paper and silver, jovially demanded rent for the use of the block, and withheld a coin. Or maybe it was the story of good William Jackson, a candlemaker in their flock, who begged the loan of a copy of last Sunday's sermon. Since he spoke from notes, Horace never willingly lent his manuscripts, but this worthy man he could not refuse. When Mr. Jackson brought back the paper, he handed his minister a box of candles with it, gravely remarking that it was an "exchange of light."

On the heels of such quaint anecdotes, Horace would mention casually to his wife that he had been elected to membership in the Wednesday Evening Club, being almost the first non-Harvard man to be invited to that exclusive social organization. In addition to a number of his clerical colleagues, the rolls included the Honorable Josiah Quincy, a classical scholar and statesman, and Dr. John Warren, the distinguished physician and scientist. The meetings of the Club brought together some of the best minds in the country.[10]

From the start of his ministry, Horace's powerful preaching had filled the small frame meetinghouse to overflowing, and it was soon clear that it must be replaced. Much important building was going on in the town. The year the Holleys came the orthodox Trinitarians completed a beautiful church on Park Street, designed by an English architect, who adorned its steeple with Ionic and Corinthian capitals. The Park Street Church was the last word in ecclesiastical style, and, like all Boston, Horace Holley saw it every time he walked along the Mall or had business on Beacon Street. He probably had it in mind when he persuaded his congregation to erect an elegant new building in Hollis Street.

As a first move the shrewd men who managed the affairs of the Society sold the Bulfinch building to a small congregation over in Braintree, who had it carefully removed and were able to put it in excellent repair for generations of pious service. As soon as the sizable rectangular site on Hollis Street was cleared, work began on a much larger structure of brick in the modern style of the Park Street Church.[11] Its spire would not overlook the Common, but it would dominate the South End for some distance. And its three flights of steps at the entrance would impress the crowds come to hear the Reverend Mr. Holley preach.

An immediate problem was to find a place to hold services during the year or more it would take to build. This was happily solved. The Reverend Mr. William Emerson invited the Hollis Street Society to unite with his flock at the First Church in Chauncey Place on Summer Street, suggesting that he and Mr. Holley preach on alternate Sundays. Mr. Emerson was a quiet liberal, who had no sympathy with Calvinism, and he entertained no objections to the increasingly unorthodox views of the man whom he invited to share his pulpit.[12] Moreover, he was in poor health, and it was a boon to him to be required to preach less often. Such an arrangement allowed him time to devote to the *Monthly Anthology*, an ambitious review which he edited for the Anthology Club, the scholarly rival of the Wesdnesday Evening Club.

That is how it came to pass that each Sunday until the new building was finished, the members of the Holley household walked a half mile or so to the "Old Brick," as the First Church was popularly known, starting early in order to be sure that Horace arrived in time to follow frail Mr. Emerson as the two of them mounted the rostrum. Mary and her companions, as was proper, occupied a pew opposite the regular minister's, in which sat devout Mrs. Emerson with her older boys, William and Ralph Waldo, and sometimes, also, her sister-in-law from Concord, Miss Mary Moody Emerson. Miss Emerson was said to be very intellectual and far more vigorous than her brother, and it is likely that she approved of little that she heard from the pulpit that year, whichever minister filled it.

For the course of this arrangement, Mrs. Emerson and Mrs. Holley greeted each other properly and listened to their husbands' sermons, but the contact seems to have gone no farther. Mrs. Emerson was so reserved that both of them may have found conversation difficult. Mary knew, of course, that the Emersons were numbered among the first families of New England in spite of being poor and given to such economies as sending the boys out to pasture the family cow on the Common. She must have respected Mrs. Emerson, as did all who knew her, but Mary Holley found women who took a back seat for their husbands and children to be a trifle dull. She would genuinely have enjoyed talking with Mr. Emerson about some of the articles and reviews in his magazine, especially a notice about Madame de Staël, but the families did not pursue their opportunity to become friends.

When Mr. Emerson died of an organic affliction of the stomach not long after the two congregations stopped worshipping together, his widow elected to attend services in respectable, rich Federal Street, where the saintly William Ellery Channing's liberal preaching was to continue for almost another decade before it shocked anyone greatly.

Horace Holley, on the contrary, had a gift for disturbing people. Proof of that came early in his life in Boston. When the "comely, symmetrical little building," as somebody with a flair for good architecture called the old church, was sold over in Braintree, the congregation there asked him to preach the rededication sermon, which was to be accompanied by the ordination of a new pastor of decidedly Calvinistic tendencies.[13] Soon after Mr. Holley accepted the invitation he was waited upon in a body by the other ministers who were to participate in the ceremonies, all of whom asked him to withdraw. It would have been diplomatic of him to do so without making any fuss about it. But he liked an argument too well to accept that easy solution of the difficulty. First he made them admit that the request came because they considered him to be no Trinitarian. Then he turned on them with the keen dialectic skill he had learned in his own Calvinistic training, and compelled them to acknowledge that their own views on that difficult subject were contradictory and confused. He won the debate, and then graciously agreed to stay away from the ceremonies. His visitors retired in silence. But he had made enemies of them all, and they never had any relations with him again.

Actually, Horace Holley was not unique in his theological views when he came to Boston. There were in the city and its environs any number of unorthodox ministers who delivered their sermons in low,

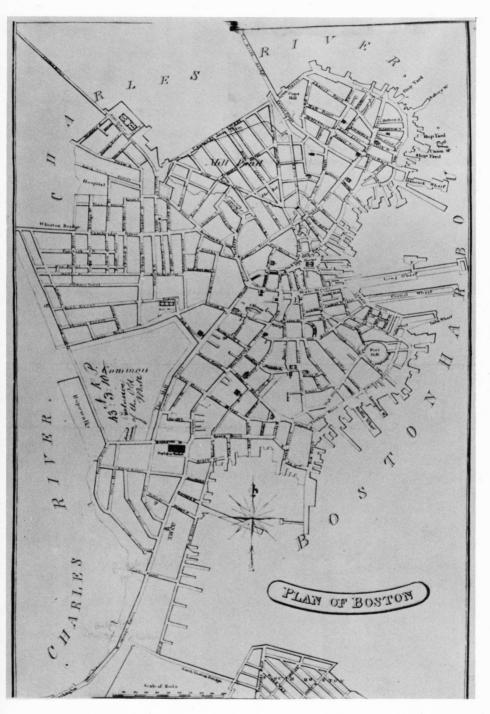

Boston as the Holleys knew it. From the *Boston Directory* for 1818. Courtesy of the Boston Public Library.

scholarly tones, with a personal humility that became the hallmark of early Boston liberalism. Such a man was the elderly James Freeman, who more than twenty years before had quietly resigned as rector of King's Chapel because he could not accept certain points of Episcopal doctrine, whereupon his parishioners had agreed to follow him instead of the Thirty-nine Articles and had retained him as their minister, without consent of any Bishop.[14]

"Liberal" was the term usually applied to all such unorthodox clergymen, although in the City Directory their churches continued to be listed as Episcopal or Congregational, or the like. These gentle Boston liberals, who stated rather than argued their convictions, promptly recognized Holley as one of their number when he came to their community. Dr. Freeman called him "the man dearest to my heart of any of the ministers of Boston." Astute old John Adams, from his watcher's post at nearby Quincy, spotted Holley as liberal enough to suit a rational deist like himself. In the intoxicating air of liberty that blew in from the Harbour, the new pastor on Hollis Street became bolder than most of the other liberals. By temperament and training he was a debater, and he never acquired the unobtrusive Boston manner.

Mary became a thoroughgoing Bostonian overnight. She fit into their new surroundings more easily than her husband because she was town-bred, and also because religious tolerance was no new enthusiasm with her but a perfectly natural attitude. What she found invigorating was not so much intellectual liberty as intellectual curiosity. Everybody they knew read books or at least respected them vastly; many of their friends and acquaintances were authors and bibliophiles. The town supported a music store where she purchased Haydn scores whenever she could afford them, and Professor Gottlieb Graupner's assembly hall presented concerts devoted entirely to the latest German and Italian composers.

She found time to resume the study of French, and to attend the readings and recitations of Monsieur Artiguenave, formerly of the *Théâtre Français*.[15] M. Artiguenave greatly improved her pronunciation, and became a good friend of the family. It was at this time, also, that she took up the serious study of botany, probably patronizing the lectures on the subject delivered by Dr. Biglow, a member of the congregation. Bostonians were interested in landscape gardening and horticulture, especially if they had homes in the country.

Dr. Warren was the exemplar of the kind of broad culture that flourished in Boston.[16] Related to the hero of Bunker Hill, he belonged to the best clubs and social circles, and was recognized to be one of the first-rate surgeons of the day. His country seat in Roxbury was the old family homestead, spacious and comfortable, built with one story at the front in the West Indian manner. Noble elms and lindens and horse chestnuts abounded, and the Doctor imported other trees from Europe to try them out in this climate. He was likewise an antiquarian who collected human skulls and all sorts of anthropological specimens. The Holleys were often entertained in the Warren homes, both in town and in Roxbury. The friendship probably began during the year Horace preached at First Church, which the Warrens were attending at the time. The Doctor was their family physician, the most understanding one Mary ever had.

Little Harriette was an unmitigated pleasure to her parents. She grew prettier, with big, blue eyes, fair hair, and fine features. Mary took pains to write her mother-in-law that the child "inherits her father's mind and constitution. She looks altogether like your family."[17] Horace adored her, and treated her as if she were an adult even before she could talk. She loved everybody, as a healthy child usually does, but it was her mother whom she adored.

During one of their early summers in Boston it was decided that Mary needed a trip to Stafford Springs to improve her indifferent health. In addition, she wanted her relatives to see her precocious little daughter. It was the first time she had gone away and left Horace at No. 92 Orange Street, and ere long he wrote plaintively about having to return to an "empty house." That was just an affectionate little joke. He was finding it no hardship to stay on in Boston to supervise the painting of a portion of the new church building. Orville was there to keep him company, and he was being wined and dined by the Davises and the rest of the congregation.

She held his letter to her heart as she read the ending: "My mind is delightfully devoted to yours and I prize nothing higher than the idea and testimony of your affection. My best love to you all. Your ever affectionate Husband."[18]

The new meetinghouse was finished in 1811, and the dedication set for the last Sunday in January.[19] The large brick building was impressive inside as well as out, with an elegantly appointed interior that was almost theatrical in effect. Galleries encircled the auditorium and looked down on a wide center aisle leading toward a massive pulpit flanked by winding stairs. Rich curtains were draped behind it, and the font stood just below it. A large organ was installed behind the rear gallery, and already the Widow Davis had donated three hundred dollars for a proper clock to be placed at the center of the gallery, facing the preacher. Money was pledged for a steeple clock, also, and for silver communion cups.

Music played a large part in the elaborate dedication service. Horace had long since forgotten his youthful debate about the moral value of music and his Calvinistic objections to choral compositions. When he came to Hollis Street he found an excellent choir, called the Singing Society, under the competent direction of Jacob Guild, a housewright. The new minister encouraged it by attending rehearsals, sometimes bringing his wife, whose musical talents were well known. Mr. Guild outdid himself in arranging the program for the great occasion: two psalms, two hymns, and the Hallelujah Chorus. The printed Order of Performance omitted all names of persons, and gave the music priority even over the sermon. Nevertheless, the crowd that filled the new church came to hear the words of Mr. Holley.

As the strains of "Old Cambridge" died away, the young pastor, barely thirty, vigorous and handsome in his flowing black silk robes, with snowy collar tabs, mounted the pulpit and began the sermon that placed him in the front rank of Boston's liberal clergymen:

I say that the bible is a better creed than any of you can make, and Christ is a better teacher than any other you can follow. . . . Were Jesus now before you in person, what would he say to your minister? "Preach me, and not Calvin, nor Arminius; not Edwards, nor Priestley; preach the bible, and not the creed of Scotland, Saybrook, Cambridge, or Savoy; preach peace, and not war; preach love, and not hatred; preach practice, and not speculation; preach union, and not division; preach effort, and not sloth; enlarge your charity and stint it not. . . ."

For these divine objects you have erected this beautiful temple; you have borne with patience your losses by conflagration; you have struggled through numerous difficulties and trials; though a young, you have become an active and independent society; you have called and are now to settle a pastor, whom, we trust, God will guide and enrich with all spiritual graces—who, we sincerely pray, may go in and out before you with a pure conscience and the gospel of peace. . . .

And now, O God, what wait we for? Our spirits and our cause are thine. Accept our souls; accept our offering. To thee, to Christ, to thy free grace, we consecrate the house our hands have built. Oh! Let thy spirit here abide. Here show thy love, and here exalt thy name.[20]

Silence was absolute as he stood, hands uplifted, after the final empassioned words of the dedication. Then with psalm and prayer the service rose to a new crescendo in Handel's triumphant music.

It was a day the Hollis Street congregation never forgot. Long afterward, when they celebrated the fiftieth anniversary of the dedication of the church, they reprinted the Order of Performance of that service in 1811. Even in bare outline it still recalled to them Horace Holley's golden voice and the thrilling hallelujahs of Mr. Guild's choir.

7. HIGH TIDE
1811-1817

The years that followed the dedication of the new church marked a high tide in Hollis Street, and the Reverend Mr. Holley was in great demand as one of Boston's most popular orators and beloved ministers. The urgent calls of his position invigorated him, but the management of the big house taxed Mary's strength until she rose in the morning weary and fell into bed at night utterly exhausted. Her poor health was one reason for asking her sister to live with them, and, moreover they wanted to make Henrietta's social life more lively than it could be in the shabby old home in New Haven. It turned out as they hoped, and very soon she had an eligible suitor in James Dall, son of a well-to-do merchant on Washington Street, both father and son being pew-holders and generous contributors at Hollis Street. Horace performed the wedding ceremony for the happy couple, uniting the two families in a satisfactory and lasting alliance.[1] The Dalls revered Horace Holley to the point of adoration. On Sunday mornings they sat under the sound of his voice, and in the evenings they came to the house to join the small, intimate group of worshippers who recapitulated his points of doctrine and cogent arguments.

About a year later the Holleys gave up the residence on Orange Street and leased quarters nearby on Boylston, overlooking the Common and the Mall.[2] It was a better residential street, and much quieter. Their apartments were in the large brick establishment of Schoolmaster John Haskell, a parishioner. They had their private parlor and adequate living rooms, but were served their meals from Mrs. Haskell's kitchen. Thus they could live in dignity and comfort with the least possible trouble or expense. The arrangement set Mary free for her music and reading, for daily walks, and even for occasional trips out of town. In spite of her husband's sincere desire to spare her, she had been greatly restricted during the seven years of their married life, often subordinating her personal interests to his. Both husband and wife were distressed and a little embarrassed that they had had no other children since their first, especially when letters from their various brothers announced a great many additions to their households. Part of the object in lifting the load from Mary's shoulders was to give her more rest and recreation.

It was Henry Austin, as often happened, who touched off the spark of adventure in her. About the middle of September, after they had got nicely settled with the Haskells, he happened to drop in for a little visit and proposed that she go with him to Saratoga and Ballston Springs.[3] He was not feeling well himself—Henry oscillated between violent activity and distressing symptoms—and why should she not pack her trunks and start off at once with him? So she did, all in a flurry, leaving Harriette in Mrs. Haskell's competent hands, with "Aunt Dall" promising to look in on her frequently. The trip by stage to Ballston Spa was somewhat strenuous for ailing travellers, and they thought the weather chilly for the prescribed regimen of eight or ten tumblers of the water before breakfast. Mary gulped them down in spite of her shivering, and soon was eating voraciously with no ill effects. Henry found a few days of the cure enough and departed.

Among the many genteel guests the most congenial proved to be a Mrs. Banks, also of Boston, with whom Mary planned to go down to New York City. This was the first time in her life that she had been thrown on her own resources among strangers, and she felt a little timid, even as a married woman of twenty-eight. Her confidence returned when she and Mrs. Banks, with all their trunks and boxes, took the Ballston hack for Albany, where they would board a steamboat for the trip down the Hudson. As the hack rattled along the bankside road Mary had a good look at one of the new craft, the *Fire Fly*, on its way to Troy, and vowed she had never seen a prettier object. The chance to ride on a steamboat was one of the main reasons for coming on this jaunt in the first place.

Albany was livelier than the Spa had been, as she wrote Horace the day after they arrived:

This is the gayest place I have seen, nothing but officers in full uniform everywhere. We have several at our table, among them Major McPherson of Philadelphia, aide to General Bloomfield, so handsome and so graceful that I distinguish him by the title of "Snowden's Knight." He is a particular friend of my friend, Mrs. Banks. Before being introduced to me, he had occasion to speak & he addressed me by the name of *Miss*. What do you think of that? Do you think the waters have renovated me?

Whatever the cause, the waters or the good company, her spirits rose. The two ladies "walked all over Albany & looked at whatever is worth looking at." They inspected the neat and elegant accommodations on the *Car of Neptune,* which they engaged for the trip down the river. They received a formal call from the wives of the patroon and the mayor, who came expressly to invite them to a party at the latter's home on the evening before their departure.

The venture into Albany society turned out sadly, but Mary made an amusing anecdote of it:

In my last letter, No. 4, my dear Husband, I mentioned our proposed visit to the Mayor's. I go on now to give the particulars of that memorable occasion. Mrs. Hubbart, who came with the ladies to call upon us, whispered to Mrs. Banks that we must *dress ourselves very smart,* for all the officers were to be present. Of course, we expected a very brilliant party, & prepared accordingly, taking considerable trouble to unpack our trunks. We saw nobody to enquire the time of visiting in Albany, but wishing to observe a medium, after consulting each other, fixed upon ½ past 7. We accordingly went at that time, but to our no small mortification, the company *had taken tea & gone home* except Mrs. Patroon Van Ranseleer & Mrs. Hubbart, whose carriage was waiting for them at the door when we drove up. They staid as long as civility demanded, & then departed, leaving us with the Mayor & lady, waiting till ½ past 9 for our carriage. They entertained us with great hospitality, expressing some regrets that we had been so formal. You may depend upon it we felt foolish enough, for nothing was farther from our minds than a wish to appear in the extreme of the fashion. . . . If you are as much amused with this adventure as we were, you will laugh heartily. We thought it would do credit to the good Vicar of Wakefield's family.

The Boston visitors were too excited about the journey down the river to worry much about the impression they had made on the Dutch aristocracy. At nine the following morning they were attended on board by the young major. He was beautiful—tall, straight, in blue uniform and a grenadier's hat that glittered with gold and was adorned with four tall white plumes. Small wonder that the two young matrons, secure with wedding rings and social entrée, permitted themselves a small flirtation. Mary enjoyed a chance to tease her husband in her next letter: "It is well for you, my dear, that my heart is pretty secure at home, or it might have to commence a long campaign. So much for fun!"

She had learned that Horace was pleased when other men were attentive to her, just as he praised her letters when they matched his own in wit and literary style. The two of them took pride in each other's accomplishments and triumphs, even small social ones.

As the *Car of Neptune* pulled out into the current, the "Knight of Snowden" vanished, never to be seen or heard of again by Mary Holley; but the trip on the steamboat was memorable. They met three sloops loaded with soldiers and sailors on their way to the northern frontier, who struck up martial music as they passed. With one hundred and fifty passengers on board it was too noisy to sleep even when the ladies retired to their snug berths. Mary sat up to peer out the tiny window; and as soon as the day began to dawn she arose and went on deck to view the grand scenery of King's Mountain and West Point.

She wanted to know all about everything, and picked out the most intelligent looking passengers to ply with questions—what was the landing they had just passed? or what kinds of trees were those just there along the shore?—but the other early risers seemed monstrously uninterested.

"There is not one sentimentalist on board," she vowed scornfully at breakfast to Mrs. Banks, "nor a person that even knows the name of botany!"

She could not understand how people could fail to have *some* curiosity and *some* feeling when they travelled. Later on in the day she found a secluded spot in which to finish her letter to her husband. She balanced her writing board precariously, and her hand shook with the motion of the boat as she set down her early morning impressions:

The views are the finest I have ever seen, and it was not difficult to imagine one's self among the stupendous cliffs & beautiful lakes of Scotland. The river winds so as to appear like a lake, frequently. I stretched my eager eyes among the rude chasms & verdant peaks of the mountains in search of the dappled grey steed and the wedding plumes of Fitz James, but in vain, we had left him behind. . . . no musick saluted my ear, but the horn of our boatsmen giving warning to passengers who might apply at the next landing.

Already on this first of her countless excursions through the inland waters of America, she was keeping a journal of her travels.

When they docked at New York City she was "something fatigued," and hastened immediately to her lodgings with a Mrs. Taylor in White Hall Street. What she desired most was a message from Horace. It was there, awaiting her arrival, Mr. William Dall having fetched it down a few days earlier. She had been so sure of finding it that she had not closed her own letter on the boat, and now she added a postscript to say she was sorry that he and Harriette had both had colds. Then she thrust the folded sheet into the hands of a fellow lodger who was taking the night stage for Boston. It was almost as if she and her husband had conversed *vis-à-vis*. Letters fairly flew across the country nowadays, if one used a little contrivance.

The fortnight in the city was pleasant. Friends heard she was stopping at a boarding house and called to convey her to their homes for visits. One day she took tea with some of her Phelps relatives out at Bloomingdale. Occasionally she looked around in the shops, fingering the "lace footing" and eyeing the stylish dress patterns.

She attended church in a discreet manner, making mental notes on a strong Trinitarian sermon by the well-known Dr. Mason in order to report it to Horace, but dismissing a commonplace discourse heard at Grace Church as not worth remembering. She was careful not to discuss theology openly.

Most of all she liked to take brisk morning walks and to inspect the curiosities of the metropolis—along Broadway to the shaded park of the new City Hall, or to Columbia College and the Academy of Arts and the Panorama of Paris. She wanted very much to attend the theatre but dared not lest it be thought a sin in the wife of a clergyman, even a Boston clergyman. Perhaps if Horace were with her, they would go anyway. She felt lonely without him.

What made her a little low in mind was really the letter she received from Charles Austin, giving a dreadful account of things in New Haven, and even proposing to break up the household in Whiting Street and sell the furniture. The serious youth had just been graduated from Yale and wanted to study for orders in the Episcopal Church. It upset him to think of leaving his mother and small half-brother with only Mr. Lewis to look after them. He went so far in his letter as to call his stepfather poor and lazy, strong words for Charles to use.

Mary disagreed with her brother about breaking up their mother's home and marriage: "If every woman quit her husband because he is poor and lazy," she admonished him, "many a man would be abandoned who has now a comfortable home."

She had never had much to do with Elisha Lewis, but she did not consider him a nonentity, as did most of the rest of the family. He had sailed the seven seas in his time, and he had been very kind to the boy Henry on that long voyage to Canton. Also he had recently spent a year or two pioneering on the Mississippi River, and she was inclined to be lenient in her judgment of him, at least until she got to New Haven.

There she found Aunt Maria Brown Austin, wife of Uncle Moses, visiting in her mother's home. Maria had come East the previous year with her two younger children, Emily and James Elijah Brown, to arrange for their education as well as to try to settle several of her husband's tangled business deals. Moses had employed Elisha Lewis to convey her down the Mississippi on a barge loaded with furs and lead and feathers to be sold for her expenses; but she and her escort had fallen out with each other long before the end of their journey to Baltimore via river craft and ocean vessel. Because of Elisha's bad management, so Maria said, her goods had been wasted and she was now relying on Henry Austin to supply her with cash. Henry was on excellent terms with Uncle Moses since his own trip West, and both he and Maria agreed with Charles that Esther ought to "make a vendue" and get rid of the house and furniture at once in order to compel Elisha to go to work. There the matter stood during Mary's visit home to New Haven, and she apparently remained neutral in the controversy.

Meanwhile Maria, a hearty and practical woman for all her aristocratic Philadelphia background, entertained Sister Esther and Niece Mary with detailed accounts of her experiences on the barge and of the trials of poor Mrs. Timothy Phelps while she lived in Ste. Genevieve, hardships which undoubtedly accounted for her low state of health and death last summer immediately after her return to Staten Island. Her ailment, Maria thought, was a "quick Consumption," hastened by "her own Imprudence." In more cheerful moments Maria exchanged recipes with her relatives, even some of her inherited treasures. She took great pride in her "Tomata Marmelade" and "Yellow Pickle" and a special "Ginger Wine."[4]

Esther Lewis ignored the unflattering discussion of her husband and made her own plans to spend the winter with her daughter Henrietta as a paying guest in the Dall home. She had enough left of Mr. Sanford's money to do that and to put Phelps in school. She intended to travel to Boston along with Mary, leaving the house and Mr. Lewis to get along as best they could without her for a season.

The relatives in New Haven did all they could to make up to Mary for the lugubrious state of affairs on Whiting Street. She dined with her aunts and drank tea with Cousin Charlotte Beers Ives. She attended serveral fashionable weddings, but many of the people she had known were missing. Uncle Timothy had gone to sea not long after bringing his wife back from Missouri. One of his daughters had been adopted by the Daniel Wadsworths in Hartford; the other members of his household were scattered or dead.[5] One Sunday Mary went with her family to services at Trinity, only to find their pew occupied by some of the crowd of representatives in town for the Legislature, and a new curate substituting for old Dr. Hubbard, who was on his last sickbed, failing daily. New Haven did not seem the same any more.

She was heart-hungry for her husband and child; and more than glad when she and Esther, after considerable bustle and confusion, were on the stage for Boston. Safe home again after nearly a month away she heard all over again that Harriette had been good and that they had talked of *her* every day. Horace had written delightful accounts of how the child would wake up early asking for her, and want to be entertained with accounts of her whereabouts and doings. He had a genius for managing children.

He captured the happy mood of this reunion in a poem he wrote about his small daughter:

> From a Husband to a Wife on Seeing
> Their Daughter, a Little Girl, at Play
>
> See, see, my Love, where Harriette goes
>   With rosy cheek and sparkling eye;
> Her fairest gifts fond health bestows,
>   And balmy breezes round her fly.
>
> See Innocence her breast adorn,
>   And infant Mirth her steps attend;
> Young life now hails her rising morn,
>   And golden hues their radiance lend.[6]

Life had a golden hue and things went right for the Holleys in those days. Orville won honors at Harvard.[7] The Hollis Street congregation grew apace, justifying the expense of the ambitious new building. Horace delivered a powerful sermon before the Ancient and Honorable Artillery Company, one that became famous in the annals of Boston oratory because, although the setting was a house of God, the audience spontaneously broke into outright applause. He addressed the Roxbury Charitable Society, and preached an eloquent discourse on the death of the Reverend Mr. Joseph Buckminster.[8] The eulogy on Buckminster, in particular, deserved to be widely circulated according to the custom of the time, but Horace was publishing none of his Boston speeches. He may have wished to revise and polish them; he may have been reluctant to trust the printed page to convey his personal eloquence. The result was that his great reputation as an orator rested upon the memories of those who heard him speak.

In the field of theology he was the author of one published item, a review titled "A Contrast between Calvinism and Hopkinsianism" in the *General Repositary and Review*.[9] His liberal views, here clearly expressed, served to widen the breach between him and the Yale Seminary. Not that it mattered to him now whether Dr. Dwight approved of him—or so he thought.

Horace had outgrown narrow sectarianism. Through his friendship with John Cheverus, a French priest who had been exiled to America in 1796 and had become the first Bishop of Boston,[10] he was aware for the first time of the age-old beauty and truth inherent in the Roman Catholic faith. The high masses celebrated in the modest Catholic church on Franklin Street may well have been the first ever witnessed by either of the Holleys. They in turn extended many "polite attentions" to the good Bishop, who not only considered his host to be *aimable* but complimented *"madame son épouse très aimable et instruite."*

In much the same fashion Horace Holley widened his political horizons. He was still a Federalist but not of the "Standing Order" variety, falling in readily with the broad conservatism of Boston's elder statesmen like John Adams and Josiah Quincy. He declined to speak at outright political gatherings, but he joined in the patriotic good works of the Washington Benevolent Society, which included among its contributing members nearly all the leading men of the Federalist Party. The Society's monthly debates at the Exchange Coffee House culminated annually in an oration held, not on the General's birthday, but, with Boston individuality, on April 30, the anniversary of his inauguration as President. These orations were customarily published and thus preserved for posterity.

In the course of such activities Horace Holley became well acquainted with President John Adams, who was living in retirement at Quincy, sorting his papers and corresponding with erstwhile foes like Thomas Jefferson. The austere old man openly said that Holley was a "rational Christian" and declared him to be "a shining light in a dark place."[11] Such words from the elder Adams would give any man a reputation, not only in Boston but over the whole country. Horace came to know the son, John Quincy, after the younger Adams returned from diplomatic posts in Russia and elsewhere, when they met in various clubs and as fellow guests at informal dinners. On such occasions fifteen or twenty of the town's leading citizens would enjoy a good repast and equally good conversation in which every man around the table revealed himself as an authority in some field or other. The Reverend Mr. Holley was deferred to chiefly on points of theology; but he found himself more and more often drawing on law and philosophy, literature and language, for the materials of his arguments.

"Mr. Madison's War with England," as Boston people called the second conflict with Great Britain, went on indecisively. American victories at sea were offset by the capture and burning of Washington City. Edward, one of Luther Holley's younger sons, served as an army lieutenant, although he got no farther afield than Hartford. Henry Austin was captured at sea by the British and held prisoner a long while, after which he came home to marry a sweet, timid New York girl of a substantial family which was in business with John Phelps Austin there. Horace Holley served as Chaplain for Colonel Messenger's Regiment, of which one company, called the "Rangers," was stationed at Fort Strong on Noddle's Island; and he rowed or sailed out at proper intervals to conduct services for the men. He got great satisfaction from this participation in the military activities connected with the defense of Boston against possible attack.[12]

In spite of war clouds Mary went for a visit that autumn of 1814 with her mother, now back in New Haven, and then on to Salisbury, where her husband would join her.[13] She was enough of a seasoned traveler now to set out with only her little daughter as companion, and to get a pleasant excitement out of learning that the stage they had almost taken was overturned on the highway. She was in good spirits, and in sufficiently good health to relish the abundant clingstone peaches and fresh oysters and excellent port at her mother's table. Charles was at home with his harmonica, and there were enough of them to sing together and to dance to the strains of "Light Fairy, Little Sue."

One day when she was browsing in the bookstore on the Green she eagerly bought a copy of the new book by Madame de Staël on Germany. In Boston's literary set there was great interest in this celebrated female exile from Napoleon's France, who was reportedly planning to emigrate to her estate in northern New York. Mary intended to save the volume for leisure reading in Salisbury, but she could not resist beginning it at once. At the chapter on "Enthusiasm" she was gripped and held. Mary hastened to write Horace that she had scarcely seen anything that gave her so much pleasure as the new book. It expressed her own ideas better than she had ever been able to put them into words.

Oddly enough, just as she was discovering her own mature philosophy in the pages of a somewhat shocking French book, she had to listen to a superlative example of a Calvinistic hell-fire sermon. On the last Sunday she spent in New Haven she attended services where a Mr. Taylor discoursed on "The Shivering Horrors of Hell," assuring his hearers that many of their loved ones were doubtless groaning in flames and would continue to do so through all eternity. She was flippant about the sermon in describing it to Horace, but she was serious as she summed up the matter: "I am thankful that I do not worship a daemon, but an indulgent Father." She knew that he had long since come to agree with her.

When Horace wrote her that he likewise was reading the new book on Germany, she felt sure that both of them were enjoying the rapturous feeling described in it as "the happy portion of kindred souls." She pored over the volume late into the night, after callers had left and the harmonica was still. She found herself setting down her impressions of it with care, polishing the phrases of her self-criticism: "I like the book more & more. I think there is in it such a glow of feeling, & such *elevation of sentiment*, & such fullness of thought, that it transports one almost beyond this scene of things. This, I suppose, is what she calls the feeling of infinity."[14] More than most women of her time, Mary Holley had a philosophical turn, and she recognized in Madame de Staël's romanticism the essence of her own credo. Fortunately her husband encouraged her to express her philosophical ideas.

At a little after four o'clock on a Monday morning in late September Mary and Harriette and Charles got off to Salisbury. The weather was fine and the coach was snug and easy, with four good horses and no other passengers besides themselves. They bowled along at about eight miles an hour, fully as comfortable as if they had been travelling in their own carriage. Mary had written to the relatives to have a wagon meet them at Canaan, but, alas, none was there when the coach left them by the roadside in the late afternoon. Poor Charles, who was no countryman, finally rented a thin horse and broken-down wagon, paying hard money in advance for them; and the party struggled after nightfall toward Luther Holley's homestead. The mountain road was in bad condition after neglect during the war years.

The bright moonlight enabled them to find Brother Milton's farmhouse; and Orville—the family called him "Quash"—walked on from there beside the wagon to guide them. Of course her letter had not arrived, and Mary vowed that Luther and his wife were only half glad to see the rest of them without Horace.

Sarah Holley was always prepared for company, and they fared well enough on her fruit pies and boiled dishes while she saved the best hams and plumpest chickens until her son arrived. Harriette trailed around after her grandmother, who called her "Little Horace." Other times she played with her Uncle Milton's small daughter, also named Harriette; and then Grandmother had to call her "Harriette Williman."

One day the two children solemnly buried a fly in the garden and sang a sad hymn in their high treble.[15] If Mary and Orville observed this scene, they found it amusing and were witty about it. Orville could be as clever as his older brother when he was minded, and he had lived in their household long enough to be good when it came to punning and word combats. Charles had already returned to New Haven, and he wouldn't have been witty with them anyway. He was far too gentle and kind.

Luther Holley lived comfortably in these later years, having added several rooms to the house to please his wife. He kept good stock, enough for all of them to take horseback rides over the hills. On one of these daily excursions Mary and brothers Milton and Orville stopped by the post office, where she found a letter from Horace—her first at Salisbury. She knew the others were eager to hear the news and so she waited to break the seal until they all reached the top of Town Hill where they could face the horses about and take a fine view of the lake. Imagine her surprise when the first words she read were lines of poetry:

The pure and peaceful lake, with magic rays . . .

She had to explain that the reference was not to Lake Wanscopomac, but that Horace was translating Madame de Staël's prose version of a German poem about the Swan and the Eagle, symbols of the Contemplative Life and the Active Life. She read the poem over twice as they sat there on their horses. The brothers nodded or frowned in a critical manner. They agreed that the subject matter was good and the lines in general were justly ordered and very poetical. Then they began to exchange quips about swan feathers and eagle feathers, which seemed very amusing at the time. Soon they clattered down the rocky road to finish the day's ride.

The Holley brothers all had fine minds, Mary thought, although none were so brilliant as her husband, save maybe Orville. She and Horace had high hopes for Orville's future, being more impressed with his

qualities than was his father. Luther thought this youngest son was procrastinating too long about choosing a profession, now that he had
graduated from college.

Horace came in early October for his first visit in four years. The
weather was glorious, and they spent whole days in the saddle explor-
ing trails over the mountains. One Saturday Mary went with Horace
and Orville and their sister Caroline, now fourteen, to the top of Brace
Mountain, and on the following Monday set out for a three-day trip into
the Catskills. She and Caroline were good enough riders to keep up
with the men on the rough trails in spite of the handicap of side saddles,
and wrung a compliment from Horace that they were "enthusiastic and
free from troublesome feminine fears and fastidiousness."

They truly earned his accolade the day the party determined to
reach Cascade Falls. On and on they rode, and then they walked for
several miles through the bright leaves, with pheasants fluttering near
at hand, and a deep view of the river with fog shredding over it. Down
the side of a ravine they all slid, the ladies clinging to the skirts of the
men's coats and letting their own flowing habits drag over the rocks and
shrubs. But the view of the Falls was thrilling, and they left their names
carved rudely on the tablerock. Once they sat for a while without anyone's speaking, the silence broken only by the tinkle of a faraway cow-
bell. They were moved by the divinity of nature.

During leisure hours at Salisbury Mary read all of her husband's excellent translation from the German lyric of "The Swan and the Eagle."
These ancient poetic symbols, the singer of love and harmony contrasted
with the fierce bird of courage, seemed to stand for the two sides of his
own divided nature. His final lines were a ringing affirmation of his
faith:

> The immortal soul unveil'd and free shall rise
> A radiant phoenix to its native skies,
> Its destiny divine with joy pursue,
> And death's own torch perennial youth renew.[16]

Horace Holley's argumentative, intellectual self came out clearly
when he delivered, by request, a series of sermons at the little White
Church at Salisbury, one of which began at one o'clock in the afternoon
and lasted until sundown. At the close he invited his listeners to engage in an open debate, but none stepped forward.

Meanwhile, in a fine burst of creative energy, Mary filled her sketchbook with views of the countryside. Especially for Horace she made an

India ink drawing of the Lake and composed some lines dedicating it to him. They delighted to surprise each other with such gifts:

> Of that sweet spot which Nature hath arrayed
> In all the charms of colour, form, and grace,
> This faithful outline, with its light and shade,
> Is all my hand unpracticed now can trace.
>
> Let Memory then for thee the pencil take,
> (Since Art defeated owns her feeble powers,)
> And deck the woods, the mountains, and the lake,
> With colours drawn from childhood's happiest hours.[17]

Soon the Holleys were back home, engaged again in the activities incident upon being fortunate dwellers in the "hub of the universe," as its complacent citizens called Boston. They kept making new friends, among them the Benjamin Busseys, who lived on Summer Street next door to the Davises. Mr. Bussey, after serving in the Revolution, had made his fortune in Boston, first as a silversmith and then as a shipper, and he was content to spend it in this city.[18] He was just now completing an imposing country estate, located on a hilltop just below the Neck in adjoining Roxbury. It was surrounded by three hundred beautiful rolling acres, which he had in mind to bequeath to Harvard College some day. It was he who presented the Hollis Street Church with two handsome tablets of the Decalogue and the Lord's Prayer, executed by the Roxbury painter, John Ritto Penniman. The Busseys owned no pew there, and the gift must have been made out of personal regard for the minister.

That April of 1815 Horace Holley was selected to deliver the Washington Benevolent Society oration. It was a notable triumph. Four thousand boys, wearing patriotic ribbons on their breasts, and headed by a magnificent standard and twenty banners, drilled in front of Fanueil Hall, which was packed to the windows with an audience come to hear the speaker of the day deliver a sympathetic commentary on Federalist principles as they were understood in Boston.[19] The Federalist Party all over the nation was falling to pieces so rapidly that the Society would never stage another annual oration; but happily, as Mr. Holley spoke extemporaneously with great brilliance to rounds of applause, he did not know that.

His failure to complete and publish this important address could easily have been excused on account of the many demands on his time. He was no longer chaplain of the Massachusetts House of Representatives, but he still held membership on the Board of Overseers of Harvard, a responsibility which he took very seriously. He and his wife were frequent patrons of the musical events of the city, such as the elaborate Peace Concert which was given at Dr. Freeman's church to celebrate the end of the war with the British. Out of that event came the impulse for founding a Handel and Haydn Society, and for the Society's tremendous Oratorio on the following Christmas Eve, an event attended by all music lovers of the region.

The Holleys made good their offers to help their younger brothers and sisters. Charles Austin was in their home while he waited for a chance to carry out his wish to prepare for holy orders. Caroline Holley spent the winter with them, bringing instructions from her father to "finish" her education properly. Arrangements were made for dancing school and riding school and French instruction; but every step must be patiently explained to Luther, who got alarmed about the matter of expense.[20] One agreeable feature was that she could take lessons in penmanship from Charles, who wrote a beautiful hand, and had nothing else to do, at least until he accepted an offer to be a tutor near Baltimore where the James Dalls now lived, while he studied theology under the Bishop of Maryland.

Although Horace put off preparing his sermons and addresses for publication, he found time to contribute an article to a new magazine, *The North American Review*, which was the successor to poor Mr. Emerson's *Monthly Anthology*. The first editor, an amateur critic-author who had got rich shipping ice to South America, modelled the journal on the great English reviews and then turned over his post to a youthful lawyer, Willard Phillips, son of a prominent family. Willard's practice did not as yet require him to spend much time in his modest office on Court Street, and he was better known as an editor of the *General Repositary*. He was also one of the witty, literary young men in the Holley's intimate circle of friends.

After Willard took charge of the *Review*, he often spent Sunday evenings with them on Boylston Street, coming early for a slice of cold fowl and a glass of wine. Then he would spread manuscripts on the table to sort out the ones for the next issue. All the articles were published anonymously and it was flattering to be in the editor's confidence. The cheerful fire crackled, and their puns and quips crackled, too, especially if they were joined by the Walter Channings or one of the younger Everetts. Channing had contributed to the first volume of the magazine an article on the peculiarities of the American language.

Horace Holley's essay, "On the Pleasure Derived from Witnessing Scenes of Distress," appeared by the end of the year.[21] It was a trifle dull, needing condensation and a sharper conclusion, but the ideas in it were forward-looking and significant. People derive pleasure from witnessing scenes of distress, ran the argument, because compassion and sympathy are an inherent part of the mind of man when he is "in a natural or benevolent state." Such feelings, like those of curiosity and action and love of novelty, make us interested in our fellows, all of us being the children of God.

The author of this essay had departed so far from Calvinism that he was now a man of sentiment, a translator of the German romantics, and a lover of Byron. If President Dwight and the other authoritarians in New Haven ferreted out the authorship of the essay, they surely shook their heads over this case of hopeless apostasy.

Mary liked these gatherings in what she might well think of as her salon, where she could match her wit with the quick-tongued young lawyers and advise them about their love affairs. Sometimes the talk turned to the latest concert or the portrait that brusque Gilbert Stuart had recently painted of Mr. Bussey. Sometimes she accompanied their songs on her guitar. It did not occur to Willard Phillips to ask her to write for his *Review* since it did not include women among its contributors. He might well have given some consideration to at least one poem in her portfolio, the lines about Niagara written during the summer of 1815.

That season she and her husband planned a long sight-seeing trip with a Mrs. Minot and her daughter in their commodious carriage via Buffalo and the Falls to Montreal and Quebec.[22] In late June they set out, armed with letters in French from Bishop Cheverus to ecclesiastical dignitaries of his church, for their first glimpse of a foreign land. Enthusiasm compensated for rough roads and uncomfortable lodgings across war-torn New York State on the way up to Niagara. When they gazed upon the Falls, its grandeur made them all feel poetic, but while the others groped for adjectives and quoted famous lines, Mary was silently composing verses, which she set down upon her return to her room almost exactly as she had conceived them. They were in the new-style blank verse, freer and better than any she had written heretofore:

> No language can describe, nor pencil paint
> This wondrous spectacle. He who would know
> Himself must come, and see, and feel the scene.
> For ages thus, e'er since the world began,

Thy torrent has poured down, wave after wave,
Ne'er to look back, or reascend the height.
The ancient forest shed its dying leaves
On the same brink where once in youthful pride
It waved the green luxuriance of Spring.
And centuries, whose birth saw thee roll on,
Went down the abyss of time and left thee here
In sacred solitude unknown to man.[23]

The travellers never got to Montreal and Quebec because both Mary and her husband were seized with the "disease of the lakes," as the ladies politely termed an illness caused by bad water and poor food. He was violently ill, so that for the first time he had need to fortify himself with that bright hope of a future life which he had preached so often to others. Both invalids recovered quickly, however, and while the trip down the St. Lawrence had to be abandoned, the party did cross into Canada and circle Lake Ontario on that side before starting back to Boston.

The year of 1816 began in peace and prosperity for the nation and for the Holleys. Save that they longed for a son, Mary felt that there was little that a kind Providence had denied them. In her deep contentment she reckoned without her husband's growing reputation and his consciousness of his own powers. In January a letter came from Lexington, Kentucky, written by a Mr. James Prentiss on behalf of the Board of Trustees of Transylvania University, offering Mr. Holley the presidency of the institution.[24] Neither Horace nor his wife knew much about the University, the town, or the Commonwealth of Kentucky, although she had heard more concerning them than he. She knew at least that several years earlier the boy Stephen Austin had proceeded, not to Yale, but to Transylvania for his education, because his mother and sister were in Lexington at the time and his father had numerous business connections there.

To Bostonians any mention of Kentucky brought to mind the Honorable Henry Clay, the War Hawk Congressman who had gone with John Quincy Adams to Ghent to negotiate the Treaty of Peace with Great Britain. Mr. Clay, it seemed, was a member of the Board of Trustees of Transylvania. Could the offer have come through that channel?

However it came, Horace was pleased by the invitation and gave it deliberate and proper consideration. In his reply he suggested that perhaps he should come to Kentucky for a personal interview; but before his letter reached its destination the offer was rescinded by the Board on March 22 because some of the Presbyterian members had forced the action after learning that Holley's religious views were unorthodox.[25] Horace received a curt notice of the Board's withdrawal of the offer, but he dismissed the matter from his mind without grudge.

The Transylvania invitation merely served to point up his growing interest in the field of education. He took an increasing part in the affairs of Harvard. Young John Everett, prodigy of the Sophomore Class at the time, often sought his assistance in revising his orations. John's older brother, Edward, a brilliant young minister, had just resigned his pulpit to accept the chair of Greek at Harvard, and had gone to Germany to perfect his studies.[26] In the light of all these events, Mr. Holley's own election at this time to membership in the American Antiquarian Society must have given him considerable cause for satisfaction. The Society fostered the collecting of materials for "history and the arts and sciences," and the certificate of membership bore the signature of Isaiah Thomas, a venerable and distinguished printer and bookseller.[27] Horace was discovering within himself and in the expectations of others a call to greatness that he had not yet fulfilled.

Mary saw no shortcomings in her husband's present position; nor could she imagine a life more ideal than theirs in Boston. She loved the salt air. She had grown attached to the green expanse of the Common, ringed about with the State House dome and many spires. She relished the succulent oysters and flaky white fish brought daily to the markets; she looked forward each autumn to purple grapes and rosy apples from the inland hills. She liked the way Boston people took pains to live well no matter how busy their minds were.

Where but here in this town would a surgeon like Dr. Warren be prouder of the Roxbury Russeting Apple originated on his father's farm than of all his professional honors? Or a former President of the United States take time from sorting his papers to arrange his peaches and pears so that they would rot properly on his shelves in order to produce seed for the future? It seemed so preposterous to her that her husband would even consider giving up the place he had made for himself in the most cultured city in America that she did not take the first letter from Kentucky seriously, although she was relieved at the notice that the offer had been retracted.

In the spring she welcomed an opportunity to withdraw a while from social activities and take Harriette with her for a visit to the Busseys on their Roxbury estate. She packed a few simple gowns made in the plain style of the day and a half dozen books, including her beloved Madame de Staël and also Madame Roland; then she was ready, in her husband's gay phrase, "to hie to the country."

The Bussey place, although it was no more than five miles from the State House, was an idyllic spot, even more sylvan and romantic than the Bronson acres in Greenfield Hill.[28] From the main residence on top of Bussey Hill were views of Boston and Cambridge to the north. Looking down through the oaks and ancient white pines of the farm itself, one saw the steep cliffs of Hemlock Hill, so densely covered with mighty trees that few rays of sun ever pierced their branches. On her daily walks Mary scrambled across the brook and up the dark hillside to catch glimpses of birch and sugar maple, and to count at least three varieties of oak that would be glorious in the fall season.

Ever an early riser she slipped out in the garden, as soon as it was dawn, to the vine-covered bower to read or strum her guitar lightly, inviting the birds to trill in response. Then came the welcome call to breakfast and companionship. Poor Horace, she mused, shut up within dusty brick walls to write sermons and orations and answer dull correspondence. Times were hard over the nation lately, and a pastor had to stay in his study and share the financial troubles of his flock. His solace, he wrote her, was in composing poems to her, or as he cleverly put it, "in the Muse that delights to sing only for you."[29]

Later on he joined her in the pleasures of Bussey Hill, and of evenings he and Mr. Bussey held long conversations about education. Like so many self-made men of the new nation, the old gentleman had great respect for scholars, and cultivated their friendship by hospitality and benefactions. Roxbury contained a surprising number of these quietly learned men who were retired ministers or schoolmasters or just lovers of books like Mr. Supply Clapp Thwing,[30] with whose wife Mary struck up a friendship. In the community was a suitable school for small girls run by Mrs. McKeige, where Harriette was placed during the visit.

As time went on, it looked rather as if Horace Holley was not to have an opportunity to progress from the pulpit to the university professor's chair, as his friend Edward Everett was doing. Despite President Kirkland's friendship no invitations came for him to lecture on rhetoric and oratory at Harvard. Jeremiah Day was President of Yale now, and firmly settled in Dwight's succession there. The Reverend Mr. Holley must be content with the continuing honors being paid him in his own field. He was asked to deliver the Anniversary Discourse, before the Pilgrim Society of Plymouth on December 22, 1817, to commemorate the landing of the Fathers. The occasion would challenge his best efforts, and he decided to spend several days in Plymouth beforehand to get the feeling and inspiration necessary to compose his thoughts. He wanted to view the Rock again and talk to an old deacon of the town. He grew so interested that he wrote out the speech in full, perhaps to justify his position as an antiquarian as well as an orator.[31]

While he was in Plymouth there came another letter from Transylvania University, which had been forwarded through the courtesy of Henry Clay's office. Mary's hand shook a little as she laid it on the desk in the study. She was sure now that she was once again pregnant. They could hope for a second child in the summer. What would she do if Horace decided to remove to Kentucky?

8. THE FIELD IS WIDER. . . .

1817-1818

The letter that Mary Holley laid on her husband's desk was an official communication from the Board of Trustees of Transylvania University notifying him that on the fifteenth of November last he had been elected a second time to the presidency of that institution. It diplomatically explained the misrepresentations that had caused the 1815 appointment to be rescinded, and stressed the fact that this newest action by the Board was unanimous. The same Mr. Prentiss with whom the previous correspondence had been held was on the Committee authorizing this letter. Along with the formal invitation was included considerable information about the curriculum, the medical and law colleges, and prospects for increasing the enrollment and the income. The salary offered the newly elected president was $2250 a year.[1]

Horace read the letter when he got home from Plymouth, in that fine afterglow that always enveloped him at the conclusion of a successful oration. Any resentment at Transylvania's cavalier treatment of him in withdrawing the earlier offer was brushed aside as he considered this one with an open mind. He took up his quill on the day after Christmas to reply to it in a gracious mood:

Gentlemen: I am happy to acknowledge your letter . . . The style of the communication is grateful to my feelings, and the unanimity with which the election has been made, after so much discussion, is highly flattering and auspicious . . . I will write to you again in a few days and either seek by letter all the information which is necessary to regulate my decision, or comply with your suggestion, and make you a visit during the winter.[2]

Mary was deeply opposed to the idea of his going to Kentucky. She felt that she needed his companionship and support during the months of waiting for their child. To be sure, before Harriette's birth she had encouraged him to set out on the preaching tour; but at that time he was never very far away from her. Moreover, she had been a younger woman then by several years and in better health.

She begged him to decline the invitation outright. With all the persuasiveness at her command she urged him to count the blessings of their present life—the loyal Hollis Street congregation, the companionship of beloved friends and associates, the liberty they enjoyed to think and say openly what they believed about religion and politics and morals.

She was wasting her words. While she talked he paced back and forth before the hearth, as in their courting days at Uncle Timothy's. When she had done, he bared his heart and mind to her, propounding unanswerable arguments in favor of making a preliminary visit to Lexington. He had come to feel that no single parish, not even Hollis Street Church, which he loved devotedly, was a broad enough field for his life work. This invitation to head a university that might well rival Harvard and Yale was conceivably the design of that Divine Providence which had guided his whole life to good ends. He must at least investigate what opportunities it offered him for a more useful career and a wider sphere of influence.

As always, he had his way; and he immediately began to make his plans. First, he laid the matter before the leaders of his church, taking them into his full confidence and throwing himself upon their generosity. With bewilderment and grief upon their kindly faces, they heard him—Mr. May and old Mr. Dall, Mr. Barzillai Homes, who had been their old neighbor on Orange Street, and the others. Their first reaction was astonishment that a successful Boston minister would even think of going anywhere else. When they knew him to be in earnest, they gave him permission to make the trip and added their blessing by supplying his pulpit during his absence at their expense.[3] Horace had only to decide upon his route of travel, put Mary under Dr. Warren's care and Mrs. Haskell's charge during his absence, and place Harriette in Mrs. McKeige's school. He intended to be gone only four or five months, and would be back before time for the birth of the new baby.

Since it was to be a costly trip, with a chance that he would not be reimbursed, he determined to make the most of every mile. He would go by stage to New York, then to Philadelphia and Washington City, and on down through Virginia to Richmond and Monticello before crossing the mountains. One of the things he most desired was to meet Thomas Jefferson, and to this end he asked President Adams to write a letter of introduction. Esteem for the Virginia statesman-philosopher was rising among Boston's liberal thinkers, and Mr. Adams had previously written a number of such letters for New England scholars who went South to pay their respects to the famous man of Monticello.

Horace's own Federalism was by now well diluted with Republican ideas, and he was strongly attracted by Jefferson's belief in the essential goodness of all men.

The letter John Adams wrote to Jefferson insured a welcome to its bearer: "You will find him frank enough, candid enough, social enough, learned enough, and eloquent enough. He is indeed an important character. . . . I regret his removal from Boston. . . . He is one of the few who give me delight."[4]

Any number of other prominent and solicitous friends gave him introductions for the journey. Dr. James Freeman wrote to a kinsman in Washington City; the Honorable Josiah Quincy addressed his good friend Judge John Rowan of Bardstown, a village in the interior of Kentucky; Mr. James Lloyd, one of Boston's financial and political leaders, recommended him to Henry Clay; and Colonel Perkins, the art connoisseur, to the governor of Maryland—all in terms of the greatest good will and esteem. Even Monsieur Artiguenave pressed upon him a missive addressed to some titled compatriot in New York. "The accomplished Mr. Holley," wrote Monsieur A., "will perhaps be lost to us, and *ce que sera très affligeant pour les amis de la vraie et belle éloquence.*"[5]

In the bustle of packing her husband's satchels and cramming his trunk with heavy coats and boots as well as lighter clothing for spring in the South, Mary must have read these laudatory letters with a mixture of pride and melancholy. Horace was as excited as a boy about the trip and she did not want to dampen his enthusiasm. It was not in his nature to realize that every beginning is necessarily also an ending, a breaking off with some part of the past. He was so sanguine that he seldom stopped to reckon up his losses, which, so far, had been few. He had never known real hardship or a great sorrow, and had never experienced defeat.

At the request of his friends, Mr. Holley planned to keep a detailed journal of his impressions on this trip, especially of such experiences as the visit to Monticello. He hit upon the idea of doing so in a series of letters to his wife, which, of course, she would carefully preserve. Thus, as he explained in a long formal introduction with which he began the journal, he could share his varied adventures with her and "offset the uniformity of her life at home." What he meant was that he hoped to alleviate the loneliness of her long months of waiting for their child, but good taste forbade his being indelicate in a composition intended for eyes other than hers.

He left Boston early on the afternoon of February the third—the year was 1818—and it seemed best in consideration of Mary's health on a wintry day that he say goodbye to her and his daughter in their rooms on Boylston Street. Tenderly he embraced and kissed them, and promised to write them both as often as he could. Then, wrapping his heavy cloak about him and putting on his well-brushed and shining hat, he was out the door and gone.

For the rest of the winter and spring, and on into early summer, Mary Holley lived a strange, divided existence. She was surrounded by devoted friends who relieved her of all possible responsibilities, rendering her free to think first of her own health and of her unborn child. All her lifelong resources—books, music, sketchbook—were ready to hand. Yet in her mind she was constantly following Horace, first in realistic detail as far as her experience could go, and then in fancy as she read and reread the letters that told her of his progress toward the West.

It seemed a long time before the first letter came from Philadelphia.[6] He had stopped overnight in New Haven, and then for a few days in New York, where he had seen Henry, now a merchant, and Orville, who was one of the editors of the thriving *American Monthly Magazine and Critical Review*. Clever Orville, after procrastinating for years, had finally found his niche. Even here in Philadelphia where there were no relatives, Horace warned her, he would be very busy. She must ask for news of him when she consulted Dr. Warren, to whom he would be writing often on business.

The Reverend Mr. Holley's journey to the West really began in Philadelphia, where he was received cordially by the literary and professional society of the city, as he managed to hint to Dr. Warren in a lengthy letter. Mr. Nicholas Biddle, Bishop White, General Cadwallader, and a certain Dr. Charles Caldwell of the university there, were among the persons with whom he discussed educational and political problems of the time. On all sides he was advised to accept the Transylvania offer. When he reached Washington City the last of March, he met with an even more optimistic view of the opportunities in Kentucky. His spirits rose steadily.

As was customary when eminent divines were in the city, he was invited to preach in the hall of the House of Representatives on a Sunday. He was met by a large and flattering audience, to whom he delivered a carefully prepared discourse setting forth the view that the reality, truth, and importance of religion are independent of the authority of written revelation. He spoke extemporaneously, relying upon his eloquence to sway his hearers.

The effect of his sermon was all that he could have desired. A few evenings later when he was calling upon President and Mrs. Monroe, their daughter, Mrs. Hay, pressed him to preach again. "You have made a convert of me," she declared. "Your sentiments are rational, and I like them. I have always felt so, but I did not know how to describe and phrase such feelings. You brought out that it is not necessary to be unnatural in order to be religious." Then, as the servants passed ice creams, cake, wine, and lemonade to the guests assembled in the drawing room, Mr. Holley and Mrs. Hay continued to converse vivaciously about their little daughters, who were the same age, and about how handsome Mrs. Monroe appeared in her rich white gown and matching turban, with delicate gold work at her breast, where hung a chain of brilliant topazes.

He dined with the John C. Calhouns, and talked over the problem of slavery with the austere Secretary of War from South Carolina, who had been his fellow student at Yale. The talk ranged farther afield to include Jackson's defeat of the Seminoles, and the status of literary institutions, primary schools, and religion. Holley wrote for his journal a considered opinion that Calhoun was "candid, discerning, philosophical, and comprehensive." He also set down a transcript of the gay conversation he had carried on with charming Mrs. Hay, just to give Mary an idea of the social life in Washington. Since that letter from Washington was marked No. 41, he must have been writing to her several times a week. He was also corresponding with various Boston friends, insisting over and over that he was keeping an open mind about the Transylvania offer. "My equilibrium is unchangeable till I have examined the place, the institution, and the circumstances for myself," he declared to Dr. Freeman. To him it was sufficient proof of an open mind to be willing to debate a proposition.

He was so busy in Washington that he may not have attended the session of Congress when a bill was introduced by Representative Joseph Desha of Kentucky to change the national flag of fifteen stars and fifteen stripes so that in the future there would be only thirteen stripes. Horace was only mildly interested in flags, although his wife was fascinated by them. In this event it would have been profitable to him if he had taken the trouble to observe the Honorable Mr. Desha with care, noting in particular his "small deep sunken eye" and his manner, which was reputed to combine the "condescension of a courtier" with great pride of office.[7] Unlikely as it seemed then, he was to see much of Joseph Desha in the near future.

Among the letters he received from home was one in his small daughter's childish writing. He replied promptly, addressing her at the school in Roxbury. He had just seen some little girls near his hotel who were getting on the stage for Boston, and he had kissed them goodbye because they reminded him of her. He did not comment on what these little misses said when a handsome gentleman, somewhat bald and by his coat a clergyman, kissed them right out on the street of the capital city. He took it for granted that they liked it. People always found Horace Holley charming, whether friends or strangers—or even enemies.

Mary wrote to him faithfully although there was nothing to tell beyond the small gossip of their circle. Dr. Walter Channing was elected to the Wednesday Evening Club. Would her dear husband like to hear a "tell" for *him* from Mrs. Warren? Or an account of the evening she herself had spent at the Perkinses where she saw that pretty Mrs. Hull whom he always found so attractive? Even as Mary scribbled the news of their happy world she knew that he would read it with only half his mind. He was intent upon Lexington, and her letters would have no part in the momentous decision to be made there.

Meanwhile, she pored over the map—the Austins liked maps as well as flags—to follow him as best she could on his way from Washington City down to Richmond and over into the mountains where Jefferson lived. As she traced the route with the tip of her quill it seemed a long and almost fantastic side trip for him to make on the mere chance of having a talk with a stranger about the prospects for education in Kentucky.

The trip to Monticello did turn out to be a disappointment. Jefferson was away from home when Horace arrived and so he dined only with the family.[8] However, the ladies proved hospitable and intelligent, and he got to see the famous cannonball clock and to take a faraway look at President Monroe's smaller home on a neighboring elevation. As he rode down from the top of Mr. Jefferson's mountain he was not sorry he had come, although he had now to travel all the way back to Frederick in Maryland to obtain a vehicle to the West.

Horace Holley's instinct was sound in seeking an interview and an exchange of ideas with Jefferson before proceeding to Kentucky. Later on in the summer Jefferson called a committee to meet at Rockfish Gap Tavern to draw up plans for the Central College of Virginia to be established in an "academical village" at the foot of his mountain where he could watch his dream of a state-controlled, nonsectarian American university come true. If Holley had found the master of Monticello at home, the old statesman could have given him some valuable advice concerning Western politics, and in turn have received from his visitor some equally valuable information about methods at Harvard and Yale for his own educational project.

As it was, about the middle of May Horace took the stage from Frederick over the Cumberland Road to Wheeling and boarded the boat down the Ohio to Maysville, formerly known as Limestone, a village on the Kentucky shore where the main-travelled road to the southward led off to Lexington, sixty-five miles away. The stage wound its way among the hills and over Stoner's Creek, bypassing a village called Paris to make a stop at Captain Johnson's comfortable inn. Then on for twenty more miles over rich, level land to the thriving metropolis of Lexington, named for the first battle of the Revolution, and the county seat of Fayette, so called in honor of the French hero, General Lafayette. In the middle of town the driver turned onto a paved street, eighty feet across and with footwalks on either side, and then halted before a sizable tavern, clearly the best in the place. As Horace got out he was greeted by the proprietor, Mr. Keene, and shown to commodious quarters, including a drawing room for receiving guests. His arrival had been expected for days, and everybody in town seemed to know it as soon as he inscribed his name upon the register.

The next day callers came in such numbers that it was a relief as well as a pleasure when Henry Clay, just back from Washington, came to ask his company for a stroll through the town. After the amenities of introduction, they proceeded along Main Street, passing several three-story painted brick stores, toward the public square and the courthouse. After that, the way led over to the poplar-shaded College Lot, a little to the north. Signs of prosperity and of culture appeared on every hand —a small public library room and a Masonic Hall and numerous churches. The citizens of Lexington required the services of half a dozen bookbinders and printers, two professional portrait painters, many silversmiths and carriage-makers, and a first-rate French confectioner. Mr. Clay showed him the Athenaeum, a club supported by gentlemen of literary and scholarly tastes, after which they called at several substantial homes in the vicinity. The Senator was introducing him to the inner circle of Lexington's established families, the circle of which Clay had become a member when, as a rising young lawyer from Virginia, he had married the daughter of Colonel Thomas Hart, influential landowner and brother-in-law of the Commonwealth's first governor. This was Horace Holley's first impression of the town, and it won him completely.

He dashed off a hasty note to Mary to acquaint her with his safe arrival, but for many days he had no time for recording experiences in letters to her. Early the next morning, after his walk about the town, Mr. Clay sent his carriage to the tavern to convey the visitor to Ashland, his residence a mile and a half out in the county, for breakfast and a look around at the extensive lawns and stables and well-tended gardens.[9] His host then rode back to town with him to the college, where the Trustees and professors and the students—there were fewer than a hundred of them—were gathered in the largest hall to hear a short address by Mr. Holley. Afterward he was taken on a tour of the Old Seminary, the shabby two-story structure in which they met, and then to the handsome new College, a three-story brick edifice, crowned with an ornamental cupola, which was set midway of the College Lot in front of the Seminary.

There was not a great deal to inspect. The library consisted of a small collection of books housed in one room; of scientific apparatus there was virtually none. The three professors who taught the arts and sciences were a formidable group, all big and middle-aged, and Presbyterians to a man. Mr. Bishop was a gaunt Scotsman, with a broad accent and, it was said, a high temper. Mr. Blythe was a square-built man with a harsh, deep-toned voice, who was admittedly firm in the classroom. Mr. Sharpe, the Latin teacher, was popular with the boys, maybe because of his jolly habit of singing the ballads of Robbie Burns to lighten sessions devoted to Caesar's Commentaries. In the confusion of the first introductions none of these pedagogues made a strong impression upon Holley.

"Everything is to be done," he wrote in his notes for the journal, "and so much the better, as nothing is to be reformed. Almost the whole is proposed to be left to me to arrange."

In considering the offer from Transylvania to become its president he would have been wise to inform himself carefully about the past history as well as the present state of the institution. Its beginnings went back nearly forty years to certain large land grants from the Virginia General Assembly for the purpose of establishing a seminary in the County of Kentucky. Chartered in 1798 as Transylvania University, it had been under the control at times of strict Presbyterians and at other times of more liberal theologians, ranging all the way from the gentle, flute-playing Reverend James Moore, rector of the Episcopal

Church of the community, who served as acting president in the early days, to various presidents of deistic and Unitarian tendencies. The present Board of Trustees was controlled by a majority who were conservative liberals in religious matters and liberal conservatives about politics and money. They were well-to-do men, who deposited their funds in the Lexington Branch of the United States Bank, and disapproved both of the Relief Measures and of the state banks that were flooding the area with unsound paper currency. Their intellectual openmindedness and their economic prudence made a combination rather like the Boston Federalism to which Holley had become a convert. Henry Clay himself was notedly more conservative since his return from Ghent.

Such denominational and political controversies seemed to Horace Holley to have no place in the administration of an educational institution. If he should come to Kentucky, he would have no share in them, would be identified with no sect or party. He was aware, of course, that many orthodox Kentuckians, especially among the clergy, had opposed his appointment ever since 1815. Shortly after his arrival in the city a prominent minister called upon him expressly to show him some anonymous letters that were being circulated against him. After preaching in the Episcopal pulpit on the subject of the Trinity, he quipped in a letter to his wife: "Persons came from neighboring towns eager to learn whether I am a heretic or not!" But he was sure he had convinced them that he was indeed no heretic, especially when his drawing room at the hotel continued to be visited by preachers from all the denominations—Presbyterian, Baptist, and Methodist—most of whom invited him to preach before their congregations.

Unfortunately for him, he underestimated the bitterness of the theological dispute which had impeded Transylvania from its beginnings; and he failed to realize that this was a political controversy as well. The University was inevitably a pawn in the contest for control of the government of the Commonwealth. Each faction wished to dominate it just as Timothy Dwight had coveted Yale for the Standing Order in Connecticut. If Horace Holley, who had been trained by Dwight, had been in possession of all the facts, he would surely have realized that he could not be President of Transylvania and remain aloof from the religious and political arena. But he listened only to what he wanted to hear and convinced himself that it was possible for him to take such high ground, repeatedly telling the men with whom he conferred that he intended to do so. He was not surprised at the ease with which he seemed to win their confidence and assent. He was accustomed to convincing his hearers.

What did surprise him was the community to which he had come. He confided to his journal: "The town is handsomer than I expected, and has a more comfortable and genteel aspect." He had not anticipated that there would be clean, paved streets, lined with ash and locust trees and set with solid-brick dwellings.

Any notion he had harbored of finding frontier crudities was dissipated once and for all the day he went with a party of twenty ladies and gentlemen some nine miles out in the county to the seat of Colonel David Meade. His elderly host, a Virginian of the old school, greeted them in square coat and great cuffs, short breeches and white stockings, to escort them around gardens that were adorned with Chinese and Grecian temples, an English hunting lodge, and a large lake. The grounds were astonishingly beautiful, and at this season the landscape was drenched with the Maytime sweetness of honeysuckle and climbing roses.

The guests were invited inside to enjoy the coolness of the big octagonal parlor, where the walls were lined with family portraits, one by Sir Joshua Reynolds. Mrs. Meade, in cap and ruffles, greeted them graciously, and played the pianoforte cheerfully until Old Dean, the lordly black butler, announced dinner. They sat down at four o'clock in the walnut-panelled dining room to a long table loaded with the delicacies of the region—ham and chickens, puddings and hot breads, cakes and pies. The conversation was as good as the viands, and when they arose it was time to start back to Lexington. Even with memories of Bussey Hill fresh in his mind, Mr. Holley had to admit to himself that in all New England there was no establishment like Colonel Meade's Chaumiere du Prairie.

He was almost equally impressed by his inspection of several large ropewalks in the town, and the thriving cotton-bagging manufactory belonging to John Brand, from Dundee, Scotland, which could turn out one hundred and twenty yards of bagging a day. Rose Hill, the new Brand villa on the north edge of town, was one of the finest homes in the community.[10]

A few days later the trustees escorted him over to the capital located in the village of Frankfort some twenty-five miles to the west, so that he could meet Governor Slaughter and the numerous judges and officials who lived there. Since the University depended upon the Legislature for its chief income, it was all-important that the political leaders approve of the new president. The Legislature was not in session, but the Governor was cordial, receiving them in his home, and promising support to the new administration if Mr. Holley decided to come. Gabriel Slaughter, a conservative Republican, had appointed most of the present trustees. Other officials were friendly, also, among them a number of prominent Baptist clergymen. Horace made a mental note to write his mother about this last, mindful of the fact that she was the daughter of one such.

After a fortnight of conferences and inspections, trips out of town and hundreds of callers, the trustees met in order for Mr. Holley to address them formally. When he had withdrawn they voted unanimously that a committee headed by Mr. Clay should offer the post to him, requesting that he give them his answer at the next meeting three weeks hence. The salary was raised to three thousand dollars, to be paid in hard money, with the diploma fees extra, and a liberal allowance for bringing him and his family out from Boston. Meanwhile, since Lexington was the chief town of the inner bluegrass country, which was dotted with prosperous small communities, it was proposed that he visit various towns nearby in order to form his opinion of the region and its people.

Horace had resumed his regular letters to his wife, telling her the good tidings:

The proofs of cordial cooperation are multiplying . . . Dinners are made nearly every day for me, and there is a party almost every evening. But attention of this sort, however agreeable, and however flattering to my self-love, do not bias my mind . . . The road which I am now pursuing, is the most direct one to useful power, to honorable fame, to the attainment of public confidence, and to the full application of all my faculties. You will not only be contented in Lexington, but you will be pleased and delighted. . . .

You may make your power and efforts very valuable, and most extensively useful in various ways. Our house will be a resort for persons of the best minds in the region, for the students of most promising talents, for the professors, for resident graduates whom we may wish to encourage, for strangers of distinction, and for all who shall have any claims to literature, refinement, manners, music, and accomplishment. . . .

For the sole purpose of doing good, I had rather be at the head of this institution than at the head of any Eastern college. The field is wider,—the harvest more abundant, and the grain of an excellent quality.[11]

These first letters from Kentucky began to reach Mary in early June, each more enthusiastic than the last. She was heavy with child—her baby was due to be born within five or six weeks—and she was heavy of heart. She could read between the lines that her husband had virtually made up his mind to accept the post. Although he had promised himself and her and the Hollis Street leaders to delay his decision until he got home, he was about to settle the matter before he left Kentucky, before she and his Boston friends could counsel with him.

She wrote him immediately, with all the vigor she could muster. Once more she described the beauties of the Boston countryside, the infinite variety of scene and historic association, the wisdom and goodness and happiness of the people. Where could he find a better place? Was he *sure* that he was not making a martyr of himself, burying himself and his talents in a remote province? She implored him not to be deceived by the gala dress of Lexington—not to make his decision there—to come home soon.

She found a messenger, maybe the Haskells' hired man, to hurry off to the post office with her letter; and then she must have sunk back on the couch in their inner chamber where he had bade her goodbye and covered her face with her slender hands to hide the tears. She was not one to weep easily, but never in her life had she felt more helpless than in this summer of 1818, as she watched her husband led on to his destiny as if by a principle of fatalism.

Her urgent letter reached him in Lexington, probably before his decision was publicly announced; but it did not alter his mind. As always, he answered her arguments triumphantly:

I am not about to bury myself, nor take my talents, humble as they are, from an active and conspicuous sphere. The whole Western country is to feed my seminary, which will send out lawyers, physicians, clergymen, statesmen, poets, orators, and *savants*, who will make the Union feel them . . . The course I am pursuing is a high and honorable one, entirely above the region of the clouds and storms of sects, and in a clear and pure day. I breathe an atmosphere more agreeable to me in the large view that I take than I have breathed before . . . A great inquiry is made of me, "How will you like my determination?" I answer always that you will leave Boston with reluctance and pain, but that you will follow my fortunes cheerfully and perseveringly . . . I shall accept of the appointment.[12]

On the twenty-fifth of June he withdrew to his room in the tavern and composed his formal letter of consent to the Board for its meeting two days later.[13] The die was cast. He then wrote immediately to notify the Hollis Street congregation, and plunged into making plans for his return in the fall. He made arrangements to rent a large residence on Limestone Street—some still called it Mulberry Street—only a short walk from the College Lot. It belonged to the estate of the late Thomas Hart, Jr., of which Henry Clay was executor. Thus the business was easily concluded, and the new president could be at rest about a proper home for his family. He was detained longer in Lexington than he wished, and before he reached Boston, his wife gave birth to her child, on the nineteenth of July.[14] As he arrived to embrace her tenderly and to look upon his longed-for son and heir, he assuredly felt that his cup was running over, and that goodness and mercy were following him all his days.

For Mary Holley the whole year had been a medley of fatigue and emotion. Not that she lacked excellent medical care or solicitous friends. She could call not only upon Dr. Warren but upon Dr. Walter Channing, now professor of obstetrics at Harvard.[15] But there was little joy for her in the coming of their second child, and, even after Horace's return, scant time for hovering over the cradle and making plans as they had for the infant Harriette.

His first task was to explain to his stricken congregation his reasons for leaving, and to dissolve the connection formally. The Hollis Street Society dismissed him on August 24 with profound regret and affection.[16] Then began the ceremonies of leave-taking. He received Resolutions of Respect from the School Committee and from the Association of Congregational Ministers and other official bodies. There were farewell dinners with various clubs and personal friends. He called on President Kirkland over in Cambridge and the Busseys in Roxbury.

Mary had little strength or time for these affectionate attentions. Whenever the baby was sleeping, she must put her mind on which of their possessions to take and which to leave behind. The pianoforte and their many books and the few prized *objets d'art* they had collected must be packed to stand a journey of a thousand miles across the mountains. She must decide upon suitable clothes for herself and Harriette for travelling in sharp autumn weather, and plan how to care for an infant on such a trip. No wonder she did not regain her strength as she should have, and looked peaked and wan.

Somehow, with everybody helping, the necessary chores were done. Horace was at his cheerful best instructing the servants just how to pack the barrels and boxes, just where to place this article and that book. He presented numerous volumes from his library to friends, each with a cordial note. He sorted out his voluminous records and papers, but this time he did not burn his old sermon notes, as he had done when they left Greenfield Hill. The doctrine he had proclaimed from the

Hollis Street pulpit was his final faith. He believed, on the basis of everything he had been told in Kentucky, that with such a doctrine he could unite all parties there.

He announced his views to Mary and to the friends who gathered in their parlor to hang on his words as long as he was among them. "There will be a unanimity of sentiment and operation that nothing could secure but that real and permanent catholicism in religion and politics which I cherish, and which you know I have been a good while obtaining and confirming," he declared. They all knew how sincere his words were, and nodded their assent as he went on. "I belong to no set of prejudices, or obstinate and silly peculiarities; and for this very good reason, that I have tried them all, and found them nonsense, by experience!"[17] As he spoke there seemed no reason why he should not be able to free Transylvania from sectarian and party strife, and make it a great center of scholarship and culture in the West. Mary resolved that, whatever it cost her, she would follow her husband's fortunes perseveringly and, if she could, cheerfully. He always detested "dolefuls"—and so did she.

One of Mr. Holley's pressing problems was recruiting faculty members for his new University. In the late summer a letter from Henry Clay authorized him to procure two tutors in the classical languages to replace Professor Sharpe, who had just resigned.[18] He promptly engaged eighteen-year-old John Everett, the Harvard youth whose orations he had supervised; and, for the second tutor, he selected Charles Walker, another one of the spring crop at Cambridge. Both agreed to accompany the President on the trip West, and it seemed a fortunate circumstance to have two stout young men as companions on such a journey.

Finally, on the afternoon of the first Sunday in October, the Reverend Mr. Holley bade an eloquent farewell to his flock and a great crowd of assembled citizens. The pews and aisles and the rostrum steps were packed, while late-comers stood outside in the street. At the conclusion of the services he slowly descended the pulpit stairs to the baptismal font, where he christened his son, naming him Horace Austin Holley. Then Mr. Guild's choir sang "Whilst Thee I seek, protecting Power," and the throng filed silently out.[19] Many were in tears, and Mary wept in spite of herself.

One last tribute to their beloved pastor came from the heart of the Hollis Street congregation. Shortly before Mr. Holley's departure, James Barker, a prosperous Orange Street cabinetmaker, requested the privilege of commissioning Gilbert Stuart to paint his portrait. Nothing could have pleased Horace more greatly, or given Mary more satisfaction. The first citizens of the town were having Stuart do them nowadays, and his recent likeness of John Quincy Adams was counted as good as the one by the famous Copley. Therefore, in the midst of the packing and leave-taking, Horace Holley and Mr. Barker made many trips, often before breakfast, down to a shabby studio near the Harbour, where the gruff, arrogant artist would receive them, his clothes disordered and spattered by the snuff he dipped continually from a large round tin wafer-box, sometimes as much as half a pound a day, so people said. He talked incessantly as he worked.

With the intuition of a great painter, Stuart chose to portray his subject just as James Barker and the Hollis Street people would always remember him—in his dark silk robes, with a book in his firm, scholar's hand. The very last sitting was on the morning of the day the Holleys were to leave, and Gilbert Stuart became strangely gracious. As he put down his brush for the last time, he turned to Mr. Barker.

"I never wish to paint him again," he said slowly. "This is the only picture I have ever painted that I have no desire to alter."[20]

The portrait was one of his masterpieces. He caught Horace Holley at the supreme moment of his life, and showed him as he really was —the fine forehead, the thoughtful eyes, the sensitive mouth. Stuart's portrait reveals the same man of whom John Adams had written the preceding spring in a letter to Jefferson: "As Holley is a diamond of superior water, it would be crushed to powder in any other country. Even in this he is a light shining in a dark place."[21]

In early October they were ready to set out for Kentucky, the Holleys and their children and the tutors.[22] Since Transylvania had been generous about expenses they purchased a green travelling carriage with good horses and engaged a driver. The young men would ride horseback alongside. All the leave-takings, public and private, were over.

At last came the early morning, before any vehicles save the market carts were abroad, when the little party jogged along Orange Street toward the Neck and the mainland beyond to start the journey. Mary sat in the carriage, wearing her plain blue habit, with the baby clasped in her arms. It was hard to believe that they were leaving Boston for always, and she turned back again and again to catch the last familiar glimpses.

The rolling of the carriage wheels set up a rhythm in her poet's mind:

> Since Boston with its dark dome and glittering spires
> Faded from my sick'ning sight away—[23]

Then the jolting over the cobblestones set her to remembering one of her husband's letters from Kentucky. He had written boldly, as if he were pounding out the words in a speech:

I cannot now balk an enterprise into which I am so far entered, which has cost me so much time and money, which is connected with so many sacrifices of ease and comfort, and which is leading to results that will be glorious in success, or painful in defeat. *I must on to the end of it.*[24]

The journey had to be made in easy stages, encumbered as they were. They stopped a few days in New York City, and sought diversion by visiting Trumbull's newest painting. His admirers reverently spoke of it as "The Picture," but Mary cared little for it.

"So many men in a familiar dress and attitude, without women or mystery is too much like common life to make a powerful impression," she remarked critically to the gentlemen with whom she was viewing the work of art. She had become a real Romantic under the influence of de Staël and Scott. Later on she found Mr. Trumbull to be interesting and his wife to be lovely when they came calling at the hotel, and she may have revised her unfavorable opinion of the painting.[25]

After the respite in New York the party proceeded to Baltimore to visit the Dalls and to let Horace accept an urgent invitation to preach at the dedication of their congregation's new church building.[26] Then they took the westward route Horace had travelled the previous spring over the Cumberland Road and across the long Pennsylvania mountains. Never would Mary forget the climb up "Sideling Hill," when everybody else got out of the carriage, leaving her to clutch the baby and try to brace herself while Wallingford, the driver, shouted at the straining horses. The season was getting late, and the brown fields were white with frost each morning as they set out in the fog. Horace pressed forward as fast as possible to be ahead of the early snowfalls.

Mary was grateful to get to Wheeling, where they sent the horses overland and exchanged the lurching of the carriage for the gentle roll of the steamboat down the Ohio. She listened languidly as her husband paced the deck, pointing out the landmarks along the shore to his little daughter and the eager tutors. On the northern bank was the thriving settlement of Marietta, founded by Revolutionary veterans from New

England; and midstream lay Blennerhassett's Island, where Aaron Burr plotted treason, as all good Federalists believed. Then farther down they could see Gallipolis, where a hundred French families had been settled by the same Joel Barlow who was one of the Hartford Wits. Even John Everett, for all his certainty that most of the country's history had taken place within sight of the Boston State House, was genuinely impressed. He was a youth of taste and wit, who made himself agreeable on the trip. Young Walker was a gentlemanly lad, but dull, who rode day after day without contributing a romantic comment on the scenery or a line of poetry, or even a pun.

They were all excited as they moved swiftly down La Belle Rivière. The world was altering, not alone for themselves, but everywhere. People hardly knew what denomination or political party they belonged to any more. To Horace Holley this change was a welcome one, however his companions felt about it.

"The single fact that I am of no party," he declared, "is of the greatest service to me. I shall act upon more minds than any man on this side of the mountains, and shall reach more sympathies."[27]

The paddle wheels could not turn fast enough for him as their boat took him deeper into the fertile Western country that was to feed his seminary.

9. HARVEST MORE ABUNDANT

1818-1821

It was dusky dark on Saturday, the twenty-first of November, when the driver of the Holleys' carriage pointed with his whipstock and called back over his shoulder, "That must be Lexington—yonder where you see the lights." Soon, the twinkling windows of houses set back from the road gleamed more frequently, and Wallingford cracked his whip to bring the horses into the outskirts of town more briskly.

"Farther on, this road becomes Limestone Street," Horace announced knowingly, "and that's where our house is located."

Then the carriage made a sharp turn to the right that brought them in sight of the new College, illuminated in their honor with rows of candles set in the windows and on the roof. In spite of the chill a crowd of students and townspeople were gathered to cheer as they came to a stop, and to greet them with good news. The fall session had begun two weeks earlier with a substantial increase in enrollment. Support was coming in from many quarters, and no less a dignitary than General James Taylor of Newport—a Kentucky town on the Ohio—had personally brought his son to enter him as a student.[1]

Such a welcome at their journey's end fulfilled all the promises Horace had made to his companions, and their weariness dropped from them as they listened to the soft, hearty voices and looked into the smiling eyes around them. Mr. Clay was not there to meet them. He was on his way to Washington, and somewhere en route might even have passed them. But the Holley family went directly to Ashland, as he had written them to do, and stayed a few days until their belongings could be set out in the new home.

The President immediately organized the academic program, grouping the students into four classes, and taking over the supervision of the juniors and seniors himself. To the young tutors he assigned numerous tasks, beginning with classes in Latin and Greek, and the custody of the library. Some improvements had been made since his inspection in the spring, but not enough. For the library he ordered new cases, a compass-stand, and stout hooks on all the shutters. He tactfully had Professor Bishop's classroom improved with a platform like the one in Professor Blythe's room. He did nothing to improve the two small offices assigned for his own use on the first floor of the new building.

Donations to the library came from friends in the East whom he had solicited. Judge Story of Salem sent his personal copies of Faber's *Thesaurus* and Postlethwaite's *Dictionary* and Swammerdam's *History of Insects,* with a gracious letter of transmittal to wish the University well and to recognize "President Holley's exalted talents." Old President Adams devoted part of Christmas Day to composing an appreciative letter predicting a great career for his esteemed friend Holley.[2]

Within a few weeks came a letter from Henry Clay, written in Washington. He had actually been in Baltimore at the same time they were, without knowing it. Along with a warm, personal welcome, the canny statesman offered his new friend some sober advice. He warned that the orthodox religionists would not cease their attacks; he knew that from experience. Holley would do better to be an educator, not a reformer, and to avoid preaching in local pulpits or affiliating with any one denomination. "The main thing," wrote Mr. Clay, "is to make men live better." Horace agreed with this philosophy, and resolved to follow the admonition to be neutral in religion and politics.

Four weeks to the day after his arrival the new President was inducted into office in a ceremony of such proportions that it had to be held in the nearby Episcopal Church instead of the University Chapel. Mary, with her little daughter, sat in a prominent pew where they could watch the long procession of trustees, professors, students, and citizens. Someone played a proper prelude on the little organ in the gallery at the rear. Robert Wickliffe, chairman of the Board, presented Mr. Holley with the keys of the institution, a Bible, and a volume of science, after which the faculty members, including the new tutors, were sworn into their offices.[3]

Finally Mary heard her husband's voice, first low and mellow, then full and golden, as he spoke to his spellbound audience. She scarcely noted his address for remembering other words of his: "... I cannot balk an enterprise into which I am so far entered . . . *I must on to the end of it.*"

Thus far the enterprise had led him to stand with the keys of Transylvania in his hand and the people of Kentucky pledged to help him.

She had her doubts and fears as to what would be the "end of it," but since it was his destiny, it would be hers likewise.

Her immediate responsibility was to set up a household in a strange community, as she had done twice before in their married life. The Hart house, as people called the place, was a commodious dwelling, built for hospitable living, which was set back from the street in a wooded lawn. The carriage house, smoke house, fences, and other improvements were in good order. It was an establishment big enough for the family and the tutors from Boston, who were to live with them, and for the kind of entertaining that Horace proposed to offer to the college and the community. The Widow Hart, who had been residing there, may have left some of her larger pieces of furniture, but much had to be purchased. The pianoforte and the books, the chairs and the pedestals which had been carted over the mountains, had to be supplemented with cherry chests and tables and bedsteads. Connecticut clocks and marble statues from Italy looked stylish, but it was necessary to arrange at once with Mr. Blanchard, the silversmith, for five dozen spoons, suitably engraved, and other silver pieces for dining and evening parties.[4]

The household servants were Negroes, leased temporarily from their owners. Mary found their presence disturbing. Her father had not owned slaves, as had a few of his New Haven neighbors; and she was awkward in directing them for a while, much more so than her husband. That and her poor health accounted in part for the long time it took to get the house settled and her duties spread out before her each day. She was so meticulous and slow about it all that her husband laughed at her, and vowed she wasted her days in waiting for a "good time" to attend to the stacks of unanswered letters on her desk and to resume her reading and practice hours on the pianoforte.

She admitted his charges of over-much "nicety" in requiring everything to be in order before she could concentrate on more intellectual things, claiming that it was but a woman's weakness. She knew herself well enough to realize, however, that she was playing the martyr about housekeeping because she was still homesick for Boston. Cocky young Everett shook her out of her self-pity. She had moped in a cloud of gloom for months, all during the Christmas season and especially while her husband was in Frankfort addressing the Legislature in behalf of funds for the University. At last John bluntly told her that her face was growing long and its lines were getting angular and "drawn down." Her mirror confirmed the truth of what he said, and that was more than her vanity could bear. Humbly she accepted his masculine rebuke and resolved, as she said, "to try *hard* to be civil, respectful, and obliging to all . . . and to be *agreeable* and to look *interestingly!*" The last resolve was what mattered most. Even in a melancholy mood she had no intention of being unattractive.[5]

Before long she discovered that her new servants were industrious and obedient and wonderfully kind, especially with the children. A time was set apart for her to give daily instruction to Harriette, as in the past, and to add lessons in history and geography. In arranging her house she reserved for herself the little back parlor, where she put her favorite books and the small table covered with well-worn green baize on which for years she had done her writing. Her guitar hung on the wall. At last, listening to her daughter's recitations or turning the pages of *Childe Harold*, she felt almost at home, and her ideas and feelings flowed as they were wont to do. To this refuge she could withdraw sometimes to fill a long sheet of news for Mrs. Davis or frame suitable replies to clever letters from Willard Phillips or Orville. Thus fortified, she found it much easier to keep her resolve to be agreeable to the crowds of guests who came to call.

The ladies of Lexington paid their respects properly and promptly, according to the town's social customs. Forenoon visits were in vogue, and Mary was astonished to see her callers arrive in silk and satin dresses and spencers trimmed in plush as if they were going to an evening function. No Boston lady would ever be so conspicuous. She learned that Lexington took its style in all things from Philadelphia, and that many of her new acquaintances sent there twice a year for their most important articles of clothing readymade.

"How is Dr. Holley?" her guests would ask politely, as they adjusted their flounces, scarcely touching their backs to the parlor chairs lest they form a wrinkle or disturb a hair. "And how are the children?"

After that greeting it always devolved upon her to supply the rest of the conversation, which flourished best when they talked of babies and recipes and clothes. For all their expensive dresses, these ladies apparently had little social life, and only the young and single ones ever enjoyed dancing. At least, none of the others admitted to such a frivolity.[6]

Her visitors were just as critical of her sober-colored day dresses and stout walking boots, designed for damp New England weather, as she was of their impractical finery. And they hardly knew how to begin a conversation with her because the word was out that the new president's wife was a bluestocking, who spoke French and talked philosophy with her husband and his friends. Later on, when many of the ladies turned out to be avid readers and lovers of music like herself, they all got along very well. Mary struck up a lasting friendship with Theodosia Hunt, daughter of a wealthy merchant whose big home faced the College Lot. Theodosia was a versifier, too, being addicted to translating from the Greek and Latin poets.[7] The two exchanged new books and magazines and ideas.

Nevertheless, for a long time after coming to Kentucky Mrs. Holley continued to be critical and more than a little condescending in her judgments, although she had the diplomacy and good sense to air her views only to fellow New Englanders. In letters to Boston she could not resist the temptation to mention all the ways Kentucky suffered by comparison with the East—burning hot summers without benefit of ocean breezes; the unthrift of farmers who left corn standing in the field all winter; and peculiarities of speech that she and her husband called "Kentuckyisms." Although it developed that a few married women *did* dance occasionally at the balls, they performed in nothing more interesting than the everlasting cotillions taught by the local dancing masters.

President Holley, on the other hand, liked his new home "lock, stock, and barrel," to use a Kentuckyism. If there were still those who resented his coming, he resolved to win them as friends for the University, or, failing that, to ignore them. The doors of their home were opened wide with a hospitality that the institution had not previously known. He presided over dinners that taxed the capacity of the ample dining room; and invited large companies to evening parties where they were offered not only a stylish collation but music and dancing and polite conversation. While the servants passed coffee and small cakes and sweetmeats and, for those who wanted them, wine and fruit, someone played the piano or sang or recited.[8]

On such occasions he and his wife were not solemn, official hosts. They circulated informally among the guests, and sometimes the President broke away from the stiff groups of gentlemen standing in the middle of the room to mingle with the ladies seated around the walls and bring a flush of pleasure to their cheeks with his apt compliments and bon mots. The guests included the trustees and their wives, and the faculty families, plus all the circle to whom Clay had introduced Horace upon his first coming, and most of the other established families who resided in the well-kept brick homes in town and country. On occasion the students and their parents were entertained, as were visitors of distinction.

As the fields took on a green tinge in the fickle Kentucky springtime, it did seem that many of the new president's dreams were being fulfilled. In spite of hard times, the Legislature granted money; students came from all over the Southern states; many of the local newspapers supported the University loyally.

Among the frequent callers at the big house on Limestone Street was young William Gibbes Hunt, a New Englander and no relation to the Lexington Hunts.[9] He edited the *Western Monitor*, the town's Federalist newspaper, which strongly supported the Holley administration. He was a popular bachelor, and a budding literary critic who needed only the support of some important man to embolden him to start a magazine of belles-lettres in Lexington. Within two or three months after Horace Holley's coming, such plans were under way. Except for a short-lived periodical many years earlier, this would be the first literary journal in Kentucky, and, more important, the "first-born of the West."

Busy as he was with administrative duties and official hospitality, the President, and also his wife, found time to have a large share in the launching of Hunt's project, which was called the *Western Review and Miscellaneous Magazine: A Monthly Publication devoted to Literature and Science.*[10] They were more conversant with current literary trends than anyone else with whom Hunt could have consulted, and their knowledge of the editorial processes of the *North American Review* proved invaluable. The new magazine was planned to include literary criticism and scientific articles, of course, together with other less formal matter, such as pioneer reminiscences designed to give it a Western flavor. There would be considerable original poetry. Volume One, Number One, was scheduled to come off the press on August 1, 1819.

Horace agreed to do a full-length article on education for the first number, in spite of the fact that several important manuscripts of his were due to be readied for the printer. Both his inaugural address and his speech before the Legislature were still unpublished, although he had been urged to give both to the general public in order to win a wider following over the state. As always, he found it dull work to try to recapture the eloquence of an address or sermon; but creative writing was another and livelier sort of challenge. Hunt's magazine fit in precisely with his dream of the University as a center of culture radiating out over the Western country. He proposed to take full advantage of this opportunity to state his educational theories and to prove that Kentucky could become the home of higher learning.

His essay on education was well and boldly written.[11] He advocated for his University a standard of scholarship not only as good as that in other American and European institutions, but even better—more languages, a larger library, a longer period of academic residence. He meant this article to be his first formal publication as president of Transylvania.

Hunt wanted other contributions from the Holley household, too, whether poetry or travel sketches or essays. He knew that Horace and Mary had been writing in a genteel amateur fashion for so long that they had only to look through their portfolios to find suitable material for a journal like the *Review*. Mary turned over to him three of her poems—the one on Niagara Falls, the one written in the Catskills in the summer of 1815, and a romantic description of the lake at Salisbury. Horace offered a dozen of his own verses. Some were clever occasional pieces, which he revised carefully for this later purpose, and a number were spirited translations from the several foreign languages which he habitually read. These felicitous paraphrases were his best achievements.

In the initial number of the magazine Hunt included only one poem, Mary's romantic verses on first viewing the Catskills. The authorship was disguised after the usual manner of polite amateurs, but not very completely. Horace composed a proper introductory note for it, explaining the origin of the piece, and she signed it "M." It may have been gallantry that prompted the editor to give her the honor of being the first poet to appear in the magazine, or it may have been his critical taste. Her poem on Niagara appeared in the second issue, along with an excellent verse translation by her husband, the "Swan and the Eagle," written that summer the two of them discovered Madame de Staël's *Germany*. In the October issue President Holley's chief contributions were an excellent criticism of Byron's *Mazeppa* and a review of the current *Report* of the American Colonization Society.[12]

In the latter he set forth his considered attitude toward slavery, taking a middle-of-the-road course very like that of Henry Clay and most Federalists in Kentucky or, indeed, in New England in 1819. Holley condemned slave traders who sought to extend the traffic, but sanctioned humane ownership of Negroes for labor in field and home and factory until such time as colonization could restore to them their natural rights. Since he had already purchased servants for his household since coming to Kentucky, this review seemed a proper occasion to express his views without becoming deeply involved in the matter.

The founding of the *Western Review* was a great satisfaction to both of the Holleys. In it Mary made her literary debut, and through its medium Horace found expression for his educational theories and his creative talent. They spread the news of the publication to a wide circle of friends in the East and, where they could, requested good notices for it.

"I hope you wise men of the east will smile upon its infant numbers," she wrote to Willard Phillips; and Orville was asked to comment favorably upon it in his *American Monthly*.[13]

Mr. Holley's desire to be official host to important visitors was amply fulfilled in early July when President Monroe, with General Jackson and a considerable party, visited Lexington on a grand tour of the Ohio Valley. On the first morning the dignitaries were greeted at the College Lot by the combined Union Philosophical and Philomathean Societies, all the members dressed to within an inch of their lives, wearing massive white cravats beneath choker collars so razor-stiff with starch that they dared not turn their heads lest they slice their ears. Mr. Holley delivered a short speech of welcome. It was not a very carefully prepared one, as he was scheduled to speak twice more for the guests during their stay. But Mrs. Holley and the other ladies who were privileged to be present thought the occasion eminently successful.

Only gentlemen attended the large dining at Keene's Hotel, where one of the numerous toasts warmed Holley's heart: "Transylvania University—the pride and hope of the state." Such occasions, with military parades and salutes, crowds of important personages, the familiar routine of delivering public addresses, and the spontaneous applause, made him feel more at ease than since he left Boston. Surely he was justified in feeling that he was now one of the accepted leaders in his new home.

A few days after the visitation Hunt asked to run Holley's welcoming speech in the *Monitor* for July 27.[14] Wishing to accommodate a friend, Horace turned over to him the brief manuscript from which he had spoken, without taking the trouble to expand or polish it. A newspaper account of a welcoming address did not seem important to him, not as compared with his forthcoming essay in the *Review* dealing with education. If he had reconsidered his draft of the speech, he would have seen that it was stiff and deprecatory. In trying not to be boastful about the University and Kentucky, he had been a trifle apologetic, although his personal delivery had no doubt counteracted that effect. What he overlooked was the fact that for every reader who would ever see the essay in the *Review* a hundred readers would scan this newspaper version of his Monroe speech. Both his friends and his enemies would form a judgment of his scholarly and literary ability from this hasty draft of a minor effort, because it was his first appearance in print since coming to Kentucky.

Holley's enemies took full advantage of his carelessness. Within a couple of weeks a withering communication signed "Common Sense" addressed to the editor of the *Monitor* was published in that paper. It ridiculed Holley's speech as ungraceful in style, lacking in oratorical climax, and snobbish in tone; and it quoted examples. Hunt did what he could to soften the attack by including an editorial defense in the same issue, but it was in vain. The inadvertent publication of the Monroe address by a friendly editor sparked the controversy regarding the new president of Transylvania. In due course of time, copies of the *Review* containing his thoughtful essay on education were for sale on the shelves of Worsley and Smith's bookstore and elsewhere in the town. Many people in the community who were concerned for education and literature, as well as others in the East, read it with respect; in all probability Mr. Jefferson saw it. But far more people read the acrimonious controversy in the *Monitor*.

The renewed attack against Horace Holley took many forms. Not only did his foes ridicule his scholarship, they charged him with infidelity and declared that his social life was immoral and his home life worldly. His wife was not mentioned by name, but she was included in the general attack.[15]

To their embarrassment the Holleys learned that the pleasure they had taken in entertaining was not shared by all their guests. Some of those at the President's parties did not approve of the hospitality they accepted. While they nibbled the sweetmeats and sniffed the wine, they cast stern glances toward a marble bust, undraped and femininely revealing, that ornamented the parlor. Others gave ear to the music chiefly to decide how worldly it was. Some one who signed his articles "Spectator" came out in a Presbyterian weekly up in Ohio to denounce these entertainments as scandalous: "Sabbath evening parties are pretty frequent at Mr. Holley's, where instrumental music and all kinds of tunes and songs are used for the entertainment of the company."[16] "Spectator" declared that the President had recently advised a student to prepare his lessons on the Sabbath if he had not the time to do so on

Saturday; that regular family worship was not observed in his household; and that he associated by choice with none but the most irreligious men in town.

Mary Holley deeply resented the charges against her husband's character and their home life, and urged him to defend himself immediately by telling the public the truth. It was undeniable, of course, that visitors sometimes called on Sunday evenings, just as had been the case in Boston. Once, she recalled, instrumental music had been played, although only sacred tunes. She had been at the piano herself, and had led the songs. Of that she was not in the least ashamed, but she felt her blood boil at the thought of having done so under the sour gaze of "Spectator," whoever he was. And the silly matter of advising the student to study on Sunday concerned an assignment in Butler's pious *Analogy!* The accusation that they neglected family worship and associated with ungodly persons was a libel worthy only of scorn; but she insisted that all the slander ought to be denied in the newspapers for the good of the University. She believed that if he did not take up his pen to answer his enemies, the public would be misled. Let him join battle with them from the start!

President Holley, however, chose to ignore his villifiers, listening to those cautious advisers like Clay, who urged him to "maintain a dignified silence . . . as his best reply to the slanderous falsehoods." She deplored the passiveness of his course; no Austin was ever passive by choice. It was the first time in their happy years as man and wife that she did not bow to his judgment in a matter of serious consideration. Some of their adherents did reply to the damaging attacks, among them William Hunt, who agreed with Mary that the only way to fight merciless enemies was to meet them in the open. His editorials in the *Monitor* defending Holley were restrained and without rancor, but he insisted that he had been *assured* that "Spectator's" charges were not true. It seems inevitable that he got his assurances from Mrs. Holley.

The controversy died out when the local minister who was suspected of writing the articles signed "Spectator" moved away, and the second year of the Holley administration opened auspiciously, except for a situation in the Medical Department to which the President now directed his attention. Nobody was quite sure how the trouble started, but it was generally known that Dr. Dudley and Dr. Drake, two outstanding members of the faculty, quarrelled over a post-mortem examination of an Irishman of the town who had been killed in an altercation. Some had it that Drake refused Dudley's challenge to a duel, and that Dr. Richardson, another of the professors, fought in his stead. However it all came about, Doctors Drake and Richardson engaged in an affair of honor, in which the latter received a wound so serious that he would have bled to death had not his opponent staunched the flow. Drake's friends vowed he was never challenged and so did not decline to fight; but he resigned at the end of the session to pursue a successful career in Cincinnati.[17] Shocking as this affair was to the new President, since duelling had long since been unheard of in New England, it permitted him to add new professors of his own choosing. He secured the Dr. Charles Caldwell whom he had met on his way out to Kentucky; and he wisely recalled Dr. Samuel Brown, internationally known for his successful use of cowpox vaccine. Enrollment in the Medical Department doubled within the year.

The most extraordinary member of his entire faculty was Professor Constantine Samuel Rafinesque, who sometimes added Schmaltz as his last name. Born of a French father and a German mother in Greece, he had lived at one time in Palermo, Sicily. He seemed to have taken all knowledge for his province, and astounded the students and townsmen to whom he lectured. From time to time he disappeared on botanizing expeditions that took him to the Indian country at the western extremity of the state. He was a prolific writer of scholarly articles for the learned journals as well as for popular magazines like Orville Holley's *American Monthly*. He overwhelmed William Hunt with contributions for the *Western Review*. In addition he organized classes for the public in Italian and French and Spanish, wrote poetry, sketched clever portraits, and on social occasions bowed deeply to kiss the ladies' hands in the European manner.[18]

The sharp-nosed little man's disorderliness and irresponsibility were a great trial to President Holley, but Mrs. Holley forgave his faults because she recognized the spark of genius in him. Muddy boots and arrogance were easier for her to bear than dullness. She found Lexington livelier and more interesting for the presence of the eccentric Constantine.

Life was proving pleasant for her in this new environment in spite of the smouldering hostility of certain groups toward her husband. One could, she discovered, learn to live with such enmity, as with a chronic ache or pain, and still enjoy each day as it came. She liked to go out in her carriage on the streets crowded with handsome vehicles and high-stepping horses, leaving her children with the nurse while she went the round of her errands, first to the small red frame post office, and then perhaps to Mr. Robert Todd's excellent grocery on Cheapside near the Court House, and over to Monsieur Giron's superior confectionery, with perhaps a look into Wenzel's music store. Other times she and her husband paid town calls or drove out to see the Clays.

She liked Lucretia Hart Clay, a small, auburn-haired, friendly woman, who was a little older than herself. Lucretia had been no beauty even in her youth, but the years had bestowed on her the poise and dignity that were her birthright. She had married for love at sixteen, and was still devoted to her famous husband in a realistic sort of way. Their house was set in twenty acres of native trees and shrubs, with a garden that L'Enfant planned for them. As Clay liked to tell his many important visitors, he had acquired this manor for himself, not inherited it; and he proudly pointed out to them the panelled library and the silver knobs on all the doors and the handsome yellow draperies he had bought in France.

Mrs. Clay was more practical than her husband. On afternoons when Mary called, her hostess was likely to be busy with the small children or conferring with young Amos Kendall, the tutor for the older boys, while she directed the servants in preparations for a formal dinner. When she "rested," she usually picked up her needlework frame. Her husband supervised the blooded cattle and the racing stock on his extensive farms, but it was she who made Ashland a home place, rooted like the copper beeches and the ashwood trees that shaded it, in a permanence that Mary Holley had never known.[19]

In many ways Mary's own life was becoming more orderly and routine. Her little son, old enough now to begin to talk, was healthy and contented in the care of his Negro nurse. He was not so precocious as their first child, but he was only a baby yet. His parents had lofty plans for his future. Harriette, as rosy-cheeked and happy now at twelve as she had been when her father wrote the charming verses about her, liked her new home in Kentucky from the very start. Already she had a dozen friends of her own age with whom she visited and played, including Ann Clay and one of the younger Hunt girls named Henrietta. Her mother still gave her lessons at home, and this year they were studying French as well as Latin, learning them together, so their little joke went. Mary was pleased with her daughter's quick, retentive memory, and longed for the time she could begin to teach her son. To keep her own mind alert she was attending Rafinesque's class in Italian, and writing occasional pieces for the *Review*. One recent contribution was a criticism of Madame de Staël's style.

"I could," the little essay said in conclusion, "while reading her book, fill a volume as large with my own thoughts."[20]

About this time, at the end of its first year, the *Western Review* stopped identifying its contributors, even by an initial. No reason was announced for the change, but undoubtedly Editor Hunt wished to make it less obvious that only a few loyal contributors were filling his pages. The offerings of the Holleys and of Professor Rafinesque were by far the most numerous, and probably for this reason President Holley had been using three different signatures. Mary and her husband continued to write for the *Review* in spite of their disappointment at having their work unidentified. Rafinesque, who always insisted upon signing his name in full to everything he published, broke off relations with Hunt and founded a literary journal of his own. The one and only number of his *Western Minerva* remained in the back room of Mr. Thomas Smith's shop because the printing bill was not paid; but Constantine's withdrawal hurt the *Review*.[21]

William Gibbes Hunt had some influence in solving the matter of church affiliation for the Holley family. He was a faithful member of the small Episcopal congregation which, in spite of numbering influential families like the Brands, Harts, Wickliffes, and Bradfords among its members, did not prosper greatly until, in the summer of 1820, it had the good fortune to call an extremely able New England clergyman, George T. Chapman. Being a methodical man, the new rector began his duties by establishing a "Record of Communicants" and in July he added "No. 45—Mrs. Mary Austin Holley" to the roll.[22]

There was no Congregational or Unitarian Society in the town with which Horace Holley could identify himself, and he would have been neither welcome nor congenial in the churches of his Presbyterian enemies. Many of the Transylvania trustees and a number of his personal friends were in the Episcopal congregation. Therefore, when he accompanied his wife and daughter to hear George Chapman's learned and correctly enunciated sermons, he felt more at home than in any house of worship in Lexington. Within a year's time Mr. Chapman was made a trustee of the University; and after Professor Bishop resigned for a more congenial post elsewhere, the rector was appointed as a member of the faculty empowered "to teach History, Geography, and Chronological Antiquities" at four hundred dollars per session.

Mary's renewal of the tie with her own church was important for her young daughter. On Sundays Harriette sat decorously in the large square pew, as contented as her mother had been at that age. The preacher's chubby face was ringed by a halo of unruly hair, and it was fascinating to watch him remove his surplice before ascending the pulpit, where he preached in black gown and black silk gloves. A score of the children she knew were likewise sitting properly beside their parents, and it is possible that even at this time she noticed William, oldest son of Mr. John Brand, accompanying his pious mother down the aisle every time the church doors were opened. He was a freshman at the University, and Harriette was only twelve; but he was the kind of youth that a little girl would remember to think about later on.

This second summer in Kentucky was full of changes. Both the Harvard tutors resigned to go back to Boston. John Everett had made his mark in Lexington as a brilliant orator and good scholar, and likewise as an ornament to local society. He had been an especial favorite of the Meades out at Chaumiere. He had done some clever editing and writing, and contributed polished Latin "Enigmas" to the *Review* in praise of "a lady who bears the Virgin's name." It was not hard to guess who the lady was, and President Holley sometimes made his wife's cheek flush a little when he teased her about her devoted young admirer. She was sorry to see John go. His departure made Boston seem farther away than ever, and his subsequent letters full of the "little news" of that cultured city did nothing to make her miss it less.[23] The University replaced the tutors with promising Transylvania graduates. It was already producing scholars of its own.

The place of the tutors in the Holleys' home was promptly filled when James Elijah Brown Austin came to board there for a season. Brown, as he was called, was her Uncle Moses' second son, who had been sent to Kentucky for schooling. He had been under the tutelage of Mr. Wilson in Nicholasville, a village in the next county, for the past year or so, but he was not a good scholar like his older brother. Many people in Lexington still remembered Stephen Austin as a studious youth, especially the Todds and Carrs and Hawkinses, in whose homes he frequently visited. Brown was a happy-go-lucky sort of lad. Born in Spanish territory and brought up a nominal Catholic, he showed no interest in preparing for the classical studies at the University; and, probably through no fault of his own, was always short of money. He was a pleasant person in the family circle, however, since he was good-looking and good-natured and full of interesting talk about the frontier and about Stephen, who was now in New Orleans studying law.

Moses Austin's investments in Missouri were turning out badly, and he saw no future there for his sons, as he indicated in a letter asking

Mr. Holley to use his influence with Henry Clay to get Brown appointed to the United States Navy.[24] Moses was contemplating yet another move into new country, this time southwestward into the Spanish Province of Texas, provided he could obtain a grant of land there to establish a colony of settlers. He proposed to make a trip to that region before the year was out. Brown, who had no more desire to enlist in the Navy than to study the classics, waited impatiently in Lexington for his father or brother to send him money to pay his overdue bills and return to the West.

Horace Holley was sufficiently interested in these accounts of the Western country to make a trip to St. Louis that fall. The original plan was for all the family to go in their carriage to visit Mary's oldest brother in Ste. Genevieve, but eventually Horace went without them on what he referred to as a "tour among the prairies and rivers of the West." In St. Louis he delivered an impressive sermon on "The Immortality of the Soul; or Victory over Death!" If he went to Ste. Genevieve, as seems likely, he found Moses Austin on the eve of starting "down the country" to Texas. The President got back to Lexington on October 1 to find that the University had opened its doors the previous Monday to a goodly number of students, many of them from a distance.[25] The handsome sum of seventeen thousand dollars had been raised to purchase books for the library, five thousand from the Legislature, six thousand from six individuals in the community, and the balance as a loan from the city. Dr. Caldwell was authorized to proceed to Europe to search the book stalls and private libraries, especially in post-Revolutionary France, for volumes on which to base the study of medicine and other branches of higher learning.[26] Soon no college library in the nation would surpass Transylvania's.

At this time President Holley gave up the imposing residence on Limestone Street, which was proving to be more costly than he could afford.[27] His lease being due to expire at the end of the year, he obtained permission to remove his family to the Old Seminary, which was being used as a steward's house, refectory, and lodging for a few students. Years before, the west side of the building had been occupied by Professor Blythe and his growing family, and with considerable renovation, it could be made into a comfortable apartment. Soon after the President's return from the West quantities of shingles and glass and hardware were ordered so that workmen under the supervision of Matthew Kennedy and John Shryock could put the rooms in good condition. By cold weather the Holleys' new quarters were ready, and proved ample for the pianoforte and the choicest pieces of furniture and all the books. Their meals were served in the refectory under the same roof, and their needs were looked after by Tim, the University's Negro servant, who was leased by the year from his owner, General Leslie Combs.

One stormy Sunday evening soon after Mary got the new home settled, she sat down at her writing table to compose a letter to Orville. Her husband was attending a meeting in the town.

Our new arrangement is commodious and comfortable, cheap and convenient for your brother . . . I have nothing to do but to take care of my children and study, their improvement supplying a motive; and I am not obliged to give my time to frivolous or tedious company. . . . I like the plan right well, and have not been so happy since I have been in Kentucky; and because—my mind is so completely and agreeably occupied.[28]

Now that she was freed from the burden of morning callers and domestic planning, she discovered once more that "the heart will be quiet in proportion as the mind is active." Here she could examine the University's new books from abroad as the boxes were uncrated in the library, and listen to table talk by scholars, even if some of them spoke in the slurred accents of the West. She presided over an official visit to the University by twenty members of the Legislature, who were conducted for two days through all the exercises of the classrooms, shown the horrendous pictures of diseased victims in the new medical books, and permitted to listen to orations in Latin and Greek. Some of the legislators told the President's wife as they bade her goodbye that they had learned more in those two days than in all their lives before. She was touched by their earnestness, and began to share Horace's faith in the latent possibilities of the new country.

She learned to know the students better, now that she was living in their midst. They respectfully kept off the grass near the Seminary, and never trampled the shrubs and flowers she set out. Despite their reputed fondness for billiards and cards, these Southern lads were well-bred. They had been brought up to say "ma'am" to her and even to Harriette; and when she invited them into her parlor they made a fine figure in their blue swallow-tailed coats with well-polished brass buttons and smartly ruffled linen shirts. Before long her daughter would be watching some tall student and thinking him handsome the way she had once followed Horace with her eyes as he strode across the New Haven Green.

Honesty compelled her to admit that the meals in the refectory were very plain. There were five large poplar tables with benches for the students; and a special one for the President's family and several bachelor professors, at which were placed a few split-bottom chairs, the brass candlesticks, and the silver spoons. The food was abundant. Each day began with a breakfast of coffee, milk, wheat or corn bread and butter, and one's choice of beefsteak, mutton chops, bacon, or salt meat.[29] No wonder little Horace was getting fat.

The Holleys dined sometimes in their own rooms, however, and their quarters were adequate for informal entertaining. Frequently Mary would send Tim around the neighborhood with invitations to the Hunts and the Harts and the McCallas—General McCalla was a Democrat and a Presbyterian but at least he was neutral toward the Holley Administration—and to the household of General Thomas Bodley, who was one of the trustees. They and other friends would come to drink a dish of tea or sip a glass of wine while they rendered an opinion of the new portraits which Matthew Jouett had just executed of President Holley and his wife.

Tall, thin Jouett was a man of wit and taste, who was considered the best portrait painter in Kentucky. He had studied for a while in Boston under Gilbert Stuart.[30] His likeness of Holley, done in the same style as Stuart's, showed a gentler, more tolerant countenance, probably because he was an intimate in the President's home and a personal friend. As a mark of esteem he presented Horace with an original drawing of the new College, titled "The Principal Building of Transylvania University, Inscribed to President Holley."

The portrait of the President was a commission from the University to be hung on its walls. The painting of Mrs. Holley, a smaller one, looked well in its special gold frame as an ornament in their private parlor. She wore a fashionable costume of black, save for a small white collar at her throat, and a large, sweeping hat that gave her a romantic air. The artist's brush brought out the delicate pink of her cheeks and the deeper color of her lips. There was a glint of gold in her brown hair. Matthew succeeded in making her look considerably younger than her thirty-six years, and she had no objection to that.

It was possible now for the Holleys to think of making a trip back East the following summer. Mary planned it to the last detail, writing the good news to her friends many months in advance. They would go in their own carriage on a round of visits to the relatives all the way from Baltimore to Salisbury, with Boston as the grand finale. When

Horace told her in the spring that he would be compelled to remain at the University all summer to encourage prospective students and promote political support, she verily felt that she would die if she had to spend another hot season in Kentucky. Horace always was minded for her to be happy, and he remembered that it was nearly three years since she had loyally followed him to the Western Country. He put no obstacles in the way of her making the trip if she could find suitable travelling companions.

10. THE PAST REVISITED 1821-1822

It was mid-June of 1821 when Mary Holley set out for her visit to the East with her two children, a nursemaid, and a clutter of baggage. She travelled in her own carriage under the care of an excellent white driver named Cooper, who knew the route thoroughly. It had required a stout heart and much good fortune to enable her to carry out her plan.

Her good luck started along in May when the Benjamin Gratzes invited her to make the trip over the mountains along with them.[1] They were companions she would have chosen gladly for such a trip under any circumstances, and in this case it was enormously helpful to be sure of Mr. Gratz' protection en route. He was a young merchant from a well-known and wealthy Philadelphia family, who had settled in Lexington about the same time as the Holleys. His wife, born Maria Gist, was the daughter of a Revolutionary officer now residing on the fertile acres of a large military grant in central Kentucky. The story of their romance was famous. Benjamin had beheld Maria from a distance while she was visiting in Baltimore, and had written immediately to his older sister Rebecca, "I have seen but not yet met the lady I am to marry." He promptly managed an introduction, and after he was established in Kentucky, wooed and won her. Now they were going back for a visit to his people, taking their first child, a son born in April. Maria was as glad to have an older woman's reassurance on the journey as Mrs. Holley was to travel in the company of an attentive gentleman.

Cooper was a fortunate choice. He came originally from Maryland with first-rate recommendations. Then, to add to Mary's comfort, Mrs. Robert Wickliffe offered the services for the trip of a well-trained, reliable nurse, named Kitty, to take full charge of little Horace. Mr. Wickliffe assured Mr. Holley that the woman could be trusted to make the journey north for the summer.

Mary's heart sang as she made her preparations. Carefully she sewed a store of precious silver dollars in the linings of her travelling dresses, and sent her watch to be tested for accuracy. All the while she joked with her husband about her running away from him, since this was the first time she had set out on an independent excursion since coming West. It was a safe and innocent joke. He knew that her eagerness to go back to Boston was heightened by her resolve that he should not be forgotten there.

Once on their way, she found conditions much more pleasant than three years before. The weather was mild and bright, and the road down to the Ohio was considerably improved. Cooper cracked his whip at Emperor and Prince, his good horses, to keep in sight of Mr. Gratz' carriage every so often and insure that they would be together when they got to the river at Maysville, where the party would take the steamboat while he rode the horses overland.

Mrs. Holley's stateroom was too small for four, and too near the boiler for comfort; but in all other respects the days on the river were ideal. Kitty managed nicely with Horace, and the tiny Gratz baby obligingly slept in his basket much of the time. His young mother had not fully regained her strength, and the two ladies had a chance to "accommodate and sympathize with each other perfectly," as Mary wrote in a long letter to her husband describing the boat trip. She could well appreciate Maria's difficulties in travelling with a very small infant. Even in the June sunshine she shivered at the memory of jostling across the frosty Pennsylvania hills with her own baby son.

Although the boat was crowded with passengers, getting on and off at every landing, the ladies spent much of their time on deck. Mary and her daughter "took sketches," in the phrase of the time, and of evenings joined with the other travellers, who chatted and sang until a late hour. Benjamin was all attention and kindness, seeming to think of nothing but to spare his charges any trouble or fatigue, and *never scolding*, as one of them made sly mention in her next letter home.

As their boat chugged up the current, Mary got to know the Gratzes better. They talked not only of Lexington but of his relatives in Philadelphia and about his beloved older sister, who was the person in real life from whom Scott had modelled the character of Rebecca in *Ivanhoe*. Scott had learned about Rebecca Gratz through Washington Irving, whose late fiancée was her lifelong friend. Benjamin took less pride in such romantic fame than in his sister's unselfish labors for the orphans and poor women of her city. His family, devout believers in the Jewish faith, were trained from youth to assume philanthropic responsibilities, and he intended to carry on that tradition as a citizen of Lexington. They talked also of books and music and painting. Perhaps Maria recalled the copy of *The Backwoodsman,* with its descriptions of the very scenery they were passing, which her husband had presented to her while they were courting.

At Wheeling the party waited a day or so for the drivers to arrive with the horses. On the second evening Mary had gone to her room in the Symmes House, a far more comfortable hostelry than the one three years before, when she heard Cooper's voice and the clatter of hooves outside. All was well, he assured her when she put her head out the window to inquire, and both Emperor and Prince were in fine shape to start bright and early in the morning.

Not a single thing went amiss on the drive across Pennsylvania. The well-travelled road wound among fields and farms and dark green forests, with the blue mountains fading in the distance, ridge behind ridge. All of the travellers grew very sunburned and black.

"Shall I say I'm a Cherokee or a Choctaw?" laughed Maria Gratz, who by now was feeling much improved.

When they let small Horace out on the road to stretch his legs, he found a tortoise, and watched it with fascination as it put out its head and crawled away.

"Let's carry it home and show it to Father," he kept saying.

At Hagerstown in Maryland, the Gratz carriage took the road toward Philadelphia, and Mary proceeded via Washington to Baltimore for the first visit of her trip. The travellers all agreed that she should see them in Philadelphia on her way north to talk over plans for their return together. She felt safe in going on with Cooper to manage for her. In Hagerstown she had learned that he had an "unimpeachable character" and came from very respectable stock, his mother being a cook in an excellent family from Boston. She directed him to drive at an easy pace through the picturesque hills and broadening valleys, and settled down to a restful drive after achieving the trip over the mountains. Prudently, she waited until she was in the privacy of her sister's home before she ripped out the coins left in her linings. She had used some of them to reimburse Benjamin Gratz for money advanced; and as she counted the balance, she figured the trip had cost ninety dollars up to now. The shining dollars she extracted were rubbed and polished as brightly as if they had just come from the mint.

They spent three weeks in the large, comfortable Dall home on the

Reisterstown Road, a few miles out from the center of the city. Little Horace played with the Dall children on the shaded lawn while Harriette wrote to her father and her young friends, and the ladies went sight-seeing. Baltimore's new Exchange Building, crowned with an imposing dome, won a compliment from Mary, who said it looked as if it belonged in Boston. Much of her conversation was about Boston, especially when James Dall was present. He still esteemed Mr. Holley above all ministers of his acquaintance, and was worried about rumors from friends in Hollis Street that their former pastor was no longer widely remembered. James was as anxious as Mary that her husband's prestige in the East should not be lost.

Charles Austin was now an ordained Episcopal minister, serving two small "chapels of ease" in the vicinity, whose communicants were mostly the landed gentry and their tenants. He was also master of a little school attached to one of his parishes, and considered himself well enough established to become engaged to Ann Buckler, a young lady of excellent family, who was willing to share his modest prospects. She was as kind and unassuming as her future husband. Mary was pleased with Charles' fiancée.[2]

In a week or so John Phelps Austin came down from his home in Perth Amboy to drive back up the coast with Mary. He was in business in New York City, and a contented family man; and she found it reassuring to jog along through the well-farmed countryside with her brother talking prosaically of trade and shipping and prices. He sounded like Uncle Timothy and Mr. Sanford. As they passed through Philadelphia she missed seeing the Gratzes, but going home seemed so remote that she gave the matter little thought. It was a pity for her not to meet Rebecca Gratz while she still presided over the big family mansion on Chestnut Street.

The days at Perth Amboy were sheer delight.

"Curried chicken, fresh oysters, sea air, sea bathing, and above all, a view of the glorious ocean!" she bubbled over to her husband in a letter posted in early August.

She might have compared such fare with the mutton chops he was eating for breakfast in the stifling refectory, but she chose to generalize.

"Every breath I draw is pleasure to me. I *could* say, but I *will not,* that a day here is worth a year in Lexington, if it were but just the difference in the air."

When they went fishing, Harriette caught the longest string, to everyone's satisfaction. Small Horace laughed loudly to see the quick, shining fish jump out of the water, but he did not much like being dipped in it. Instead he trotted back to the house with Kitty, where he chased the peacock and gathered snails and was a contented little boy.

By this time Mary was receiving frequent letters from Lexington, and she found space at the end of one of her replies to say she was glad to hear that Commencement had gone well. She tried not to think often of Horace's working steadily on through the heat while she breathed invigorating ocean air.[3]

A few days later she ordered the carriage made ready. Since her party would include an elderly aunt as far as New Haven, she decided to take the route around New York instead of through it. When they stopped with friends on the outskirts, however, she could not resist the temptation to drive into the City for a call on Uncle Timothy's oldest daughter, Amelia, now the wife of the Reverend Mr. Wainwright, who was so popular at Grace Church. It was said that he was sure to be a bishop. She was glad she had taken the trouble to go, not only for the visit with her favorite of Aunt Jennett's children, but because Amelia's foster mother was there. Mrs. Wadsworth invited Mrs. Holley to stop overnight with her party when she passed through Hartford. There would be plenty of room for all of them.

After that excursion Mary drove on next day toward Greenfield Hill to keep her promise to spend a night with the Bronsons. With them, as with Mrs. Wadsworth, her sizable party would be no burden. She instructed Cooper to press on in spite of the gathering darkness, but at Greenfield, where she had planned a sentimental pilgrimage to wellloved places, she ran into her first untoward circumstance.

It was already night as they drove up the dogwood avenue and saw by the dappled moonlight that all the doors of the big house were closed, the shutters, too. There was nothing to do but rouse the gardener, and he, stupid man, could not locate the keys. So they all spent the night in the cheese room with their clothes on. Breakfast next morning at a boarding house run by two of the village housewives cost Mary five dollars in the United States currency for which she had exchanged her silver. Her disappointment was keen, but she made a joke of the affair in her next letter and declared to her husband that she had felt for all the world like Rip Van Winkle.

This brief visit was the last time she ever went back to Greenfield Hill; and it was just as well. The shadow of President Dwight was very long there, falling even across the Bronson gardens, which were famous because of him, like the school and the church. The Holleys had left the place to get out of that shadow.

Despite the night's discomforts, Mary's spirits were high as they drove up to her mother's home just after noon. For a wonder, Mr. Lewis, with the aid of Phelps Sanford, had recently painted and repaired the house and fences until she had to admit that the old place never looked better. Letters were waiting for her, not only from Kentucky but several from Mrs. Charles Davis in Boston, who was urging her to come there as quickly as possible. One of Mrs. Davis' messages included information of such vital importance that Mary lost no time in relaying it to her husband:

She says the story that I had from Mr. Dall was nonsense, that there are gentlemen enough in Boston that are not only ready to relieve you of any debts but to subscribe any sum for a church for you, provided they had any hope of your accepting. They are only waiting to know your course. She wishes me to say whether you could possibly be prevailed on under present circumstances. I shall not say you *will* but I only hope you may have the offer. If you could once more breathe this air you could not hesitate. She speaks confidently about it.[4]

When Mary walked with her daughter up to the New Haven Green she felt as if she, too, were a stranger. The bodies in the old burying ground where Elijah Austin had been laid to rest were being moved out to an extensive area on the edge of town called a "cemetery," a change that was unpopular with many citizens. On the Green had risen a new and larger Trinity Church, set right in the midst of the orthodox meetinghouses. She thought it the handsomest such edifice she had ever seen, and made sketches to send home. The town boasted several other new buildings, including the grand mansion of Mr. De Forest, who had made a fortune in Buenos Aires and was spending it on lavish parties for his friends.

Mary stayed in New Haven only long enough for her mother to enjoy the children and for the relatives to see them. It may have been on this visit that Esther gave her granddaughter an oval-shaped locket, prettily enamelled in green and white, and just the size to look right hung round a girl's slender throat. Harriette treasured it all her life.

The visit to Salisbury was not a very extended one either. From Perth Amboy Mary had written to Orville, who was now editing a newspaper in Troy, of her plan to take the children to Salisbury,[5] and promptly upon her arrival all the brothers and sisters within range gathered to see them. At dinner each evening they drank a health: "To President Holley!" Thanks to Kitty's care little Horace was no trouble, and his grandparents pronounced him to be a fine, plump boy. Harriette proved that her mother was right in thinking that she took after the Holleys. She was completely at home with them and corresponded with some of these cousins long afterward.

Luther was avidly reading Madame de Staël's history of the French Revolution, which he discussed in detail with Mary. Although he belonged to the aging generation of the American Revolution, he was still remarkably tolerant toward new ideas. His daughter-in-law never ceased to wonder at his elasticity of mind and his intuitive perception of what was just and right. Her conversations with him were the best part of any visit to Salisbury.

She was eager to get on to Boston; but Mrs. Davis, in whose house she planned to stay, was visiting somewhere in upper New York and proposed to come by Salisbury on her way home so that she could have a seat in the Holley carriage for the rest of the way. After a fortnight and more of fruitless waiting Mary's patience wore thin, and she departed, setting out in the general direction of New Haven. Just beyond Canaan they met the stage—with Mrs. Davis a passenger in it.

"Stop! Stop!" screamed both ladies, and in a trice they were on the ground, embracing and laughing and all but weeping. Mary let Mrs. Davis beg her a little to carry out the planned visit to Boston, which she had no real intention of missing.

They went by Hartford and spent the night with Mrs. Wadsworth at lovely Monte Video, where Mary had often been a guest. In the evening came Dr. Silliman, a friend of Horace's and an intimate of Myron Holley's at Yale, to pay his respects to her. They all sat until midnight while Mary told them of the Western country and showed them her drawings made on this journey. The doctor, author of *A Tour from Hartford to Quebec*, joined with the others in urging her to write a book about her own travels. She was flattered to have the suggestion made by Silliman, whose *Tour* had recently been the subject of a favorable criticism by Horace Holley in the *Western Review*. She wrote her husband of the compliment that had been paid her, and kept the idea in mind as something to think about.

A thousand long miles separated her from Lexington when at last she reached her goal. Pedestrians along Boston Neck that September afternoon must have turned to stare at a dusty carriage in which two ladies were pointing out the sights to a pretty girl and a wide-eyed Negro nursemaid and a plump little boy. At Mrs. Davis' home messages from her friends awaited Mary, and within hours came a stream of visitors. She found two notes from John Everett,[6] whom she had kept posted about her coming through Mrs. Davis. He had sailed for Europe a short time earlier to become secretary to his brother Alexander in the American Legation at The Hague, and he was overwhelmed with regret at missing her. His messages were more ardent than usual. He had kept up a sentimental correspondence with her ever since leaving Kentucky, which she had never taken seriously; nor had her husband, with whom she shared the young man's charming letters. John's departure on the eve of her arrival made her know that he had never been serious either. He was far more ambitious than romantic. How well the brilliant Everett brothers made the most of their opportunities; so much more shrewdly than Horace Holley.

She was very weary, but too excited to admit it, and she welcomed the scores of Hollis Street parishioners and other people who came to the house. Within a fortnight she proved her gratitude to them by returning all their courtesies. She drove in her carriage up to old Mr. Dall's at the head of Orange and then walked down the length of the street, stopping at each house in turn. Elderly Mrs. Johnson Jackson kissed her and wept openly and said they had quit going to church at all . . ., and shy Mrs. John Pierpont, wife of the new minister, received her without a trace of resentment or envy. Mr. Pierpont was not a very lively preacher, people whispered to Mary, but he was a good man and a scholar and a poet.

She arose at daylight and filled long sheets to post at once to Kentucky with the heart-warming news.

"By the middle of the day I can no more write than I can fly," she explained, as she noted the early hour. The chances were that she had not slept much after these exciting days in the world she loved best.

"I called upon all who have visited me, and upon one personage who has not. Who do you think this was?" she queried. "No other than the Reverend Horace Holley . . . at Mr. Barker's warehouse!"

She had gone to get her first look at the Gilbert Stuart portrait, which Mr. Barker now proudly displayed in his business establishment since reverses had robbed him of his nice home. Nothing would have induced him to part with it.

"There it hangs," she scribbled, "and there your friends, countrymen, and lovers go to pay you their worship. There are ladies who never walk up to the South-End without stopping to pay their respects. Everybody says to me, 'Have you been to see the portrait?' just as 'Have you been to see Athens?' "[7]

She thought Stuart's painting had a different character from Jouett's but refused to admit that either did him justice. Both were official portraits, and she may have wished for a likeness that revealed the warmth of his nature and his natural gaiety.

She let Mrs. Bussey take Harriette to Roxbury for a visit, and sent Kitty and little Horace around to all the Hollis Street friends for them to see him. Then she virtually collapsed with exhaustion and was ill for a few days. Dr. Warren said she was worn out with travel, and prescribed salt water baths and rest. Ere long she was out again and able to accompany the doctor and his wife to St. Paul's Church, of which they were now communicants. After long study he had read himself into the Trinitarian faith. Mary did not take communion that morning with the Warrens, and she thought the rector looked at her reproachfully. Perhaps she felt a kind of loyalty to the Hollis Street congregation. When she told Horace about the matter, she offered no explanation, assuming that he would understand her action.

The letters he addressed to his wife and daughter in Summer Street were full of news. To Harriette he wrote affectionately, admonishing her to improve her speech and rid herself of "Kentuckyisms" with her mother's help. He told her that upon her return she would go with all her young lady friends to an excellent academy just opened by Colonel Dunham. She would find her own room in their apartments much improved. Wig Turner was making a new rug for the floor. A door was being cut connecting it with that of her parents, and some shutters made for privacy and for shutting out the heat of the sun. The temperature reading, he added a little sadly, was eighty-one degrees at three o'clock in the afternoon as he penned these lines to her.[8]

Harriette was more delighted with these plans for their return than was her mother. Mary caught the significance of her husband's decision to put their daughter in a regular school instead of continuing the lessons at home. There was an ominous note for her in his having the room done over to suit a grown young lady's needs and taste. Clearly he was strengthening the ties that bound them all to Kentucky, and it may have been when this letter arrived that she required Dr. Warren's attentions again.

The excitement of her return to the East and the widespread discussion here of inviting Horace Holley to come back to a Boston church built up in her mind an almost irrepressible desire to have him do so.

She knew that she was procrastinating overlong if she had any idea of going back to Kentucky with the Gratzes, but she did not wish to leave Boston before some definite offer was extended to her husband. With a reckless hope of staying on until spring she wrote Benjamin Gratz an offer to let him use her driver and the horses on the way home if he would advance her two hundred dollars for her winter's expenses. As might have been expected, he had made other plans and the Gratzes departed from Philadelphia without her. There followed an exchange of letters with her husband as to what she had best do; and finally, with the safe season for travel virtually over, he agreed for her to remain in Boston if she could make some arrangement about Cooper and the horses.

She remembered that Edward Holley had told her in Salisbury that he could sell the pair for her at a good price if need be, and she took up the matter with him by letter. A local man offered her two hundred dollars for Emperor and then backed out of the deal. Edward wrote her that he could find no offers for the horses. It seems certain that she ended by sending Cooper back to Kentucky with them, since Horace Holley rendered the carriage and pair on his tax list in January, 1822. Mary kept the nursemaid with her in Boston. Kitty showed no inclination to run away, and she proved so satisfactory that Mary purchased excellent new leather shoes for her and suggested in a letter home that her husband make Mr. Wickliffe an offer for the woman.[9]

Thus, by a combination of good planning and bad planning, Mary Holley spent the winter of 1821–1822 in Boston. Horace was agreeable and understanding about her long absence. She had managed to leave the final decision to him; and, after all, had not he himself been compelled by circumstances beyond his control to be away from her at more than one important period in their lives? They were both strong-willed persons and often differed in their opinions, but each respected the other's ultimate wishes.

Mary exerted herself during the winter to send new books and periodicals which she thought might interest him and their Lexington friends. Such were the first numbers of Mr. Dana's *The Idle Man*, of which she marked No. 4 as especially intended for Theodosia Hunt.[10] She forwarded to him the long letters she was receiving from John Everett describing his adventures in various European capital cities. They were observant and witty, and the ardent regard for her expressed in them was only a part of the gallant pose which the young tutor had struck while he lived in their home. Horace thought the letters interesting and showed at least portions of them to their friends in Lexington. Mary also kept her husband posted as to what Boston was saying about Henry Clay, and about Kentucky in general.

He, in turn, informed her that the *Western Review* had expired with the issue of July, 1821, in spite of all that its few loyal supporters could do. Toward the end he had gone deep into his own files for contributions, and into hers, also. In next to the last number he had given the editor that letter about music which she had written him before they were married, and he thought she would be pleased to see what an informative article it made. In the final number William Gibbes Hunt had written a stinging valedictory in which he got Kentuckians well rebuked for "neglect and scorn," but nobody seemed to care enough to rescue the little journal. With more help it might have rivalled the *North American Review.*

Sometime in the fall he wrote her that Brown Austin had gone back home to Missouri. Uncle Moses had died several months earlier, and, according to a communication reported in the Lexington *Public Advertiser* on August 4, Stephen was on his way to the province of Texas to take possession of lands granted to his father for the purpose of settling three hundred families there. Brown intended to go on at once to Texas.[11]

President Holley's letters that winter to his wife and to friends like Mr. Bussey were vibrant with good news of the University's progress.[12] Never since his coming had it been so prosperous. The legislators who visited the institution in the spring took back so favorable a report that the Commonwealth made a grant of twenty thousand dollars, and in early December the governor invited him to address both lawmaking bodies. He did so, with excellent response. He wished Mary had been in Frankfort to hear him; and he wished for her, too, when he gave a witty toast at the Washington Day Dinner before the ladies departed.

Students were enrolling from the South and the West. A lad from Ste. Genevieve travelled on horseback all the way from Missouri with letters of introduction to prominent citizens in his pocket and a trunkful of stylish clothes following by boat and stage. Scions of well-to-do families in Tennessee and Louisiana came and planters' sons from Mississippi, like the fourteen-year-old Jefferson Davis, who struck up a friendship with Henry Clay, Jr. Both boys had their hearts set on West Point, as had a personable young student from down near Maysville named Albert Sidney Johnston.[13]

The President made it a point to know small personal details about his students, such as the proper spelling of their names, and their family backgrounds. There was, for example, young Craik from Virginia, grandson of General Washington's personal physician, who rode his excellent saddle horse over the mountains to enter the Medical College, but when he presented his credentials, Mr. Holley perceived that the young man was a born speaker and persuaded him to study law instead.

Winter and spring went by, and Horace offset his loneliness by working incredibly hard. He ordered inventories taken of all the furniture in the refectory, and encouraged the organization of a new student literary society. He planned a series of lectures to be given by himself on the philosophy of the mind, and obtained the approval of the trustees for it.[14] He paid social visits to the Hunts and the Caldwells and the Prentisses. Very often before he retired he took time to pen a message to his wife and close it meticulously with his favorite seal of two clasped hands. Early next day he would take the letter to the post office and inquire for mail from the East.

Mary's letters had a double emotional excitement for him. Their correspondence was always that of lovers. This separation, the longest they had ever known, meant no diminution of their affection. She wrote of a visit with dear friends of theirs when they drank rare wine and often called his name: "If it is not named," she added, "my heart always whispers, 'I wish he were here!' " Then, too, she never ceased to tell him that his Boston admirers were eager to recall him. Resolved as he was to go on to the end of this task in Kentucky, his pride was touched by their belief in him.

Mary made no haste to return to Kentucky, although the roads were open by late May. She had little money left, and even if she had been able to afford the trip, a party as helpless as hers would have had difficulty making the arrangements. She let it be known that her husband was coming to Boston for her during the summer. Dr. Warren wrote Horace to inquire if perhaps he could bring along an Indian skull;[15] and other persons sent him word not to delay his journey. He steadfastly completed the college year with an impressive exhibition of public examinations, declamations, and debates before starting East in early July. His expenses were being paid by Mr. James Morrison, president of the Board of Trustees, who, according to the discreet Minutes of the Board, provided "the means to accomplish the object of Mr. Holley's visit to Boston." The public-spirited Mr. Morrison did not want Transylvania to lose its brilliant new president. Nor did the Trustees, who passed a resolution of appreciation for his services and recorded it in the Minutes.[16]

While President Holley was in Boston he was invited to preach several times in the lofty pulpit of the Hollis Street Church he had built.[17] Among his subjects were "The Nature of Man" and "The Nature and Sources of Human Happiness," themes that showed clearly his increasing concern with philosophy and education rather than theology. The congregation listened spellbound, as they had always done. He was widely entertained, presented with gifts, and congratulated by everyone on the succcess of his Western university. He found it good to be able to say with quiet confidence: "No institution pretends to be our rival in the West." He may have mentioned casually that he had recently been elected a member of the Physico-Medical School of New Orleans.

He brushed aside his friends' suggestions and his wife's earnest pleas to look into several opportunities for returning to Boston, and started back to Lexington with his family in time to reach Transylvania for the opening of the fall session. The Trustees were expecting him to return and bring his family with him.[18]

As they drove through New Haven they picked up his sister Caroline, now twenty-one, to take her back for the winter with them, an addition to the party which must have crowded them uncomfortably unless Horace rode with the driver or was himself the driver on this trip. At any rate, they paused only for a brief critical glance at Yale, and then proceeded southward, avoiding New York, but stopping in Baltimore and in Washington. In the capital they took the young ladies to see the usual sights, and to call upon the Monroes in the presidential mansion. They reached Lexington by October 22, a little late, but they found a fine student body of about 350 young men from many states. It was true that Transylvania had no rival west of the mountains.

11. GREEN HOLLY AND THISTLE

1822-1825

The apartments in the Old Seminary seemed to Mary Holley like a place she had never seen before when she came back that October of 1822, not because of all the improvements which Horace proudly showed her but because for nearly a year she had cherished the hope that she would not dwell there again. Her impractical idea had only wasted her time and made trouble for her husband, who was increasingly determined to carry out his plans for the University. When he went to Boston to bring his family home, President Holley may have told Mary plainly that she must never go there again without him; or he may have trusted her to realize that her actions had embarrassed him. She never went East again while they lived in Kentucky, not even when he did.

There was no time for brooding over the past. She was soon engulfed in the responsibilities of being the President's wife and the chaperone of two attractive girls and the mother of a four-year-old son. Their surroundings were not designed for the needs of a little boy, and she wished he were old enough to be studying his books. He was a more difficult child than her daughter had been.

Harriette had little leisure to enjoy her new rug and shutters. At Professor Dunham's Female Academy near the College Lot she was promptly enrolled for classes in history and geography, rhetoric and arithmetic, piano and drawing and dancing. Thanks to her mother's tutoring and the polite conversation to which she had listened all her life, she did well in all of them except arithmetic; and Mr. Clarke, her obliging teacher, soon remedied that shortcoming. Julius Clarke's serious mind was set on the law, but in the meantime he was an excellent schoolmaster. The giggling girls in his classes were wholly uninterested in his sound Whig views and his New England common sense, but President and Mrs. Holley approved of his political opinions as well as his pedagogy.[1]

At the Academy Harriette made her first bow to society. In its classes was at least one young miss from nearly every influential family in Lexington—Bledsoe, Clay, Wickliffe, Brand, Humphreys, Tibbatts, and so on—plus many petticoated and bonneted scholars from other towns and states. Her dearest friend from the day she enrolled was Ann Wilkinson Taylor, daughter of the General in Newport. Together they wrote their compositions, often in verse, and brushed their hair a hundred strokes a day, and lowered their glances properly when they passed groups of grown-up college men on afternoons when Harriette took Ann home for tea with her mother and Cousin Caroline.

The University refectory had been discontinued during Mary's absence, and she found herself once more in charge of the kitchen and dining room of her own household. She had good servants and enough money, however, to live well, and she resolved to be a part of the town's social life. If she could only get Boston out of her mind she could find Lexington interesting and its people distinguished. The Benjamin Gratzes, for example, were her close neighbors since purchasing a handsome home across the street. This year Mary was one of the many ladies present at the Washington's Birthday Ball to raise her glass with pride when Horace proposed the toast: "Our fair country-women assembled in honour of this anniversary—with such living monuments of our Washington's glory, who would ask for mementoes in brass or marble?"[2]

President Holley and his wife patronized the theatre, and sometimes entertained the performers in their home, occasions on which Horace liked to advise the young actors on the art of public speaking. One such guest was a handsome juvenile named Edwin Forrest, who performed that winter at Usher's Theatre with the company starring Mrs. Eberle. The students at the University were so entranced with young Forrest that they raised funds to enable him to proceed to New Orleans to make his first appearance as a tragedian.[3] As might have been anticipated, many people did not approve of such worldliness on the part of a college president and his family, being of the opinion that attending Mrs. Eberle's benefit was almost as sinful as watching horse races with Mr. Clay. Some of the students, for all their politeness and friendliness, criticized the President's social habits. One student wrote garrulously to an out-of-state friend:

It is admitted by all that Mr. Holley has no religion. Young men when they enter college enter it with that impression and do not suffer themselves to be led away by him, which he is not disposed to do and if he were disposed to inculcate his doctrines (provided he has one) the whole town with whom the young men associate would be a check upon him. He is a great man and only wants religion to make him capable of doing as much good as almost any man that ever lived.[4]

If Horace Holley had known what was behind this young man's respectful smile in the classroom, he would only have laughed and quipped that he was glad so harsh a critic thought him a great man. He could not hope to please everybody all the time. Even his enemies did not object when he was elected president of the Lexington Literary Society, founded that year, and delivered learned papers on "The Moral and Religious Opinions of the Ancients" and "The Peculiar Manners of the Inhabitants of Northern Virginia." Or when Mrs. Holley set out her strawberry beds and a tomato patch, and took drawing lessons from a worthy clergyman.

In the spring of 1823 a serious misfortune befell the Holley Administration in the wake of a great benefaction to the University. It came about with the death of James Morrison and Holley's oration eulogizing him. Mr. Morrison, a faithful and generous trustee of Transylvania, had instructed his attorney, Henry Clay, to write into his will a gift of twenty thousand dollars to the University for a professorship, and fifty thousand more for a building to be named in his honor. A man of high moral character and public-spirited generosity, his religious views were generally understood to be liberal in about the same measure as those of Jefferson and John Adams and the rational deists of that earlier generation.

Under the circumstances, the president of Transylvania was expected to deliver a memorial address, paying tribute to the late Mr. Morrison's character and benefactions. Horace composed his speech carefully, preparing a clean manuscript to go immediately to the printer for publication. With sincerity he praised Morrison as a great and benevolent philanthropist, beloved of men for his good works and certain of favor with God. He arranged with Mr. Chapman to use the Episcopal Church for the ceremonies on the nineteenth of May, and appointed a Committee on Arrangements headed by Trustee Thomas Bodley to see that the sexton mended the stove pipe, cleaned up properly, rang the bell, and assisted the musicians.[5] As was expected, a large crowd heard the oration, and the newspapers were complimentary. Shortly afterward there issued from a local printing office a pamphlet titled *A Discourse Occasioned by the Death of Col. James Morrison, Delivered in the Episcopal Church, Lexington, Kentucky, May 19th, 1823, by the Rev. Horace Holley, A.M., President of the Transylvania University.* It was too bad that the honorary degree of LL.D. conferred upon the author by Cincinnati College the following fall came too late to adorn the title page of Horace Holley's best-known publication in Kentucky.[6]

The Morrison pamphlet was the first sermon ever published by Horace Holley, and, as it turned out, the only one. The style was smooth and his critics could find no slightest fault with the syntax; but they attacked the *Discourse* on far more serious grounds than those for which they had ridiculed the Monroe speech. They declared the author to be an infidel, and combed the pamphlet for evidence of heresy. Following these charges a series of other violent attacks began to appear in the press.

Pursuing his established policy of ignoring his enemies, the President planned an extensive trip for himself and his family that would remove him from the scene of the controversy for most of the summer months. He had several speeches to make in the western part of Kentucky and an invitation to come to Nashville, the metropolis of Middle Tennessee, for an important interview about an educational institution there. Mary had not forgotten the idea of writing travel descriptions and she was delighted at the opportunity to see the new country. They took the "young ladies" with them, and that term now included their daughter as well as Caroline Holley. Little Horace could be left at home in good hands. It was a gay party of travellers in the carriage that wound along the ridges and then down to cross the Kentucky River and proceed southward to the Tennessee line.[7]

President Holley was in extraordinary good spirits on this vacation despite the ominous reception of his Morrison eulogy and his wife's urging that he defend himself openly. After he decided to forget the unpleasant situation, it seemed far less dangerous. Whatever the Presbyterian and Baptist parsons said against him personally, the University was in favor with Governor Adair and was growing with each new session. This invitation to Nashville had to do with Cumberland University, a small institution in search of a president. It had perhaps come to him through General Jackson, whose namesake-nephew, Andrew J. Donelson, was a law student at Transylvania, or through the lawyer Whartons of Tennessee, who had nephews there.[8] He thought it most unlikely that an offer, if made, would tempt him to leave Lexington; but it was good to know that his reputation was spreading. Any prospect sponsored by eminent men was worth investigating. He was keeping abreast of his professional opportunities, and only lately had written his friend, Jeremiah Day, to inquire what salary and perquisites the president of Yale was currently receiving. He had learned, to his considerable satisfaction, that his own emolument, when paid in specie, was better than Day's.[9] He really needed more money than Day, however, as more was expected of him socially and his territory required wider travel.

He might have admitted to himself, too, that his family was getting more expensive. Mary was spending a good deal for the bonnets and laces and flounces needed by a young-lady daughter. He had been compelled to purchase a third horse for this journey, a good bay that he rode alongside the carriage. They could not live comfortably in their college quarters without at least two servants, and owning Negroes was not cheap, as he was finding out. He was increasingly conscious of the necessity for financial security, and was trying to pay off the debts accumulated in his early married life. He had succeeded in retiring over a thousand dollars of the old loans since giving up his large home on Limestone Street.

He turned these personal matters over in his mind as they followed the usual route, just as they had marked it on the map, southward to Harrodsburg past the old fort where the early settlers fought off the Indians, and to Danville, where they could not resist the chance to stop a few miles south of town and pay their respects to aged Governor Isaac Shelby at his pleasant home called Travellers' Rest. Mrs. Shelby, sister to Lucretia Hart Clay, welcomed them at her long dining table, and afterward they conversed on the veranda and viewed the General's swords and a special gold medal struck off in his honor. They remembered chiefly a courtly old gentleman who looked like the pictures of George Washington.[10]

By easy stages they drove on to Nashville, where they ferried over the Cumberland because the big new bridge was not finished. The Inn was comfortable, and over on Court House Square the ladies promptly found Mr. Earl's Museum of Natural and Artificial Curiosities located up over a confectionary. He was a popular portrait painter, and included likenesses of various famous men among his curiosities.[11] Seeing the relics reminded Mary Holley that she might find an Indian skull for Dr. Warren while she was in Tennessee.

Governor Carroll and General Jackson called upon President Holley the evening of their arrival, and the General invited the party to be his guests at his home a few miles out of town. The gaunt white-haired Jackson would have to be hospitable at any season to the president of his nephew's university, but this summer he had an even better reason.

He was a candidate for the presidency of the United States in next year's election, having permitted his Tennessee "Junto" of followers to pit him against such formidable seekers for the office as Henry Clay and John Quincy Adams and John C. Calhoun. Holley was one of the few men in the West on familiar terms with all three of his rivals, a fact of which Old Hickory was well aware.

The Hermitage, as the Jackson place was called, was a roomy mansion of brick, burned on the premises, with a wide, two-story piazza. On the well-mowed lawn were gigantic forest trees, and someone, long years before, had set out a border of cedars, in the Tennessee fashion, along the guitar-shaped driveway.[12] Rachel Jackson, a plump, sweet, unfashionable woman in her fifties, greeted them in the wide hallway and sent their bags up to the ample guest rooms above. It pleased her to have Harriette and Caroline make merry with her houseful of foster children and nephews while she showed Mary all the gifts her husband had received. There was a large silver vase from some ladies in South Carolina, and also a sword manufactured in Middletown, Connecticut, which she tactfully called the most beautiful of all.

Mary spent much of her time at the Hermitage in the garden, and she made three drawings of the house for her sketch book. In the evenings she and the girls danced to the music of the flute with the other guests while the General regaled Horace with anecdotes of the Indian Wars and elicited his opinions about a Democratic candidate's chances in the East.

The Holleys returned to the Inn for a few days to look over the college and to be looked over. President Holley preached in the Baptist pulpit on the following Sunday on "Opposite Tendencies of Religion and Scepticism," and was well reported in the Nashville papers. The college, being in financial straits, made no offer that could be considered seriously, but the conference was wholly friendly. An unexpected compliment in the city was Mr. Earl's request to be permitted to execute a portrait of President Holley to add to his museum. Earl had married Mrs. Jackson's late niece, and now lived at the Hermitage, where he had a rare opportunity to portray prominent subjects. He did not have much chance to study Holley during the few hurried sittings but he completed the painting, which remained in Nashville as a souvenir of the visit.

Mary found the skull for Dr. Warren as they were spending the first night on their return journey at the home of venerable Mr. Craighead, whose wife was a sister of Dr. Brown of the Transylvania Medical Department. It was plain to see that the house was built on top of an

Indian mound, and when her host mentioned Indian graves nearby, full of complete skeletons, she commandeered the services of two young men on the place to excavate a section of turf and choose a well-preserved skull. Getting it home posed a problem, which she solved by carrying it in her personal travelling bag, to the horror of her daughter and niece. It was worth any amount of trouble to be able to send a perfect specimen to Boston for display in Dr. Warren's fine case of Indian relics along with a card identifying it as her gift.

On the way back Horace spoke on behalf of the University at several towns. The most gala affair was in Hopkinsville, a cultured little community in a rich farming region, where the citizens arranged a banquet at the hotel. From her room Mary could hear them roaring their approval as he spoke on "The Interests of Learning and Humanity, Especially in Kentucky." She was taking advantage of an evening's leisure to write Dr. Warren about the skull and to philosophize about the good people of the West who had been so civil to them and who "wanted only education to put them on a level with their fellow-creatures in more enlightened regions." She was still somewhat supercilious toward people reared west of the mountains.

In Bowling Green, another town where President Holley spoke, he made so good an impression that a party of ladies and gentlemen accompanied him and his family for a few miles out of town to have a farewell melon party. The route led next to Mammoth Cave for a strenuous three or four days of sight-seeing. They quizzed the guide about Indian relics and the saltpetre works as they followed his torch along the tunnels, peering at the Devil's Armchair and the Gothic Chapel.[13] After the rest of the party were exhausted, Mary and Harriette went on to explore an extra cave. They had more melons and fresh-water fish at the hotel, and in the evenings the ladies sang and the younger people sometimes danced.

They made only one more important stop on the road toward home. At Bardstown, a well-established town in good agricultural country, they visited the Proto-Cathedral to hear mass and to see the fine religious paintings, mostly by famous European artists. Horace still insisted that there was too much "mummery" about the Roman Catholic service, but for all that he was deeply impressed to find an Old World shrine at the edge of the frontier.[14] Mary found nothing uncongenial in the formal ritual although she, too, rejected the thought of dogma. They visited the small Roman Catholic college, to which Horace had previously given his cooperation, thereby showing the same friendliness that he displayed toward the educational institutions recently established by the Baptists at Georgetown and the Presbyterians at Danville.

Holley practised the tolerance he preached. Near Bowling Green they had passed through a Shaker settlement, and he had stopped to talk a while with one of the leaders of the community, who told him they had just mowed four and a half tons of timothy off of one acre. Luther Holley's son knew enough about farming to realize that a blessing was being bestowed upon workers who could reap that kind of crop. In the long letter that he wrote his father about the journey he spoke with respect of the Shakers. The Holleys reached Lexington by the middle of September to find their little son well and happy, and the affairs of the University unusually tranquil.

Nothing of consequence resulted from the long trip to Tennessee but it enlarged their horizon, both geographical and political. When General and Mrs. Jackson paid a visit to Lexington some months later Horace arranged for a military escort of Transylvania students to accompany their carriage drawn by four blooded gray horses in the long parade,[15] and with his wife attended the ball given for the great Democratic leader.

Prudence dictated that the president of the University and his wife remain neutral in politics, and in public places she let him speak for the two of them. Her interest in such affairs, however, was keener than his, and he welcomed her opinions and enthusiasms even when they were not his own. He was, for the day in which they lived, unusually broad-minded in his attitude toward women, even granting permission to his students to "introduce their lady friends to his classes."[16]

President Holley's tolerant ideas were of no advantage to him in his battle with his orthodox foes for the control of Transylvania. They had continued their attacks while he was absent on the trip to Tennessee, not only on theological but other grounds. In praising James Morrison's good works and noble character as sufficient for eternal salvation, he had, so his foes declared, showed himself to be no true Christian. As time went on, the range of the charges grew wider. "A Citizen" denounced him not only as an infidel but as a frequenter of the theatre, the ball room, and the card table, and as a blasphemer. Occasions were cited when he had ridiculed religion. Two of his own students were found to testify that the President had spoken scornfully of "those who go about the country braying like asses, telling God what poor Hell-deserving scoundrels they are, and who burn brimstone under the noses of the people."[17]

Petty accusations like these were hard to deny specifically. As he would have been the first to admit, and as his wife and adherents well knew, he might carelessly have said something to his students rather like the remarks in their testimony. He was prone to talk to them as if he were discussing current topics with his peers at Mr. Clay's table. And when the boys laughed at his slightly irreverent anecdote about religious fanatics, it never occurred to him that some of them were shocked and offended.

Although Holley did nothing to answer the attacks upon his character, the agitation roused him to look into the bookkeeping system of the University. When the refectory closed because it was losing money steadily, the students were left to board out in the homes of townspeople, sometimes paying more than their parents thought just. The committee of the Legislature which made the annual investigation suggested that the institution "dispenses its blessings to the rich alone." In most other respects the report was fair and, on the whole, generous, but this charge of favoritism was damaging.[18]

Leniency was not to be expected from the new state administration which came into office in Frankfort early in 1824. Governor Joseph Desha was opposed to Henry Clay and all his works, of which he considered the Holley regime at Transylvania to be a prime example. He was the same Joseph Desha who was a Democratic Congressman from Kentucky, when Holley spoke in the Hall of Representatives on his first trip West, and he had never pretended to approve of the new president.

Holley was not unduly alarmed at the unfriendliness of the Desha officials. He had been well treated by the two preceding governors, and he relied upon the trustees to defend the University against charges of snobbishness and extravagance, hoping they would also improve the financial management, which was in truth careless and unsystematic. He devoted his time to his own academic duties, lecturing regularly to classes in law and natural philosophy; and he was responsible for disciplinary problems, as when young John Pope Trotter refused to write a theme in his own class because he did not approve of his professor's religious views. Before the lad was finally persuaded to apologize for publicly insulting his mentor, a pamphlet appeared about the fracas and some of the professors took sides in the argument.[19]

Discipline sometimes involved the faculty members, also. Constantine Rafinesque was one with whom he had numerous disagreements, which were all the harder to handle because the "Grecian Bard," as he signed himself, was a favorite of Mrs. Holley's. She saw that he ate his dinner, after she had made him wash his face and comb his lank, black hair. She encouraged him in his plan to establish a botanical garden for the University,[20] and he advised her about her roses and jasmine. She personally improved the appearance of the grounds near the Seminary with plantings of honeysuckle and lilies until they all but rivalled the Gratz and Hunt lawns across the way. She was concerned not only to beautify the environs but to have a place for her son to play with his puppy or kitten, and flowers for him to fetch in to show his father.

The family's life began to center around Harriette. In late January her proud parents attended the Elocution Day Exercises at the Female Academy at which she delivered a speech. Her subject was "The Cause of the Greeks," on which she had composed a well-phrased essay. She recited it with animation and gestures: "It is the cause of a noble, an oppressed, an injured people, bursting the bonds of tyranny, and striving to throw off the debasing fetters which have hitherto bound them, to gain the freedom of their fathers! And shall we not assist them by every means in our power?"[21] After the exercises all the sweet, demure misses came down from the platform to be presented to their elders, girls from a dozen states and a foreign land or two. It required diplomacy and tact for the Holleys to keep from smiling when Miss Florida Louisiana Georgia Pope from Springfield, Kentucky, courtesied to them.

Ann Taylor and Harriette were still inseparable, and their fondness for each other was now redoubled because they were being courted by swains who were likewise friends. John Tibbatts, of Lexington, a graduate of the University who had been a tutor before taking up law, was Ann's avowed suitor and already was begging to be allowed to press his case with her father.[22]

Harriette's beau was the Brand boy she had known ever since coming to Kentucky.[23] He was a college senior, and handsome in a masculine way, with high forehead, firm jaw, and steady hazel eyes. He was popular with the young people as well as earnest and studious. On the bright summer day when he stood with the graduating class of 1824 to receive the sheepskin diploma inscribed to Gulielmus Moses Brand, he was ready for the place in the family business that his energetic father was saving for him. He was also mature enough to want to marry and settle down at once, provided he could persuade Harriette and her parents that she, too, was old enough.

Her father and mother approved of William. There was no reason why they should not. Son of a gentle, pious mother and a highly respected father, the young man was what was called in the town "a good catch" for any girl, even for one's own daughter. He must have gotten formal permission from her father to ask his daughter's hand in marriage very soon after graduation, certainly before the President set out for the East to take his sister home and to pay a visit to the elder Holleys.

His departure left heavy responsibilities for his wife. She was the head of the household and, as his representative, of the University; and she was in charge of her daughter's romance. She very certainly did not put any impediments in the way of true love. Harriette made up her mind to have William before her father got as far as the Ohio River, and overtook him with a letter at Washington, Pennsylvania, to tell him the joyful news. He found time to write an affectionate reply, approving her "choice," and hoping that she had felt free to make up her own mind.

"Don't be coquettish with Mr. *****," he admonished her. "He is an honorable young man." Horace Holley's fairness and generosity were never better revealed than in the letter giving his parental blessing to his cherished only daughter.[24]

He wrote home frequently to describe how he and Caroline played chess and backgammon on the boat, and how they paid a call on the Gratz family in Philadelphia.[25] But for once Mary had no longing to be travelling with him, not even to the East. She enjoyed being duenna for the young lovers; and she rather liked the authority that she exercised when problems arose in the institution. Two students, one being Andy Donelson, got into an altercation with the principal of the Female Academy; and brusque Professor Bishop quarrelled with another member of the faculty. She was successful in persuading Andy and the other youth to apologize to the principal; and she soothed the professorial tempers and feelings. She was tempted to take the liberty of sending the manuscript of her husband's excellent speech for the senior class to the printer, as the students, including William, had asked him to do. She refrained, since she would have been compelled to fill in his notes and polish the style. Meanwhile she had both pianofortes tuned.

Her main reason for being satisfied to remain in Kentucky for the summer was to chaperone her daughter and Ann and their suitors on a little journey to the Taylor home down in Newport, just across from the thriving town of Cincinnati over in the state of Ohio.[26] She could take little Horace along with her in the carriage. Since young Tibbatts had not yet won consent to ask for Ann's hand, the whole trip took on a gay and almost conspiratorial air of matchmaking. Problems of the University vanished from Mary's mind.

Ann came to spend the night on the eve of their departure, and at sunrise the young men rode up to the door for an early start. A dismal rain kept them waiting, but everybody drank innumerable cups of tea and peered out at the sky until ten o'clock, when the sun burst through the clouds. The ladies and Horace occupied the barouche as they drove out of town, with the men and Jenny, the nursemaid, on horseback alongside. Sometimes they swapped places, giggling at the chance that one of the girls might gallop off with her lover. Mary felt young and romantic herself.

In the big Taylor mansion overlooking the river they took their ease. Little Horace, enchanted with the water and the boats, rambled along the bank with Jenny and Ben, the driver.

"Please, Mama," he begged when he had her alone, "let's live here and never go back to Lexington."

She would have been wise to observe her small son's decided likes and dislikes, which already revealed that he was happiest when he was out of doors, doing things with his hands, but just now she was engrossed in her daughter's plans. Harriette and William were the center of attention and she shone in their reflected romance. Poor Tibbatts could not persuade the General to consent to an early marriage for Ann, and sadly took his departure while the rest of them stayed on for the appointed visit.

Mrs. Holley's room, with a sweeping view of the river and the spires of Cincinnati in the distance, was an admirable retreat in which to read new books or write. One day Mrs. Taylor took her over to the city in a rowboat—the Ohio was low at that season—both of them dressed in their best for an elaborate dinner with a lady from Philadelphia. The wines and finger bowls and formal service reminded Mary of "old times," as she always called Boston society in her own mind. They crossed on another day for a large party given especially in her own honor by a Mrs. Lymus. Here she was welcomed by the *literati* of the town, already a center of cultural aspiration as well as trade.

She stopped that day at the bookstore run by John Foote of Connecticut, who had recently founded the *Cincinnati Literary Journal*. In its early issues had appeared a Latin poem praising Horace Holley, and some precocious verses by a girl in Professor Dunham's Female Academy. It was inevitable that Mr. Foote should ask Mrs. Holley for a contribution to his magazine.[27]

Inspired by his request, she composed "Lines by a Lexington Lady, on Leaving Cincinnati," just before the end of her visit. The lines sound as if she wrote them rather hastily as she sat by her window in the Taylor home:

> Genius of the stream, farewell!
> Farewell, lovely Ohio! . . .
> Who knows but in yon busy mart
> Full many a heart beats high,
> As genius waits the touch of art
> With thoughts that Heav'nward fly?[28]

John Foote found a place for her poem in an early number of the *Journal*, and thus established her among the female poets of the Ohio Valley. The recognition pleased her, all the more because it had come to her personally. She was as eager for the satisfaction of seeing her words in print as her husband was indifferent toward it.

The barouche got back to Lexington under William Brand's care, and already Mary found it natural to have this dependable young man look after her. They were home a couple of weeks before Horace returned, because once more he had travelled far to pay a visit to Thomas Jefferson at Monticello. This time the old statesman was there. He conducted his guest over the buildings of what he called his "Academical Village" down in the town of Charlottesville, where his university would open its doors for the coming spring term. The Monticello ladies remembered Mr. Holley's former visit and were again most cordial, especially an intelligent and interesting granddaughter, Miss Randolph, who greatly impressed the stranger.

The two men talked late into the night about their theories of education, exchanging suggestions and offers of assistance.

"It matters not to a liberal mind," said Jefferson, as they faced each other across the long drafting table cluttered with architect's plans and maps and stacks of letters, "whether good is accomplished in one's own or another institution." He had long been recommending to Virginia youths that they cross the mountains to study at Transylvania.[29]

At Monticello Horace Holley at last came in personal contact with a mind that could have polarized his own unstable liberalism, but the meeting came too late to determine the course of his career. It probably did not occur to Jefferson to offer the President of Transylvania a professorship in his proposed university, and Holley would not have considered accepting such a demotion in rank. He would have been fortunate had such an arrangement been effected, because the new University of Virginia, freed from sectarian control through the design of

Jefferson, was the one institution of his day where Holley would have been able to make his full contribution to liberal education.

Jefferson and Holley corresponded for a time, sending each other copies of the administrative rules and reports of their institutions. The memory of his visit seems to have been in Horace's mind as he delivered his annual Introductory Law Lecture early in November of that year on the subject of "The Advantages Arising from the Study of Law and Politics in the United States." In the course of his address he remarked that he had never been "entirely weaned" from his first nurse, the Law . . . "from whose fountains I have not infrequently been tempted to think I ought never to have strayed."[30] With that sentiment his wife fully agreed, whether or not she was so tactless as to say so at the time.

Other contacts her husband had made during his trip to the East were of interest to Mary. In Frederick, Maryland, he met up with Benjamin O. Peers, the Transylvania graduate who had replaced John Everett as tutor for a while. Peers was just back from Switzerland, where he had learned how to conduct a Fellenberg school based on the advanced principles of the venerable Pestalozzi. The Holleys had long agreed with the Pestalozzian ideas which argued that education must be moral and free and closely related to life; but they rejected his teachings when he relied upon intuition more than reason. They differed, too, with their Boston colleagues like William Ellery Channing, whose ways of knowing "transcended" reason. They belonged to the older, rational school of Jefferson.

These discussions of politics and education were overshadowed for a time by the importance of Harriette's wedding in early January. Both families agreed that the young couple knew their own minds, and gave their approval for an early marriage. The usual preparations went on apace, and besides the cutting and sewing and fitting of the trousseau, all the uncles and aunts must be notified. The news was promptly relayed to Scotland and New York and Baltimore, so that the bride's Uncle Archibald Austin was moved to mention to Cousin Stephen out in Texas that Mary Holley's daughter was being married to a "Mr. Brant of Kentucky."[31]

John Brand gave his son a home located near his own handsome residence and within easy walking distance of the bride's parents. The small house was adequate for the present, and he proposed to build them a proper mansion in due time. He intended to do that for each of his numerous sons and daughters, because he had prospered mightily since his arrival in America empty-handed and in debt. A story went the rounds that after recouping his fortunes he made a trip back to Glasgow to invite his old creditors to a dinner where they found the sums due them under their plates. He was generous to his wife; her rugs and chairs and china came across the mountains from Philadelphia. Now that his eldest son was through college and ready to take over some of the responsibility of the various business enterprises, he himself hoped to have more time to support the political campaigns of his friend Henry Clay, and to serve on the newly organized City Council, and to supervise the breeding of the racing stock and fine cattle on his farms. He was a loyal supporter of the University and of President Holley.

William's mother was gratified when it was decided that the wedding ceremony would be performed by Dr. Chapman according to the Episcopal rites. Her daughter-in-law would naturally attend Christ Church, as the rector was insisting that it be called now; and some day when a bishop made a visitation she could be properly confirmed. There was no doubt that Harriette was expected to become a Brand.

Everything was done in an efficient manner. On the day before the wedding Horace Holley addressed the Clerk of the Court of Fayette County, authorizing him "to give Mr. William Brand a certificate or license, according to law, for the purpose of a marriage between him and my daughter . . ." The next day, which was the eighth of January, 1825, the groom and his father gave surety for fifty pounds to the Commonwealth. The bride's name on the document was spelled wrong, probably by her future father-in-law, since he was the one who signed the bond.[32]

After the ceremony an elaborate collation was served. The table was heaped with viands around a masterly wedding cake, and many healths were drunk. Only one toast was written down for the young couple's descendants to remember: "Scotland, New England, and Kentucky, a union of the thistle's defense with the evergreen of the holly and the abundant cornfields of the West!" That was the toast of the bride's father.[33]

The chief feature of the entertainment arranged for the guests was undoubtedly the idea of the bride's mother, and may not have met with much approval from President Holley. Professor Rafinesque composed a formal "Epithalamium or Nuptial Ode for the Wedding of Harriot Holley and William Brand," which he inscribed in handsome lettering and signed "Constantine the Grecian Bard." When he presented his gift of verses to the newly-wedded pair, he must have recited them in full to the assembled guests:

> Jovial friends and festive crowd,
> Now assembled in the hall,
> Join the minstrel, at his call
> A nuptial chorus sing aloud.
>
> The bride is the daughter of beauty and worth,
> And a tender young flower from the land of the North;
> She has chosen for mate and is blessing for life
> A genuine young Son from the land of old Ossian.
>
> The green holly and thistle in garlands are blended;
> The fond joys are beginning, the sorrows are ended;
> Since the thistle and holly have lost all their thorns
> And the crown that they weave, the fair bride now adorns.[34]

As the Grecian Bard read on and on to the end of his long poem, the guests agreed that Harriette was indeed a "fair charming youthful bride" and her William a "hopeful worthy mate." They complimented Mary on the festive and unique arrangements, knowing that she had planned it, even to the minor matter of the bride's crown of holly and thistles from which the thorns had been clipped away. Harriette's wedding was far more attuned to her mother's temperament than to her own, or to the sober style of the elder Mrs. Brand.

Through this marriage Mary was at last reconciled with Kentucky, not as her own spiritual dwelling place but as her daughter's home. William's prospects were secure and dignified enough to satisfy the fondest parents, and his young wife would fit admirably into the clannish Brand family circle. At the wedding feast it was extremely satisfying to Mrs. Holley to look down the long table and see John Brand rise to propose a toast in his broad Scottish accent to his dear, dear children.

The Holleys had continuing reason to be proud of their son-in-law. The following spring when General Lafayette visited Lexington[35] on his grand tour of the country, William was on the Committee for the Ball at the Grand Masonic Lodge, the only young man to be named along with Mr. Hunt and Mr. Gratz and other such prominent citizens. Both President Holley and his wife had a share, too, in the festivities, Horace having actually extended the initial invitation to the hero to come to the city. They managed so that the schedule of the visit called for the first stop to be made at Translyvania, featuring ceremonies in the chapel and a reception in their residential apartments. They then set about preparing a "literary repast" for the visitors, designed to demonstrate the excellence of culture in the West. The President wrote a short speech of welcome; students and members of the faculty composed laudatory poems in Latin and French and English; Mrs. Holley contributed an Ode, in English. The "repast" was printed in full, ahead of time, so that the pamphlet could be distributed on the great day.

Rain was falling that May morning when Mary rose early to arrange her basket of orange blossoms and roses and honeysuckle to decorate the General's room at the tavern. Later the sun broke through, as great crowds of people, wearing Lafayette cockades, watched the parade come in from the Old Keene Place, a few miles out in the country, where he had spent the night. President Holley rode with the trustees and students pretty far back in the line, while Mrs. Holley and the wives of other dignitaries waited at the tavern to be presented. Mary and Mrs. Dunham had the pleasant privilege of presenting their floral baskets in person.

The ceremonies at Transylvania were an unqualified success. Lafayette sat on a comfortable sofa in the crowded chapel, listening patiently to the many speeches, and responding graciously to each in the appropriate language. He accepted an honorary degree from the University at the hands of Dr. Holley. Mary's poem, well declaimed by a talented student from the western part of the state, was given the place of honor among the poetic tributes. At last all the notables repaired to the Holleys' apartments to partake of refreshments, to be presented to the General, and to press his hand.

The day was packed with excitement. Military companies paraded on the high ground beyond the College Lot, after which followed a huge open-air dinner and then a visit to the Female Academy, newly renamed the Lafayette Female Academy. Here Mary heard another of her poems for the occasion sung by the pupils to the air of "Strike the Cymbal."

> Welcome La Fayette!
> Let shouts of myriads sound!
>   With us uniting
>   For Freedom fighting,
> Our arms with victory were crowned.

That evening she donned her best velvet gown and in company with hundreds of other ladies and gentlemen climbed the stairs of the barely completed Masonic Hall to the two big rooms on the second floor, where the ball was held. The members of the Committee and their wives had wrought wonders in a brief time. The rough walls were hung with portraits of Lafayette and Washington, Clay and Shelby; and Matthew Jouett had devised a large transparency of Daniel Boone between the two rooms. On a long table were huge bowls of punch and a magnificent castellated cake achieved by Monsieur Giron, who was a good Mason.

At nine o'clock the General promenaded through a double line of guests to his seat of honor before the table. He departed at eleven, but the dancing and celebrating went on much longer. After the honor guest was gone, somebody, perhaps a member of the Committee, suggested that they not cut the cake that evening but save it for the Masonic breakfast next morning. At the breakfast it was so much admired that it was not cut then either but preserved intact until the next meeting of the Grand Lodge in order to encourage attendance.

Nobody minded saving the cake, certainly not Mary Holley. She was in the gayest of spirits as she admired the transparency and occasionally permitted one of the gentlemen to lead her out for a cotillion. She was well aware that she danced more gracefully than many of her daughter's friends. No morsel of M. Giron's cake could have been as sweet to her as the events of the day. She could still hear in her mind the ringing sound of her own verses and feel once more the satisfaction of receiving the famous guest in her own salon. Now the sight of Harriette, lovely in trousseau lace and silk, moving modestly through the assemblage on her proud young husband's arm, filled her heart to overflowing.

A few days later the *Kentucky Reporter* carried a long account of the visit, omitting no detail, not even the floral baskets. She pasted the clippings in a scrapbook she and Horace had purchased when they first came to Kentucky. It was labelled "A Collection of Articles Relating to Transylvania University from 1818—," but they had never got around to putting anything in it but odds and ends such as invitation cards.[36] She resolved at this season to do better by the Transylvania Scrapbook, and beginning with the Lafayette visit, she added material from time to time. She had a profound respect for every written or printed paper that pertained to herself or her family, and she meant to see that Harriette's and William's children knew they were Austins and Holleys as well as Brands.

12. ON LEAVING KENTUCKY 1826-1827

Lafayette's visit was the last gala time President Holley and his wife were to know at the University. The Desha Administration attacked Transylvania again; and at last in an address to the Kentucky Institute, a select organization for promoting the arts and sciences, Holley flung back a dignified retort: "While my tongue can move, or my pen can shed its ink in intelligible characters, I will assert and pursue the liberty of philosophical, political, and religious investigation, unawed by civil or ecclesiastical power . . ."[1] But he still refused to enter the dusty arena of political controversy, as he made clear in a letter to Henry Clay, now serving as Secretary of State under Adams, who had defeated both Clay and Jackson for the Presidency. Holley took high ground, as usual:

I am threatened with a political attack from the Relief Party, although I have always avoided all interference with the political opinions of our students, and have taken no part in our local politics . . . I shall wait calmly for the result in the next legislature, but shall maintain the course I have pursued, without either defying or fearing public opinion.[2]

He accepted with good grace a demand from the Legislature that the trustees answer a series of pointed questions regarding the University's debts, the salaries and fees of the president and faculty, the fees for private instruction, diplomas granted, and so on, together with proof of the answers. He personally prepared a report to the trustees to explain the various ambiguities and irregularities in the system of bookkeeping.[3]

Very likely Governor Desha would not have been placated by any kind of report, but a special circumstance intensified his antagonism to Horace Holley. It was customary at the time for the students to deliver extemporaneous speeches on current events in the chapel, and, as ill luck would have it, one youth spouted a tactless denunciation of the Governor.[4] From that day Desha was the irreconcilable foe of the University and its president. The struggle between them was clearly approaching a crisis. Mary's sensitive spirit felt every implication of these baleful happenings, and her sky darkened with ominous clouds.

Letters from her brothers in New York told her that Henry was now heavily involved in the operation of a cotton gin on the coast of Mexico, and that Stephen and Brown Austin were making good progress in Texas. In Lexington she heard less favorable news of the Texas Colony from Littleberry Hawkins, who had spent a year there trying to sell land to recover the money which his deceased brother Joseph had advanced for the venture. Littleberry called on the Holleys at intervals with uncomfortable tidings of the Widow Hawkins' poverty and of Brown's still unsettled debts in the town. For all that, he was sure that Stephen would someday pay off everybody. Stephen's colonists had unbounded faith in him, it seemed.[5]

Business more urgent than family news demanded attention during the summer. Professor Bishop, long restive under Holley's liberal policies, departed to become president of a university in Ohio. His going was fortunately without incident, but Professor Rafinesque's severance of relations was more violent. Constantine had always exercised the privilege of absenting himself from his University duties at will, usually to go on scientific excursions, from which he would return with large boxes and bags of specimens to pile into the two rooms reserved for his use in the Old Seminary building. Early in the summer of 1825, he set out on such an excursion, and at the beginning of the fall session he had not returned.

In the meantime the President found a real need for all the extra space in the building. He decided to take into his own domestic household twelve scholars from lower Louisiana who were enrolled in the Preparatory Department, and in this way augment his personal income somewhat. The boys were about of an age with his own son, and the parents were mostly wealthy planters, who were pleased to place their sons in the home of the President, under the immediate supervision of his wife.[6] In order to accommodate the boys, he ordered one of Rafinesque's rooms cleared out and the plunder all put into the other one.

When Constantine got back along in the fall he was furious. The President had broken into his rooms, he raged, and piled the invaluable collections and precious inventions in a heap. He was also displeased that he had been relieved during his absence of the post of librarian. He at once removed himself and his belongings to lodgings in town. He left the college, as he set down in his autobiography, "with curses on it and *Holley*."[7] He lingered in Lexington and the vicinity for several unhappy months before he dispatched his forty boxes of collections to Philadelphia and left the Botanic Garden to its fate. Rafinesque was ever a trial to Holley, who did not grieve over his departure. How could the President foresee that the exasperating little man's fame as a scholar would reach farther into the future than his own?

As Rafinesque angrily gathered up his belongings he took with him a portfolio of portrait sketches of prominent persons. It included General Lafayette, Governor Shelby—Constantine also visited at Travellers' Rest—Dr. Chapman's wife and young daughter, and a dozen others. One unidentified sketch showed a slight lady, guitar in hand, who could be no other than Mary Austin Holley. Inscribed around the drawing in the artist's script were these lines:

> *Emblèmes sincères de douceux et beauté*
> *Ces fleurs sentent dire la simple vérité.*[8]

Rafinesque's maledictions on the University and its President did not include her.

Horace Holley made one last trip to Frankfort in the fall, prepared to present the Trustees' answers to the investigation and to defend the University in a speech before the Legislature; but upon his arrival he found the hostility of the Governor so great that it was not practicable to deliver his address. On the long, cold ride through the winding hills back to Lexington he faced the stark fact that he had lost the fight for control of the institution, at least during the present administration. He pondered how to break the news to his wife. Actually she was less surprised at the outcome of his trip to the capital than he was. One can imagine her asking him how he could possibly have hoped to argue rationally with Joseph Desha or to soften the hatred in that "small, deep, sunken eye."

The rebuff in Frankfort shook Holley at last out of his attitude of calm indifference toward his enemies. Within a fortnight he made up his mind that he was not willing to be subservient to Desha for the rest of his term as governor in the tenuous hope that the next election might restore the University to favor with the politicians. A day or two before Christmas he sat down at his desk and took up a freshly sharpened quill to address a communication to Mr. John Bradford, editor of the first newspaper in the West, and now chairman of the Board of Trustees of the University: "Dear Sir: It is my intention to resign the office of President of this institution at the close of the academical year which will be on the last day of September next."[9]

He added that he would willingly carry on his duties until that date, thus giving the Board ample time to secure his successor. He went on to explain that he contemplated carrying out a long cherished desire to visit Europe. He closed with "Sentiments of the highest regards" and affixed his seal of the two clasped hands.

Out of consideration for the festivities of the season he may have delayed dispatching his communication to the venerable Mr. Bradford until after the New Year. His own household contained a dozen small boys who must be entertained to keep them from being homesick, and there were the usual family dinners with Harriette and William and with the Brands. At Rose Hill the crystal chandelier was reflected on John Brand's long polished table set with English china and mono-grammed silver, and loaded with spicy, well-cured ham and delicately browned fowl. If President Holley announced from his place at Mrs. Brand's right that he was sending his resignation to the Trustees, he did so with emphasis on his new plans for extensive European travel.

Harriette was expecting a baby in May, and her mother joined in feminine concern about the event. They calmly sewed fine seams and discussed the requirements for a good nursemaid while Horace busied himself finishing a complicated outline on which he had been working lately, a "compressed tabular view" of Brown's *Philosophy of Mind*, designed to facilitate its use as a text. The chart was a neat pedagogical device, but only that, and hardly worth a scholar's effort.[10] Shortly after the holidays he had it printed for use by his senior students, disregard-ing entirely the fact that he had just attempted to sever his official con-nection with them.

While her husband was losing his political battle with the Governor, word came to Mary Holley that John Everett was dead, just before his twenty-fifth birthday. Since returning from Europe he had continued to write her occasionally about the theatre or the new books or their mutual friends, but he had apparently outgrown his romantic infatu-ation for her.[11] She put his youthful, foolish letters away, and felt some part of her own past wither. In the next Transylvania catalogue a star appeared beside the name of Johannes Everett, former tutor.

As might have been expected, Mary found herself a foster mother to the little French boys from Louisiana, whose ages ranged from ten to fourteen. Her favorites were the five Labranche cousins, all from plan-tations on the German Coast, as the banks of the lower Mississippi River were called.[12] Their great dark eyes filled with gratitude when she con-versed with them in their own language and guided their clumsy fingers as they wrote dutiful letters to "Maman" and "Papa," in which they said that they were gaining weight and learning to speak English better as time went on. Nemese, aged ten, was the only son of Mr. Hermogene Labranche, owner of the Good Hope Plantation, situated a few miles above New Orleans. Eusebe and Cyprien and Drausin were his first cousins, and Romuald was a cousin once removed. They had beautiful manners, and brought with them many trunks full of quaint, elegant clothes that were entirely unsuited to Kentucky winters. She relished buying their extra wardrobes, since she had *carte blanche* from their indulgent parents. Her own son, although a little younger than the strangers, got along well with them. That fact, together with the extra money from the boys' board, more than made up for the trouble of keeping them. She taught the cook to prepare dishes to their taste, and she saw that they said their prayers as they had been taught by their pious Catholic mothers.

The group of preparatory school boys in the household played a considerable part in the President's plans to leave Transylvania. Ever since his teaching days at Greenfield Hill he had been interested in the training of youth. He had tried out his theories on his daughter, and now he was observing firsthand the development of his own son and these other boys in his household. In his mind began to crystallize the idea of an experiment in ideal education, and he produced an outline for it which he called "A Plan of Education for the few who can afford it." He jotted down only the essentials:

1. A small group of pupils.
2. Instructors and pupils to constitute a family.
3. Languages necessary to a complete education, in order of importance: English, French, Spanish, Italian, Greek, Latin.
4. Residence in different cities and towns, and learning all things relating to them on the spot.
5. Proper exercise, amusement, study, attention to health, etc.
6. Paris to be the chief place of residence.
7. Excursions to London, Edinburgh, Dublin, Rome.[13]

He was combining educational theories with wishful thinking. If he could organize a group of scholars whose fathers were able to pay for such a plan, he would be able to finance a lengthy sojourn abroad with his own family. He and his wife could be instructors and at the same time enjoy travel in Europe. Such an expedition would not be quite the *wanderjahr* of romantic travel that the fortunate Everett brothers had been privileged to enjoy in the universities and cities of Europe, but it would fulfill his own and his wife's long-cherished dreams of seeing the art treasures and the scenic beauty of the Old World.

After the Trustees received his letter of resignation they held several meetings to persuade him to remain; and he finally agreed to stay "for a while."[14] During the following spring came word of the death of Luther Holley, at peace with his world and his Maker; and the consequent postponement of Caroline Holley's marriage to her devoted swain until autumn. Horace inherited a tract of land from his father's estate, and sometimes he spoke rather expansively of going back to "find peace in cultivating it," but he did not speak in earnest.[15] Neither he nor Mary wanted to live out their lives in Salisbury.

The news of Holley's proffered resignation spread rapidly over the state and the whole South. In spite of reduced tuition fees the enrollment dropped sharply during the year 1826, even in the Medical Department; and the Law Department was abolished by order of the Legislature. The same legislative order reduced the president's salary one thousand dollars per annum as of the coming September.[16] For some time Holley had been depending to a considerable extent upon the income from boarding the Preparatory boys, and when this further financial reduction was announced, he hastened his plans to leave.

He wrote to the parents of the Louisiana boys describing his Plan for Education and proposing that they commit their sons to his charge for five or six years for their education in Europe under the personal supervision of himself and his wife. Other pupils of like station in and near New Orleans would be welcomed. By the end of the year, after he had received replies from them expressing interest in his Plan, he felt justified in making the final break with Transylvania. He determined to organize his travelling school immediately and to set out for Europe.

As he read the letters from Louisiana he did not realize that the planters whom he addressed were unaccustomed to speaking or writing in English. When some clerk or kinsman had read and perhaps translated President Holley's communication to them, they were apparently not clear about the specific proposal he was making to them, although their replies expressing admiration for his educational theories were undoubtedly sincere.

On January 10, 1827, Holley addressed another official letter to Mr. Bradford:

Circumstances which have become known to me within a few days put it within my power to carry into execution a design which I have long cherished, of going to Europe. My earnest wish is to take the voyage at a season of the year which will be least dangerous and oppressive to my family, who are to accompany me. May or June is best for this purpose. As I have to visit Louisiana before I leave America, it will be conferring a great favour upon me if the Trustees will allow me to resign my office of President at the end of the half yearly session . . . on the first Monday of March next.[17]

The trustees accepted his resignation this time, and, although John Brand was a member of the Board, made no further attempt to dissuade him. The announcement of his early departure appeared in the local newspapers the following week. There were fewer than thirty students enrolled in the Academic Department, and their instruction was turned over to Dr. Chapman and to Benjamin O. Peers, now back as a professor.

After enduring a long period of indecision and inaction, the Holleys made rapid preparations to leave as soon as possible. They gave to their daughter, or left in her keeping, their choicest furniture and silver. Their practical household equipment in the old Seminary must be disposed of immediately, as well as the long shelves of books, the carriage and horses, and a good milk cow. Horace set to work at once on a very long report to the trustees in which he outlined the future needs of the University, producing the best writing he had ever done in his official capacity, and indulging in no hint of rancor or resentment.[18] It was doubtless Mary who prompted him, while he was reviewing the records in order to compile his report, to make careful notes and copies of such of the minutes and items as pertained to his own career, beginning with his being twice called to the presidency. These notes became a part of the family papers which she took pains to preserve.

Then while Mary packed and sorted and ran the establishment with diminishing supplies, Horace put the University buildings in order for his successor, keeping meticulous financial records now, as if to refute somehow the unproved charges that his administration had been untrustworthy about money. He set down in his account book such items as cleaning the stovepipe and mending the gates, or putting in new glass and paying postage on magazines. These were expenses he had often neglected to charge to the institution before, and his listing them now was the only sign of scorn he allowed himself as he left the place to which he had been welcomed with such fanfare. He reckoned up his own financial condition carefully, too, and wrote to Orville that he was leaving Kentucky worth at least six thousand dollars, counting his books, furniture, land, and two slaves. He had paid off all his debts. He felt prosperous enough to commission Matthew Jouett to do miniatures of his daughter and her husband to take with them on their journey.[19]

Early in March the newspapers advertised a public sale "at the dwelling house of Dr. Holley, (in the rear of Transylvania University) of All his House and Kitchen Furniture."[20] When the townspeople read that, they knew the Holleys would be leaving soon. On Wednesday, the fourteenth, after the crowd gathered, the auctioneer pounded his gavel, and Mary looked on while her beautiful clock was sold, and the countless books she and Horace had read and kept, until finally somebody led the cow away. There remained the tiresome matter of collecting the money from all the buyers, even down to four dollars for a bedstead from a Mrs. Saunders. They had their own petty obligations to settle, too, to the last penny. Horace was emphatic about not leaving the smallest bill unpaid.

He was completely absorbed in this new travel venture, and for months had been obtaining letters of introduction from his friends everywhere to prominent persons in Europe. He had long since applied for a passport for himself and his family.[21] His wife found leaving much harder. She had put down roots in Kentucky, however reluctantly, and she was loath to leave behind a daughter and a grandchild and congenial friends. She wished to be well remembered.

In such emotional moods she was likely to rise at daybreak and go to her writing table. There, by candlelight, she would compose letters, or sometimes poetry. When John Tibbatts, now Ann's husband, lost a young sister in January, she contributed memorial verses to the *Reporter* titled "On the Death of Miss Susannah Agnes Tibbatts."[22] The poem that she called "On Leaving Kentucky" appeared in the same paper on March 10, the day the advertisement of the auction was run:

> Farewell to the land at whose call I deserted
> A dearly loved home and the place of my birth!
> In sorrow I met thee, with eyes half averted;
> In sorrow I quit thee, thou bright spot of earth!
>
> With the wide world to rove in as in life's early day,
> But with spirits less buoyant as chastened by time,
> Reflecting in sadness I tread the lone way,
> As homeless I leave thee, thou beautiful clime.
>
> Shrubs and trees, which I've planted and nurtured with care,
> Geraniums, roses, and myrtles, adieu!
> Who your first fruits and flowers hereafter will share,
> And who will e'er show such devotion to you?
>
> To the church too farewell, where with weekly devotion
> My heart and my voice in full unison were

With the organ's deep tones, as with lively emotion
I joined in the concert of praise and of prayer.

But how to the friends who have cherished me ever
Shall I utter the word, or but think we must part!
Let Destiny rule as she chooses, O never
Shall their sacred remembrance be torn from my heart!

May they too forget not they once loved the stranger,
Whatever her mood was, grave, gay, or serene;
Though a pilgrim henceforth, in far countries a ranger,
She will still love to dwell on the days that have been.[23]

Mary's poem was a literary echo of Schiller's "Joan of Arc's Adieu to Vaucouleur," a lyric that Horace Holley had translated from de Staël for the *Western Review*, especially in the lines bidding goodbye to her flowers around the Seminary walks. As a lady of letters she chose this romantic way to express her genuine sense of loss at ending a chapter in their lives. Again, as when she came to Kentucky, she calls it destiny that compels her husband to pursue his restless career. There is a melancholy and strangely prophetic note in her reflections on the "lone way" she must tread in the future. Several newspapers reprinted the poem, and Horace had it run off on a convenient sheet for distribution among their correspondents. It was better known and more admired in the Ohio Valley than anything Mary wrote during her years at Transylvania.

Loyal friends called daily to offer their services, adding to the confusion of the dismantled establishment that was occupied chiefly now by the bewildered small scholars from Louisiana. Horace took long walks with young William Leavy, one of his early students who remained his unswerving supporter, to calm himself by reviewing the situation from every angle. It might have been a mistake, he admitted, to attend horse races, but such errata were of no matter now. The young man persuaded both Doctor and Mrs. Holley to accompany him to a studio where all three had silhouettes of themselves done for Leavy to keep as treasured souvenirs.[24] Horace always aroused this sort of reverent admiration among his followers.

The trustees contributed five hundred dollars toward the former president's expenses upon leaving, and filed an official letter of appreciation of his services, in which special mention was made of the "grounds around the tenement occupied by the President . . . handsomely ornamented by Mrs. Holley." The student societies and the newspapers expressed their regret.[25]

On Sunday evening, March 25, Horace Holley delivered a valedictory address in the crowded chapel of the University. At last—and too late —he publicly defended his administration, speaking extemporaneously for nearly two hours. It was probably the best oration he delivered in the West, but all that remained of it was a page of outline notes preserved by his wife.[26]

A few days before they started to Louisiana, Dr. Chapman christened their grandson, William Holley Brand.[27] Innumerable farewells were said, and on the twenty-seventh they set out in the Brand carriage, accompanied by their daughter and her husband as far as Louisville, and escorted for several miles out of town by a complimentary escort of forty ladies and gentlemen on horseback. The boys and the servants and the baggage followed in another carriage. Among the outriders was William Leavy, eager to pay honor to the "most accomplished and elegant Lecturer and Speaker to whom I ever listened," as he duly set down in his recollections of the day.

At last the escort halted and waved goodbye. Horace Holley had come to the end of this more abundant harvest which he had envisaged in the West; and no person, he declared, ever possessed a conscience more pure than his in regard to it. He was leaving behind him few visible signs of his impact upon Transylvania. No building had been erected during his administration; no stone was inscribed with his name; only the Jouett portrait in the chapel would bear witness to his personal presence. He had to be content that his fame was preserved in the memory of young men like William Leavy, and in the continuing opposition of orthodox minds.

They drove westward on the road to Louisville, the busy town at the Falls of the Ohio where travellers embarked for New Orleans. While they waited there for the boat Horace busied himself with trivial tasks like giving William the exact amount of money to pay a small forgotten debt. When the time of departure came, Mary and Harriette clung to each other and had to be torn apart by their husbands and led weeping away, one to her stateroom and the other to the carriage for the long, sad drive back to Lexington.[28] Between mother and daughter, so different and so devoted, was a tie even stronger than their natural relationship. To Harriette Brand her mother was always a great and important person. Throughout the unending journeys of Mary's future, her gentle daughter was her lodestar.

When Mary had rested in her commodious stateroom for a day or so, and wept until she had no more tears to shed, she made a careful toilette and came on deck to find her husband in cheerful conversation with a group of gentlemen, including a judge and other men of prominence. The boat was moving with immense rapidity, its rate being estimated at some twelve miles an hour, and she permitted herself to be made comfortable in a chair by the rail where she could watch the unending panorama of wooded shores, still dark and winter-gray, broken at intervals by the inlets of creeks and rivers, all pouring brown spring freshets into the Ohio, which soon would swell the Mississippi below. It seemed fitting that they should begin their journey into an uncharted future on these swift rivers, and on a boat called *Fame*. She relaxed to her heart's content. The servants, under Horace's supervision, were managing well with the boys. The food in the dining saloon was excellent.

The grandeur and romance of the rivers vanished when the *Fame* stuck for two days on a sandbar near Chickasaw Bluffs because it was too heavily loaded with barrels of flour and hogsheads of tobacco. They waited for a rise in the river while countless other boats passed by, some stopping to take off several passengers who were eager to proceed on their way. Not until the *Fame* was once more in the current did Mary begin a letter to her daughter:

No. 1, April 8th.   Mississippi River just below
                                              Memphis (Chickasaw Bluffs)

My dearest daughter, The blue mist has faded on my sight and is far, far away in the distance. When shall I see Kentucky again, and what may not first intervene![29]

The rest of the message was not sad, but a newsy account of the people on board, which she closed and sealed in time to hand to the purser for an upriver boat they passed. When their steamboat tied up a few hours at Natchez, friends came aboard to invite the Holleys to take a drive through the winding streets of Natchez-under-the-Hill, haunt of gamblers and desperadoes and women of ill repute, and then in the Upper Town past spacious homes with wide galleries and graceful ironwork. Mary savored this land of shadow and sunlight, especially the deep green trees hung with trailing Spanish moss, and the splashes of bright wild flowers. When she handed her latest letters into the care of Mr. Martin, their host, she bade him add a message on the outside of the one to her daughter to say that he had seen them and that they were well.

They planned to visit for several weeks at the river plantation homes of their scholars before going down to New Orleans. Dr. Holley made this arrangement in order to allow the boys time to visit their parents before departing for Europe with him, and to give opportunity for other planters in the vicinity to enroll their sons likewise. He and his wife anticipated gracious hospitality during their stay, but they could not possibly have foreseen the extraordinary community into which they were welcomed as they descended the gangplank of the *Fame* that April day onto the private landing of the extensive sugar plantation of Mr. Hermogene Labranche, twenty-nine miles above the City.[30]

This was the German Coast, settled a century earlier by immigrants first from Germany and then from France, who intermarried until the various great families were inextricably related to each other.[31] Their land holdings extended along both the Right and Left Banks, and they had grown rich, especially since the introduction of the sugar cane. In the parishes of St. Charles and St. John the Baptist, near the community of Bonnet-Carré, lived several brothers of the extensive Labranche connection. Descended from a German immigrant named Zweig, the family had changed its name to Labranche when it intermarried with the Acadians, especially with the Fortiers and Trepagniers. Hermogene's plantation lay on the Left Bank, measuring thirty arpents, or nearly a mile, along the river between those of his brother Drausin and of the kinsmen of his wife, née Elizabeth Aimee Trepagnier. The Holleys already knew one of the Trepagniers who had fetched the boys up to Lexington when they came to school.

Across the river on the Right or West Bank lived an older brother, Jean Baptiste Labranche, whose wife was also a Trepagnier; and a mile or more upstream was the home of Edmond Fortier, their cousin germane, who had married a Labranche. People who liked the French style of architecture, with its outside gallery stairs, counted the Fortier place the most beautiful house in the area. Each plantation had its own landing where the steamboats stopped to load sugar, and often the officers and prominent passengers were invited ashore to dine or at least pay a social visit.

The mansions, which all faced the river, were set well back in groves of magnolias and live oaks, with flowering gardens which led down to the top of the river bank or levee. The pianofortes and carpets and inlaid chests, the silver and linens and china were imported from France by New Orleans merchants.[32] The planters usually owned hundreds of slaves for house service and labor in the fields. They dealt with their Negroes according to the custom of the country but, on the whole, more kindly than some of the other masters. These Creoles all spoke French by preference and many of them by necessity, but they wanted their children to be educated in the American language and customs. For that reason the Labranches and other parents had risked sending their young sons on the long journey to Kentucky.

The visitors were graciously received and royally entertained. They went across the river in a rowboat to dine at the homes of the relatives. They attended mass at the church a couple of miles below Good Hope Plantation. Officially it was the Church of St. Charles Borromeo, established in 1741, and adorned with fine oil paintings from abroad, but it was best known as a landmark for river pilots because its red roof could be seen from far off on the flat landscape. As boats came down the river, the Red Church was the last landing before the City, and the crews were paid off there.[33]

Mary found Madame Hermogene's company congenial, and grew fond at once of Baby Melazie. Young Horace fell into the ways of the plantation as if he had lived there all his life, making friends with the servants and the horses and dogs. He felt good in this soft, warm Louisiana springtime. His mother did, too, and was well pleased to prolong their stay on the German Coast.

Not so with Dr. Holley, whose thoughts could not be diverted from his travelling school and the departure for Europe. After the round of formal visits he broke through his hosts' polite delay and pressed for a conclusion of the arrangements to which he understood they had already agreed. To his utter astonishment the Labranches and the other planters told him that after considerable pondering they had decided not to send their sons to Europe with him. They gave him good and natural reasons. In the first place, if their boys stayed abroad for several years, they would become strangers to Louisiana and unused to its climate and customs. To some of them the plan seemed too costly, while others admitted that they could not bear to part with their children for such a long time. *Mais, mon cher docteur,* they added gently, since they all esteemed him as the best of possible educators, surely a plan of the same sort, more or less, could be arranged to establish such a school in or near New Orleans where it would be equally remunerative to him and more agreeable to them. A little patience would be required, because the prospective patrons who could be persuaded to subscribe the necessary funds were now withdrawing from the City and even from the Coast to their remote plantations for the summer season.

The shock and humiliation that Horace Holley suffered at the sudden collapse of his much publicized European tour is hard to estimate. He had already told or written everybody he knew that the plan was a *fait accompli.* He had in his possession a great many flattering letters of introduction from President Monroe, President Madison, Edward Everett, and other influential personages. Since arriving in Louisiana he had received his official passport, signed by Henry Clay as Secretary of State. It was No. 1147, beautifully engraved, wanting only that he fill in the descriptions of himself, his wife, and his son. He put it aside uncompleted, and with it the bundle of laudatory letters. He might need them some day, but they seemed irrelevant at present.

This stroke of ill fortune wounded him more deeply than his defeat at Transylvania.[34] There he had at least had the satisfaction of making his own decision to resign. This cherished travelling school was blighted, not by his enemies, but by kindly strangers who suggested that he change his plans in as casual a manner as if he were an itinerant tutor. Yet he realized that he had no alternative but to accede to their wishes. He had burned his bridges behind him in Kentucky, and he had refused all offers from Boston for so long that he could not suddenly go hat in hand to ask for a church there.

While his son went fishing with his playmate Nemese and the plantation colored boys, and his wife performed on the excellent pianoforte in the drawing room for Madame Hermogene's pleasure or walked with her in the gardens, Horace Holley retired to the airy guest chamber that was for the time being the only home he had. The weather was growing warmer, and he was glad to have off his unsuitably thick clerical coat and cravat. Back and forth he paced behind the long shuttered windows that opened out onto a wide gallery. Neat women were moving quickly to and fro, bearing piles of snowy linens and pitchers of fresh water to the various chambers. The Labranches were so genuinely hospitable that it would be proper and easy for him and his family to stay on here indefinitely while he conferred at leisure with the prominent men he knew in the City. What was the old Creole proverb someone had quoted to him: "What you lose in the fire, you will find in the ashes"?

Leisure and patience were all very well for these German Coast planters, but it was not in Horace's nature to wait for things to work themselves out. He felt that he must do something positive about the situation, and at once. Already he had the nucleus of a boys' school in the pupils he had brought with him from the Preparatory Department. If the planters wished to educate their sons near home, why not start an academy at once in a building he had heard was vacant over on the Right Bank? He had been informed that it was an almost new brick structure of four rooms, with a gallery and glass windows, situated at Bonnet-Carré, very near the sizable Church of St. John the Baptist.

During the second week in May, the New Orleans *Argus* ran a formal announcement of a projected "literary and scientific institution . . . for the instruction of youth" at Bonnet-Carré. The advertisement was written in English, and bore the dateline of May 25. It proposed to offer all the branches of a liberal education in French and English according to a "new, concise, and methodical system," and further promised to give instruction in Latin, Greek, Hebrew, Italian, and Spanish. Patrons could send their sons for a whole quarter before paying any tuition, and then "if indubitable progress, or change, intellectually as well as morally, is not affected (in the pupil) in that time, the proprietor will absolutely refuse any pay."[35]

The proprietor did not sign his name, directing that inquiries be sent to him in care of the postmaster at Bonnet-Carré; but there was no other person on the German Coast that spring of 1827 who could have offered such a range of instruction but Dr. Holley. Nor was it likely that any other pedagogue would have waived his pupils' tuition until the parents were ready to pay it gladly.

The advertisement ran for many weeks, with intermittent revisions. At times it also appeared in French. If Mary helped her husband translate it, she took occasion to polish the style and make a few corrections in it. Meanwhile, having made this appeal for patronage along the Coast, Dr. Holley and his family proceeded to the City and took rooms in a first-rate boarding house to pursue the matter of financing a school with the help of friends there. The Labranches and other planters were actively supporting him, but he also had influential connections of his own. The Erwins and the Duraldes, both related to Henry Clay, and families like the Addickses and Charbonnets who had been patrons of Transylvania, were all potential helpers in his project.

Matters went well. Soon a "Prospectus of a College near New Orleans" was being circulated, in both French and English.[36] The education it proposed was similar to that advertised in the *Argus* with the omission of Hebrew and the addition of gymnastic and military exercise. In spite of the absence for the season of many likely subscribers, the sum of twenty-six thousand dollars was quickly pledged. In the light of these developments, Horace naturally gave up the idea of a school at Bonnet-Carré and addressed himself to the task of organizing the college at New Orleans, and especially of taking care of the needs of the boys he had brought with him from the Preparatory Department, who had been out of school now for several months. Summer was a poor time to begin classes in the climate of Lower Louisiana, and all his friends, experienced in the temper of a semitropical season, urged him to wait until autumn. Why not spend July and August as a guest on various plantations? His wife urged him to go back to the Labranche plantation, but against everybody's advice, he undertook the new task at once.

Negotiations were begun for buying a suitable location for the College four miles below the City near the old Battle Ground where General Jackson's frontiersmen had whipped the British. The Holleys rented a large dwelling in the same vicinity so that they could provide temporary quarters for the boys' school and could be on the scene to supervise the erection of future buildings. Mr. Charbonnet,[37] merchant and negotiant of New Orleans, assisted in the business dealings, but Horace supervised everything, making innumerable trips back and forth to town. He taxed himself writing letters to his family and various acquaintances, some of them wholly unnecessary, in order to describe his prospects and to philosophize on the customs of the region.[38]

Mary found herself meagerly equipped even for her family's personal needs. They had brought with them only clothes and belongings suitable for travel abroad, but she worked unstintingly to see that by the end of June the house was sufficiently furnished for word to go out that classes would begin at once. The parents promptly purchased mattresses and other necessaries as they were directed, and responded that they were ready to fetch their sons to the new institution.

The setting of their home was romantic, if only its mistress had possessed the leisure to enjoy it the way people did in this languid atmosphere. Perpetual sunshine gleamed on ever-blooming flowers and luscious fruits, and on the glassy river, low between its glistening green banks. The air was heavy with the smell of flowering and fruiting and rotting. At night the awesome blackness of the water was flecked with the light of torches from the fruit and vegetable boats, reflected on the waves and on the backs of rowers chanting in endless, mournful cadence on their way to the markets.

Mary looked upon this strange scene with interest, as if she were beholding a foreign land, but to Horace it suddenly became unbearable. The river at noonday was a sea of melted glass. The midnight chant was a death knell.

"One breath of air," he cried out as Mary begged him to lie back on the couch by the window and let her fan his brow, "one breath of air from the Northern shore of freedom, though borne upon the eastern gale, were worth all the boasted luxuries of the ever-smiling scented South, alluring but to destroy!"[39]

Strange that he should be echoing her own words from Perth Amboy that summer in the East about a breath of pure air; but she had not the heart to chide him for that. Ever since his defeat in Frankfort she had watched him struggling like some giant bound by silken threads as he tried to extricate himself from the past and make a fresh start. These recent weeks he had exhausted himself in the debilitating heat, and for almost the first time in their married life he admitted that he was ill. He was covered with a prickly rash that felt like needles over his body, and sometimes he vomited. He could not, he shouted at her, remain in this suffocating house and listen all night to these mournful cries. He bade her send word to the parents not to bring the boys now. He must take passage on the first boat sailing for New York.

She knew that he was more heartsick than physically ill. All this frantic work in a half-empty house by the lonely river had been an attempt to regain confidence in himself and his destiny. But at last his stubborn will was broken, his courage spent. He was afraid of the climate, he confessed in a scrawling letter to Harriette and William, and added, "I intend to fly from it."

Desperately she begged him to stay on here and rest even though they did not open the school until fall; and the prospective patrons who had subscribed to the new College tactfully urged him not to abandon so promising a project. He hardly heard what they were saying. He hastened to book passage for himself and wife and son on the *Louisiana* two weeks hence, and spent his scanty strength making preparations to leave. Most of his ready cash had gone toward equipment for the house and school, and a few days before sailing he was compelled to sell their excellent colored woman named Susanna for the sum of four hundred and fifty dollars, with Mr. Martin Duralde as witness to the transaction.[40]

They sailed from New Orleans on a Sunday, the twenty-second of July, after a gay and almost festive dinner at the boardinghouse with a party of companions who went down to the levee to see them off.

"A prosperous and speedy return!" called their friends as they waved goodbye.

"Health and happiness to you!" replied the Holleys from the deck, as the boat started downstream under the full pressure of sails and steam and current.

The subscribers in New Orleans and along the Coast expected Dr.

Holley to come back in the fall to complete the plans they had so confidently made, although they realized when he left that he was too shattered in health for anyone, even his wife, to press him for details. Yet on board the boat he rallied at once, and as they passed by the Battle Ground, he pointed out their house and talked boldly of his College. The farther away they sailed, the more enthusiastically he discoursed about it, and upon the history of Louisiana, about which he proposed to write at some future date.

For the first time in his life he did not know what he wanted to do next. Indeed he did not know exactly where he proposed to go when he arrived in the East, but it was good to surrender himself to the pleasure of a placid voyage with no business, no cares, no decisions to make. Even when the pilot departing at the Belize near the mouth of the river pointed out an unfortunate vessel anchored in quarantine because its captain and half the crew were dead of yellow fever, the tragic ship seemed remote and shadowy in the gray mists.

Mary and other passengers were bothered by wretched *mal de mer* for the first few days out, but on the fourth day, which was very fine, she brought out her guitar to join a sociable group gathered around her husband. She was surprised and a trifle intrigued to be the only woman on board, but in such polite and considerate company she felt at ease. Everyone was well by now save a gentleman whose indisposition appeared not to yield to simple medicines for seasickness.

After a bright sunset the wind suddenly stiffened, and by nightfall a tempest was raging. Other terrified passengers found refuge inside but Mary huddled on a settee in a sheltered corner of the deck, preferring to endure the wind and blowing rain to the stifling cabin where her husband and son had gone. She was ill again and did not hear the groans of the poor gentleman who was indisposed. He died at midnight, and the ship's officers buried him next morning as best they could in the midst of the gale.

At daylight Dr. Holley staggered up from below, clutching to any handhold, blinded and weak with nausea and headache. Since there was no physician aboard, he kept asking the officers if seasickness could be so terrible; and they, intent upon saving the ship, assured him that there was no cause for alarm. The other patients dosed themselves for seasickness and sucked at lemons, and most of them, including little Horace, improved with the weather. All but President Holley and his wife. He lay on deck on an improvised pallet, shivering in the sunshine and racked with pain. His illness was clearly not seasickness but the dread yellow fever, and now it was too late for any help from aromatic camphor or calomel or opium mixture.

Mary lay helpless, too, on her settee, while her son kept crying in his child's voice, "My father, O, my father!" Gradually her symptoms began to abate, but she did not know when her husband's suffering ended or see them wrap him in his cloak for burial. All she could ever remember was the smell of burning tar, the report of the pistols, and the splash below as the sailors dropped their burden over the side. They told her that he died on the thirty-first of July, and that he was buried off the Dry Tortugas.

Her son, spared by the plague that had smitten his parents, wandered about the ship like a small ghost, singing softly to himself. He was a badly frightened, lonely boy who had just seen his father buried at sea. Now he was not only homeless but fatherless.

During the voyage up the coast Mary recovered slowly, but she might well have perished had not the crew and her fellow passengers nursed her gently. As she regained her senses she found a measure of relief for the desolation that engulfed her by pouring out her heart in a poem to her husband's memory. It was the only kind of communication she could establish with him. She found the strength to set it down on paper during the days they were nearing their destination and while their vessel stood out in New York Harbour waiting for the quarantine officials to come aboard:

> O! had he lived to reach his native land,
> And then expired, I would have blessed the strand,
> But where my husband lies I may not lie:
> I cannot come with broken heart to sigh
> O'er his loved dust, and strow with flowers his turf;
> His pillow hath no cover but the surf;
> I may not pour the soul-drop from mine eye
> Near his cold bed:—he slumbers in the wave!
> O, I will love the sea, because it is his grave![41]

Even as she wept out her story to the brothers and friends who gave her haven in New York, her sorrow was sublimated by her pride in being the wife of a great man.

13. RADIANT PHOENIX

1827-1829

The news of President Holley's tragic end spread quickly over the country. The obituary notices in the New York papers were copied and enlarged in Boston and New Orleans and Baltimore.[1] A busy statesman like John Quincy Adams made a long entry in his diary for August 12 about the career of his late friend, whom he termed "a man of genius, learning and eloquence."[2] Already the faithful flock on Hollis Street had met after the Sunday services to request of Mr. Pierpont that he deliver a memorial discourse on their beloved former minister. Faraway in Lexington at the opening of the fall session of the University the students of the Medical Department asked Dr. Caldwell to pay a formal tribute to the late President.[3]

Mary Holley remained in New York only a few weeks, and then went up to Boston, instinctively seeking the place where her husband had been most loved and honored in his lifetime. In the haven of Mrs. Davis' home she received innumerable callers, and furnished Mr. Pierpont with materials for his sermon such as the details of the death scene and her own poem on the subject, along with a copy of the pamphlet of the Transylvania Trustees defending the Holley Administration. On December second she must have sat, shrouded in widow's weeds, in her accustomed pew to hear his excellent "Discourse . . . occasioned by the Death of Horace Holley, LL.D." It ended with a long quotation from her poem, which Pierpont called "the wail of the widow."[4]

John Pierpont was a sincere friend of the man he eulogized, whom he had known at Yale and in whose home he had dined. No orator himself, he nevertheless praised Holley as a "pulpit orator at the top of the nation" and as a great intellect. With scrupulous honesty he also pointed out his subject's shortcomings, admitting that he was too versatile, too reckless in private conversation, over-generous toward his enemies, and careless about publishing his eloquent speeches.

Pierpont gave the widow a number of copies of the published *Discourse* to send to the relatives of the deceased and to distribute in Kentucky. It was followed very soon by a laudatory obituary in one of the Boston papers by Gerry Fairbanks, a deacon in the Hollis Street Church, who was not inclined to recognize any possible faults in Horace Holley.[5]

Tributes continued to be offered to the widow. While she was with Mrs. Davis a committee from the Church called to present an official letter of condolence, beautifully engrossed in fine script. The committee, which included Mr. Samuel May, stated that the whole congregation would "feel no small pleasure in knowing how we may best contribute to your comfort while you are among us, or lighten the heavy load of your affliction."[6] Already a fund was being raised among them for the benefit of young Horace.

By this time Mary knew full well the one thing which would serve to lighten the load of her affliction. There must be published as soon as possible a true and worthy memoir setting forth Horace Holley's achievements, not only those which were recognized in Boston but his contributions to education in the West. It must be the full, public defense of his character and career that he had never been willing to make for himself. His fame must not be allowed to die at the hands of his enemies, but, like the "radiant phoenix" in the poem he had translated, it must live on . . .

> Its destiny divine with joy pursue,
> And death's own torch perennial youth renew.[7]

She was determined to erect a monument to his genius, and as her strength returned, she spent it wholly on this project. When Mr. May called again to tell her that the fund for her son had been invested under his supervision, she talked with him about the need for the memoir. He agreed, and suggested Orville Holley as the best person to write it. Mary thought so, too, and wrote at once to her brother-in-law at Troy.

She wanted to ask advice also from Edward Everett while she was in Boston. Her ties of friendship with the Everetts were so strong, not only during the years of her residence here but also during the time when John had lived in their home in Lexington, that she felt she could turn to Edward for advice about the memoir. It was often noted by their friends that his career resembled that of her husband, both being brilliant orators and preachers who later became educators. She asked him to assist in the actual writing of the tribute, but received from him only a sympathetic and noncommittal promise to criticize the manuscript before it went to press.

In mid-September she accepted an invitation from the Busseys to bring her son out to Roxbury, where there was plenty of room for him, and to stay as long as she wanted to remain in the vicinity. She accepted and renewed her strength in the autumn garden and in the gold and scarlet woods while she continued to press her plans. When she had not heard from Orville after several weeks of waiting, she wrote him again, more urgently: "I hope I shall get an answer to this one; if not, goodbye forever & aye. Yours, M.A.H."[8]

Orville did answer her second plea, and agreed to contribute some memories of his brother if they would be of any help. He, too, seemed reluctant to be Horace Holley's advocate. Following up this idea of personal recollections, Mary wrote to Milton and Myron, asking for their reminiscences and any family letters and records they could send her. Before long somebody at Salisbury, probably her husband's mother, sent her a large collection of the family papers.[9]

The winter was coming on. Harriette, who was expecting her second child, urged her mother to come to Lexington immediately, but the Dalls insisted that she stop en route for a visit in Baltimore. Before she made any move she must make some decision about her son's schooling. Finally, it seemed best to place him under the care of a Mr. Wells in Cambridge, who already had charge of educating several boys from the German Coast.

The stay in Baltimore calmed her nerves and assuaged her grief. The Dalls still lived out from town, at the first gate on the Reisterstown Road, in the roomy, comfortable house that was quiet and peaceful. They, too, were grief-stricken. All their memories of Horace Holley were fond, proud ones, and they heartily approved the idea of a book about him. Gradually the clouds lifted for Mary, and her natural buoyancy asserted itself. When she took up her pen to write friends, she drew upon the philosophy of courage by which she had always lived. In a long communication to Mr. Clay, addressed to him in Washington, she wrote: "There is that in the human mind, when worthy of its high origin, which makes it go on under all circumstances, adverse as well as prosperous."[10] Sometimes in her letters she became a little gay and witty.

She had thought that going back to Lexington without her husband would be even harder that the leaving had been, but it was not so. Harriette and William and all the Brands made her feel that she was coming home. Friends rallied to console her, and Horace Holley's enemies were stilled for the time being by his misfortunes. Few of them had desired any such tragic fate for him. They had called upon Providence to punish him but not to make a martyr of him.

One evening early in January Dr. Charles Caldwell called upon the widow at the Brand home to pay his respects. As they sat before the marble fireplace in one of the front parlors he produced from his pocket the oration he had delivered on the genius and character of the late President at the opening of the Medical School and read it aloud to her. She sat with tears in her eyes and a proud smile on her lips as he proclaimed in learned style and sonorous phrases Holley's greatness. He read for nearly two hours, and when he had finished, gallantly offered the manuscript to her if she wished to publish it, promising any aid in his power.[11]

She accepted without hesitation. By this generous act the brilliant, arrogant doctor dispelled any bitterness that she might have felt toward the University because of her husband's fate. Dr. Caldwell's speech was animated by the same desire to defend Holley against his detractors which she herself felt but had not been able to arouse in Edward Everett and Orville Holley. She decided to center the memoir around Caldwell's address and to gather the rest of the material herself without further deliberation. Words from de Staël which she and Horace had read together long ago came back to her, the passage about enthusiasm as "an asylum from the utmost bitterness of sorrow." Enthusiasm stood her in good stead now, saving her from rancor and brooding.

She wrote a great many letters, taking them to the post office herself to get a little exercise in the winter afternoons. She posted one to Milton Holley, instructing him to get Orville or Myron to do a sketch of her husband's boyhood. Others went to Boston seeking some one to write of her husband's years there, and initiating arrangements for a publisher and subscribers. The book must issue from a Boston press; and already in her mind's eye she could see an elegant volume, ornamented with suitable engravings. The Gilbert Stuart portrait would be included, of course, and Jouett's drawing of the 1818 Transylvania building, and perhaps one more illustration. Her pen fairly flew as she explained over and over to her various correspondents the details of the project and just what each of them must do immediately.

She qualified in the local court as administratrix of her husband's estate, with William Brand on her bond in the sum of four thousand dollars,[12] although his conservative upbringing made him dubious about both the chaotic condition of his father-in-law's finances and his mother-in-law's extravagance. There were assets and liabilities outstanding in New Orleans that only personal attention could settle. Some of the fund intended for the European tour was left, and this Mary was willing to spend in order to publish the memoir if necessary, although she expected to make a profit eventually from the book. William took care of the business of the estate, giving her the backing of the Brand name. Her own son could not have been more helpful.

The houseboy who tended the fire in Mary's upstairs room during those winter days must have wondered at the long hours she spent sorting and arranging the papers and clippings spread out on her writing table. In the box from Salisbury were letters Horace had written home when he was at preparatory school in Williamstown and still others from New Haven. Many were dated long before she met him, and revealed facts about him which she had never known and family relationships that she had shrewdly guessed. In her own files were their letters to each other through the years, and copies of the *Western Review*, and his sermon outlines and manuscripts, together with heaps of certificates and diplomas and official papers of all kinds.

As she read and reread Dr. Caldwell's manuscript she realized that it was in no sense a biography. It was a eulogistic defense of President Holley, but in order to understand its significance, a reader must also meet the living man who was revealed in the Stuart portrait. Arrangements had been completed to have Mr. T. Kelly, an excellent engraver, execute a copy of Mr. Barker's canvas for the book.[13] The more she thumbed through the papers and clippings, the more she knew that no matter what help she could get from Myron or Orville or anybody else, she herself would have to write the story of her husband's life and character. She was aware that biography was a form of literature rarely undertaken by women, who usually confined their efforts to poetry or novels; but there was no one else to do it. The memoir would be published over the name of Dr. Caldwell, and although it seemed unfair that her own would not appear on the title page, there was no alternative if she was to achieve her great end. Sheltered in her daughter's home she labored during the early months of 1828 composing the biographical narrative and arranging the contents of the volume.

She set up the formal title page with great care to get just the right effect. It read in part: *A Discourse on the Genius and Character of the*

Rev. Horace Holley, LL.D, Late President of Transylvania University, by Charles Caldwell, M.D., Professor of the Institutes of Medicine and Clinical Practice in said University; with an Appendix, containing Copious Notes, Biographical and Illustrative.[14] There must be no doubt of the University's connection with this tribute to its late President. To make sure of that she was willing to sacrifice recognition of her own joint authorship.

She titled the "Discourse" as Part I of the proposed book, estimating that it would occupy about the first one hundred pages. Part II, called the "Appendix," had various sections, referred to as "Note A," "Note B," and so on. The arrangement was not an attractive one, but it enabled her to give Caldwell's essay the prominent place it must have, and to add other "episodes and souvenirs" almost at will. It was the quickest way to put the book together, and she felt that time was of the essence.

"Note A" was her narrative of the life of Horace Holley up to the time of his coming to Kentucky, based on the family letters and a delightful autobiography that Luther Holley had done at her husband's request, plus her own recollections. The narrative was completed with no help from the Holley brothers although she wrote Orville once more offering to "interweave" anything he might send her.[15] Eventually he did contribute a few memories, which she included.

The compilation and publication of this memoir to her husband was a bold and ambitious undertaking for Mary Holley. She already had a modest local reputation as a poetess and correspondent, but she had never undertaken a full-length book before. She sorely needed as collaborator somebody other than Dr. Caldwell, who did not have a logical mind, either. The rest of the "Notes," from B to G, were miscellaneous enough to seem like a scrapbook. To make up, as best she could, for her husband's not having published much during his lifetime, she included two items from the *Western Review*, a portion of "Education in the West," the best statement of his mature educational philosophy, and "The Imperfection of Language." "Note E" was virtually a reprint of the 1824 trustees' defense of the Holley Administration. She included Horace's outline on "The Philosophy of the Mind," perhaps because it was the last thing he composed, and added several excerpts from manuscript sermons.

As the final "Note" she resumed her biographical narrative in order to recount the departure from Transylvania and the last days in Louisiana. When she wrote of her husband's death at sea, she boldly stepped out from the shadows of anonymity and described the dreadful experience just as she remembered it, ending with an eloquent declaration of the confident religious faith in which he had died:

While his friends, therefore, have reason to rejoice in the abundant splendor and usefulness of his life, his enemies can gather from his death nothing to serve them as a ground of triumph. He exhibited, at all times, that sereneness and calm confidence of soul which belong only to the man

> Whose yesterdays look backward with a smile,
> Nor like the Parthian, wound him as they fly.[16]

After her aching fingers had penned that last page, she methodically sewed together the sheets of the complicated manuscript, and at once began to make her plans to go East to obtain enough signatures on the subscribers list to satisfy the publisher. Dr. Caldwell promised to meet her in Boston along in June to see the book through the press.

She went first to Washington City to visit the Henry Clays in their well-appointed house near the State Department, and in spite of being in mourning found herself in the midst of the fashionable society of the national capital. At first she only drove out in the mornings with Lucretia to take the subscription lists to friends who offered to pass them around in the Senate and House. It encouraged her to see Mr. Clay's name down for five copies and Daniel Webster's for the same number. Everybody was sympathetic and interested in her cause. Senator Everett took the manuscript to criticize, as he had promised, and engaged himself to read it at an early date.[17]

After a fortnight of semiretirement friends convinced Mrs. Holley that in order to push the subscriptions she should go to the sessions of Congress and accompany her hostess to official parties where she could meet more people, especially newcomers. That was how she happened to attend the amazing *soirée* at the Russian minister's home, of which she wrote at length to Harriette. In past years she had grown accustomed to filling her letters to her husband with accounts of such experiences, and it seemed natural now to describe them to her daughter. Alas, however, she could not indulge so freely in the sharp comments and puns and worldly gaiety that had enlivened hers and Horace's correspondence. Harriette was too kind and too good to be worldly, and also much influenced by the growing fashion that required ladies to be retiring and proper. The new fashion bored Mary, who preferred the more forthright manners of the early Republic in which she had been reared. She took cognizance of the current mode, of course, but she did not diminish her personality to suit this new reticence in women.

She wrote to Harriette about the *soirée*, with a caution not to mention her going out in society except to say that she had talked with Mr. George Ticknor and Mr. William Prescott about the book, and a request not to show her letters around to anyone at all.

The Russian Minister's party was beyond anything Mary had ever attended, in Lexington or even in Boston. Servants in red-and-white livery escorted the guests upstairs to the Yellow Ballroom with its orange trees and blooming plants. On the service table were "various disguised dishes of cold meats" and strange sorts of confections and ices, lighted by gleaming silver candelabra. To all the eminent persons she met she mentioned the memoir of her husband. She hoped that Harriette would understand that going out into the world so soon was not only a way of keeping up her spirits but of keeping his fame alive.

Edward Everett returned her manuscript promptly with some candid advice. He had found Caldwell's "Discourse" dull reading, and thought it should be used merely as a supplement to her narrative, which the public would certainly regard as the most interesting part of the book. He suggested that Mrs. Holley should "reduce" her style, which was sometimes too light and "playful" for such a serious composition. He astutely pronounced Luther Holley's autobiography and letters to be "extremely good."[18]

Mary accepted his criticism with humility and gratitude. His preferring her narrative to Dr. Caldwell's oration more than compensated for his comments on her style. She crossed out the "playful" comments, and deleted the clever phrases that were out of key. But she could not change the original plan of using the "Discourse" as the title article, no matter what Everett advised. Dr. Caldwell was already in the East, having gone by Troy to demand from Orville his still unwritten contribution and then proceeded to Boston to confer with various persons about publishing plans. He was expecting her arrival there soon.

Reluctantly she made herself leave Washington, having thoroughly enjoyed the privileges of being a member of the Clay household. Sometimes she assisted the Secretary himself by copying letters for him when he was ill, and she relieved Lucretia of various responsibilities. She received her own guests in the little upstairs drawing room before a blazing fire.[19] She liked this world of polished diplomacy, and was remarkably well versed in parliamentary procedures and political tactics. For example, she understood better than most of the people she met the harsh fact that General Jackson and his Western Democrats were likely to win the presidential election in the fall and so sweep Adams and Clay and their polite society out of Washington City. She had had painful and illuminating experiences with the power of politicians in the West.

In Boston an agreement was reached with the publishing firm of Hilliard, Gray, Little, and Wilkins to bring out the memoir,[20] and she spent the following months supervising the publication. The printer was Hiram Tupper in Bromfield Lane, who did professional work for the Hollis Street Church. Whatever assistance she had, she must have read and reread the galley proofs herself carefully to achieve the all but flawless format.

The memoir appeared in the late summer of 1828 as a volume of nearly three hundred pages, beautifully printed on excellent stock, with three full-page engravings. It cost more than was expected, and Samuel May generously stood security for the publisher's bill until collections could be made to meet it.[21] Caldwell's *Discourse*, as it was generally called, was promptly placed for sale with prominent booksellers in Boston, Philadelphia, and Baltimore, and ere long with Mr. Flint in Cincinnati and several dealers in Kentucky. Subscribers expected to receive their copies individually, and on Mary fell the responsibility of collecting the money from them.

Her brother Henry set her mind at rest about the publisher's bill. While she was visiting in New York that autumn he came there on a brief trip from Mexico to see his wife and children. He was genuinely grieved to see his favorite sister a widow, and proud of her courage in bringing out the memoir. He promised that before he left New York he would send Mr. May the money to meet the publisher's demands. It is probable that he eventually forwarded a check to Boston; however, the bill had not been settled in full as late as the following spring. The episode was characteristic of both Henry and his sister, of his impulsive generosity often unfulfilled and of her carefree way with money. She continued to press the collections but worried no more about the debt.

While Henry was in New York he declared his dissatisfaction with his cotton gin and other investments in Mexico. He wished to undertake another and more ambitious venture. There was a fortune to be made, he believed, in operating a steamboat up the uncharted Rio Grande River that flowed between the states of Texas and Coahuila. He was as optimistic about this new project as he had been about the experimental date palms he had once brought home from a voyage to the Orient, or any other of his bold ideas. Stamping up and down the room he shouted that the steamboat was his "hope for retrieving my ruined fortune and of laying a foundation for an estate for my family by securing a large tract of land." What he had in view was to obtain a grant in the new Austin Colony, and he had written several times to Stephen Austin about the matter.[22] As he talked about penetrating the upper reaches of the unexplored Rio Grande del Norte, his timid wife, born and reared in New York City, silently hugged her children closer and trembled at the thought of going to Texas to live.

By the end of the year Henry was on his way to Mexico, with his confidence in his projects bolstered by the promise of a certain amount of financial cooperation from his brother John. In New Orleans he bought a steamboat called the *Ariel* and set out in her for the Rio Grande. Before departing from the States he felt moved to "lay before the Government a Memoir on the western boundary pointing out the advantages of an exchange of the territory west of the Rocky Mountains for the land between the del Norte and the United States . . ."[23] Henry always thought in large, even grandiose, terms, and assumed that his opinions were of importance. He greatly resembled his Uncle Moses in appearance, and was more like him than either of Moses' own sons.

Mary Holley was too much concerned that summer with the publication and sale of the memoir to take an active interest in the Austin Colony. Her husband had not considered going farther west when his Kentucky venture failed, but had turned back toward the East and Europe. While he lived she, too, faced in that direction. Now, in the dead center of the storm of misfortune that had wrecked her life's hopes, she heard her brother's plans for the new frontier with detachment, as if they had no relevance for her.

Dr. Caldwell's *Discourse* was a success, if one might judge by the good notices it received. For Mary the most important comment was Edward Everett's full-length discussion in the *North American Review* soon after its publication. Very adroitly he omitted any significant comment on Caldwell's eulogy, of which, of course, he had disapproved in the manuscript. Instead, he paid an open compliment to her share in the work, saying that her biographical notes were "written with simplicity and ease which would do credit to a practised author." He remarked, too, upon her "gracefulness of manner."[24]

Since other reviewers also recognized her share in the memoir, Mrs. Holley was justifiably proud of her first published book. She had not only lifted the name of Horace Holley above the slander of his enemies, entrusting his fame to the verdict of the future, but she had herself become a recognized author. She knew that were he alive, he would approve of her tribute to him. He always encouraged her creative efforts, never begrudging her any of the praise she won.

Year's end found her again visiting the Clays on the eve of their dismantling their Washington home to return to Kentucky. In a matter of weeks Old Hickory's victorious Democrats, pouring in for the inauguration of their President, would take over the White House and the Capitol and the city's social life. Henry Clay, gaunt and melancholy, lay on a "sopha" in the little drawing room with his dark cloak thrown over him while Lucretia tiptoed around holding up a finger and pointing to her husband. "He sleeps," she would whisper to Mrs. Holley or the lady callers who came to inquire about him.

Mary had recently brought her son down from Cambridge to Baltimore to put him under the care of her brother Charles. Horace seemed to like his uncle's school at the Garrison Forest Church, and so she had come to Washington for a brief visit. It had to be brief because her hostess was arranging to sell most of the furniture immediately and depart for Lexington. Once she got there, Lucretia meant to stay.

The new Washington, on the brink of change, was not distasteful to Mary. In spite of the collapse of the Adams-Clay regime she still had many friends who entertained her hospitably—the English Minister's wife, and the Porters from New York, who were related to the Holley family, and a delightful Mrs. Johnston from Louisiana. Everywhere she went now she was flatteringly introduced not only as the widow of her famous husband but as Mrs. Holley, the authoress.

New Year was ever a special day for her. Remembering her Latin mythology she always looked both ways, backward to shed a few tears over the past and forward to gather up her resolution for the future. On this January 1, 1829, she found herself at a time of change and decision. Almost singlehandedly she had produced and published a book, making the long trips across the mountains several times, not always with an escort. Never strong physically, she had surprised herself by the stamina and endurance she possessed when urged on by a driving purpose. That task was accomplished, and now her chief concern was money. She had expended her husband's modest estate freely in order to achieve her aim, and there was not much left except the uncollected accounts in Louisiana.

She could solve her financial problem by going back to make her home with Harriette and William, who urged her to come. She was in her forty-fifth year, and many a widow of her age with a meager income would count herself fortunate to be able to spend the rest of her life rocking her grandbabies and remembering the past. In going back to the Brand home, however, she would encounter a problem. Reluctantly she was having to admit, at least to herself, that young Horace was a rather difficult child. He was seldom well and learned slowly save when he chose occasionally to apply himself to some task he liked, such as drawing pictures or hammering nails. She hoped he would be content to stay with Charles until he was ready for an education for some profession.

She was weighing such considerations as she attended to her correspondence during the final days of her visit in Washington. Almost the only person who had not acknowledged the receipt of his copy of the *Discourse* was Orville Holley, and she carried out a New Year's resolution to write him and ask why. She also wanted very much to hear his opinion of the book. He was often procrastinating and selfish, but he could be charming when he liked, and she never got really angry with him. During all the years that he lived in their home she had made allowances for this spoiled younger brother of Horace's.

Writing to Orville always inspired her to be gay, and her pen ran on lightheartedly: "As to the books, did you receive them? And can you send me the money? If so, let it come under cover to Mr. Clay. . . . Send me any criticisms you care to make unless perhaps you are jealous that I have run away with praise belonging to you!"[25]

She went on to tell him that she was proceeding from Washington to Lexington within a short time, and "perhaps on to Louisiana, where I have a plan if I choose to act upon it." She had already decided that she was not going to settle down in her daughter's home to transform herself into a useful and comfortable old lady. Neither then nor later did she ever contemplate such a career for herself.

As she had feared, Horace insisted upon returning with her to Kentucky, and Harriette offered to have him stay with her during their mother's visit to Louisiana on business. While she waited in Lexington for favorable weather to make the trip down the rivers, she received such flattering recognition from the University that she could almost believe that her husband's labors had not been in vain. Interest in culture had been revived and a new literary magazine, *The Transylvanian*, launched with the blessing of President Alva Woods. Its editor, a mathematics professor, was also a "suitor in the bower of the muses," and he requested her permission to reprint "On Leaving Kentucky" in the first number, together with a complimentary foreword which praised Mrs.

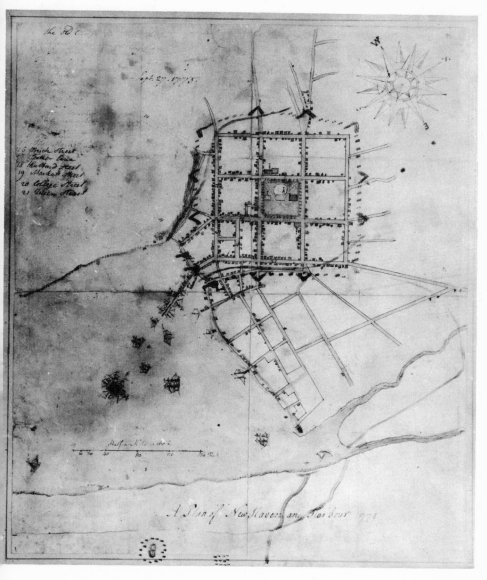

Plan of New Haven, 1812, by Amos Doolittle. Courtesy New Haven Colony Historical Society.

Hollis Street Church, Boston, dedicated 1811 during the ministry of Horace Holley. Courtesy Boston Public Library.

Letter from Horace Holley to Mary Austin Holley during a visit she made to his parents in Salisbury, Connecticut. In it he relates his service as a chaplain during the War of 1812. Courtesy of Transylvania College Library.

Portrait of Horace Holley by Gilbert Stuart in 1818 on the occasion of Holley's departure from Boston. Frontispiece in Caldwell's *Discourse*.

THE PRINCIPAL BUILDING of TRANSYLVANIA UNIVERSITY, INSCRIBED TO

PRESIDENT HOLLEY.

Erected in 1818 before the inauguration of Horace Holley as President of Transylvania University, this Main Building burned in 1829. This drawing by Matthew Jouett is included in Caldwell's *Discourse*, opposite p. 190.

Drawing by C. S. Rafinesque believed to be of Mary Austin Holley. Courtesy Transylvania College Library.

Rose Hill, Lexington, Kentucky, built by John Brand about 1812. Courtesy Lafayette Studio, Lexington, and the present owners, Dr. and Mrs. G. Davis Buckner.

Mary Austin Holley's letter to her daughter describing her first visit to Texas in 1831. From a photostat, courtesy Barker Texas History Center Archives.

The last page of Mary Austin Holley's letter to her daughter, January 6, 1832, describing her first visit to Texas. From a photostat, courtesy Barker Texas History Center Archives.

TEXAS.

OBSERVATIONS,

HISTORICAL, GEOGRAPHICAL AND DESCRIPTIVE,

In a Series of Letters,

Written during a Visit to Austin's Colony, with a view to a permanent
settlement in that country, in the Autumn of 1831.

BY MRS. MARY AUSTIN HOLLEY.

WITH AN APPENDIX,

Containing specific answers to certain questions, relative to Colonization in Texas, issued some time since by the London Geographical
Society. Also, some notice of the recent political events in that
quarter.

BALTIMORE:
ARMSTRONG & PLASKITT.
1833.

The title page of Mary Austin Holley's first book on Texas. From a copy owned
by Rebecca Smith Lee.

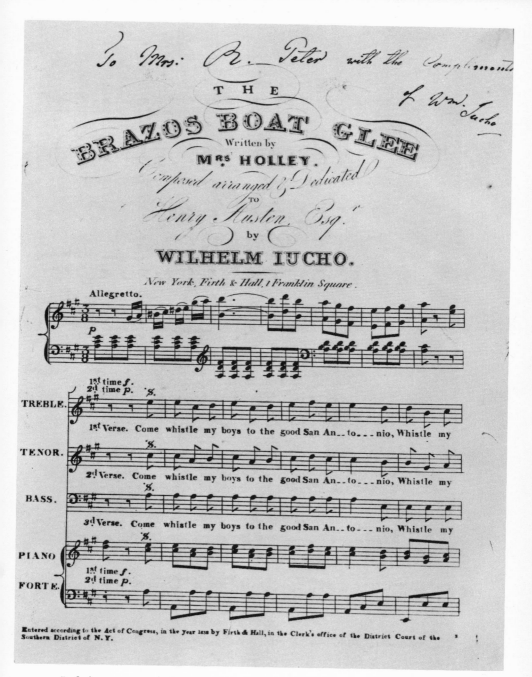

Iucho's arrangement of Mrs. Holley's *Brazos Boat Glee*. Among Mr. Iucho's music pupils were the daughters of Dr. Robert Peter, professor at Transylvania University, and Mrs. R. Peter, to whom this copy was presented. Courtesy Transylvania College Library.

Portrait of Stephen F. Austin in the Senate Chamber of the Texas State Capitol in Austin. Painted in 1836 in New Orleans for his sister, Mrs. Emily Perry, it was presented to the State of Texas by her grandson, Guy M. Bryan, Jr., in 1919. Courtesy Texas State Archives.

Stephen F. Austin's tomb at Peach Point Plantation in the family burying ground. From the Hally Bryan Perry Collection, courtesy of the Barker Texas History Center Library.

Sketch of Peach Point Plantation Homestead by Mary Austin Holley, probably made during her visit there in 1837. Courtesy Barker Texas History Center Library.

Mary Austin Holley during her later years in New Orleans. Courtesy Barker Texas History Center Library.

The famous "iron lace" balconies of the Labranche buildings at Royal and St. Peter Streets, New Orleans, built by Jean Baptiste Labranche in the mid-1830's. Photograph courtesy of Grant L. Robertson.

DIED.—on the 2d inst., in the 60th year of her age, Mrs. MARY HOLLY, widow of the Rev. Dr. Holly, late President of the Transylvania University. Her husband was for a time, minister of the Gospel at Greenfield, Connecticut, and afterwards in Boston, when his great talents placed him in the foremost ranks of his profession. He was then called to preside in the University of Kentucky, when on a visit to New Orleans, he fell sick and died of the same disease that put a period to the life of his widow. Mrs. Holly afterwards emigrated to Texas under the protection of her distinguished relation, Mr. Austin, where she wrote the history of that country, then struggling for its liberties against the embodied forces of Mexico. The work is written with great purity and elegance of style, contains much information, and first turned the attention of the public to a country destined soon to become a subject of the deepest interest to the civilized world.

Mrs. Holly was well read in the literature of the three most enlightened nations of Europe as well as of her native country: she understood their philosophy and formed opinions for herself. She was skilled in all the doctrines of theology, her favorite study; and having weighed them with an even hand, attached herself to the Unitarian School, whose interpretations of the scriptures she thought most reasonable and just.

Mrs. Holly was no less gifted in person than in mind. Her form was slight and graceful, and her finely turned features glowed with animation, when aroused by her subject. She was sought after in every society where she appeared; admired for the justness of her sentiments, her benevolence of heart and cheerfulness of temper that sustained her under the multiplied ills of which she had her share.

She expired on the ninth day of her illness, which she bore with an unbroken spirit. Her body was attended yesterday by her friends to the grave, where the funeral service was performed by the Rev. Theo. Clapp.

Obituary of Mary Austin Holley in the New Orleans *Courier*, August 3, 1846, attributed to the Reverend Theodore Clapp. Photostat courtesy of Library of Congress.

Holley's treatment of nature as superior to that of Mrs. Hemans, the popular poetess.[26]

Among this small circle that was trying to rekindle the fires of creative culture was Benjamin O. Peers. He was no longer with the University, but had become an ordained Episcopal minister and a teacher of boys in the town. To the first issue of the new magazine he contributed an article setting forth the educational theories he had imbibed in Switzerland, even signing himself "Pestalozzi." Mary did not wholly agree with these views, any more than had her husband, and she proceeded to exchange opinions with Peers in what she called "conversations on education" that appeared in subsequent issues of the *Transylvanian*. She signed herself "Philopaidos," a pen-name that may well have echoed the "P. P." which President Holley used sometimes for his contributions to the old *Western Review*.[27]

The "conversations" ceased when she announced in the April number that she could reply no further because "other objects will occupy me." She was on the eve of departing for the German Coast to pay a visit to Madame Hermogene Labranche. "Pestalozzi" soon tested his theories by founding the Eclectic Institute in a large house near the College Lot, where, in his own fashion, he kept alive in Kentucky a liberal point of view regarding the education of the young. Mary remained in touch with him by correspondence, and not solely for the exchange of ideas. She had an eye to putting her son under Mr. Peers' tutelage when it suited her needs.

When she first arrived in Louisiana she spent a week or ten days in New Orleans but accomplished practically nothing toward settling her husband's neglected affairs, and then she sent word up the Coast that she was ready to come there. The Labranches dispatched a coach and four driven by the Trepagnier kinsman who had brought the boys to school. It seemed selfish and also a trifle dull to enjoy such a luxurious ride with only Trepagnier (was his name Jules or Hypolite?) for company, and she offered to convey Mrs. Humphreys, a Kentucky friend encountered in the City, to her son's plantation up the Coast. Mrs. Humphreys' daughter in Lexington had recently married the widower, Mr. Robert Todd, who had a houseful of wilful children by his first wife, and Mary would have relished hearing the new stepmother's side of that much discussed alliance. However, Mrs. H. had other plans and declined the invitation.[28]

N'importe, thought Mary, with a feeling of having found just the right French phrase for the carefree, comfortable feeling with which she settled herself and all her bags in the large carriage. It was really more pleasant to make the little journey by herself so that she could listen for the notes of the birds, some of them strange to her, and watch the flicker of sunlight through the festoons of gray moss hanging from the trees. In spite of painful memories of those tragic weeks she had spent with her husband in the all but empty house near the Battle Ground, she loved this wide, gray river and the rank green fields stretching out behind the levees on either bank. She was more alone than she had ever been in her life, without the companionship of husband or child or kinsman; but it seemed entirely natural to be back in Louisiana.

Young Trepagnier willingly told her the plantation news. Things were much as usual except that Nemese was away in the East at school. Nothing else had changed. Sure enough, as they passed the Red Church and came into the fields of the Good Hope Plantation, she recognized all the landmarks. She must call it "La Bonne Espérance," she reminded herself, and she must say "Madame Labranche," because she recalled that her hostess spoke only French. The countryside seemed even lovelier as she contrasted it with the late, sooty Kentucky springtime she had left behind; and she made a mental note to tell Harriette in her first letter that the orange trees were blooming and the mockingbirds singing everywhere.

Mr. Labranche kindly arranged to collect the sums due her on her husband's accounts, and thus relieved her of that annoyance. In return, she tactfully offered to give music lessons to little Melazie; and naturally the child's parents accepted with pleasure. Everyone inquired affectionately about young Horace, who apparently had not seemed unsociable or odd here on the plantation. Best of all, many people on the Coast wanted to buy the *Discourse*. The copies she had brought with her were soon gone, and she could have disposed of scores more if she had had them. Ere long the cape jasmine under her window filled the night with fragrance.

The days tinkled on as sweetly as the little tunes she taught to her small pupil, and incredibly soon it was time to take the boat up the river if she meant to go back when Mrs. Humphreys did. But Mary let the *Hibernia* and Mrs. Humphreys go without her, and instead she attended an elaborate Sunday dining across the river at the Jean Baptiste Labranche plantation. She explained to everybody that she did so to please Cyprien and Eusebe, sons of the household, who were not yet too big for her to embrace and call her little Louisiana scholars as she had done when they were her charges in the Old Seminary. When she did finally leave, at the beginning of the hot season, she had engaged herself to return in the fall as Melazie's governess with the privilege of bringing her son.

After these months in the polite, formal world of her rich Creole patrons it was something of a jolt to come back to the problems and changes that awaited her in Lexington. Harriette's third child had arrived in May.[29] They named her Mary Austin Brand—the first daughter had been called Elizabeth Hay for William's mother—and Mary's pride should have been expansive. Actually, she was not much interested in tiny infants. It was when children began to talk and could be taught that their activities seemed important to her.

Earlier that same month Transylvania's new college, where the candles gleamed in the windows for Horace Holley the night he arrived to become President, had burned to the ground. Everybody knew how it happened because young Cassius Marcellus Clay, a cousin of the Senator's, living as a student on the third floor, owned up to the cause.

"My black servant stuck a tallow candle to the steps when he blacked my boots, went to sleep, and the flames went up like powder," he admitted.[30]

The students had run out in their nightshirts, and with help from the townspeople had saved part of the books and apparatus. No lives were lost; the Seminary and the kitchen were unharmed, but the blow to the University was severe.

When Mary Holley looked at the blackened rubble, the scorched shrubs, the trampled lawn, she was torn between divided emotions. She hardly knew whether to mourn for the ruin of so much of her husband's lifework or to count the fire as retribution due for the institution's rejection of him. She put aside the temptation to feel unworthy satisfaction in Transylvania's misfortunes, and before leaving for Louisiana in the autumn she made a gift to the library, badly depleted and housed once more in the old building. She gave it the scrapbook in which were pasted the clippings about Lafayette's visit and considerable other material, inscribing on the inside cover: "Transylvania Library. Presented by Mary A. Holley, October, 1829."[31] She thus indicated that with the successful publication of the memoir vindicating her husband's character she had made her peace with the University. Most of the men now laboring to revive his dream of liberal education in Kentucky were either his colleagues or pupils he had trained. If his enemies would cease to attack his memory, she was willing to sign a truce with them.

The season of her leaving for Louisiana saw changes in her family.

Her daughter became a member of Christ Church when the eminent Bishop Ravenscroft journeyed to Lexington from North Carolina at Dr. Chapman's behest to confirm seventy-one persons, including Mrs. Lucretia Clay and her daughter, Mrs. Ann Erwin, of New Orleans, and also the well-known Dr. Ephraim McDowell, a surgeon in the nearby town of Danville.[32] Thus Harriette became more completely a Brand.

Sad news came to Mary that her mother had died in New Haven in early August, aged seventy-two, and for the third time a widow since the death of Elisha Lewis a few months previous.[33] Esther had been alone in the house on Whiting Street since his death and the marriage of her son Peleg Phelps Sanford to his cousin, Mary Phelps; but she had relished life to the end, content with her home and attended by an ever increasing clan of relatives. Her mother's death broke Mary Holley's last tie with her youth in New Haven, and made her more willing to begin a new life on the German Coast if she could somehow get herself and her son ready for the journey. She was down with chills and fever when she should have been packing, and it took heroic doses of quinine and calomel to get her up and about the house to begin her tasks.

She spent whole days storing papers and linens and special articles in the large trunks bought for their trip to Europe that were now stored in Harriette's upstairs back bedroom. Clothes for winter and spring in the South must be put in smaller trunks for this journey. She was determined to take her guitar with her, but was baffled by the problem of packing it. She ended by carrying it in her hand. As she and her daughter filled the trunks she took the opportunity to give Harriette some practical advice—how to spread a shawl over her winter supply of peaches against the cold; how to preserve sweet potatoes in clean pillow cases; and the proper way to sew up the hams at hog-killing time in tow cloth the way it was done by thrifty housewives in the North. She felt that Harriette had yet to learn how to set an ample table for her growing household. The two of them talked so much at their work that Mary forgot to lock the big trunks or to pay the cobbler for Horace's shoes, which were not worth that much money anyway because they wore out on the steamboat.[34]

There was no end to trivial exasperations. As Mrs. Holley and her son jolted along in the coach to Louisville over slippery autumn roads, a pompous fellow passenger whom she happened to know, looked askance at her guitar and then inquired in a solemn manner how she explained having no religious scruples about taking the Sunday steamboat.

"And how, Mr. Butler," she replied sharply, "do *you* explain that God permits the river to flow and the sun to shine on Sunday?"

Whether or not the sun shone as they left the Falls of the Ohio, it was shining gloriously when they stepped off the gangplank at the Good Hope Plantation landing to find the Hermogene Labranche family there to greet them. First there was an "animated breakfast," and then they all drove off in carriages to attend services at the Red Church, where Father Segura's entire congregation consisted of themselves, one other family, and a cluster of house servants. The broad altar of polished mahogany and the twelve handsome oil paintings of the Stations of the Cross seemed overwhelming for such a meager gathering, but just outside in the churchyard were so many marble gravestones of the departed Labranches and Trepagniers and Fortiers and their neighbors that the little group of worshippers was greatly augmented by their presence.

Afterwards the Labranche family crossed the river in skiffs to Brother Jean Baptiste's, taking the priest with them to baptize an infant. That ceremony was promptly performed, and then there was singing and dancing—even waltzing, with the good Father looking on in approval. The dinner that followed was sumptuous, especially the pungent gumbo served in Madame Jean Baptiste's famous solid silver tureens. She was the dear Tante Melazie, for whom Madame Hermogene had named her own daughter. As they were rowed back across the river, the oars dipping rhythmically and the lights of the plantations shining on either shore, Mary Holley compared her new friends with sour Mr. Butler of the stagecoach, and found French customs far more to her taste.

Next morning her pupils numbered four, Melazie and two little girl cousins from neighboring plantations, and Horace. She instructed them in the three R's and also in drawing, music, and dancing. The girls were more diligent at the pianoforte, but Horace excelled with the crayons. In the evenings she played for them to dance cotillions and waltzes while Madame Hermogene did needlework and Mr. Hermogene read his French newspapers from the City. When there were visitors the elders sometimes joined in the dancing. Even Horace was willing to try a few steps now and then, but he preferred to be outside with Carlo, the dog which had been given him for his very own. In the plantation carpenter shop he pieced together a little cart for Carlo, with the assistance, of course, of both *les charpentiers.*

"He is as happy as the day is long," his mother wrote to Harriette in her Christmas letter to Kentucky. It was the first time in a long while that she had seen him so.

She did not find time to finish this letter until late on New Year's Day, which was a holiday for everybody on the plantation to celebrate "finishing the sugar." The weather was perfect for merrymaking, soft and bright and warm. After the slaves had feasted on fresh beef and casks of wine, they donned their best black coats and dresses, the women wearing colored kerchiefs round their heads and the men waving bright scarves as flags. Then they paraded in the dusk to the door of the big house shouting *"Bonne Année pour vous!"* and making their bows to the master and mistress, to the noisy accompaniment of violins and kettle drums and tambourines.

There was one ceremonial Congo dance, done in the old, old manner. The most elderly of the men approached the master, bending first on one knee and then on the other, singing all the while in a weird minor key. It was an ancient ritual of homage from a faraway homeland, and the sight of the rapt black faces moved Mary Holley profoundly and in a curious way. She felt that Mr. Hermogene and the dancers were actors in a strange and primitive drama, controlled by inexorable forces, a drama in which she herself was not personally involved. By thus detaching herself from the tragic implications of the scene, she arrived at the mixed attitude toward slavery held by most of the people she knew in Kentucky. As she closed the letter to her daughter she could still hear the throbbing of the drums in the quarters half a mile away, and she commented that the "rigors of slavery seem softened since I have seen these poor wretches in their gala time and witnessed so much benevolence in their master and mistress."

Her eager curiosity had ranged over all the processes of sugar making, the steam engine that crushed the cane, the huge kettles in which the juice boiled furiously, and the long lines of men and women, besmeared with sugar drippings, carrying it in buckets on their heads to great vats where it stood for the molasses to accumulate. Her season's gift to the Brand family was a barrel of sugar from Good Hope Plantation, which would be loaded at the levee next day. Another like it was marked for shipment to the Dalls in Baltimore.

As a suitable souvenir of the season each of the little girls presented her parents with a crayon drawing which she had painstakingly achieved, and they in turn politely thanked Madame Holley for her thoughtfulness. All in all, Mary had reason to think that the coming year of 1830 would be a prosperous one.

14. GOOD HOPE

1830-1831

Mrs. Holley beamed with pride on the evenings in the great parlor of the Good Hope Plantation when Melazie adjusted her small self and her stiff petticoats on the brocaded stool in order to render *The Caliph of Bagdad* for her admiring relatives. Even Uncle Alexandre, patriarch of the family, complimented the child and noted what a pretty picture she made in the soft candlelight that shone from the sconces at either end of the keyboard. He complimented her teacher, too. But a whole winter of such placid domesticity would have become monotonous to the Labranches because, as Mary expressed it, "the French *will* be gay and happy & amuse themselves." When Hermogene and his brother Jean Baptiste announced that their families would go into New Orleans for the opera season, everybody was delighted, including the new governess.[1] City-born and city-bred, she had no real talent for country living; and since all the children were to remain at the plantation, she would have a holiday from lessons.

The previous summer the two Labranche brothers had purchased an excellent town house in the heart of the Vieux Carré, as the French section of the City was called. It was *un demi-terrain* on St. Peter Street between Royal and Bourbon, and it cost fourteen thousand piastres unfurnished.[2] Even yet it was only partly outfitted, and one of the chief intentions of the Mesdames Labranche during their stay was the choosing of furniture and linens and silver requisite for family use and for much hospitality. Nothing could have pleased Mary more than the prospect of giving aid and advice in such a task.

Consequently, one fine day in mid-January the Hermogene Labranches, together with a staff of servants and a drayload of baggage, boarded a downriver steamboat and after a brief trip debarked at the wharf on Levee Street just in front of the Palace d'Armes amid a great confusion of flatboats and other steamboats and even ocean-going vessels. In the family carriage that had been driven down to meet them they were whisked in no time past the parade ground with its rows of sycamore trees and then the Cathedral and the Cabildo over to St. Peter Street and the new house. The place was already lively and bustling with the Jean Baptiste family and servants, and their early visitors. It would continue to be that way throughout the season, and Mrs. Holley was told that she, too, was welcome to invite guests to breakfast or dinner or whenever she chose. She had ample leisure to visit with her own friends in town, so that when Senator Clay and his wife arrived to be with their daughter, Mrs. Ann Erwin, she called immediately to greet them and to get the letters they had fetched to her from Harriette. A little later it gave her considerable pleasure to arrange for an exchange of calls between them and the Hermogene Labranches.

The Vieux Carré contained the shops of many merchants and craftsmen, especially cabinetmakers. Just around the corner from the Labranche home at 55 Royal, a Frenchman named Mallard had opened a shop well stocked with beautiful dressing tables and tester beds, mostly of rosewood, which, according to him, withstood the damp climate of the lower country better than mahogany.[3] Mary was enchanted with this sophisticated French-style furniture which the Labranches were buying, and spent whole mornings examining the various types of construction and finish.

She executed a commission for Mrs. John Brand for a "rocking chair à la Boston." It cost twenty dollars, which was a trifle more than William's mother had said to spend; but, as Mary wrote Harriette, "When she knows the comfort of it she will not regret the money." The first price had been twenty-five dollars but by going in on a deal whereby Mrs. Labranche purchased two of the Boston rockers, one for herself and one for Madame Holley, Mary managed a bargain for everybody. Mary was tempted to buy the senior Mrs. Brand a handsome full-length dressing glass priced at sixty dollars but thought better of it. While she was in the shop she purchased and shipped to Kentucky three little rockers for her grandchildren and impulsively added a special chair for her own use "at the piano, harp, or writing desk." She longed with all her heart, since William could so well afford it, to embellish her daughter's house with these elegant pieces that had so much more chic than the plain designs of the Kentucky cabinetmakers.

Getting herself the little chair to use at the harp was not as fanciful as it probably seemed to the Brands when they uncrated the shipment in Lexington. She was now enjoying the free use of a handsome harp at the plantation, and during this sojourn in the City she took some lessons from Mr. Lewis, a musician she had met coming down on the steamboat this last trip. She got along well in spite of a certain stiffness in her fingers, an infirmity to which she admitted very reluctantly. She even priced harps at one of the music shops, but found that a good one would cost three hundred dollars. That made her enjoy the opportunity to perform on the fine instrument at Good Hope all the more.

Life was gay and amusing among the wealthy French families during the season. Callers came to the house on St. Peter at all hours, and among them were several former Transylvania students, now important young men in officers' uniforms or tall beaver hats, who came to pay their respects to President Holley's widow.[4] Several evenings each week the family attended the American Theatre or heard an opera in the *très gentille* seclusion of their loge, from which they saw everything through a lattice without being seen themselves. This private loge cost six dollars a performance, but money seemed to be no consideration with the Labranches. Mary boasted a little about these extravagances in a letter to her daughter soon after their arrival at the house in town: "You never saw people spend money so freely. They go out & send home the most elegant articles, paying the money down without a word. Mr. and Mrs. Labranche are every day asking me if I do not want money, telling me to spend just what I like, but I only do so for what is necessary."[5]

She felt that she repaid their kindness when her taste and wide experience were a help in furnishing the house, because neither of the Trepagnier-Labranche sisters knew fashion outside Louisiana. They would, no doubt, have purchased the massive sideboard and eighteen matching chairs for the *salon à manger* even without her advice since scarcely a meal was eaten without several guests. She had influenced them, however, in such refined selections as the pair of inlaid playing tables and the small cherry-tree armoire with its graceful accompanying stand.

The social season, alas, ended suddenly for the Labranches when Uncle Alexandre died, although they remained in town for a while afterward. Mary observed the household's formal mourning, and gave up seeing the great Clara Fisher perform at the Theatre; she did so willingly out of friendship and respect, and made the most of her extra leisure to shop or go walking to the Place d'Armes and over to the French Market. The Market was as large as the one near Hollis Street in South End Boston, and far more exotic with its striped awnings above the counters heaped with red and yellow and purple fruits and vegetables. The place was redolent of chicory and garlic and the special blend of spices that Louisiana cooks called *"filé."*

On her strolls through the French section it was inevitable that Mrs. Holley should discover Miss Carroll's Bookstore at 149 Chartres Street.[6] Mary Carroll was an English gentlewoman of uncertain age, with fine eyes and pleasing voice, who had come to New Orleans a few years before and established herself as a milliner in a good location next door to Madame Fox's genteel boardinghouse directly across Chartres Street from the best drygoods emporium in the French section of town. Everybody knew of the "philosophical milliner." It was said that she advised her customers concerning the latest Parisian modes and at the same time directed her assistant, a comely mulatto girl, how to construct a bonnet or *chapeau*, both in fluent French. While the ribbon and wire were being twisted and tacked into an impressive shape Miss Carroll might also be carrying on a learned discussion in English about metaphysics with various distinguished gentlemen and ladies sitting in the corners of the shop. Everybody of talent who came to New Orleans made a point of calling at her place of business, even her sharp-tongued fellow countrywoman, Mrs. Frances Trollope. That lady later admitted in print that Mary Carroll had "a pretty air of indifference" that made her seem superior. She was indeed a superior person, and it was not surprising that she and Mary Holley struck up a warm friendship.

By this winter of 1830, in which the two ladies met, the "philosophical milliner" had given up hats for books and was offering her customers the latest publications from the Eastern cities and abroad, as well as up-to-date educational supplies from Boston and many radical journals. One of Mary's first purchases was a set of special educational instruction cards, together with several useful prints, for which she paid the considerable sum of seven dollars. This was surely one of the necessary expenditures for which she let Mr. Hermogene pay because she got them to use for her pupils at the plantation.

She found the versatile ex-milliner to be conversant with the most modern ideas of pedagogy, such as those she herself had discussed with Benjamin Peers, and rather more "advanced" than either of them. The two ladies agreed that the teaching cards were "full of information about everything that a child wants to know—almost," and Mary promised to report on her success with them. She had found a kindred spirit, even if she did not approve of Mary Carroll's ideas about politics and marriage. They saw a good deal of each other whenever Mary was in town for the next few years. The bookstore on Chartres sometimes received her mail, and acted as her agent to sell her books. When Miss Carroll's wealthy patrons began to neglect her, it was Mrs. Holley who managed to lend her a little money.[7]

On the Labranches' return to the plantation all reports indicated that life had gone on as usual. The day they arrived Horace was inconsolable because Carlo was locked up until it could be determined whether he had rabies; but on the whole the lad had got on all right without his mother. Lessons were resumed; and in all probability the teaching cards helped to answer almost all the childrens' questions. Steamboats stopped several times a week to load the sugar crop, and often some of the officers and the more important passengers were invited to dinner at the house. As spring came on, with fine prospects for another good yield of sugar, Mr. Hermogene, ever an indulgent man, decided to humor his wife by taking her on a tour of the eastern seaboard and a visit to their cherished son.

When they invited Mrs. Holley to go with them as companion and interpreter, she pretended briefly to hesitate. Her letter at the end of March explaining to Harriette why she felt that she should accompany the Labranches instead of spending the summer in Kentucky was a masterpiece of understatement and diplomacy:

There is some talk of making the whole journey with Madame Labranche. She wishes me to go and will have need of an interpreter. The opportunity offers so many advantages as not to be resisted, though I have thought all along I would not be tempted, and could not give up the pleasure of passing the summer with you for any consideration. I should have a very agreeable journey, *leisurely and without expense*, while my salary is going on. It might benefit my health, as *motion* is my element.

We go by the Lakes & the Falls, which I should like to see again—perhaps Montreal & Quebec, & pass a little time at Saratoga, & all the cities. Do you not think I ought to go? I shall place Horace with Mr. Peers whether I go or not . . . I have some unfinished business in Boston I should like to attend to. What a curious destiny is mine to keep me forever on the wing![8]

Mary already knew, as she signed the letter "Love to all friends, farewell, Mother," that she could not possibly resist this opportunity for luxurious travel that would cost her nothing.

The Labranche party that boarded the *Washington* from Good Hope landing in April was a sizable group. There were Mr. and Mrs. Hermogene; and her two grown Trepagnier nephews, who meant to make the whole trip; and two of his Fortier nephews who were schoolboys going to Lexington to be put under Mr. Peers along with Horace; and

Mrs. Holley and her son, who brought along his dog Carlo. Mr. La-branche was generous about expenses and very considerate in per-mitting Mrs. Holley to leave the boat at Louisville and take the boys by stage to Lexington while the rest of the party went on to Cincinnati to wait for her.

Horace got sick in Lexington, as he often did at any change or stress, but his mother resolutely enrolled him in school and bade Harriette see that he took some calomel. There were times lately when she felt that she must be free for a while from the responsibility of looking after him, and although she was unwilling to admit it, his sister had more success than she in managing the boy. Maybe Mr. Peers' Pestalozzian methods would be beneficial in this case, even if they were wrong in theory. Horace had not minded coming to school in Kentucky if he could bring Carlo with him.

She was feeling altogether like her old self as she kissed her daughter goodbye and let William place her in the best seat in the stagecoach for Cincinnati.[9] She was actually amused when the place next to her was taken by the Reverend Mr. Blythe, stern spokesman of those orthodox religionists who had driven her husband away from the University. As the coach rattled along the streets they passed numerous Presbyterians, who all stared in amazement to see Dr. Blythe and President Holley's widow calmly rolling along side by side.

During the long ten miles to Georgetown, where her solemn fellow passenger would alight, they talked "like the fox and the cat," and she listened to the good man so attentively and conversed so demurely with him that he assured her of his conviction that Providence was directing her present activities to some good and great end. As he left, he "shook hands double" and wished he could continue in such pleasant company. He would have been less amiable if he had known that she was laugh-ing to herself at his ignorant pronunciation. Fancy a college professor's calling attention to the "lun*a*tic *a*sylum" when they drove out of town past that institution! At the same time she found it flattering to have a stiff-necked man like Blythe bow so readily when she condescended to be diplomatic with him. After he had departed from the coach she won-dered if she could have won over some of her husband's opponents if he had let her try.

The Labranches were genuinely glad to see her when she reached the genteel Cincinnati boardinghouse where they were lodged. They needed her help in coping with their remaining nephew. Hypolite had already gone home, and now Jules was ill in bed of a fever, refusing to let the landlady call a doctor or to take any medicine. Mary counseled patience, and entertained Madame Hermogene by taking her about the city shopping and calling. They missed several good boats while Jules was making up his mind what to do.

She did not object to the delay. Cincinnati had become a city of twenty-seven thousand inhabitants since the summer she visited the Taylors across the river, and she relished a few days of sight-seeing. Word soon got around that Mrs. Holley was in town, and all the friends who had been in her home in Lexington overwhelmed her with kindness. At parties in her honor she sang and played the pianoforte while various talented gentlemen performed on the flute or lyre and still other guests delivered original declamations. One day she crossed the river to Newport to call on Ann Taylor Tibbatts and her pretty children so that she could write Harriette about them.

Her most interesting new acquaintance was that inveterate traveller and writer, Timothy Flint, who had known her Austin kin in Missouri and had preached for a while in upper Louisiana.[10] He was the author of a popular book of travel, *Recollections of the Last Ten Years . . . in the Valley of the Mississippi*; and in the pages of his *Western Monthly* had recently written a very sympathetic review of the memoir of Horace Holley. More than any other critic, he openly praised her share in the book, stating that whereas he found Dr. Caldwell's style wordy he would not wish to change more than a sentence of Mrs. Holley's contribution.

The morning that Mary went with a friend to call upon Mr. and Mrs. Flint she found him sitting in the parlor at a large center table, surrounded by books and pamphlets and manuscripts, compiling the next number of his magazine with the patient help of his wife and their pretty daughter. Work stopped while they all talked of Transylvania and Lexington, and of the German Coast and the Province of Texas in Mexico. Flint had published a novel laid in Texas, and had corresponded occasionally with Stephen Austin.

The Flints were well informed about the cultural life of Cincinnati and the whole Ohio Valley region. One of the sons ran an excellent bookstore on Main Street opposite the Presbyterian Church, where all the bookish people foregathered. In the course of the morning's visit the talk got around to the late and unlamented "Trollope's Folly," that Gothic, arabesque bazaar down by the river in which a lady from England had mixed lavish displays of imported merchandise with more lavish murals of the infernal regions—to her financial ruin. She had recently departed and proposed to write a book about her travels in America, or so it was rumored. Nobody in the city had said a good word about the "veritable old Trollope" within Mary's hearing except Timothy Flint, who thought her an intelligent woman. But he thought well of everybody. Mrs. Holley could add a little information about Mrs. Trollope, obtained from Miss Carroll, who had known the lady well ever since she landed in New Orleans with her delicate son, two daughters, a man servant, and the young Frenchman who painted the murals. When Mary consulted her watch she was properly astonished and shocked to see that she had visited with the Flints for more than two hours!

Cincinnati boasted twenty-five church buildings, several of which Mary visited during her stay. The Unitarians were thriving in their new Gothic-style edifice, and seemed to be in close touch with the Hollis Street Society, having invited John Pierpont to be a visiting preacher. On her last Sunday she attended morning mass at the Catholic Church, and admired the music. That evening she heard a sermon by Mr. Alexander Campbell,[11] "one of the reigning stars at present," whom she praised somewhat faintly. She was becoming as nonsectarian and eclectic as her late husband; except in Lexington, where she was drawn with her daughter's family toward her old faith.

When Jules Trepagnier finally tottered downstairs at the boarding-house, he decided to go back to the German Coast on the next boat, and the Labranches promptly booked passage on the *Mountaineer* for Wheeling.[12] It proved to be a "shaking kind of a boat," but at least it permitted them to start their journey to Baltimore and up the coast to New York and Boston. The Labranches were interested chiefly in hastening on to Cambridge to see their son. Fifteen-year-old Nemese was well and making good progress in his studies; but he was far more mature than his classmates, and eager for his education to end. Nothing he had learned in school altered his wish to spend his life as master of a Louisiana sugar plantation. After parting reluctantly from him, his parents halfheartedly permitted their interpreter to conduct them on a tour of the beautiful Hudson Valley.

Mary looked forward with keen anticipation to revisiting this romantic region, and to seeing Orville Holley again. He was a link for her with the literary world where people not only read books but wrote them. She had long since forgiven him for neglecting to send materials for the memoir of his brother, remembering only the idyllic journey in this region on which he had accompanied her and her husband. She went to a good deal of trouble to arrange her party's itinerary so that he could spend a day with them at Saratoga.[13] She was sure that she had her emotions and her memories well under control.

She was mistaken about her emotions. When she first saw Orville coming across the street toward her and her friends, he looked so the image of her husband that she thought for an unreal moment that it was veritably Horace. After hasty introductions she proposed that the two of them take a stroll, and began talking excitedly about anything and everything except what was on her mind. The same illusion came again and again during the short hours they were together. That evening while she was attentively trying to show the Labranches how to dance a figure on the ballroom floor a glimpse of Orville standing at the far end of the long hall became once more the beloved image reproaching her for having so soon forgotten that she had first beheld these scenic beauties while clinging to his arm . . . and once more she seemed to see the waves rolling off the Tortugas. It was out of the question to mention the matter to Orville in the midst of the crowd, and, as she was to learn later, he would have been indifferent to her resurgent emotions. He was a self-sufficient person, who preferred to have no part in the dreams and problems of others.

Mary was glad when they reached New York City, where her hosts set out for home, leaving her to come on later after a visit with her relatives there. By parting company with the Labranches she avoided the bad luck that dogged them on their return journey. Mr. Hermogene was ill of a fever most of the way, and had to be carried off the boat at the plantation landing by his relatives and servants, all of them weeping for joy that he had not perished on the dangerous journey.

The visit with her brothers in the City was what Mary needed to banish her melancholy memories. Both of them were doing well in the commission business, and for some years had been exchanging infrequent letters with Stephen Austin regarding prospects and investments in Texas. He sent them long, formal explanations of the affairs of his Colony, one of which contained information so useful for emigrants that Archibald caused an excerpt from it to be printed in the *New York Journal of Commerce*. Stephen placed a large order with them for oak timber, and commissioned them to shop for items for his personal use. Once he sent a Mexican doll and other gifts for the children of his New York cousins. They in turn kept Stephen posted as to the news on the Atlantic seaboard regarding finance and international relations, and sent him seeds for his garden and lent him a copy of the Austin genealogy that Mary had furnished to them. Henry's latest letters from the

Rio Grande announced that he now proposed to sell his steamboat and secure land in the Austin Colony to make a home for his wife and children.[14]

All this exchange of letters and business warmed Mary Holley's heart. Here was a second generation working together to restore the family fortunes. In her childhood the Austin dreams had been of ships to China; and in her youth the lead mines in Missouri had seemed to promise fortune. Now Moses' sons in Texas were corresponding with Elijah's sons in New York to ask credit and advice in return for incredible grants of land if they would come to the Colony to claim them.

She reconstructed what she knew about Stephen Fuller Austin. She remembered a serious, well-mannered boy in Greenfield Hill, and recalled the good reputation he had left behind him in Lexington, and then added her impression of the man who had written so earnestly about his Colony. She felt herself drawn to him as much as were her brothers. John had named a son for him, and Archibald was talking about emigrating. The phrases in one of the letters lingered in her mind: "The natural resources and wealth of Texas, in fertile lands, timber, pasturage, etc., are incomparably finer than any country I have ever seen . . . We need nothing which nature could supply, but we do need population."[15]

Stephen's words carried conviction with them, and rang with the sincerity of the man. He was offering a league of land for settlers like herself and her son. She would not have been her father's daughter if she had read the letters without wanting a share in the Colony.

The few weeks she spent in Lexington in the early autumn were a dull interlude in her long journey. She decided that William and Harriette "lived too low," that is to say, too frugally and soberly. She tried to persuade her daughter to go calling with her or shopping or just walking, only to have her beg off because she had no proper dress or suitable shoes. The grandchildren were obedient and respectful to their elders. Too much so, Mary thought, and she protested at the scoldings and whippings they got.

"You are breaking their spirit," she declared to her daughter. "I would rather have Horace's bad manners than the loss of his affection and confidence or an iota of his independent spirit!"[16]

Children could and should be reasoned with by their elders. She had insisted upon this basic truth in all her "conversations" with educators, and she wanted her grandchildren to have the benefit of her advanced ideas.

The truth was that she had returned to Lexington from her travels in a critical mood and was prepared to lecture its citizens for past or present shortcomings whenever she observed them. One day while taking her walk she was accosted by a gentleman who asked her to show him Transylvania University, which he had been unable to locate. She took a certain satisfaction in pointing out to him the ruins of the building that had burned, and in writing a poem about the experience:

> Stranger, you ask (and sad are the thoughts that spring
> From memory's hoard of painful recollections!)
> "Oh, where is Transylvania?"[17]

The remaining fifty or more lines bewailed the fact that the University "lay in dust and ashes," which was not an accurate statement in this fall of 1830. Transylvania's enrollment was well over one hundred, and the distinguished Lexington architect, Gideon Shryock, was designing a new and grander building than the one the fire destroyed, to be erected with the funds left by Colonel Morrison. Shryock's plans were given final approval by the trustees while Mrs. Holley was in Lexington, although she possibly may not have known it.[18] When she composed her elegiac verses she was really thinking of the oblivion which had engulfed her husband's contributions to the University. Whether or not she sent the rather mediocre verses to the inquiring gentleman, she kept them in her portfolio.

When she left for Louisiana she enrolled Horace in Mr. Peers' new Eclectic Institute. He would board with Mr. Bradford, and, his mother hoped, Harriette would look after him generally. Income from the fund for his education which Mr. May administered in Boston would help pay his expenses, and possibly some additional collections from sales of the *Discourse* would be forthcoming. Mary looked forward to a winter in the South when she could read and sketch and practice on the harp, and perhaps do something about getting land in the Austin Colony. At the heart of her cheerful outlook as she set out for Louisville to take a boat down the river was the possibility of joining her brother Henry in the Texas venture.

When the wheels of the stagecoach began to turn, she felt that "her lucky star seemed to be in the ascendant," and her spirits rose with it.[19] Somewhere near Frankfort the woods on either side of the road were on fire, making the scene look like some enchanted forest in a fairy tale. The moment she reached Mrs. Langhorne's select boardinghouse in Louisville and before she could lay aside her bonnet, an invitation came to a great fête at Bell's new tavern, where all the fashionable society of the town gathered. As usual she was urged to sing for her fellow guests, and when at the close of her number she announced that she was "at home" to her friends at Mrs. Langhorne's, she brought upon herself a stream of visitors for the rest of the time she was in Louisville, and invitations for every remaining evening.

Mary's intuition for important people rarely failed her, and she accepted an invitation to spend her last evening in Louisville at the home of the George Keatses. Mr. Keats, a thriving merchant, was brother to the famous English poet, and himself a man of literary taste.[20] It was a small party but a distinguished one, made up mostly of local personages. There were Judge Fortunatus Cosby[21] and his charming wife, whose son had attended Transylvania and who had entertained Mary at their home only the previous evening; and Dr. Caldwell's son Leaming,[22] likewise a former Transylvania student, now "grown fat and almost handsome," as Mrs. Holley laughingly observed in greeting him; and Mrs. Worsley, wife of a well-known bookseller and Whig editor.[23] To round out the company were Alexandre Graihle,[24] prominent New Orleans lawyer, and Mrs. Holley. She had introduced Mr. Graihle to this inner circle of the town's society, and he was probably her escort for the occasion.

The American reputation of John Keats had risen of late to unprecedented heights, especially since N. P. Willis' articles in the *American Monthly* the previous spring. His poems were reprinted in numerous magazines and the copies of his published works had become rare items in the United States. Mary had all this in mind when she elected to spend a literary evening with the poet's brother and his pretty wife Georgiana. She thought their home in beautiful taste, and openly complimented the large center table with pillar and claw, on which was placed an astral lamp. She had priced lamps like that only yesterday in the local shops, longing to send one to her daughter.

Books were everywhere in the Keats home, and her host invited Mrs. Holley to peruse some of the poems in a volume of his brother's work. It was the only one he had, he noted with regret.

"Exquisite!" exclaimed Mary Holley, turning the pages reverently, and feeling loath to relinquish the precious book. She perceived the full flame of greatness in this poet's perfected lines as she had recognized sparks of it in Rafinesque's botanical searchings and her husband's orations. In the presence of genius she was always reverent.

The talk that evening ranged widely, and it was good. Her host knew many business men in Lexington like John Brand and Benjamin Gratz, and was, indeed, associated with them in promoting a pioneer railroad in Kentucky. The Cosbys and Keatses were among those Louisville Unitarians who often welcomed Boston preachers to their pulpit, and were on the verge of erecting a handsome new church building. The gentlemen in the company were Whigs to a man, who were eagerly awaiting the new official campaign biography of Henry Clay. It was being written by George D. Prentice, a young Yankee from Connecticut who had recently located in the town to edit the pro-Clay *Louisville Journal*. It was very probably after her return from spending such an evening among the literati of this busy little metropolis at the Falls of the Ohio that Mary composed what she termed "a few lines containing some compliments" which she turned over to Mr. Cosby for the local newspapers.[25]

As she boarded *The Planet*, a smallish steamboat which would take her all the way to the German Coast, she was more at ease with the world and herself than she had been for a long while. Everyone in Louisville had received her as a person of importance, and on the boat she was greeted by several passengers who knew who she was and had heard of her career. One incident touched her deeply. On the first day aboard, a plain young man who said he had been born and reared in Salisbury—he had the look of a journeyman printer or the like—told her that when he was residing in Lexington he had often seen her. He remembered distinctly that the last time he beheld her she was standing on the steps of the Episcopal Church; he even recalled the dress she wore and the color of her bonnet. Little things like the shy man's remembrance of her had a lasting value for Mary, enough to cause her to mention them in letters to her daughter, thus preserving a record of them, although, of course, in a casual and deprecating manner.

Good Hope Plantation seemed like home when she waved goodbye from the landing to Alexandre Graihle and the young man from Salisbury and the other companions of the twenty-day trip on the *Planet*. The Labranches were there to embrace her and pour out the tale of their own wretched journey after they parted from her. Grinning black faces crowded around her, with Tom and Jose asking after Master Horace while they carried her bags and boxes up to her spotless chamber and bowed their appreciation when she complimented the great bowls of oranges and late roses.

By now she knew the German Coast well enough to be aware of the great contrasts it offered. In the midst of luxury and security a dreadful abyss would suddenly open up. On a quiet evening as she and Madame Hermogene sat with their needlework before a small cheerful fire, the gentle Frenchwoman—she was entirely of French descent, not part German like Mr. Hermogene—would relate awesome stories about her family—how her uncle had been murdered during a slave insurrection, and how her own father had simply walked out of his house there on the Coast one morning during breakfast and had never been seen again. Or did she say it was the father who was murdered and the uncle who disappeared?[26] Mary could never get all the Trepagniers straightened out in her mind, let alone the rest of the entangled families. These tales to which she listened over and over were part of the undercurrent of danger and excitement that she discovered beneath the smooth surface of the plantation's formal life.

Texas must be dangerous and romantic in much the same way, she kept thinking, but if the Austins were courageous they could establish landed estates for themselves and their descendants like these along the German Coast. Their experiences would be no more grim than those which the polite people on the Coast had endured.

All through the fall and early winter she waited impatiently to hear from Henry about his plans, but the year ended without word from him. January of 1831 found her with the Labranches in St. Peter Street for the season, and soon Mary withdrew from the sociability of the household to compose a letter that had been on her mind since the previous summer. She wrote to her cousin, Stephen Austin, addressing him at San Felipe, the capital of the Austin Colony.

Her action was not an impulsive or hasty one. She had decided after long deliberation that she wanted to go to Texas with Henry to secure a grant of land near his and to carry out a promising project of her own. This first communication deserved to be written with the utmost care. Since Stephen had indicated in one of his letters to New York that he recalled his visit with her in Greenfield, it seemed appropriate to begin by renewing that old acquaintance. She could take it for granted that he knew something of her later life as wife of the president of Transylvania. Even on a remote frontier he must have heard a good deal about her. She proposed to appeal to him as a kinsman for aid in recuperating her fortunes:

New Orleans
January 21, 1831

My dear Cousin,

I am far from having forgotten you or your visit to Greenfield, as you suggest in your letter to my brother John. Indeed, I often find myself employed in tracing the progress of the "puny boy" through the daring career of the enterprising man. Little did either of us, at that time, contemplate the condition in which the present anniversary finds us. I have been more frequently led to these reflections since I have been living comparatively near to you—since I have been left alone to mark out the future destiny of myself and my son.

More particularly with regard to my son, I have thought I would write to you and renew our acquaintance, in order to learn what prospect Texas would offer to him, looking some distance ahead; whether it would be an object for me to take any steps with such views—securing land—etc. . . .

I have thought, too, if my brothers could make it their interest to remove to Texas, we could there build up our fallen family in new hope and happiness . . . I saw your letters to my brothers, and pamphlet while in New York. Are there persons among you who want education and accomplishments such as I could give? . . . Be so good as to write me on these points, and others concerning yourself. . . .

Is your sister and her family with you?

Mary Holley

That seemed rather an abrupt ending, and so she added an informal postscript:

I lately heard from New York and New Haven. All well. I am obliged to hurry to send my letter.[27]

She sealed the sheet and posted it, and ere long went back to the plantation and her classroom. For months there were no letters from Texas, either from Stephen or from Henry. In early March she managed to get to the City again and was dismayed to learn that her brother had been ill there for the past few weeks and was now gone up the Coast to find her. Like impetuous Austins they were crossing each other's paths without knowing it. A hurried message to the plantation caught Henry there. Somewhat reluctantly he left the hospitable Labranche ménage and the fresh strawberries to join her in town, where, in spite of all their blunders, they spent a happy week together. They were both "full of Texas," as Mary put it, and although they had long been out of touch with each other, their views were as similar as if they corresponded weekly. They were sure that this was the great opportunity for the Austins to make a new start toward fame and fortune.[28]

Henry had adventures to relate. He had plied his *Ariel* up the Rio Grande, her tall smokestacks belching woodsmoke and her side paddles chunking, as far as the Mexican village of Mier. That was far enough to convince him that he wanted his Texas land to be located in Stephen's colony on the Gulf and not in the arid land along the Rio Grande. The *Ariel* was now anchored at the mouth of the San Jacinto River on the Texas coast until such time as he could find a buyer for her. Meanwhile he had secured grants through Stephen for land up the Brazos River in the Colony, not as much as he wanted, but he had plans to secure more. He was bringing his family out as soon as he could arrange for their passage from New York. He gave Mary a few copies of a translation Stephen had published of various Mexican laws regarding colonization and of Stephen's original map of Texas distributed by Tanner of Philadelphia. The map represented a prodigious amount of exploration and surveying. On these copies was pencilled the portion of land to be allotted to the members of the Austin family who settled in the Colony.[29]

"Like the ingathering of the Jews!" she quipped to her brother as they pored over the papers. Her visions began to encompass not only leagues of land for herself and her son but fertile acres for Harriette and William and their children.

The important thing, Henry assured her, was to act quickly. Only the previous year the Mexican government had passed a law forbidding any further immigration from the United States except that Austin's Colony and one other were permitted to settle a few more North Americans, exceptions which were made in deference to Stephen's high standing and diplomacy. Her letter to Stephen should be in his hands by now, but she took no chances. She saw to it that her brother posted two additional messages to him during their week in New Orleans, in both of which he emphasized his sister's desire to secure a grant.[30] They agreed that she would join him in Texas after his family arrived.

While she was in the City she could not resist the temptation to talk of her prospects to her friends, especially to the Clays, who had spent the winter with the Erwins but were soon starting to Kentucky. In their care she sent Harriette a pamphlet and a map, along with a pattern of handsome blue dress material and directions for lining it throughout with stiff muslin. She always begrudged slightly the money she spent on clothes for her daughter, but there was no way to make her dress stylishly except to send her the proper material and careful directions about how to make it. One of the crosses Mary Holley had to bear was that although the Brands were rich enough for her daughter to live as well as any lady in Lexington, Harriette prided herself on being a frugal housewife and a good manager. If the Texas venture turned out well, Mary vowed she would not count pennies or skimp on presents to Lexington.

Henry stayed a long while in New Orleans to straighten out his affairs. In May he was still there, sending messages up the Coast to his sister to refrain from worry lest she spoil her beauty and lose her chances to catch that future senator about whom he had been joking her. He advised her to go to Kentucky for the summer and promised that he "would move her on to the wilderness within a year."[31] Mary liked her brother's flippancies because since her husband's death no one teased her about being attractive to the opposite sex. But she ignored Henry's advice about proceeding to Kentucky for the summer. She felt that she must make the trip to Texas as soon as she heard from Stephen, and she hoped not to be encumbered with the responsibility for her son on that expedition. Taking a calculated risk on the Louisiana climate she stayed on at the plantation during the hot season.

Midway of the summer she received a long letter from San Felipe, dated July 19:

My dear Cousin:
I see by your letter to Henry that you are looking toward Texas, and have even made up your mind for a permanent removal to this Colony . . .

Mary caught her breath as she realized that he had not yet received her carefully worded message. This letter she was reading was in response to the two hasty notes she had made Henry send from New Orleans:

It is needless for me to say that I shall be happy to see you here and anxious to serve you . . . the idea of your removal here, and of the society that will of course spring up under the influence of your wand gives me more real pleasure than anything which has occurred in some years.

Brown Austin must have talked of the musical evenings in the Holley home in Lexington and the varied social life over which she had presided there. His brother seemed to know a good deal about her:

May we not form a little world of our own where neither the religious, political, or *money-making* fanaticism . . . shall ever obtain admission? . . . Let us unite a few choice families and make a neighborhood, as we say in this country . . . A moneyed fanatic would say that I have followed a shadow, for a fortune I have not made as yet, but I shall have a competence and am satisfied. The credit of settling this fine country and *laying the foundation for a new Nation which at some future period will arise here cannot be taken from me;* and that part of my family who have ventured to follow me will be sufficiently provided for . . .

The letter was unexpectedly flattering, accustomed though she was to deference and respect. Her cousin was already sharing his own ambitions and philosophy with her. The conclusion of the letter dealing with the business of her land was brief.

I am spinning out a long letter, and I fear, a dry one . . . I will set apart a league of land for you and hold it in reserve until next winter or spring.

On the first of December I leave for Saltillo, the seat of Government for our State, 550 miles distant, and shall from necessity be absent at least seven months . . . Henry says that you wrote to me. I never received a line from you, and have now written as though a month, and not twenty-five years had intervened since we met or had any communication. I hope you will follow my example, for it will be my greatest pleasure to hear from you.

STEPHEN F. AUSTIN[32]

In the privacy of her own chamber, shadowed and cool in spite of the languorous heat outside, she turned over the long pages he had filled with flowing script and read them again. It was her first glimpse of Stephen Austin, the man. From this moment she always thought of him as a statesman and a maker of history. Sensing the significance of this message from Stephen, she labelled it "File of July 19, 1831," and preserved it carefully.

Even so, this first letter did not tell her very much about him. It was too formal, too carefully composed and full of abstractions to reveal his day-by-day personality. If she had known her enterprising Uncle Moses and his careful Philadelphia wife better, she would have understood their son more fully.

This cousin whose letter she was reading over and over was nine years younger than she, and a bachelor. At sixteen he had been honorably dismissed from Transylvania and gone home to Missouri to spend the next ten years in vain attempts to make his father's lead mines and store and farm show a profit. He devoted his youth to this hopeless struggle, and then in desperation went down to New Orleans to offer his services as clerk, overseer, or anything at all to make an honest living. There he met the older brother of one of his Lexington classmates, the former United States Senator Joseph Hawkins, a successful attorney, who generously boarded him and lent him money for books and clothes while he was reading law.[33]

Meanwhile Stephen's father was undertaking a new venture that made all his previous projects seem small. Moses made the long journey to San Antonio, chief settlement in the Province of Texas, and obtained authority from the royal government of Spain to found a colony on the Gulf Coast; but he was too old for this last and greatest gamble. On his deathbed back in Missouri he instructed his wife to lay the burden of the Austin Colony on the shoulders of his older son and charge him to restore the family fortunes. Stephen had little heart for the plan, but the request left him no choice. The ruling passion of his nature was a sense of duty, whether to his father or to his own given word or to an appointed task.

Now in 1831, a little more than a decade after coming to Texas, he had reason to be proud of what had been accomplished. He had first explored the region along the lower Brazos and Colorado Rivers which his father had chosen, and charted an original map of it. After the Mexican declaration of independence from Spain in 1821 he had journeyed to the City of Mexico to confirm his father's grant with the new Republic, correcting his Spanish in order to deal with the officials as an accredited diplomat. He had been scrupulously loyal to the Republic of which he and his colonists were nominal citizens, but had carefully remained aloof from political controversy. Most important, he had succeeded in establishing five thousand settlers in his Colony.

Stephen was land poor. He had never been able to pay off all his father's obligations or make all the reimbursements to the estate of Joseph Hawkins, who had died before the Colony became well established. Nevertheless, his position was improving, and the prospects for the Colony were so bright that he was urging his only sister, Emily, to come on from Missouri with her husband and family to take up some of the good land next to his own on the lower Brazos and also other valuable tracts. His brother Brown had died of the fever in New Orleans the previous summer, and he felt the need of gathering his remaining family around him.

In his letter to Mrs. Holley, Stephen might well have given her more information about her Texas land. The fact was that when Henry wrote him in early April that she planned to emigrate, he had immediately instructed his secretary, Sam Williams, to set apart "a good tract for Mrs. Holley, widow of the late Doctor Holley, who will remove to the Colony next fall, and be the most valuable acquisition we have ever yet received, in the female line, or probably will receive." And she would have been glad to learn that when he wrote to her he had already had a league surveyed for "Mary Austin *viuda* Holley" and himself signed the title of possession on the thirteenth day of June, 1831.[34] He probably postponed writing to her until he had the time to express himself in a proper manner and at considerable length. He was aware that he was addressing a lady who had a literary reputation.

Almost in the same post with Stephen's letter to Mary came a breathless scrawl from Henry urging her to come to Texas before Austin departed for Saltillo in order to claim her colonist's league of land and also take possession of a tract that he himself proposed to buy for her. He advised her to take the schooner *Spica* from New Orleans as far as the town of Brazoria, somewhat above the mouth of the Brazos River. He would meet her there. By that time his own family would have arrived.[35]

The Labranches consented for her to leave her pupils for the trip to Texas. Having entertained Henry in their household they doubtless had heard about the vast opportunities awaiting her there, and so realized the urgency of the journey. They expected her to return by the end of the year. She notified her daughter in Lexington and her brothers in New York and countless other people about her plans, and let Henry know that she had booked passage on the *Spica* for the middle of October. She arranged to take most of her available money, amounting to approximately nine hundred dollars, just in case she should decide to build a home on her land while she was there.

15. DEAR COUSIN

1831-1835

Texas meant more to Mary Austin Holley than land and adventure. It presented a major theme for a book that was greatly needed. No author of literary reputation had as yet undertaken to describe Texas to the world, a task for which she felt herself peculiarly fitted. She was well known for her share in a successful memoir, and had elicited praise from discriminating critics for her travel descriptions. She had contacts with Eastern publishers. Best of all, she would be able to speak about Texas with the authority of a citizen who owned land in the Colony.

During the long, leisurely days of the summer of 1831 on the plantation, she made plans to write a book about Texas.[1] Her own journey would furnish a background of fresh, firsthand impressions, but for solid content she must consult all the available pamphlets and newspaper articles. She could get Henry and Stephen to tell her the basic facts, and then interview various other settlers for their experiences. This theme of Texas united her deepest interests—romantic love of nature and the vision of a new nation rising under the aegis of the Austins. She could hardly wait to begin writing, and she sent to Miss Carroll's shop for an extra supply of foolscap paper and a large bundle of quills to pack in her writing case.

Mrs. Holley boarded the *Spica* at the New Orleans levee an hour before it sailed on the afternoon of October 18. The anchor was not weighed until after dark, but she was already keeping a careful record in her journal of what transpired.[2] The captain was a Bostonian, polite and respectable. The passengers included an editor from Michigan, a civil engineer from Kentucky, a teacher from Missouri who brought along his bride and a substantial stock of drygoods to establish a store in the new country—all in all, an interesting assortment of characters, she noted. Next morning early she was peering out the window of the small ladies' cabin when the *Spica* reached the Gulf and their towboat, the *Shark*, cast off and disappeared. Then a southeasterly wind took them out to sea, with the sixty-ton vessel rolling and pitching, and Mary put aside her journal. Never a good sailor, she reclined unhappily on a pallet spread on the deck for the four days it took to reach the Texas coast at the mouth of the Brazos River.

Once the motion ceased she revived and eagerly scanned a flat shore line that showed no signs of life except some barracks, palmetto-roofed and windowless, where sentinels in bright uniforms paced lazily back and forth on their lonely rounds. The red-white-and-green flag hung limp on its staff until the afternoon breeze from the south spread it out softly in the mellow sunshine. Along with the other lady passengers she enlivened several hours of waiting by dropping a line over the ship's rail, and by looking on with delicate interest while a gentleman with a scientific bent dissected a sunfish. In the evening all aboard joined in a vesper service, wafting their English hymns on the Spanish breeze with not the least feeling of being foreigners.

The name of the river in the soft, beautiful Spanish tongue was Brazos de Dios, meaning "Arms of God." She jotted that down to remember, along with a legend that the sailors, when becalmed, "whistled to St. Antonio for a fair wind." While they waited to start their slow progress up the river, she tasted the brackish water to prove for herself that it was flavored by minerals from the plains far up near its source; and she rubbed the rich red clay of the banks between her fingers to find that it was "slippery as soap and sticky as putty." After the pilot got the *Spica* across the dangerous bar that all but obstructed the entrance to the river, the vessel proceeded under spreading sails, and Mary resigned herself to watching the lovely countryside that glided slowly past her.

"There is nothing," she remarked to a fellow traveller at her side, "in the whole course of the Ohio and the Mississippi, for quiet beauty, to be compared with the Brazos."

All the passengers of romantic turn sat up half the night watching the fair moon and pointing out Spica, which the scientific gentleman declared to be a star of the first magnitude. It was a very good omen for all the travellers to a new land.

It took as long a time to get up the river to Brazoria as to come from New Orleans to its mouth. For the last ten miles the boatmen "warped" the vessel tediously up the crooked channel, sometimes so close to the densely wooded shores that the passengers caught glimpses of wild creatures among the trees. When the boat tied up at the Brazoria landing on the evening of the twenty-sixth it was absolutely the only craft in sight; but the total male population of the village, about two hundred and fifty in all, were there, shouting raucous greetings in various American accents and demanding that the mailbag be tossed off at once.

Henry Austin rushed aboard to escort his sister ashore and look after her baggage. He had come down the day before from his home thirty miles upstream. He could hardly wait to let her get settled at their boardinghouse, a well-run hostelry owned by a couple from New York State that was the most suitable place for a lady to stop. He wanted to show her the town. They were both as excited as happy children.

Brazoria was booming. Although it boasted thirty-one houses, three of them brick, so many emigrants had arrived recently that every man who could drive a nail had turned carpenter, and still some folks were virtually living out in the open. Mary was astonished to meet a family from Connecticut, the husband being a Yale graduate, who were keeping house in a sort of shed. On the Sunday evening when Henry took her to call upon these people, the lady had her china and glass and linens set out for a polite meal, with the children and servants bowing meekly for grace and all minding their manners. Not everyone she encountered was so well-bred as that, of course, but her brother saw that she met the best class of colonists, and waited while she plied them with questions. They went by the home of John Austin from Connecticut, no kinsman but a friend of Henry's, to whom she had been requested to fetch some strawberry plants from the plantation. As she pressed him with questions about the settlement, he furnished all sorts of information.[3]

Soon after her arrival she informed her brother that she intended to write a book about Texas and wanted to gather all possible material on the subject. He thought it an admirable notion, and offered to help her, especially with regard to the coastal country and its ports and rivers, about which he had learned by experience while operating his steamboat. That unlucky craft was now falling to pieces in the San Jacinto River for want of a way to get it out and take it to New Orleans; but her owner thought his land operations ought to offset the loss.

Henry contributed a helpful piece of information when he told her that Stephen Austin had recently received a communication from the London Geographical Society called "Questions Relative to Texas," which seemed to indicate an active interest in Great Britain regarding emigration. Both Mary and Henry saw instantly that her book might well be directed toward answering such inquiries. In short, she might profitably write a travel book in the interest of emigration to the new land. He may also have told her that a certain Dr. Branch Archer from

Virginia had been in Texas since July, reportedly collecting data for writing its history.

Mary wasted no time. During the days they spent in Brazoria she wrote to Colonel Austin—he held that rank in the Mexican Army—addressing him at San Felipe, his tiny capital farther up country, and making a number of definite inquiries. Would he approve of her publishing a book to acquaint the world with Texas and its inhabitants in the manner the subject deserved? Had he himself replied to the request for information from the London Society? Would he permit her to include in her book the story of his own share in the establishment and growth of the Colony? As a sort of afterthought she asked if her league of land could be located below Brazoria near the Gulf. She had heard of several settlers there like the McNeels from Kentucky who already had developed extensive cotton plantations.[4]

After about a week she and Henry embarked early one morning in a small sailboat for the last stage of the journey to his home at Bolivar.[5] The river now was smooth and clear and green, and they moved slowly against the current, tacking with the lazy wind or being propelled by the oarsmen. They saw flocks of tame birds and a basking alligator and along the shore a few cattle grazing, but no human beings to disturb the solitude. All the long autumn day as they sailed deeper into the green wilderness, she gazed about her with peaceful, solemn emotions. This, at last, was the "universal repose of Nature" that the poets and philosophers knew and described. The only distraction was that she felt compelled to take notes as Henry kept on telling her of things she must include in her book, like sugar trees and Mexican superstitions about eagles. His mind was a compendium of such items and he felt sure all of them would be of use to his sister in writing about Texas.

Just at sunset they reached the head of tidewater where he had laid off his town site, naming it in honor of the great South American patriot. It was located on the east bank upon a bluff of stiff, red clay clothed with heavy timber and wild peach, which, as he explained, was a kind of laurel, and a dense undergrowth of cane. With great outlay of labor and money he had cleared a tract of fifty acres, built his own log house in the shade of a great live-oak tree, and settled down to wait for the emigrants who would populate his town. None had come as yet, the colonists preferring to stop near Brazoria or spread out on farms back from the river, and his home stood solitary in the wilderness. He had recently improved it by adding two rooms in preparation for the coming of his sizable family and his sister. The furniture consisted of rough beds and a few rawhide-bottom chairs. His wife was bringing their household goods with her from New York.[6]

Bolivar House boasted no servants except an old Negro gardener, and for the present Henry expected his womenfolks to do the work in frontier style. There was plenty of milk and, with the know-how to make it, plenty of butter, and a nice late garden. Deer and turkey were at the very doorstep. Here were all the makings of bountiful living, and although Mary had never had occasion to do much cooking, she saw to it that the pumpkin and cabbage and late tomatoes were properly prepared and seasoned, and she supervised the fowl and fish and game that sizzled over the flames in the great fireplace. In time her brother hoped either to secure a Negro woman or to settle a Swiss couple on the place. The trouble about owning slaves in Texas under the new Mexican law was that they could not be owned outright, only indentured until they worked off their purchase price. For that reason Henry had only the aged gardener, who was hardly likely to want to leave.

Mary got her first taste of changeable Texas weather within a few days after her coming. All of a sudden an icy wind swept down from the northwest, whipping the tall trees and blackening the late rosebuds in the yard. She had brought only light-weight dresses, the sort she wore on the plantation, and now she shivered even inside the house, which was poorly chinked against drafts. She made a note to include in her book an explanation of the "northers," as the cold spells were called, and some practical advice to emigrant housewives about bringing warm clothing and enough blankets.

The norther was a lucky circumstance for her. In this interval before the coming of her brother's family she had leisure to gather a remarkable store of information from him. It seemed like their childhood days on Whiting Street as they sat before the glowing embers until long after midnight while he described some of the unusual plants of the region, such as the prickly pear, called also the cactus or nopal, which the Mexicans fed to their cattle; and the extraordinary "muskeet" tree, which likewise supplied food for the stock since they ate its pods. In the dim firelight she made notes on what he said until her fingers ached and her eyes smarted.

Her journal was running to great length, and her notebooks were bulging. Her mind, too, was crowded with ideas and plans of all sorts. She wanted to start writing the "large book on Texas," as she referred to her original project; but the more she listened to Henry, the more she knew that she must consult with the Empresario before she could make a working plan for it. "Empresario" was the title by which Stephen was known to the Mexican authorities, and she liked the sound of it. She persuaded Henry to get off another letter to Stephen ere setting out for Brazoria to meet his wife and children, who were coming in on the *Nelson.*

Just before Henry was ready to leave, Stephen's reply to her own letter came, brought down from San Felipe by a shivering rider who had all but ruined his horse to get there in a hurry.[7] It was a brief, feverish scrawl. Stephen had been ill, and it was apparent that he had made a great effort to write at all. He was willing, he said, to discuss her plan with her, but beyond that he added very little. He seemed not to understand her need for prompt cooperation or to grasp the urgency of her letter. Henry fumed with impatience, and vowed that his sister should talk with Stephen if he had to take her to San Felipe on horseback as soon as he got back from Brazoria. He sent notes by travellers who went up that way telling Stephen that Mrs. Holley's time was limited, that she was losing a hundred dollars a month in salary while she remained in the Colony, and anything else he could think of in order to make him see that she must not be put off.[8]

Never had Mary known solitude like that at Bolivar House during the week or more that her brother was away. The old gardener brought in her water and firewood, and there was ample food in the cupboard and storeroom. Occasionally she was visited by the ferryman's wife or the tenants on the plantation across the river. It belonged to a physician from Mississippi who had not yet brought his family to occupy it. Most of the time she was by herself, yet she was not lonely or afraid. The cold weather continued and she hovered near the fire in the kitchen-living room, a shawl around her shoulders and a kettle boiling to make countless cups of tea. With nothing to interrupt the flow of her pen and compelled to postpone her "big book," she let her kindling imagination play on all sorts of literary inspirations. She drafted the introductory chapter of a novel laid in Texas. Timothy Flint's novel, *Francis Berrian,* although about the Mexican border, had not dealt with the Brazos country, and the Austin Colony was a field white for the romancer. She hastily outlined a story for young boys, like the Peter Parley narratives, remembering that a publisher in New England was selling those juveniles by the tens of thousands. Surely lads like her own son would be thrilled by stories about the Lipan Indians. The one of these "extra" compositions which gave her most pleasure was a lyric she titled "The Brazos Boat Song," set to a familiar tune.[9] In her mind's eye she could already see the published sheet music displayed on some rosewood pianoforte, and she made a sketch of Bolivar House to adorn the front cover.

A couple of days after her brother's departure a messenger brought her another and longer letter from Stephen.[10] He was recovering from his illness. He cordially approved her plan for a book about Texas, and would attempt herein to answer her questions. Yes, he would come to Bolivar to spend some time with her as soon as possible and give her what information he could. No, he had not yet answered the inquiries of the London Society. As to her league of land, it was already located near Galveston Bay, and could not be changed now. Finally, he added, he was truly anxious to see her. Should she find it convenient to come to San Felipe, his sister, Mrs. Perry, would entertain her gladly.

Once more, in this letter to Mrs. Holley, Stephen Austin was stiff and reticent when he meant to be cordial. It would have been more friendly and informal of him to tell her that his sister had just had a baby, her fifth by this second husband, whom they were naming Henry Austin Perry;[11] but no word of this was included in his letter. Moreover, he did not indicate that he had already made definite plans to come down to Bolivar on his way to the coast to attend to some business. He stood a little too much in awe of this cousin, whom he knew to be a lady of importance in Lexington and Boston and Washington, to tell her how really eager he was to see her.

In Brazoria Henry had to wait six days for the coming of the *Nelson,* and the return trip to Bolivar took longer than he expected. Even though his wife had been obliged to leave some of her boxes and furniture in New York because the vessel had not room for them, Henry was still hard pressed to convey his family and their belongings to their new home in the little sailboat. Their arrival put a sudden end to all quiet and to Mary's productive hours of writing. The children, three girls and three boys, ranging from sixteen to four, did credit to their mother's careful rearing, but the house fairly burst its chinks as their noise and rough play spread through it.

While Henry took his sons out to explore the country, the women and girls managed to get things into some sort of order. New York furniture was set on puncheon floors, and rough shelves were loaded with fine china plates and silver spoons and forks of solid weight. Blankets and quilts were distributed among the beds and makeshift pallets while Mrs. Austin grieved that she had not been permitted to bring her feather beds or her Windsor chairs. Despite the difficulties of travel she had contrived to fetch a sizable package of drygoods that Stephen had commissioned from his cousin John Phelps Austin in New York, mostly dresses and dolls for the families of his Mexican friends. Included in it as a gift to him personally were a small box of very superior shaving soap, and a dozen shirts and a stock made especially by John's wife, like the ones she was accustomed to make for her husband. The package was set aside to await his coming.[12]

When Stephen arrived he announced that he was almost well again, in spite of a ride of sixty miles in weather cold enough to make his face ache painfully. His plan to go on to the Coast had gone awry and he had impetuously—impetuously for him, that is—borrowed horses from Mr. Perry and come on to Bolivar House to see Mrs. Holley.

Amidst sudden, cheerful confusion ten members of the Austin family were stepping over each other in the log cabin. Some of them were strangers until now. Henry hardly knew his own children apart, and had to line them up to call them off to Cousin Stephen: Mary and Emily and Henrietta, James and Edward and young Henry. There were so many Marys that some kind of special names had to be devised, maybe Aunt Mary and Sister Mary and Little Mary. After all the greetings and inquiries, Aunt Mary and Cousin Stephen paused to beam upon the uproarious family reunion and both agreed that all the children were "lovely." Then the two of them withdrew to the least noisy corner of the warmest room to accomplish the business for which he had come, which was to talk about Texas and about her book. From the moment he entered the house they were absorbed in each other.

He looked older than she had expected, and just now he was too thin and pale. But his figure was muscular and graceful. His forehead was high, his deep hazel eyes were thoughtful, and there was strength of character in his short upper lip and firm jaw. He looked more like a townbred lawyer than a frontier colonizer, especially after he donned the fashionable stock from New York.

What Stephen thought of her was recorded in an impulsive note to his sister a few days later. Mrs. Holley was more charming and much more youthful than he had imagined, he told Emily, and he added that he thought she, too, would like her cousin.[13] He had been sure that Mrs. Holley would be a "valuable acquisition" to his colony when he first heard of her coming, but he had not guessed that he would be so happy in her company.

They had not expected, these two middle-aged persons who were bent on serious enterprises, that their meeting might take a romantic turn; and apparently no one else, not even Henry, who always encouraged his sister's small coquetries, had matchmaking in mind. It was true that Stephen had been talking cautiously for years about getting married at some future date, but only after the family debts were paid. He had even corresponded with an old college friend in Lexington to inquire what had become of their former sweethearts; but nothing had come of the matter.[14] He might as well have been married to Texas for the past ten years. And Mary Holley, for all that she was more sophisticated and experienced than he in matters of the heart, had no thought of becoming seriously interested in a man the age of Orville Holley or John Everett or Willard Phillips, those young swains whose attentions to her had flattered her husband as well as herself in the happier days of the past.

Nevertheless, their meeting at Bolivar House this Christmas season of 1831 was a love affair, and during the ten days they spent there they caught glimpses of a new and happy world they could create together. He found the rough-hewn room with its unpolished floor and mud-chinked walls a veritable salon where for the first time in his life he could talk about philosophy and politics at the top level of his mind and heart with a gentle woman who knew firsthand the great world in which he had had so little experience. Texas, as he described it to her, was the Utopia for which all romantics long, where enthusiastic souls discover their own creative powers.

In her company Stephen was not in the least reserved or silent, as some had declared him to be. Eloquently he told her about the fertile colony of hundreds of thousands of acres situated here on the Brazos and Colorado Rivers, where settlers could be prosperous and well treated under the generous contract obtained by the Austins from the Mexican government. He made light of his own arduous labors and physical hardships, although he did relate to her an adventure with the Comanche Indians in which he lost his saddlebags containing a Spanish grammar that turned up later to start a rumor that he had been killed. Mary's pen raced to try to take down all he told her, particularly every scrap of personal reminiscence.

Lately, Stephen said, his troubles had been chiefly with certain settlers from the United States in the adjoining grants and even with some of his own people who would not respect the Mexican laws and officials. He himself counted an oath of loyalty given to an adopted government as a sacred obligation. He earnestly desired to prevent quarrels between Mexico and the North Americans, and now that the Mexican law required immigration to be chiefly from elsewhere than the United States, he was more hopeful of preserving harmony. He extracted from his pocket a copy of the "London Geographical Society Questions" about Texas and a set of specific "Answers" which he had just compiled.[15] She could use them in her book, he agreed, and also a manuscript he had composed titled "Emigration to Texas from Europe," which set out in an orderly manner the geographical, economic, and political aspects of the Colony.[16] He gave her a fresh copy of his map of Texas, on which he had made a few corrections to bring it up to date. Thus he supplied her with the authentic factual basis of her book, to which she could add her own impressions and such materials as she had obtained from Henry and others. She had been intuitively right in feeling that she must see and talk with Stephen, and she began the composition of her book at once, in the midst of the happy disorder of Bolivar House.

While Sister Mary and her daughters were busy in the kitchen, Aunt Mary's pen moved steadily across the long foolscap pages. She began with her impressions and experiences on the passage from New Orleans to Brazoria, feeling that she could thus be completely herself and enliven the account with poetic descriptions and light touches. Into this narrative she wove statistics and solid information about rivers and towns and the early history of the Austin Colony. She wrote in a burst of creative energy, trying to complete the first draft in time to have Stephen's and her brother's criticism of it.

Each evening they gathered around the hearth, old and young alike. As the great logs crackled and glowed, they laughed and sang and told stories. Stephen was delighted, and showed himself enough of a musician to join in the singing without spoiling the harmony. Not in vain had his father long ago instructed the schoolmaster in Colchester to give the boy a gentleman's education. Mary led the choruses and taught the others to sing her "Brazos Boat Song." It was a rallying cry, she said, for the Austin clan in this new home "far, far o'er the wave":

> Come whistle, my boys, to the good San Antonio,
> Whistle, my boys, that fav'ring gales blow.
> Spread wide the swelling sheet,
> Make fast the oaken sprit,
> And steer to our forest home,
>   Far o'er the wave.

When they had sung to their hearts' content, she read aloud to Stephen and her brother what she had written, sheet by sheet, for their corrections and opinions. Henry stamped around the room as she read, tending the fire and offering innumerable suggestions. Stephen listened quietly, nodding gravely when he agreed with what she wrote and frowning thoughtfully when he did not. Both gave her their approval of the manuscript, and heartily endorsed the sentiment of her final chapter:

One's feelings in Texas are unique and original, and very like a dream or youthful vision realized. Here, as in Eden, man feels alone with the God of nature, and seems, in a peculiar manner, to enjoy the rich bounties of heaven, in common with all created things. The animals, which do not fly from him; the profound stillness; the genial sun and soft air—all are impressive, and are calculated both to delight the imagination, and to fill the heart, with religious emotions.[17]

Her eloquent words were freighted with meaning for herself—and for Stephen. He sensed her mood, and broke through his ingrained reserve to praise her sentiments warmly. He felt strangely free here at Bolivar House, and remarked to his cousins that it had been a long time since he had been so gay, although he hastened to add that in his youth he had been sociable enough. Mrs. Holley discovered that Colonel Austin could be sociable and gay again, and in a few crowded days she came to know him as no one else ever had.

She understood how he had grown to manhood on a remote frontier, cherishing old-fashioned ideals and political theories inherited from the founders of the Republic. He trusted human nature and was as tolerant toward all religions as Thomas Jefferson. Yet in dealing with land, he was practical and single-minded like Washington; and he regarded obligations as seriously as John Adams or any true son of New England.

While the two of them sat long hours before the hearth he explained the problems with which he had wrestled in his lonely years as *empresario*. He felt no qualms about nominally accepting the Roman Catholic state church, either for himself or his colonists, whose marriages and baptisms, of course, must be performed by the padres whenever they were available. True religion, he thought, was wholly an individual matter, like a man's obligation to keep his word. Sectarianism he disliked, even abhorred, and Mary could say a heartfelt amen to that. Stephen disliked slavery, too, although slave labor had been used in his father's lead mines and he himself owned two house servants. On this difficult and unavoidable issue he found himself in practical agreement with the policy of the Mexican government. Since 1824 it had expressly prohibited slave trade although, as a temporary expedient, the North American settlers had been permitted to bring into the Texas area such slaves as they already owned for the hard labor of land clearing and cotton and sugar cultivation. Austin felt that for the present there was no alternative to these compromises unless white settlers from Europe could be induced to emigrate.[18]

He admitted that he had this matter of securing emigrants from Europe in mind when he made the hard trip to Bolivar so soon after his illness to talk with her. Her book might well prove of value in encouraging settlers from England and Switzerland and all of Europe. It was good to talk over these problems with someone from the outside world. His associates in the Colony seemed indifferent to his difficulties in negotiating on the one hand with the Mexican political leaders, who were "electrified with horror" at the condition of the North American Negroes, which was actually less cruel than the bondage of their own native Indians, and on the other hand with the wealthy planters along the Brazos, who had settled there under the tacit agreement that they could go on living just as they had lived in Alabama and Tennessee.

Mary realized his position at once. She also disliked slavery and had long favored liberation by colonization; yet for years she and her husband had owned good Susannah and Ben, the coachman. She appreciated the dilemma of her cousin, caught between his personal ideals and his Colony's necessities. He did not have to tell her that if he had to choose between the need for strengthening his Colony by admitting the Southern planters and the desirability of abolishing slavery immediately, he would do what was best for his Colony. Nevertheless, they both agreed that if European freemen could be induced to come to Texas it might be possible to put the Mexican law into effect and get rid of the "hateful institution" soon.

As she listened to him she sometimes tactfully enlarged upon his ideas, giving new turns to his thought. He perceived that she could safely be trusted to present his views about Texas to the world, and he gave his approval to her book with only one reservation. He requested that he not be made in any way responsible for it. Nor did Henry wish to be known in connection with it. It was to be solely her achievement.[19]

Before he left for business in Brazoria Stephen told her about the formal deed which he had recorded in the San Felipe Land Office for her the previous June. It was an elaborate title of possession, couched in Spanish, affirming that "Mary Austin *viuda* Holley" had been accepted as a colonist, and conveying to her, her children, heirs, and assigns, one league (4420 acres) of land known as No. 14 lying on the right bank of the arroyo called Dickson's Creek. The document was signed by Estevan F. Austin, with two witnesses. He showed her the exact location on the mainland opposite the western end of Galveston Island, and the nearby tracts owned by himself and his relatives, the Perrys. It was the first land she had ever owned in her life, and it gave her a satisfying sense of security and pride. Few persons she knew, not even William Brand's father, owned as much as 4420 acres.

As final confirmation of her status in the Colony, Stephen wrote out for her in Spanish, using the last blank page of his "Address to European Emigrants," a certificate of citizenship to permit her to return to the States for a few months without losing her league of land.[20]

They made plans for her to come back within the year to make her permanent home in Texas, and perhaps to open a small, select school. They talked of establishing an "arcadia" on the banks of the Brazos. He had recently sketched the plans for his sister's residence, soon to be built on the Perrys' lower Brazos plantation. It was a plain, generous frontier home, with a wing at one end reserved for him, but as he showed it to her, they both realized that he might well have no use for that addition to it.

The meeting between them was so exciting and so filled with urgent tasks to be accomplished that the only certainty in their minds when Stephen left was that he would see her in Brazoria before she sailed. By taking the *Spica* at the very end of December she could barely keep her promise to the Labranches. After Stephen's departure from Bolivar House she had only two or three days to sort the stack of manuscripts and determine how to proceed.

Her "big book" she titled *A Visit to Texas, with Notes on that Country, by a Lady,* and before doing anything else, she selected a fresh sheet to compose the dedication. No matter how cautious Stephen chose to be about receiving recognition, he would not refuse her that privilege:

TO
COLONEL STEPHEN F. AUSTIN

Dear Sir:

Too much praise cannot be awarded to you, for your judicious, disinterested, and generous management, of the affairs of your Colony. You have accomplished great ends with small means. You have endured more hardships, and made greater sacrifices, than often falls to the lot of man to encounter. You have a right, not only to that best reward, the consciousness of good deeds done—but to a just appreciation of those deeds by the public.

There is great pleasure, therefore, in inscribing to you, as a humble tribute to distinguished merit, this little work on your own Texas, by your friend and kinswoman.

MARY AUSTIN HOLLEY

Bolivar, Texas, December 24, 1831[21]

The smaller juvenile narrative she called *Travels in Texas, intended as a Companion to Peter Parley. Inscribed to H. A. H. by his Mother.* She had done little more than sketch out this story, which she set aside until the more important book was completed.

She wrote to an Austin relative, Thomas F. Leaming of Philadelphia, who was Stephen's agent for the Texas map, asking him to consult Mr. Tanner about permission to use it in her book. Surely Stephen's corrections on her copy would be valuable enough to compensate him for the privilege.[22] Then she approached the most difficult of her problems, that of securing a publisher. She planned to ask her brother John to attend to the "pecuniary part of the business" once a bargain was made, but neither he nor Archibald made any pretension to literary judgment. Removed as she was by thousands of miles and many weeks from any contact with the East, she turned once more to Orville Holley and wrote him an urgent appeal to be mailed the moment she reached New Orleans. There would be no time for composing it in Brazoria, and she well knew that on the voyage she might not feel like writing:

Bolivar, Texas, December 24, 1831

Dear Orville,

I am about to put your friendship to a severer test than I have ever yet done. To be brief, *I have written a book* and want it published. And I want *you,* either *for love* or *for money* to attend to it. It is a work on Texas, and I think a valuable one.[23]

She went on, somewhat incoherently, to say that she was going to send him what she had written by the first packet out of New Orleans, without even waiting to have a fair copy made. He was to arrange it in chapters and correct the style and even leave out the poetry if he chose. But the facts must stand as they were. She bade him offer the book to Harper's for its Family Library; and with superb confidence went on to suggest the proper booksellers to handle the sales, and sent a message to N. P. Willis, the critic, who was Orville's good friend, concerning the impression the book might make upon him. Her decision to risk her manuscript to Orville's indifferent care was hasty and ill-judged, but she

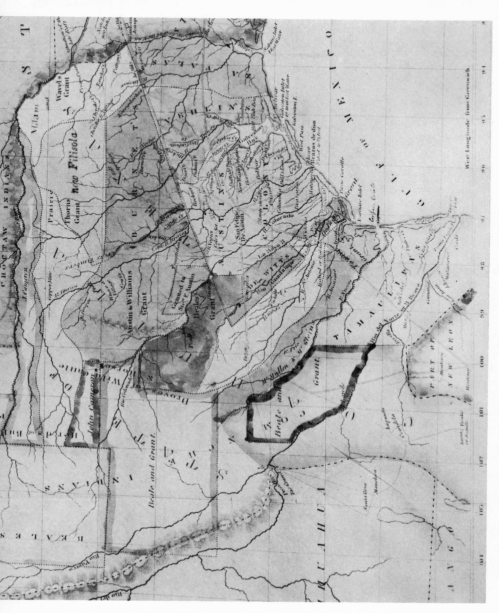

Map of the State of Coahuila and Texas included in Mary Austin Holley's *Texas* (1836). Measuring thirteen by ten and a half inches in the original, it showed the various grants in colors.

was throbbing with fatigue and her mind was racing ahead to her meeting with Stephen in Brazoria on the morrow.

Out of gratitude to her brother she was taking pretty, blue-eyed Little Mary back with her to the plantation for a long visit. Henry felt that a girl of sixteen needed more social life than Bolivar House provided. On the day before the *Spica* was due to sail, he escorted the ladies down the river in a small boat, loaded with their possessions. Mrs. Holley kept her hand on the package containing her manuscript. It was her most valuable possession.

In Brazoria they went as guests to the home of the John Austins to await their sailing. Stephen was in town, and deeply involved in the long standing controversy between some of the townspeople and the government officials regarding certain strict customs regulations imposed upon all vessels landing in the Brazos. Such regulations were impractical and unjust, the Texans declared. Stephen tried to pacify the irate shipowners and also win concessions from the government, but in vain. The day Mrs. Holley arrived an outbreak occurred in which some Texan vessels forced their way to the sea, wounding a Mexican soldier in the fracas.

Ladies were warned to stay off the streets not only because of the shooting but because the crowds were rough at the Christmas season. Nevertheless, she ventured out of the house far enough to witness scenes of violence which shocked and disillusioned her, not because she was afraid, but because such lawlessness and drunken brawling spoiled her romantic impressions of Texas.[24]

Stephen came to say goodbye to her in her host's parlor, and bade her to be very careful of her safety. He had much unfinished business to attend to before he left on the long journey down to Saltillo for the meeting of the Mexican Legislature. She promised that she would return in the fall "with her goods and chattels to take up her domicile." He spoke with a touch of melancholy of his duty to his Colony, and wondered if they would ever meet again.

"Dear cousin," she replied lightly, hoping to raise his spirits, "whatever befalls us, my first and highest duty shall be to write your biography!" And so they parted.

The captain of the *Spica* got a permit from the officials to permit his sailing, and on Christmas Day the passengers were aboard early, lined along the rail to shout their farewells. Henry decided to accompany his ladies down to the Gulf, to see them safely past customs and on their way. He brought aboard at the last moment a letter to his sister from Stephen, written early that morning. She read it there on deck, in the midst of the noise and bustle.

Stephen admitted that his note was an excuse to say farewell to her once more, but also he enclosed some additional paragraphs for the book that hinted at the future independence of Texas and disapproved of slavery. Such bold words sounded as if he were casting caution aside and openly assisting her to "tell the world about Texas" in her book. He wrote, indeed, as if the volume were their joint enterprise.

"Print the Colonization Laws and the Translation side by side," he wrote and then went on to talk of their future together. "The next year —how much happiness or how much bitter disappointment it may bring—for I hope *then* we shall all be happily and quietly settled. Farewell."

As the vessel hauled off and swung out into the current, she seemed to see Stephen's slender, erect figure standing on the shore. It was hardly possible that he was actually there, but she remembered it that way.[25] Perhaps she was blinded by tears. She would have been happier if she could have known of the letter he wrote next day to his brother-in-law. In an unusual outburst of emotion he said, "Mrs. H. is a divine woman!"[26]

Mary also felt the urge to say farewell a second time. When Henry left the boat she put a letter in his hand for Colonel Austin. This time she more fully succeeded in expressing what was in her heart. In knowing him, she wrote, she had experienced the deep pleasure of discovering congenial feelings and tastes and sympathies that very few in this cold and selfish world can appreciate and enjoy. And she told him of her resolve that, though the world as yet knew but little of him, he should become famous through her pen. It was a platonic sort of love letter, but she knew that he too spoke the language of idealism and sentiment.

He proved that he understood her message. The next day after Henry brought him her letter he wrote a long reply. It would be weeks before she received it but he could not wait. His words were responsive and eager. He wrote about himself instead of his Colony, and described his "need for a social circle": "My sister's family, and Henry's, and Archibald's, and you—my friend, you—how shall I ever thank you for venturing into this wilderness, how express the happiness of the ten days visit at Henry's . . . Yes, we will be happy."[27] He wrote to her twice more during the next three weeks.

The passage to New Orleans was long and rough. Mary was seasick, as usual, and did little more than keep an eye upon her niece and complete a few letters. Three were to Stephen, one of them being dispatched at sea when they exchanged mail with a passing ship bound for Texas. One other task she kept putting off, that of writing to her daughter. She had not sent a line to Harriette since leaving Louisiana, and had felt a twinge of remorse when she heard from her just before leaving Bolivar. Finally, as the vessel ascended the lower reaches of the Mississippi, she forced herself to begin a letter that must be posted as soon as they landed.

She hardly knew where to begin. She explained about the league of land, and then described Henry's children in somewhat unnecessary detail. There was really not much point in picturing four-year-old Henry as being like "waxwork, his skin is so fair, his cheeks so red, his eyes so black, and his hair such beautiful auburn." Eventually she told of the book she had composed and her plans for publishing it, and stated her resolve to make her future home in Texas. She mentioned Colonel Austin in two or three sentences, but said nothing that would have led Harriette Brand to guess the important part he had played in her mother's trip to Bolivar. The letter was a hasty one, and hurriedly concluded: "The City is in sight. Best love to all friends, my dearest daughter. Mother. Friday Evening, January 6th."[28]

A fog of delay settled down upon her in the City as she struggled to send her bulky manuscript to John in New York by the earliest possible packet. She wrote him precise directions about delivering the bundle to Orville immediately, and about locating a copy of the latest colonization law of the Mexican government, the one dated April 6, 1830, which was not to be found in New Orleans and must be added to the manuscript.[29] When these matters were done, she went back up the river to the plantation where her small pupils awaited her after a very long vacation. She wondered how she could possibly last out the year in the classroom.

"*Merci et bon soir*," she would murmur to her maid in the evenings as the door of her chamber closed. Now she could take out from her escritoire the packet of Stephen's letters and reread them. She counted the days on the calendar since she had seen him and the months before she could commence her career of active happiness in the Colony.

His first letters were cheerful, although sometimes he wrote late at night after long hours at his desk. He had obeyed her injunction to laugh away care and had gone dancing at a ball. Once he closed his letter with "*Adios, amiga mia.*" Then came a message full of concern because of the bold sentiments he had written in those extra paragraphs to be added to the book. "We were excited at Brazoria," he declared, and asked her not to publish those indiscreet sentiments, especially the one about independence from Mexico.

She hastened to comply with his request and sent letters to John Phelps Austin and also to Orville, although she had no way of knowing as yet that he had undertaken to assist her. She bade them to delete the offending section, explaining that it was that portion written in the Colonel's hand on note paper. At the same time she thought better of the sharp comments on the drunken brawling in Brazoria which she herself had written at the same time, and she requested that her remarks also be deleted. Her undiplomatic words might well be attributed to Stephen with dire results. In her letter to Orville she commented at length on Colonel Austin's methods: "It has ever been the policy of the Col: to move on quietly & steadily, exciting as little attention as possible, until (using his own simile) the infant should become a man & strong enough to wield its own weapons."[30]

There was good news in one of Stephen's letters. He wrote that he had authorized her brother to "chuse 200 acres out of my Peach Point survey of premium land for you, if I am gone too long." He was making sure that if she got back to Texas before his return from Saltillo, she would be able to establish her residence on the site he had selected for their future "arcadia."

To his letter she replied at once to express her gratitude for his generous gift, and he, in turn, answered the very day hers came to say how pleased he was that she was pleased. He even let his shy imagination foresee a happy day when "on our ponies we will scamper over the flowery prairies to the sea."

For the rest of the winter and spring Mary lived a double existence, her mind divided between the kindly monotony of the Labranche household, punctuated with Creole chit-chat and childish trivia, and all those other "thoughts and views so grand and glorious"—a phrase she used to describe her ideas when she turned them toward her future.

Stephen's last letter to her before his departure for Saltillo was dated February 19, but it was beginning to be spring on the German Coast when she read it:

I was made happy today by the receipt of yours of the 5th and 6th ultimo . . . It was like a dream of sunshine after days of clouds . . . I expect I have tired you out with my long letters. Taciturn as they say I am, you see I can be loquacious sometimes, and to some persons. It is long since I have been able to talk frankly as I wished. This is the last letter you will receive from me for the present . . . In a few days I shall be off, to return a free man, about June, and commence my improvements . . . You can go on preparing for your removal according to your wishes . . . Farewell, a long farewell.[31]

As she saw the "long farewell" at the end of the last sheet, she shivered with foreboding in spite of the tenderness of his words. She knew that by this time he was punishing his horses on the long road that led down to the Rio Grande and up to Saltillo. He was playing a dangerous game of neutrality on this mission, subordinating his personal interests, even his own convictions, to the welfare and safety of his colonists. How was it he had expressed it?

"Years ago," he had said, "I enlisted myself as the slave of this Colony, and I am bound in honor and duty to labor for it until its affairs are done." In such loyal servitude he would spend his strength, and until his duty was done, their arcadia, his and hers, must wait. This was the last letter she received from him for a very long time.

News regarding the fate of her manuscript in the East was exasperatingly scarce.[32] Dependable Brother John notified her that he had delivered it into Orville's hands, and had himself paid Tanner's bill for the map. A New York newspaper ran a notice of a forthcoming book on Texas without naming the author, whereupon Mary saw to it that her friends knew that it was her work. Young James Drake, of the well-known Louisville theatrical family and fellow passenger on several trips down the Mississippi, wrote from his plantation home on the Gulf to inquire when he could purchase a copy of her "Notes on Texas."[33] However, it was late spring before Orville finally wrote to say he had read the manuscript and thought her "character" of Colonel Austin was well written. He had met Stephen in Greenfield when they were boys, and apparently found it interesting to renew the acquaintance. He said little about trying to secure any publisher, and less about revising and arranging the material for the printer. Mary began to suspect what she should have known for years, that Orville Holley was a poor reed to lean on; but the fate of her manuscript lay in his indifferent hands, and since she had kept no copy of it, she could only wait on his decision.

With all her plans uncertain and tenuous, she set out for Kentucky to spend the summer of 1832. As she left New Orleans she addressed a wistful note to Stephen at San Felipe, knowing that it would gather dust on his desk until his return from Mexico: "Our book is not out yet that I know of . . . May all happiness attend you—remember me kindly to your sister and her family. Your cousin, M. A. H."[34]

She found Harriette in poor health following the birth of a baby in April, a boy that William named for his wife's father.[35] Mary's own son Horace, now a gawky fourteen, had grown up astonishingly in the year and a half under Mr. Peers, but he was no better in books than he had been in the past, and he took little interest in girls or the social entertainments Lexington offered to lads of prosperous families. He thought the prospect of living in Texas was tolerable, but most of all he wanted to go back to the plantation on the German Coast. With a sigh of resignation his mother realized that she would have to take him back with her in the fall. Whether he would fit happily into her life at Peach Point was a problem she would have to work out when the time came.

She found little to interest her in Kentucky that summer, and spent a good deal of time teaching Lizzy, the oldest granddaughter, to take neat stitches in her patchwork pieces. When she told the Brands and a few friends about her land in the Austin Colony and the new book, most of them were politely noncommittal. That was to be expected, she commented to herself, of prudent people who had handsome bank accounts. Only to her daughter did she reveal something of her feeling for Stephen and the part he played in her plan for living in Texas, knowing her to be the only person in Lexington likely to approve of her mother's dream of happiness. Out of the depths of her unwavering trust and devotion Harriette did approve, but not being an Austin by temperament, she made no effort to persuade her husband to buy several leagues of Brazos River land, as Mary urged that he do.

The hot summer precipitated epidemics of fever and cholera that swept the entire country, lasting on into the autumn season.[36] When Mary and her son made the journey down the rivers on a dreadfully uncomfortable boat early in October there was talk that the sickness was still abroad in New Orleans. Then a poor passenger died suddenly of the fever, and Mary took to the cabin with her camphor bottle and tried to shut out old, painful memories. Good Hope Plantation seemed a blessed haven although everybody there was wearing bags of camphor and garlic around their necks and great fires were kept smoking in the yard as tar was poured on them. She settled down to lessons and quiet. Horace had a horse and a gun as well as a dog, and learned to chop wood for exercise.

She found no letters at all from Texas on her return to the Coast, not even from Henry. Then, roundabout through New York, came word that

Sister Mary and Little Mary had both died of the cholera at Bolivar House, leaving poor Henry with four young children. In the same letter from New York was other bad news. Orville had been frightened by the pestilence that was now sweeping that city, and had fled, taking her manuscript with him. Her brothers had no idea of his whereabouts or of his progress toward securing a publisher.[37]

Mary could deceive herself no longer about Orville. He was a procrastinator—worse, he was irresponsible. She would never again turn to him for help or advice. Her indignation, of course, did not serve to locate her manuscript or make up for all the time he had lost for her enterprise. For the present she could only remain in seclusion and hope the sickness did not creep up the Coast.

A few deaths among the field hands occasioned great anxiety for the Labranches, and everyone worked to keep things in order. Mrs. Holley took charge of the breadmaking, and taught the cooks to use yeast instead of leaven, even keeping a little pot of yeast made of hops from the Brand household in her own room. A pretty young lady newly arrived in Louisiana from Paris who took refuge with the Labranches from the sickness in town proved to be of no practical help; but she lifted their spirits with her display of new fashions. She wore her hair twisted on the top near the forehead with a large, high comb above all like the horn of a unicorn, and no locks in front save the little beau-catcher curls at the temples. Mary took occasion to observe the arrangement carefully and describe it to her daughter. She may well have altered her own coiffure a trifle to match it.

At last she received the letter from her brother Henry which he had sent to Kentucky and her daughter had forwarded. It was the message about the loss of his wife and daughter. The epidemic and the conflict between the colonists and the Mexican officials had destroyed his glowing prospects, and his grief made him very pessimistic. Strife had broken out in Texas, just as Stephen had got back from the meeting of the Legislature in Saltillo.

Mary was told the details of Stephen's return in a long communication from Texas narrating the epoch-making events of the summer, which she knew she must include in her book to bring the account of Texas up to date. Although she carefully did not mention his name as responsible for it, no doubt Stephen Austin himself arranged to send her this communication from San Felipe not many weeks after his return in the hope that it could be added to her volume before publication.[38]

These events were important to her as a writer no matter how much they dashed her personal hopes. During Austin's absence in Mexico some of the Texans, restive under certain harsh officials of the Mexican government, had organized an uprising that resulted in two small but violent battles. The colonists were divided between one party which wished to remain loyal to Mexico and another which demanded more freedom of trade and self-government. Austin, who kept in touch with the situation during his absence, urged that the settlers seek their rights under law, without violence; but even he might not have been able to control them had not a current political revolt within the Mexican government itself furnished him with a way to effect a temporary compromise. It was a quiet, well-conducted revolt, led by Generals Santa Anna and Mexia, which had been gaining momentum for nearly a year. Its leaders called it a "liberal" or "republican" revolution agains the tyrannical government in Mexico City. Austin found these liberals to be favorable to his settlers, and returned to the Brazos in mid-July in company with General Mexia and his troops. With much fanfare and speechmaking, the Texans declared for Santa Anna's party, and more rights for themselves. Stephen Austin thus effected an uneasy truce until the October convention of all the settlers, which was called to press claims for the organization of Texas as a separate state in the Mexican nation.

The material sent to Mary Holley included documents that were the basis of any historical account of the summer of 1832 in Texas: verbatim accounts of the speeches of Stephen F. Austin and Alcalde John Austin and General Mexia; the official exposition of the Texan position and the resolutions adopted by the meeting at San Felipe. She had only to compose brief remarks to preface the new chapter in which they were grouped. This invaluable addition to her work on Texas came at about the time she heard of Orville's disappointing delays, and it prompted her to take some action about her manuscript.

Before the end of the year she wrote to Orville, demanding that he send the papers to her brother Charles at once, and she appealed to Charles to undertake the publication of her work. She wished him to add this fresh material that she was dispatching to him. She may have already agreed with Orville to delete her poetry and to arrange the narrative of her visit to Texas in the form of twelve letters. At all events she composed a new title page, calling the work *TEXAS. Observations, Historical, Geographical and Descriptive, in a Series of Letters, Written during a Visit to Austin's Colony, with a view to permanent settlement in that country, in the Autumn of 1831. With an Appendix, Containing specific answers to certain questions relative to Colonization in Texas, issued some time since by the London Geographical Society. Also, some notice of the recent political events in that quarter.* The Dedication to Stephen remained unchanged. She felt sure that the Dalls would assist Charles Austin in making financial arrangements with some Baltimore firm to publish the book and permit her to reimburse them from the sales.[39]

Good Hope Plantation was lucky enough to escape the ravages of the cholera during the fall, but calamity struck later, during the season for making the sugar. The pestilence spread from the field hands to the big house. Patience and Louise and Jean, who competently served their master's breakfast in the morning, were dead at sundown. When Mr. Hermogene himself fell ill for a few days, Mary made calf's-foot jelly and assisted with the household until she, too, was stricken in the night with a deathlike chill and could only thump on the floor beside her bed to summon help. The skill of the plantation physician and his strong medicines checked the early symptoms, and in a day or so she was out of danger and could laugh a little with him over the stiff hot toddy he made her drink.

"You must not think I am afraid to die when the *finish* comes, or that I am not always prepared," she said to him solemnly, after a few swallows. Then, with a twinkle in her eye, she added, "But I do not think it is just the epoch in my affairs when I can best be spared."[40]

Monsieur le docteur assured her that everybody was prepared to die some other time; and that made her laugh again. By Christmas week she was out of her bed, and soon was well enough to drive down the Coast along hedges of blooming roses with Mrs. Humphreys to call on a lady just back from Boston and New York, who brought messages from friends there. When the family went to the house on St. Peter Street for the season, now that it was again safe to be in town, Madame Hermogene let her choose her own belated New Year's gift. She selected a handsome clock imported from Paris. But as they went shopping in the Vieux Carré they passed Miss Carroll's and saw the shuttered windows and closed door. She had perished during the epidemic and lay buried in a hasty grave, far from her native England. Poor Miss Carroll, thought Mrs. Holley, who had liked this strange, lonely crusader and would miss their disagreements.

Her own life was unsettled and unanchored. She heard nothing from Stephen and learned about him only from news accounts in the New

Orleans papers, which reported that the Texans were demanding separation of their province from Coahuila and more self-government. She knew that Austin had no objection to separate statehood for Texas, provided the change was made under the Mexican law and without violence. She knew also about the laborious correspondence he was carrying on to bring together the various factions in a practicable union. New leaders were dominating these Texas conventions, such men as William H. Wharton and the recent governor of Tennessee, Sam Houston, who felt no need for loyalty or gratitude to Mexico. Austin found himself involved in the difficult task of acting as liaison between them and the officials in Mexico City, who did not concede to the Texans the right to organize their own state government and draw up their own constitution.

Mrs. Holley had the good sense to realize that Stephen had no time for his personal affairs, and to know that their plans were being deferred. With resignation born of long experience, she accepted the disappointment and filled her life with varied activities. When Charles wrote that he would publish her book in Baltimore within a few months, she prepared a Prospectus and set about circulating it widely in New Orleans and along the Coast. The Erwins took a list to show to their acquaintances in the City, as did the Thwings, whom she had known in Roxbury. Scores of subscriptions were paid in advance.

One friend was especially helpful and attentive whenever he was in Louisiana between business trips to Central America. This was Mr. Savage, a single gentleman of considerable taste and education, who began to pay court to her after her return from Texas. It seemed as if the visit to Bolivar House had brought her out of her widow's seclusion, because during the opera season the Labranches' box had been crowded with handsome Dr. Hunt from Lexington and Mr. Savage and other gentlemen gathering to talk with her between scenes. Her hosts playfully called her a "coquette." Mr. Savage had been an observant traveller on his trips to Guatemala, and he gave her a copy of his original essay titled "Description of a Nopalade, or Estate for Cultivating the Cochineal," explaining at length to her that the nopal, or prickly pear, was the favorite food of the cochineal insect, source of crimson dye.

Mary found Mr. S. a little garrulous and tiresome, but he served to restore her wounded ego, and she boasted about her new beau in a letter to Harriette in the late winter after it had become obvious that the plans with Stephen were to be deferred:

What would you say if I were to tell you of another project—that I have half promised myself to Mr. Savage?!! *But don't be frightened before you are hurt.* There is nothing settled—he has gone to Guatemala and will not return before July. . . . You do not know Mr. S. I never knew him well till now. I see in him much to admire. He takes an interest in Horace & is just what he requires, being at once decided and firm, aimiable and kind. You must keep my secret till I see how matters go, for after all, *je ne sais pas.*[41]

Stephen wrote her a long letter on April 20, the day before his departure once again for Mexico City to present the application of the recent Texas convention for separate statehood. It had a melancholy, disillusioned tone, from the very opening lines:

I do not know that, in the whole course of my life, I have so sensibly felt the extremes which ardent and sanguine temperaments are liable to, as during the last eighteen months. When you were here we permitted our imagination to ramble into futurity with untiring, and more than full grown wings. The result has been what calm and calculating judgement would have foreseen—an unnatural flight, and consequent disappointment. Well, so be it. I had rather at least be capable of being moved by bright visions, never realized, than to pass through the world without being touched by the recollection of the past, the events of the present, or the anticipation of the future. . . . The calamity which Henry has suffered by the loss of his wife, and by sickness is truly distressing. I am convinced from numerous examples that persons raised in cities ought never to remove to a new and thinly settled country.

Did he mean to cancel all their mutual plans? Had he changed his mind about an "arcadia" and a "congenial society?" The end of the letter was capable of various interpretations:

If I succeed in this mission I intend it shall terminate my participation in public matters . . . But, I must confess, I have done calculating for the future . . . Henry informs me that you intend spending the summer in Kentucky. I think this is a good plan. In the fall, or winter, come and pay us a visit and look at your league of land . . . I hope to be back in four months . . . Farewell—S. F. AUSTIN[42]

One thing in the message she could not misunderstand. His duty to the Austin Colony remained his supreme obligation. He felt that he had been rash to dream of personal happiness until he had fully discharged it, and lest she be disappointed, he was bidding her not count on the plans they had made at Bolivar.

He was in reality much more concerned about her future security and happiness than the letter indicated. On the previous day he had written a long, careful will disposing of his considerable estate, and had it properly witnessed by seven friends. The tenth section of this document bequeathed a league of his land "situated on the east side of Bayou Flores opposite its junction with Bayou Austin" to "my cousin Mary Austin Holley, widow of Dr. Horace Holley, and to her son in case of her death."[43] That same day he wrote his brother-in-law that when he returned, if he did return, he intended to close all his affairs and "settle myself and get a wife and be a farmer."[44]

Mary Holley knew no more than what his letter told her, and she met his cool withdrawal with a touch of bravado. She disregarded his advice and decided to remain in Louisiana for the summer. She was expecting a shipment of her books from the publisher before fall, and she wished to deliver them to the subscribers promptly. If this first edition proved popular, she wanted to return to Texas to secure information for a second one, whether Stephen had returned or not. When she mentioned this matter of another visit in a letter to Henry, he hastened to discourage it. He asked her, instead, to take his motherless children to Lexington to make a home for them there and supervise their education. She knew that she might have to agree to look after her brother's family for a while, but the idea of a second book about Texas remained in her mind.

Another reason for staying in Louisiana during the summer of 1833 was to complete her duties as governess in the Labranche home. Seventeen-year-old Melazie's education was almost "finished," and soon her betrothal would be announced to Donatien Augustin, a prominent attorney of New Orleans. For only a brief time longer could Mrs. Holley count on a salary of one hundred dollars a month and a luxurious home for herself and her son.

She assuaged her disappointment over the withering of so many of her "bright visions" by being somewhat nicer to Mr. Savage, who gallantly reciprocated by offering to take Horace off her hands for an extended trip to Guatemala. For that she was sincerely grateful. Sometimes she could not control her tall son, now openly rebellious when she scolded him for dawdling over his books. He would laugh in her face and shout for her to stop that everlasting talking, and then stamp noisily outdoors to go fishing or hunting. Her neighbor, Dr. Humphreys, examined him and tried treating him with blisters on the neck and massive doses of calomel to cure his nervousness, but to no avail.

Mr. Savage bluntly told Mary that her son's troubles grew out of his mother's indulgence and promised to manage him better on their travels.[45] Horace jumped at the chance to go to Guatemala, even promising to learn to speak the Spanish language. He would have promised anything at all in order to escape from the prison of daily lessons in the company of polite young ladies and the prospect of endless books to study.

In December Mrs. Holley and her son went down for a few days to the house on St. Peter Street to try to find out what had become of the Baltimore publisher's shipment, long overdue. The big packing box was discovered in a local bookstore where it had been gathering dust in a corner for nearly three months. As soon as it was carted to the house and uncrated, she sent Horace scurrying about the town delivering copies to subscribers, with instructions to collect what money he could.

Mary Austin Holley's *Texas* (1833) was a slender, duodecimo volume, bound in dark blue cloth with the title in gold. There were no illustrations or poetical embellishments, but the large, folded reproduction of Stephen Austin's Map of the State of Coahuila and Texas showed up beautifully.[46] The printer's bill, plus the cost of the map, came to something over three hundred dollars; and after freight charges there would be a substantial sum left if all the copies were sold. Charles, generous brother that he was, refused any remuneration or part of the profits.[47] This publication was not so pretentious as the book honoring her husband, but it carried her name on the title page as author. She must have looked long and proudly at the little book, and wondered when, if ever, Stephen would see it.

Back again on the plantation the Holleys waited impatiently for word of the vessel to Central America. In her spare time Mary took up painting again, chiefly because she found that she could interest Horace in it. He had a flair for doing clever likenesses of people that were often devastating caricatures. She could not decide whether he achieved them by accident or sly intent, nor did it matter. He would never seriously put his mind on becoming an artist, or anything else that kept him indoors. It was a relief in the late winter when she finally got him off with Mr. Savage to the tropics. While he was gone she could cherish the hope that masculine discipline and a life of vigorous action would miraculously transform Horace into the kind of man she and his father had planned for him to be.

Melazie's wedding took place in March, 1834, with all the excitement of an elaborate trousseau and family dinners and handsome gifts befitting the only daughter of the Good Hope Plantation. Mrs. Holley beamed her approval of the groom. Donatien was the son of a distinguished scholar who had emigrated from Touraine, and the young attorney himself had compiled a legal volume or two. He was twelve years older than his fiancée and not wealthy; but he was an officer in the Military Legion and a brilliant fencer, and his social position was excellent.[48] The couple would reside for a time in the house on St. Peter Street, and they both invited her former governess to continue to make that her home in the City.

Mary loved her pretty young pupil next only to her own daughter, and felt more *en rapport* with Melazie and the genial Donatien than with the more austere Brands. In the Augustin home, as on the Labranche plantations, people would never forget that Madame Holley was a literary personage who was so good as sometimes to instruct *les enfants*.

With Melazie married and Horace gone to Guatemala; with Stephen still in Mexico—so far as she knew—and Henry unwilling for her to come to Bolivar, Mary had no choice but to return to Kentucky in the late spring for an indefinite stay. She took with her the remainder of her new books to place on sale in Louisville and Lexington. She arranged for a Texas newspaper to be forwarded to her regularly. She resolved to attain the "tranquillity without indifference" that had sustained her during difficult times in the past.

In Lexington she found the Old Seminary where she had lived so many vivid years reduced now to a heap of rubble. All activities were centered in the beautiful new white-pillared Morrison College set on the rise beyond the College Lot. The Transylvania of Holley's administration was gone almost beyond recognition. Moved by the passing of an era, she pulled from her files the poem she had composed years earlier after fire destroyed the College building. This she sent, with a letter of explanation, to the *Lexington Observer and Kentucky Reporter*, confident that Messrs. Finnell and Wickliffe, the editors of this loyal Whig sheet, would gladly welcome Dr. Holley's widow to their pages. They did so, publishing her communication at the top of a column in the edition of Wednesday, June 4.[49] There could not have been a better way to let people know that she was back in their midst after nearly two years.

The town was slowly recovering from the ravages of the cholera epidemic of the year before, which had taken a ghastly toll. Harriette and William were in their partially completed new home, a large and elegant one built after the first one burned.[50] They lived in more style than formerly, and Mary was pleased when her daughter sent out formal cards for an "At Home," affording her mother an opportunity to mention the Texas book to numerous callers. They all promised to buy copies, and many of them actually did so.

Among the callers were Professor Wilhelm Iucho, the new German music teacher from New York, and his aristocratic American-born wife. He was a talented composer with a list of published titles to his credit, including the *Lexington Grand Waltz* that he had just dedicated to Mrs. Henry Clay.[51] Mary showed him some of her own lyrics, and he displayed particular interest in the "Brazos Boat Song."

In midsummer she contributed a few anonymous verses to advertise the Ladies Fair, a local charity bazaar. The lines were a mere trifle but she hoped a few of her friends would recognize their nice literary flavor.

> Come, Gentlemen and Ladies all,
> Who grace this famous city,
> Come now to the Masonic Hall,
> The mart for all things pretty.[52]

It was pleasant, as the months passed, to clip the many favorable notices and reviews of her book on Texas from publications as far apart as Boston and Brazoria. These went into her bulging files.

16. TEXAN SONG
OF LIBERTY
1835-1836

Early in May of 1835, after a long winter of waiting in Kentucky, Mary Holley once more saw the flat Texas shore line and the wide mouth of the Brazos River. When the schooner *San Felipe*, on which she was a passenger, tied up for noonday at the settlement of Quintana she rushed down the gangplank, armed with pencils and pad, to take a sketch of a large, newly completed warehouse. Bent on her task, she was soon drenched with perspiration and almost faint with the heat. The temperature, as she later learned, stood well above eighty degrees in the midday sunshine where she was working, and there was not another soul in sight. Making sure she was protected by her voluminous skirts, she deftly removed her heavy stockings and stuffed them in her reticule. Then she resolutely finished the drawing and made careful notes about some swarthy sailors who were tinkering with the windlass for the vessel's long haul up the river. She had come to Texas to get material for another book, and every minute must be made to count.[1]

Within an hour or so the *San Felipe* proceeded slowly upstream, and after a few miles somebody pointed out to Mary the boat landing used by Peach Point Plantation, which lay back from the river on the west side about ten miles south of Brazoria.[2] The Perrys were already living there in the house Stephen had designed for his sister; and somewhere off in that direction, amid the low-lying clumps of trees, was Mary's gift from him of "two hundred acres of premium land." But he was still far away in Mexico, and without his presence the gift seemed remote, too.

It was the first time she had seen Texas in the spring, and her spirits soared at the sheer beauty of a countryside where bright emerald fields were spangled with multicolored wild flowers beneath a wide, incredibly blue sky.[3] They went on past Brazoria to Columbia, a thriving new town. Here Henry was waiting with horses for them to ride up the west side of the river to the Bolivar ferry, where the boat would deposit

Mary's luggage on its way. This welcome diversion gave her a chance to see how the country was settling up, and to stop for an hour with the Phelpses, now established at Orozimbo Plantation just across from Henry's place. Dr. Phelps lived in true Southern planter style in a comfortable house set within a grove of trees and surrounded by broad acres of cotton, already thick and green.[4]

After a hearty tea and exchanges of promises to see much of each other during her stay, Mary and her brother rode on to the river and crossed over in a skiff to Bolivar, swimming their horses as they went. Even before they pushed off they could see Henry's three sons standing on the opposite bank waving to them. They were pathetically glad to see her, and everybody, including Henry, cried a little for joy and also for sorrow because of the mother and sister who were not there to complete the family circle. When Aunt Mary saw the sorry state of things in the log house under the great live oak, she understood why her brother was determined to have her take his children back to Kentucky with her. Certainly his girls needed someone besides the tenant's wife to look after them, and the boys were also shabby and unkempt.

There was plenty of news about affairs in the Colony. Stephen had been released from the prison in the City of Mexico, where he had been held for a year on a trumped-up political charge, but was still being detained in the vicinity on bail. He was well and in good spirits, according to the last word to reach the Perrys, and hoped to get home soon.[5] He had better be getting back, Henry Austin fumed to his sister, or that precious policy of peaceful adherence to the Mexican government would be defeated by agitators in the Colony like the Wharton brothers from Tennessee. He wondered if she remembered them, and of course she did, recalling both William H. and his younger brother, John A., as students at Transylvania along with General Jackson's nephew. Aristocratic, ambitious young hotheads they had been in those days, and she doubted that they had changed much.[6]

Henry was working hard for Stephen's conservative policies, and was getting fine cooperation from a young surveyor named Gail Borden, who had taken over the work of the Colony's Land Office in San Felipe, which was piling up because of the Empresario's absence and his secretary's neglect.[7] Henry kept an eye on what went on at the office because he was busily acquiring additional land by going "in cahoots" with new settlers, that is, by advancing their first fees for a share of their allotments. Along with all his other projects he was now a practicing attorney, having memorized the principles of law during his years at sea.

No household duties tied Mary down on this trip to Bolivar. Sketch pad and notebook in hand, she walked abroad to her heart's content, making notes on the handsome dahlias and stellaria, the huge geraniums, the mimosa and passion flowers that flourished in the rich Brazos Valley soil. She personally set out some rose slips in her brother's yard, some that she had brought all the way from her daughter's garden in Kentucky. Henry talked at times of selling the place and had even advertised it once in the papers,[8] but she planted the roses just the same. She liked to make a flower bed wherever she lived.

Good weather permitted her also to go visiting in the "neighborhood," which usually meant across the river to Orozimbo. There the trees and shrubs already rivalled those at Mr. Bussey's place in Roxbury. How much more luxuriantly everything grows in Texas than to the East, she noted, as she made sketches of the Phelps house and the spreading live oaks. And while Mrs. Phelps could not set a table here on the frontier to equal Colonel Meade's at Chaumiere du Prairie, her guests fared extremely well. Any day in the week the colored butler served a noonday dinner of venison steaks, Yankee pickled pork, and rabbit soup, garnished with spring lettuce and snap beans and new potatoes.

Mary would have liked to travel more widely than just around the neighborhood. She wanted to accompany her brother on one of his trips to San Felipe to see about getting some "cahoots" land for herself, and to talk with Gail Borden, who had issued a prospectus for a newspaper, one which would very certainly support Colonel Austin's policies. She did not get to San Felipe but she arranged for the *Telegraph and Texas Register* to be sent to her when it began to appear.[9]

She wanted to visit Peach Point on this trip in order to see Emily and James Perry; and she would have enjoyed the horse racing at Columbia and the annual grand ball at Velasco on the Fourth of July, had not her visit been cut short by Henry's anxiety for her to be off to Kentucky with his children. He was apprehensive about their health during the summer months when the fever was prevalent, and about the likelihood of armed conflict. He suddenly decided that they should take the *San Felipe* to New Orleans in mid-June, and so they did. She had not accomplished much research for her new book on this second visit, but her brother's insistence left her no choice other than to make a home for his motherless children in Kentucky.

At the mouth of the Brazos the schooner was delayed long enough for Mary to fulfill at least one of her wishes. While they waited Mrs. Perry came down from Peach Point to call on her in her stateroom on the *San Felipe*. The two cousins fell into easy conversation, and soon they were strolling up and down the beach in the afternoon sunshine, talking about all the many things they had in common. Emily must ask about dear Mrs. Beck, at whose select boarding school in Lexington she had spent several of her childhood years, and Mary must relate how she herself had gone to call on the poor old soul not long since in Cincinnati, to find her in sadly straitened circumstances.[10] They exchanged news of their children, and discussed the education of Henry's young ones. Emily wanted to send her older sons back to school in the States before long.

Mary remembered afterwards that she and Emily Perry spent the evening talking about Emily's brother and family. She did not recall just what they said to each other about Stephen; whether, for example, she mentioned to Emily the arcadia that was to be established on the Brazos or the two hundred acres of premium land promised to her, or whether Emily told her that Stephen was planning to settle down with a wife when he got home. The chances are that both women were a trifle cautious and guarded, speaking chiefly in pleasant generalities. Whatever they actually said, they became friends and remained so through the years. Each had a deep respect for the place the other held in Stephen's affections. And, after all, they were both Austins.

In New Orleans Mrs. Holley took her bedraggled flock of nieces and nephews directly to the house on St. Peter Street in the hope that the Labranche family would not be in residence, and had the good luck to find it empty save for the servants, who stowed the party away in comfortable guest rooms and speedily bustled about in kitchen and dining room. Correspondence with the German Coast revealed no messages from Guatemala as to the whereabouts of Mr. Savage and Horace; and by the end of the month, the travellers were on an upriver boat bound for Kentucky.

Mrs. Holley was resolved that on coming back to Lexington to reside even for a limited time she would live with dignity. The house she leased on Constitution Street was a well-built frame dwelling, which was, by an odd coincidence, within a stone's throw of the big mansion in which she and President Holley had entertained so lavishly when they first arrived in the town.[11] She liked being situated within five or six minutes walk of her daughter's residence and also near the post office and the old College Lot, near which many of her friends resided. Common sense should have told her that the thousand dollars a year which her brother had promised her for keeping his children was not enough to support them, even frugally, let alone in such ample style; but she was never practical about money matters, and just now she was in an optimistic mood over the prospect that the Texas land would make all the Austins rich.

Her new home had a comfortable stone-flagged porch at the side, opening into a parlor large enough for her pianoforte and for some of the other furniture that Harriette had been keeping. She brought over a few books from Elmwood, too, and innumerable files of papers and letters. She had amassed considerable material for her next literary project but she needed to go through it and sort it. Far more than her furniture or jewelry or even her leagues of land, these letters and verses and clippings were the legacy she meant to leave to her descendants. Her published books, of course, belonged to the world.

The upstairs of the house took care very nicely of Henrietta and Emily, almost young ladies now, and Edward and James and little Henry, who was eight, with a spare room or two besides. Nearby was the new city school, which would do for the boys until funds were available for better education. For help with the kitchen and servants Mary leaned heavily on the Brands, who were generous and practical. They welcomed the young Austins as if they had known them always.

William Brand had by now assumed active charge of the family interests, even to supervising a large breeding farm where the famous mare, Lady Adams, and her foals grazed on rich bluegrass pastures.[12] This business arrangement left William's remarkable father free to devote his later years to supporting Henry Clay's political ambitions, to serving as trustee for the Lunatic Asylum, first of its kind in the West, and to pursuing all sorts of other good works, public and private. His eldest son was following in his footsteps as director of a bank and of the new railroad being built from Lexington to Frankfort, and as trustee of Transylvania and vestryman of Christ Church. Harriette was absorbed in her home and children, and was becoming, so her mother thought, altogether too much the devoted slave of her husband.

Mary was sincerely fond of all the Brands and proud of the connection; but her son-in-law, who was more of a Scotsman than his father, took life so seriously and neglected so many interesting possibilities offered by his wealth that she thought him somewhat dull. Knowing that she could rely upon his solid protection when she needed it, she began to take his goodness for granted and to impose upon him at times. As she saw it, such demands were made only upon her daughter; but in the end it was always William who helped her.

Once properly settled, Mrs. Holley looked about her at the changes in Lexington. They were not very marked and, on the whole, were agreeable to her. The University had got rid of Mr. Peers and his "hobby Pestalozzianism"—she was sorry for his departure—but she approved of the new president, an Episcopal clergyman from Connecticut, whose administration reminded a local newspaper of the "days of prosperity under the talented Holley."[13]

Politically, the community was still Mr. Clay's bailiwick. Loyal Whigs like John Brand and Robert Todd believed that Harry of the West would yet be President of the United States, if not this coming year, then in '40 or '44. In Kentucky neither political party had taken a strong stand regarding Texas, but the issue regarding slavery was already sharply drawn between the moderates like Clay, who supported a recent state law banning the slave trade, and the Democrats like Robert Wickliffe, who opposed the law.

The most valuable addition to the life of the town, to Mrs. Holley's way of thinking, was the *Intelligencer*, a Whig sheet edited by two alert and intelligent young men, both from New England. Julius Clarke,[14] the more scholarly, had been Harriette's history teacher at Professor Dunham's School. The other editor, Edwin Bryant,[15] had come from Massachusetts as a boy, attended Transylvania briefly, and begun his career in journalism down in Louisville under the influential Clay editor, George D. Prentice. He was the politician for the paper. Julius, studious and sober, was less popular than his partner but he also was active in all sorts of public-spirited enterprises. He was a captain in the Rifle guards and president of the Young Men's Temperance Society; he was interested in the Colonization Society, of which Mr. Clay was a national figure, and in the Anti-Gambling Society, of which Mr. Clay was not considered a supporter. Under the firm name of J. Clarke & Co., Printers, Julius published books and pamphlets such as the *Transylvania Journal of Medicine* as well as horse bills and every description of job work.

It was a brisk little walk from Constitution Street to the office of the *Intelligencer* on Hunt's Row, but Mrs. Holley defied the summer heat to step down there not long after her return to town. There she could learn what the intellectuals of the town had been doing while she was away. For example, her friend, Professor Iucho, had delivered an impressive address before the local Lyceum on "The Dignity of Sacred Music."[16] It was remarkable that Wilhelm spoke English so fluently and intelligibly. She heard, too, about the Whig stand on national issues.

When she found that the editors of the *Intelligencer* were aware of the political importance of Texas to the United States and appreciative of her first-hand knowledge of the situation, she promised to give them the benefit of her direct contacts with the Austin Colony. Soon she discussed with them her plan for a second book on the subject. Julius Clarke gave her good advice, and his orderly mind and good scholarship assisted her in outlining a more solid and extensive treatment of Texas than her first one had been. Most important of all, he engaged to publish the book for her. With this good turn of events, she had reason to believe that her coming back to Kentucky was providential.

Her literary labors were unavoidably interrupted by numerous distractions. Henry's children had to be completely outfitted, especially the girls, who had not even one proper dress to wear to church. The Brands were expecting another child in midwinter and so Harriette needed her time and attention. Calls were exchanged with old friends, sometimes chiefly to learn of all the births and marriages and deaths among the Hunts or the Chinns, and again to admire Maria Gratz' elegant clothes that Benjamin's sister Rebecca had brought her from Philadelphia—turbans and walking dresses with capes to match—and to meet that famous lady in person and discover her to be as interesting as all reports had declared.[17]

She saw something of Wilhelm Iucho that summer. He came to the house to try out her pianoforte and departed with the loan of a Haydn sonata. Ere long he asked permission to dedicate to her his newest composition, a pretty air without words, which he deemed appropriate to publish in her honor. It was to be called "Lady, do not bid me sing,"[18] and the charming title may well have originated in the conversations about music in the parlor on Constitution Street. Mary was pleased at the compliment, and rightly so. Iucho was a popular composer in the East as well as in Kentucky.

In spite of such interruptions she worked regularly at her desk for some part of each day, shutting the door of her room and putting on the eyeglasses she used now for close work. It was difficult to write the story of Texas without knowing what Stephen Austin's views would be upon his return from Mexico, but she took Julius Clarke's advice and began with orderly chapters on the geography, the bays and rivers, and the products of the region. She intended this new book to be serious history and exposition without the light touches and personal experiences of her earlier travel book. A map was absolutely necessary, and she decided to use Tanner's latest edition of Stephen's official one, with a few extra place names which she herself probably wrote into the copy she sent to Philadelphia. This time she wanted the map colored in order to show the various land grants, with the Austin Colony a bright yellow in the center of Texas. She ordered two thousand of them run off, in the hope that John Phelps Austin would again stand good for them until the book paid off.[19]

She was undertaking this third publishing venture on her own financial responsibility. Henry had sent her no additional money for household expenses, and soon there would be printer's bills to pay. Somewhat anxiously she inserted an advertisement in the *Kentucky Gazette* offering to sell half of her Dickson's Creek land:

The above tract was selected for the proprietor by persons familiar with every league in the Colony—it consists of a mixture of prairie and timbered land, and is the finest that can be, for the cultivation of Cotton or Sugar, all conditions having been fulfilled, and expenses paid.[20]

Although the advertisement ran for several issues, no purchasers appeared. The town was absorbed in watching "that stupendous Aerial Ship, *Star of the West*," as it inflated for two hours and then ascended into the skies. Children and servants could enter the enclosure for half price, only fifty cents, and thereby make sure that a dog really was taken aloft and dropped in a parachute.[21] Mary probably paid the full dollar to see it for herself.

The hot summer months passed slowly, and about the first of September came the long-awaited letter from Stephen. He wrote from New Orleans on August 21, 1835, to say that he was at last back in the States and on his way to Texas. As she broke the seal her hand must have trembled a little at the thought of what he would have to say to her after this interval. His absence of more than two years had separated them with cruel completeness, and her scanty news of him had come through roundabout channels, such as newspaper reprints of his official letters to the colonists or word that he had borrowed five hundred dollars from the Dalls of Baltimore to tide him over during his stay in Mexico City.[22] A single glance at the closely written sheets told her that the bond between them was unbroken:

My dear cousin: I am, as you will see by the date, once more in the land of my birth, and of *freedom*—a word I can well appreciate. I shall leave here in a day or two for Texas. I wished to have taken a trip up the river, and thence to the north but shall have to defer it until spring. . . .

It is evident that the best interests of the United States require that Texas should be effectually, and fully, Americanized—that is, settled by a population that will harmonize with their neighbors on the *East*, in language, political principles, common origin, sympathy, and even interest. Texas must be a slave country. It is no longer a matter of doubt . . . Being fully Americanized under the Mexican flag would be the same thing in effect, and ultimate result, as coming under the United States flag.

She must have read that part over again to be absolutely sure of its meaning. Was Stephen now giving up his personal opposition to slavery in order to strengthen his Colony? Yes, that was clearly his meaning. As always, his Colony came first with him, even before his personal ideals and, as she had long ago realized, before his own dreams of love and happiness. But as she read on down the page the color rose in her cheeks. He was asking for her help the moment his foot touched the soil of the States. He still needed her:

A great immigration from Kentucky, Tennessee, etc., each man with his rifle or musket, would be of great use to us—very great indeed . . .

To conclude, I wish a great immigration from Kentucky, Tennessee, *everywhere*, passports or no passports, *any* how . . . This fall and winter will fix our fate—a great immigration will settle the question.

S. F. AUSTIN[23]

After so long a separation he was once more confiding his plans and policies to her as freely as if it were only yesterday that they had talked for hours on end at Bolivar House. He made no mention of their arcadia, and spoke of seeing her only as a hope deferred. He wrote as a man completely dedicated to his duty. His letter was essentially a call to her to use her pen and influence for Texas, and pronto, as he might have said in one of his infrequent attempts at gaiety.

She got down to the *Intelligencer* office with the news that Colonel Austin had arrived in New Orleans barely in time for the item to be inserted on the editorial page for the issue of Tuesday, September 1. The editors were gladly using all the Texas items she brought them, having just published her newsy letter from a lady in Brazoria who painted an optimistic picture of life there. The names were left blank, as was customary, but any reader whose opinion Mrs. Holley valued could recognize the communication as one to her from her important connections in Texas, especially the nice bit about a party of visitors who dined at Bolivar House and praised her roses as they drank a toast to "Absent Friends."[24] She did not, of course, furnish the editors a full copy of Stephen's New Orleans letter with its revelation of his new policies, although he had not cautioned her that it was confidential. He trusted her discretion, and with good reason.

There was much about Texas in all the Lexington newspapers from then on, mostly copied from the New Orleans press. Bit by bit the exciting events there were unfolded to their impatient historian, who pieced them together in a parlor more than a thousand miles away. Henry, who now resided in Brazoria in the midst of the action, wrote her from time to time, his pen racing with excitement. On September 10, he dashed off a vivid description of events:

Stephen has at last arrived. I rode all night through the swamp and rain to meet him at Perry's. His arrival unites all parties . . . We Republicans have striven for quiet till we learned the true Mexican Government intentions. . . . We meet in middle ground, stand on our constitutional rights, and reject the Centralists.

Then he went on to describe the grand ball given at Mrs. Jane Long's tavern in Brazoria in honor of Austin's return.

There were 60 covers and the tables were three times filled by men alone. In the evening the long room was filled to a jam; at least 60 or 80 ladies who danced the sun up and the Oyster Creek girls would not have quit then had not the room been wanted for breakfast—you never saw such enthusiasm . . . Stephen left last night for San Felipe. You ought to receive with this the newspapers and the handbill giving all particulars.[25]

Mary learned the "particulars" when the Texas papers arrived to supplement the news she had been gathering from other sources. During the period of Austin's imprisonment, the so-called "liberal" Mexican party under General Santa Anna had abandoned the Republican principles of the Constitution of 1824 and become a "Centralist" dictatorship under the General. Harsh regulations were issued to the Texan colonists, with orders for the arrest of those who resisted. Citizens met in various towns to declare that they would not submit to such tyranny, and some to ask for a "consultation" of all Texans. Many leaders emerged: the Wharton brothers, Sam Houston, Jim Bowie, Ben Milam, William Travis, David G. Burnet, and Lorenzo de Zavala, a prominent Mexican liberal who sided with the Texans. But no one of them commanded the loyalty of all the colonists, who were waiting to make up their minds until the Empresario got home.

In his "keynote speech" at the dinner in Brazoria soon after his return, Stephen Austin united them under his leadership and guided them to a crucial decision in their relationship with Mexico: "The constitutional rights and the security and peace of Texas—they ought to be maintained; and jeopardized as they now are they demand a general consultation of the people."[26] With these words the die was cast. He was directing his people to organize themselves against the ruling government of Mexico. The speech represented a great decision on his own part, one which he apparently had made during his imprisonment. He was abandoning his duty and loyalty to the Mexican government for the good of Texas, and submitting the course of the future to the will of its people.

Mary Holley grasped the significance of this keynote address although she read it in newspapers that were many weeks old. His New Orleans letter had revealed to her that he knew when he returned to Texas that separation from Mexico was all but inevitable. The speech showed him trying to make sure that separation came about by lawful means and, if possible, without violence.

In the perilous months after this speech Stephen Austin proved himself as competent a leader in war as he had been in peace. He was chairman of the committee that invited a general consultation to be held in San Felipe as soon as possible, and he immediately assumed responsibility for organizing volunteer companies for defense if the Mexican government sent troops to enforce its demands. Before the consultation could assemble to be "the voice of all Texas," as Austin's committee desired, a force of Mexican soldiers landed on the coast to reinforce the troops at San Antonio in subjugating the Texans. From San Felipe Stephen Austin issued a circular to the people of Texas: "War is our only resource—there is no other remedy but to defend our rights, our country and ourselves by force of arms!"[27] The volunteers chose him as commander-in-chief of the forces that started at once toward San Antonio to check the enemy. He selected for his officers many of those hotheads he had been restraining in his vain effort to avoid this conflict —West Pointer James Fannin, famous Jim Bowie, rugged Ben Milam, and the gallant Whartons. Under his diplomatic leadership his capable subordinates won a series of small battles and confined the numerically superior Mexicans within the fortifications of San Antonio.

How like Stephen all this had turned out to be, thought Mary, as she pored over the published accounts and tried to trace the routes on her map. Once he felt that it was right for Texas to defend itself, he had dedicated himself wholly to the struggle in spite of the poor health he had suffered since his imprisonment and his temperamental aversion to warfare. In the volunteer army with him were his young nephews, William Joel and Moses Austin Bryan, sons of Emily Perry by her first marriage.[28] When the Consultation finally assembled at San Felipe on November 3, General Austin remained with the army, but despatched to the meeting a formal communication setting forth the military situation and the critical need for men and supplies. In order to expedite the raising of funds for public necessity he authorized the November Consultation to mortgage his entire personal estate.

Most of these facts were in the public print before Mary heard again from Henry at about the end of the year. Texas was in the midst of a revolution, he wrote her, and union and harmony with the Mexican government were no longer possible. Stephen was in command of four thousand men deployed before San Antonio—but surely Mary knew her brother well enough to allow for exaggeration at this point. And, the letter continued, a norther was raging that was cold enough to freeze Indians![29]

Henry added that since absolutely no land deals were being made in these confused times, he had no money to remit to her; but he hoped to send her sufficient funds early in the coming year. He never was concerned, then or later, that she was compelled to borrow money in Lexington to maintain his family. Nor did she herself worry greatly over the matter at this particular season. As long as her son was in Guatemala he was no expense to her; and she hoped to stave off her creditors, with the help of William Brand's backing, until she could realize a profit on her book. If worst came to worst, she could take a boarder or two to occupy the upstairs rooms.

No historian of a new nation was ever more handicapped by remoteness from the scene of events. As winter weather settled down over the whole country, with snow and ice making roads impassable in the Ohio Valley, the stages into Lexington and even the locomotive mail car from Frankfort were so delayed that the items in the local papers delivered by shivering carriers at her door were weeks behind. The Texas publications were later still in reaching her. She found it hard to continue writing even the descriptive and historical chapters without knowing what fate had befallen Stephen's little army before San Antonio. Yet she kept doggedly to her task, artfully inserting Mr. Savage's "Description of a Nopalade" to fill out her discussion of natural history, and including in the chapter on Indians an exciting account of the famous fight at San Saba by one of the Bowie brothers that she probably extracted from a Philadelphia periodical.[30]

She covered hundreds of pages with neat, fine script; then she sewed the long sheets together by chapters and stacked them on the shelves of the little closet in the hallway by her bedroom door. She was determined that Stephen should have this new book to encourage immigration no matter how her eyes burned from overwork and her fingers stiffened. It must be published as soon as she could deliver the manuscript to Julius Clarke's printers, even if at the last moment the forms had to be unlocked to add one more battle.

Eventually the official reports of the November Consultation at San Felipe appeared in the Texas newspapers, telling that the delegates had voted to make Texas a Provisional State of Mexico, but only on condition that it be governed in accordance with the Constitution of 1824. Another consultation or convention was called for the coming first of March to decide upon future action. All this was in complete defiance of the Centralist Government in Mexico City; and Article 5 of the Consultation's "Solemn Declaration" set forth the right of Texas to declare its independence if it saw fit. General Austin, Dr. Archer, and William H. Wharton were named commissioners from the Provisional State to the United States to present the case of Texas and obtain assistance. Already volunteers were streaming from all sections to the aid of Texas, but the object of the mission was to obtain not only soldiers but the financial credit and political support necessary for an independent state. In line with Austin's planning, the Consultation had moved cautiously but inevitably toward independence.

The news about the Consultation that chiefly caught the eye of readers in the States was the choice of Sam Houston as major general of the Texas armies, with the responsibility for combatting a full-scale invasion which was reportedly coming from Mexico. He had resided for two or three years in East Texas and early became prominent as an advocate of independence.

The name of Houston was well known to Mrs. Holley. At the time of her visit to Nashville a dozen years earlier he had been a rising attorney about to be elected to the United States Congress as one of Jackson's protégés.[31] His widely publicized domestic unhappiness and his years spent among the Indian tribes made him seem to her an unlikely rival to challenge Austin's claim as the father of Texas no matter what military eminence he attained. The hero of her history was, of course, Stephen Austin, and she waxed eloquent in composing a full biographical chapter about him:

When, in the progress of years, the state of Texas shall take her place among the powerful empires of the American continent, her citizens will doubtless regard Gen. Austin as their patriarch, and children will be taught to hold his name in reverence; for though there have been many other respectable men engaged in the work of colonization, yet Gen. Austin began the work, and was the first to open the wilderness. All the subsequent labour of others has been comparatively easy.[32]

As she paused to read this paragraph over a time or two, she may well have mused that she was already keeping the promise made to him when they were together that some day she would write his biography.

Once again settled into the routine of working at her desk, Mary's mind teemed with other literary projects also. Some were in lighter vein. For example, when the *Kentucky Gazette* announced its annual competition for the New-Year's ode customarily distributed by the carriers in return for a seasonal gift, she entered a sprightly poem in which she managed to crowd all sorts of diverse themes—a plea for Texas, her dislike of religious orthodoxy, and a touch of romantic optimism. She overloaded the verses intended for a newsboy's handbill with such a burden of ideas that the editor awarded the first prize of a year's subscription to the *Gazette* to the mediocre verses of another contestant, but thought it diplomatic to publish hers also.[33]

Some of her musings were melancholy. A little before Christmas the town was shocked by the death of the Clays' only remaining daughter, Ann, at Woodlands, the Erwins' estate near her parents' home. Mrs. Holley surely rode in the Brands' carriage as part of the long train that accompanied the remains to the vault, and later offered her condolences in person to Lucretia Clay. She had often been a guest in the Erwins' New Orleans home, and the death broke a strand in her friendship with Senator Clay and his wife.

This sadness, and perhaps also the daily sight of the old Hart house next door, brought to mind that first winter when President Holley had opened his home and his heart to Lexington. During the gloomy, shut-in days of winter an ivory miniature of her husband, which she always kept close at hand, seemed verily to speak to her. She felt compelled to answer, and on New Year's Day, that anniversary which she commemorated anew with each passing year, she put her reply into words. Her answer was a poem, one of her most moving ones:

To My Husband's Miniature
on New Year's Day, 1836

Friend of my youth, I see thee now
In spring-like freshness still before me,
Calm dignity upon thy brow—
And love: Oh, let me still adore thee!

The "happy year," to all so gay,
Returning brings no joy to me;
It is—it is my wedding day;
He lies beneath the dark blue sea.

MARY[34]

In this mature period of her life Mary Austin Holley possessed the resources of past and future alike. She treasured the memories of earlier days, sad and happy, just as she liked to leaf through her files of old letters and records; and her youthful love and passion for Horace Holley, dead almost ten years, continued to enrich her literary powers. Likewise she was inspired by her devotion to Stephen Austin and his Texas cause. Concentrating on chapter after chapter of historical writing cleared her mind and lifted her heart. The future took on meaning and hope each time he called upon her to join him in his "bright visions."

She drove herself hard at her many tasks, and for diversion ventured out in the cold to hear her old friend, Dr. Caldwell, deliver his inaugural address as president of the College of Physicians and Surgeons in the University chapel on a Tuesday morning early in February.[35] She must surely have borrowed her daughter's carriage and driver for such occasions and for frequent trips back and forth between their houses when Harriette's little daughter was born in the dead of winter.[36]

Suddenly all Texas seemed to be at her doorstep. On the heels of a packet of Gail Borden's papers full of critical news, especially concerning the forthcoming Convention on March 1 to set up a permanent government for Texas, came a letter from General Austin, dated January 7 and posted from New Orleans:

I had hoped to have the pleasure of seeing you soon, but it is not certain, as I may not be able to visit Lexington until I return from the Eastward as we are very much pressed for time. I am bound to Washington, New York, etc., in company with Doctor B. T. Archer, and W. H. Wharton, Esq. We are commissioners for the Texas Government. Our principal object is to raise money, means, and men to sustain our cause.

One item in the letter was of paramount importance to her. *Stephen was on his way to Kentucky.* To be sure, he was cautiously warning her that he was not absolutely certain that he could see her. When, indeed, had

Stephen ever put pleasure first? She had learned in her younger days to discount Horace's too optimistic plans; but for Stephen to say he *might* do something was the same as a promise. She was very sure that he would come to Lexington.

Once she had grasped the all-important fact of his nearness, there was much else in the letter to excite her: "The war for Liberty goes on prosperously, so far, in Texas. It must, and will, end in *Independence* —a Declaration will be made in March." She had been right in thinking that Stephen had concluded his long debate with himself about divided loyalties, and had joined the Texas war party. He was declaring for Independence:

When I left Texas there was not an enemy within our limits, nor east of the River Bravo del Norte. Gen. Santanna, however, is marching on in person with all the force he can collect to *annihilate* us. We have no fears, but we must be ready for him. We need all the aid we can get in men and money, provisions, arms and ammunition.

Large contributions have been made in the United States for the extension of Christianity over the South Sea Islands by means of Missionary Societies. Is not our cause quite as important and sacred?

This part of his letter appealed to her, the thought of the Texas cause as a religious crusade. She had said something like that in her "carrier's ode," and the idea deserved to be expanded. She was nodding her approval as she read on further in the letter:

We shall stop one day in Louisville. I would like very much to visit Lexington. Some of my cherished schoolmates and companions of happy days still reside there: John McCalla, Pierce Butler, the Todds, etc.: please remember me to them. . . .

I have written hastily and must close, for I am at the end of my paper, but not at the end of the subject. It is a copious one, and I am perhaps rather enthusiastic in the view I take of it. My whole heart and soul is devoted to it. I am well.

S.F.A.[37]

He had no need to add that word about his devotion to his Colony. She knew that already. Texas was his vocation, as writing was hers.

She put on her eyeglasses for the fine print in her almanac to calculate his whereabouts. It was now the middle of February, and he must already be in Nashville or, more likely, on his way down the Cumberland to where it flowed into the Ohio in the old Indian country. She remembered exactly the gloomy, wooded shores where his steamboat would turn upstream into the Ohio, at a tiny settlement where Mr. Jefferson's sister and her family had resided for a time, as had been told her on various trips down the river. Once in the Ohio, it ought not take long for the Commissioners to come up to the Falls and the town of Louisville.

She slipped and slid on the icy sidewalks to share her news with the *Intelligencer* office. The editors had already received a report that the Texas Commissioners were being detained in the lower Ohio by heavy ice, and the exciting news that General Austin would visit Lexington must certainly be given to the public immediately.

Julius Clarke had an editorial on Texas already in type for the next issue, but he wrote another emphasizing the General's impending visit to the community. Following Austin's letter closely, and prompted by Mrs. Holley's eloquence, he penned a special appeal for aid and emigrants to the young state. She probably faced him across his cluttered desk, all but dictating such sentences in his article as "The example of the benevolent, who send men, money, friends, and kindred to the Pacific Isles . . . is adduced as an argument for removal to Texas." Clarke ran the new article over his usual signature and put it at the head of the editorial column on Friday, February 19; and, lest good typesetting go to waste, followed it with the other one he had done previously.[38] This Texas material Mrs. Holley brought to the office was not only a journalistic *coup* but also good advertising for her book that he had agreed to publish.

In giving the first notice of Austin's visit to the *Intelligencer*, Mary was indulging in justifiable partiality to her friends and future publishers; but when another message came from him, written in Nashville on February 16, she ignored private considerations and furnished all three of the local papers with complete copies simultaneously. The letter began "Dear Cousin;" and it ended "Yours, S. F. Austin."[39] There was no longer any reason for ladylike concealment of her important connection with the movement to aid Texas.

In his letter from Nashville Stephen wrote that the ladies there had "offered to furnish the means of arming and transporting a Company of Volunteers to Texas," calling this an act of "patriotism worthy of imitation." Mrs. Holley counted his words a suggestion to her to organize the ladies of Lexington, and resolved to ask his advice about how to do so when she saw him.

Before his arrival she set about rousing interest in his visit, first among his old friends, and then among younger men who might be persuaded to assist in any way. Edwin Bryant was a help in pointing out the political influences that affected the issue, and warning her that the Clay followers would be wary of being too openly enthusiastic about Texas. That meant that Austin could hope for support chiefly from Jacksonian Democrats like General McCalla and old Postmaster Ficklin, one-time friend of Moses Austin.

Ten inches of snow blanketed the region at the end of February, causing several days of anxious waiting even after the *Intelligencer* announced that the distinguished visitor was "expected hourly." He finally arrived on Saturday, March 12.[40] He was alone, and seemed weary after spending about fifteen hours on the ninety miles of icy road from Louisville to Lexington. Both he and Wharton had been ill of influenza in Nashville, and Wharton had remained there to recuperate. General Austin had come on to Louisville, accompanied by Dr. Archer, and had stayed there longer than he intended in order to deliver a formal address in defense of the Texas cause to a large and enthusiastic audience of ladies and gentlemen in one of the city's prominent churches on the preceding Monday. The doctor had gone on by boat to Cincinnati to await Austin's arrival so that they could resume their journey together to the East. These unavoidable delays were putting the Commissioners far behind their schedule, and Austin could ill afford the time and strength which this detour to Lexington cost him. He evidently wanted very much to see Mary Holley.

Before her comfortable fire in the parlor on Constitution Street he relaxed his thin, tired body for the first time in months. Hot, succulent food and a little wine restored his energy, while the melodies Mary played for him made him feel that he was truly in the Lexington of his happy memories. But there was even more for the two of them to talk about than at Bolivar House, and far less time. He was committed to be in Cincinnati on Monday, and to get there would mean another fifteen-hour journey by coach.

He remembered Henry's children and greeted them affectionately. He had actually considered bringing along his nephew Moses on this trip as a secretary. He approved his sister Emily's plan to put her older children in school in the States and asked Mrs. Holley to recommend some good institution in Lexington. Then they talked about her Texas book that he had helped her to write—they had not been together since its publication—and he told her how he had seen it for the first time in a Spanish translation which they showed him in the Mexican prison. It was a version made for the President of Mexico, who had obtained from it most of his knowledge of Texas. She privately resolved to include that interesting episode in her new book if she had to add a footnote somewhere.[41]

The General had with him the carefully prepared manuscript of his Louisville address. She read it eagerly, finding it to be a full statement of his slowly developed plans for the Austin Colony and for Texas as a whole. It was a defense, if one were needed, for his cautious policies during the early years, and proof of his self-sacrificing courage in the present crisis. The two of them agreed that the address must be published at once in the Kentucky newspapers, and she asked that she be allowed to include it in her new history of Texas.[42] Confident that she would handle the matter properly, he turned the manuscript over to her.

They discussed at length the best way to have the ladies of Lexington sponsor a company of volunteers for Texas, and he sketched a suitable flag for it. He proposed an elaborate sort of banner, with a Union Jack in the corner for Anglo-Saxon origin, thirteen stripes for descent from the United States, a sun radiating beams of liberty with a head of Washington in its center—this to represent Texas—and a green border for Mexico. The effect was much the same as a complicated design for a Texas flag which he had recently sent to Gail Borden from New Orleans.[43] She declared the flag for the Lexington company to be "historic," and promised that it should accompany the men to Texas. They both liked flags and uniforms and coats-of-arms, although Stephen gravely confessed to a "feeling that heraldry in its full sense was un-American." He had substituted a deer head for the three crosslets on the shield of the Austin arms, he said, "because he was a pioneer."[44]

While Austin was in Lexington he had interviews with numerous citizens, some of whom had previously fostered rallies for the cause of Texas in the community. Postmaster Joseph Ficklin came, as energetic and involved in politics as he had been when he counseled with Stephen's father thirty years earlier; and John McCalla, now General McCalla because of service in the Indian wars, and a power among the Democrats; and Editor Bryant, all of them pledging active support in organizing groups of volunteer soldiers and emigrants in the region.[45] Julius Clarke managed to read the address and obtained permission to publish it as a separate pamphlet. If Robert Todd came to call on Stephen Austin at Constitution Street he was not thereby influenced to make any public contribution to the cause of Texas. However, the two long-time friends may well have had a brief visit and an agreeable conversation about the first Mrs. Todd, whom Austin, too, had known when they were young.[46]

On Sunday evening at a little before nine o'clock the General took his place in the Cincinnati stagecoach and waved goodbye out the window to Mrs. Holley and the rest of the little group who braved the intense cold to see him off. These loyal supporters would spread the enthusiasm which his visit had kindled.

While the Commissioners were winning advocates for their cause portentous events were changing the course of history in faraway Texas. On March 2 the Convention at Washington-on-the-Brazos issued a Declaration of Independence, and four days later the small Texas force that was besieged in the Alamo, a fortified mission on the edge of the town of San Antonio, was attacked and massacred by Santa Anna's army. Together with their leaders, Colonel Travis, Jim Bowie, and David Crockett, a volunteer from Tennessee, the gallant defenders died to the last man. On the very day that Austin was rousing his audience in Louisville, the broken bodies of the Texas soldiers smouldered in heaps outside the walls of the Alamo, where Santa Anna had ordered them to be cast for burning.[47]

Fortunately for Stephen Austin and his cousin the tragic news of the Alamo was delayed during his visit in Lexington by tardy communications, withheld from them long enough for the two to see each other happily face to face for a brief thirty-six hours. The meeting rekindled hope in their own hearts as they joined their efforts for his cause.

Lexington became very conscious of the crisis in Texas. Austin's address appeared in full in two newspapers. News items traced his journey eastward via Cincinnati and Pittsburgh and Baltimore, sometimes quoting excerpts from his letters to Mrs. Holley, though without mentioning her name in the matter.[48] On April 8, the editorial column of the *Intelligencer* urged the "prompt attention of the Ladies of Lexington" to the matter of raising a company for Texas, "a cause equally as deserving as the Hindoo and Hottentot." A week later, when people were shocked into action by the news of the Alamo, a "City and County Meeting for the Cause of Texas" was called for noon of April twentieth at the Court House. All citizens, including the ladies, were requested to attend.[49]

The large crowd that came to the meeting effected a permanent organization for the purpose of sending emigrants and troops, with Edwin Bryant as secretary and General McCalla as one of the moving spirits.

Mrs. Holley was present, having got up a group of ladies to attend, and all but made a speech herself when the visiting Texas officer referred to her book on Texas to prove the high character of his countrymen. Contributions poured in. William Brand and his brother George probably attended the meeting, since they were listed afterwards in the papers as making suitable donations. The names of Mr. John Brand and most of the other old-line Whigs did not appear among the contributors.

The support of Texas raised ticklish political questions, and Mary found that her coworkers were, for the most part, not the men who had defended President Holley during his administration at Transylvania. This alienation from her old friends did not deter her. Without counting the cost to herself, she plunged into the thick of the agitation. During her husband's public controversies she had remained in the background as became a wife. Now, as both landowner and historian of Texas, she was resolved to take an active part in the effort to aid its cause. In private conversation and with her pen she spoke out boldly—as boldly as a lady could—and she would gladly have made public addresses if her sex had been allowed that privilege. The City and County Meeting was such a notable success that she caught the mail the next day with an exuberant letter to Stephen in New York to tell him all about it.[50]

Her personal affairs hardly warranted as cheerful a letter as the one she posted to him. Innumerable annoyances were delaying the work on her book. A few days before the meeting some one entered the house and stole her little French watch with its filigree chain and, worse still, her gold eyeglasses.[51] Her household bills were beginning to worry her. She had received only a few letters from Henry of late, and those were entirely filled with accounts of wartime conditions along the Brazos and how he had personally outfitted his tenants for army service. He sent her no funds at all during such confusion. To help out with expenses she had taken a couple of boarders and was considering renting the house adjoining hers to take others; but that would offer problems also when she had only two servants. Until her book came off the press or Henry sold some land, she would have to pinch pennies.

Many emigrants were enrolling to go to Texas, and the Ladies' Legion and other companies of soldiers were being recruited. Supplies and clothing had to be provided for all of them. More and more people must be drawn into the work in addition to her personal friends, whom she had long since solicited. She put a notice in both the *Gazette* and the *Intelligencer* during the last week in April:

Those ladies who are disposed to devote a portion of their time, and their needles, to the holy cause of the Texans, will please to call at the house of the subscriber, where may be found *materials* for this sacred charity.

M. A. HOLLEY[52]

The materials were all contributed by prominent men, including even John Brand, and the ladies had sewing parties on Wednesday and Saturday afternoons with admirable results. Emily and Henrietta Austin stitched frantically at all hours. By the time the Volunteers were ready to depart the ladies had turned out eighteen shirts, twenty-four pocket handkerchiefs, six collars, eight black shirts, twelve shirt bosoms, three roundabouts, nine hunting shirts, and one mosquito bar, in addition to some other supplies.

There was also the urgent matter of providing a flag for the Ladies' Legion. General McCalla generously donated the staff and spearhead; Mrs. Holley herself purchased the silk material and got young Miss James, a friend of Henrietta's, to paint the design upon it.[53] It required considerable ingenuity to get all the symbols arranged on the field of the banner, but the task was finally accomplished. Mary spent thirty dollars of her own on it, and did not begrudge the extravagance. It was, in a way, Stephen's flag.

In spite of these many conflicting duties the book neared completion. Julius Clarke was immensely helpful, giving her just the kind of criticism she had sought in vain from Orville for her earlier literary ventures. She acknowledged in the preface her obligations to the "distinguished young gentleman who assisted in the compilation and arrangement," without calling him by name.[54] Perhaps, as her publisher, Clarke wished to remain anonymous.

She was forced to give up a few of the good features she had meant to include, such as the special sections on geology and botany which she had vainly tried to obtain from two distinguished naturalists who had visited Texas. Both men, alas, died before she could make contact with them.[55] She realized, moreover, that her historical narrative was incomplete as long as the conflict in Texas was still undecided; but her call for emigrants must be sounded at once if it was to help Stephen. She published a notice of the forthcoming book in the *Intelligencer* on May 6:

TEXAS

In Press, and will shortly be published, and for sale at the bookstores, and at this office, "TEXAS," being a Historical, Geographical, and Descriptive work,

of Three Hundred pages, duodecimo, by
Mrs. Mary Austin Holley
Price $1.50

Within a week came the glorious news of the victory of Sam Houston's Texans at San Jacinto on April 21 and the capture of Santa Anna. Mary's immediate response was an original lyric of triumph. With tears in her eyes, she sang it to a Scottish tune when friends came to share the rejoicing in her parlor. She gave it to the Lexington papers for publication.[56]

Almost immediately Wilhelm Iucho called to praise her poem and asked permission to set it to original music for his New York publishers. He already had a melody in mind, and by leaving out two or three of her stanzas he would make a rousing song, sure to be popular all over the country.

"Ach," he cried, showing her a large paper adorned with flourishes and German script, "but just see how beautiful a sheet music it will become!"

THE TEXAN SONG OF LIBERTY
Written by
Mrs. M. A. Holley
Composed and Dedicated to
GENERAL HOUSTON
by
Wilhelm Iucho

And when she gaily gave her consent he bowed over her hand in full Continental style.

She was in the throes of concluding the last chapter of her history with Houston's official report of the battle of San Jacinto when she received a letter from Stephen postmarked at Maysville on the Ohio River.[57] He was on his way home, and excitingly near to Lexington. Never could there be a more opportune time for him to pay another visit to the city. The emigrants and about four hundred volunteers, fitted out by the citizens at the cost of several thousand dollars, were gathered in the vicinity, restless and eager to start West. There was to be a huge military parade on Friday afternoon, June 3, and a ceremony to present the flag to the Ladies' Legion, which was commanded by a handsome young Captain Postlethwaite. The crowds were getting a little out of hand, chiefly because the commanding officer was not on the ground; and a firm leader was needed to get the expedition off promptly and in good order. Austin's presence would accomplish just that effect.

While she was writing hurriedly to Stephen at Louisville, urging him to come over to Lexington, if only for a day, Mr. Ficklin came to her house, and soon Bryant and General McCalla came, too. The word of Austin's being nearby had got around town. They all felt that if he would make even a short speech at the ceremonies, the party would leave in high spirits and, in all probability, more contributions might be raised. They had worked hard, these Kentucky adherents of the Texan cause, to achieve what Austin had asked of them. His second visit, they thought, would clarify all the arrangements for the emigrants and volunteer soldiers. It would indeed crown the efforts of the Texas sympathizers. They hoped—or, at least Mary Holley hoped—up to the last moment that he might arrive for the festivities.

Austin did not come to Lexington, but the flag presentation in the late afternoon on the lawn in front of the Hart house was a notable occasion anyway, and was witnessed by an overflowing crowd. The shining banner was officially presented by Henrietta Austin in a dramatic speech which her aunt had written for her:

GENTLEMEN VOLUNTEERS,—At the request of my aunt, Mrs. Holley, and in the name of my country, I present you a Flag, designed by General Austin. . . . Take this flag, gentlemen; go plant it in the Land of Flowers, the land of the *myrtle* and the *vine*, the *bay* and the *holly*, our beautiful Texas. There let it take immortal root and reach the skies![58]

Henrietta's high young voice quavered a little as she tried to make all the emphatic points just as she had been instructed; but, according to the long account in a local newspaper, her "animating address" was well delivered. One of the officers of the Legion accepted the flag from her with "emotions of deepest sensibility" and on behalf of the volunteers tendered "to that distinguished Lady, at whose solicitation you present it, and whose name is so intimately identified with the cause of Texas, their liveliest gratitude." Mrs. Holley was pleased with the ceremonies, and consoled herself that it might have been somewhat unreasonable to hope that General Austin could or would have come so far out of his way just for the day. She had learned to accept disappointments without becoming discouraged.

She would herself have advised Stephen to push directly on to Texas if she had known all the circumstances. True, he and the other Commissioners had been successful in obtaining men and money in the United States, but while he had been away, opposing political factions were struggling for control of the new Texas government. Now it was reported that the Mexicans were massing troops on the border for another invasion. He felt that the Republic needed every man to be at his post, especially the Austins. He took the first available boat at Louisville, and all the letters from Lexington were eventually forwarded to New Orleans and on to San Felipe.

The Texas Expedition got off from Lexington the day after the ceremonies, and Mary turned her belated attention to reading galley proof from Clarke's presses. The book, because of numerous additions, was running more than a hundred pages over the original estimate, but Julius stuck to his bargain. All through the month of June Mrs. Holley was in and out of the printing shop, where typesetters argued and the presses banged, making last-minute corrections. She was a perfectionist when it came to reading proof, but it took all her will power to work at her task during the hot summer days.

Just before the Fourth of July her brother Henry paid her an unexpected visit on his way to the Hot Springs in Virginia for his dyspepsia.[59] He wept with feeling when he embraced his children and gave them all the money he could spare for their clothes and other bills, but he made no mention to his sister of relieving her of the responsibility for them.

Henry was brimful of news about Texas, which she shared freely with the visitors who came to the house on Constitution Street. Among them was Wilhelm Iucho, who listened with rapt admiration to his stories of the battle of San Jacinto, including accounts of the heroism of the Texans, especially that of a newcomer from Georgia named Lamar, and the ridiculous cowardice of Santa Anna. A perplexing problem had arisen as to what to do with that infamous prisoner, who was being kept in polite captivity on the Orozimbo Plantation to protect him from the wrath of some of the irate Texans. There was no doubt that Stephen would settle the matter when he got back. Henry liked the proofs of his sister's new book so well that he proposed to send a number of copies to Great Britain at his own expense in order to influence public opinion there. Then as suddenly as he had come, he was off to drink the waters at the Springs.

The book was offered for sale by the middle of July as a sturdy volume of four hundred and ten pages bound in tan cloth and bearing a red-leather label on the spine lettered in gold *Mrs. Holley's Texas*. The Lexington papers were complimentary, and a flattering review appeared promptly in the Louisville *Journal*, with one comment that pleased her especially: "Mrs. Holley's pen has lost none of its sprightliness and grace. She is an agreeable writer, adorning every subject and adding an interest to the dryest details."[60]

She forgave the Louisville critic's saying that the typography of the book was "not the neatest specimen of the Western press." In truth *Texas* (1836) was not as well made a book as her two earlier volumes, but the sales were better. Sizable orders came from merchants in Brazoria and Columbia to supply the demand in those places.

The summer season brought family problems as well as literary accomplishments. The Brands lost their two-year-old son, John Samuel, during the hot weather.[61] Henry Austin stopped again on his way back to Texas, somewhat improved in health but very pessimistic over the fiscal state of Texas, and practically without funds himself. And the Texan cause in Kentucky suffered a severe setback when the volunteers came home disgusted at the treatment they alleged they had received. They had gone for a fight with the Mexicans and allotments of free land, but had got neither. They aired their grievances in violent letters to the Louisville and Lexington papers, declaring that even General Austin had neglected them. Editor Bryant championed their cause, and old Mr. Ficklin wrote a sharp personal letter to Stephen Austin about the matter. Kentuckians had supported Texas all the more strongly after their sons were brutally slaughtered at Goliad and the Alamo; but when their volunteers were shabbily received, they became angry and their pride was hurt. The controversy went on in the Kentucky press for the rest of the year 1836. As young Captain Postlethwaite of the Ladies' Legion expressed it, "We confess we have lost some of the good opinion we had of Texan affairs."[62]

Mrs. Holley carefully avoided becoming involved in this fiasco. Whatever had occurred about land grants for the Kentucky recruits, she felt sure that it was not Stephen's fault. He wrote her in the fall that although he had been ill again all else was going well, and bade her pay no attention to troublesome reports. He mentioned to her that he had "accepted and entered upon the office of Secretary of State" of the new Republic of Texas.[63] She already knew through the papers that Sam Houston had defeated him for the office of president and had immediately offered him this place in the Cabinet.

Stephen was apparently devoting his whole energy to official correspondence, as she learned when Mr. Ficklin showed her a long communication which Austin had written to him at about this same time.[64] The object of the letter was to explain courteously to his "old and esteemed and dearly cherished friends" in Lexington the case of the Kentucky volunteers so far as he himself had had anything to do with it. He insisted that when he was in Kentucky that he had not promised them both land and bounties and that he had not purposely neglected them upon their arrival in Texas after the fighting was over. He explained, too, his part in preventing the Texans from taking violent measures against Santa Anna.

Mary asked Mr. Ficklin for permission to copy this letter so that she could put it in her files. She wanted no part of the controversy of the volunteers, but she must be prepared to defend Stephen. She approved of his acceptance of the post as secretary of state. In spite of his poor health he was the most competent man in the new nation to carry on diplomatic negotiations with foreign powers, and Houston had been wise to offer the position to him. Feeling that her pen and her extensive personal connections could be far more helpful to Stephen and to Texas in Washington City than on the remote frontier, she was eager to have a share in his efforts to secure first recognition and then perhaps annexation for the new government.

Her next task was to use all her influence to get the Kentucky Legislature to pass resolutions favoring the recognition of Texas as an independent nation. Working with ladylike indirection she interviewed first one and then another of the Democratic leaders known to favor recognition, and eventually even joined in some of their political consultations.

Meanwhile she was putting her house in order to extend her field of operations beyond Lexington if need be. Henry at last sent her some money for expenses, with a reassuring message that Stephen had sold two leagues of his own land and bade him see that Mary "had what she needed." Henry also wrote that the new book was in great demand in Texas, where it had been quoted on the floor of the Congress as better than any speech on the subject.[65] Characteristically, as soon as the financial strain eased up a little Mary sent her niece Emily on a visit to relatives in New York, put Edward Austin in the excellent Catholic school for boys in Bardstown, and indulged herself in the purchase of a good colored woman as a personal maid and additional household help. With Amy snugly installed in a little room over the kitchen, her mistress could turn her back on the house without having her jewelry stolen. She could also be freer to work for the passage of the Resolutions on Texas Independence.

Mrs. Holley spent several days in Frankfort during the December term of the Legislature, and put to the test her ability in political maneuvering. First she persuaded a group of prominent ladies to attend the sessions in order to crowd the chambers with enthusiastic partisans. At suitable intervals she appeared in the hotel waiting rooms and in the parlors of the town, furnishing information about Texas, either from her own book or from the late papers. She preferred not to think of herself as "lobbying," a vulgar new word used to describe politicians, but she was proud of her achievements. The lower house passed "Mrs. Holley's Resolutions," as they were being called, just before it recessed for the Christmas holidays.

She was feeling the exhilaration of success. *The Texan Song of Liberty* was just off the press of Dubois and Bacon in New York, and Mr. Iucho, to avoid controversy, had tactfully omitted the stanza about the Lexington Volunteers.[66] This recognition of her literary position gratified her, and, as if to justify it, she sent a manuscript poem from her files to the editors of the *Intelligencer* for publication at the end of the year. It was another of the verses written long ago to her husband. The theme and even the emotion were entirely remote from the political bustle in which she was spending her days this December of 1836, but it was too good not to publish, now that time had transformed the tragedy of Horace Holley's career into a noble memory. She titled it "To ——— ———" and signed it simply "H."[67] Many readers would recognize and appreciate the poem's significance; and its appearance in print would preserve it for the future.

Yuletide celebrations in the community were interrupted by the death of Mayor Charlton Hunt, who had been not only a friend to Mrs. Holley but a contributor to the Texas fund; and his burial with a parade and military honors was a civic event of real magnitude.[68] As the procession moved slowly past the long rows of silent citizens on its way to the old Episcopal Burying Ground at the edge of town, a mud-spattered stagecoach rolled alongside, and everybody on the sidewalks craned his neck for a glimpse of the foreigner who crouched inside it. News hissed along the crowd that it was General Santa Anna huddling out of sight in terror lest the Kentuckians revenge themselves upon him for Goliad and the Alamo. He was being brought East by an official Texas escort under Colonel Barnard Bee to confer with the President in Washington City.

The treatment accorded the Mexican general in Lexington was magnanimous, according to local opinion. His party lodged cozily at the best hotel for a week while Dr. Dudley of Transylvania treated a severe cold the prisoner had taken. The stagecoach company obligingly furnished two excellent four-horse vehicles, for the sum of five hundred dollars, it was rumored, to get the *cortège* on to Maysville over the wintry roads. Although everybody was curious about the infamous guest, who never once ventured outside his apartments, few people saw him except a special delegation from the Legislature and Mrs. Mary Austin Holley.[69]

Accompanied by Colonel Bee, who was a friend of all the Austins, she paid a formal call at the hotel. Santa Anna was necessarily grateful for the generous treatment he had received at Orozimbo Plantation—the Phelpses had twice saved his life, and the neighbors had been kindly disposed—and when Mrs. Holley and Henry Austin's daughters were introduced to him, he was very gallant and urbane. In greeting such well-connected ladies he said all the right things, marvelling at the beauty of the Kentucky snow and complimenting them upon their city in his best Castilian Spanish. Through his interpreter he told Mrs. Holley that he had seen her book, and spoke of Stephen Austin as *amigo.*

Sitting there in a staid hotel room two thousand miles away from Mexico, still sniffling and watery-eyed in spite of the doctor's ministrations, Señor Antonio López de Santa Anna did not look much like a cruel fiend. Mary found it interesting to meet him in person, feeling that she was there as an unofficial representative of the Texas government and its secretary of state. She was always at her best when circumstances permitted her to rise above controversial emotions to the more tolerant and civilized level of diplomacy.

The call on Santa Anna was a triumph for her, in a small way, but nothing compared with the significant part she played in the passage of the Texas Resolutions in the Kentucky Senate early in January. The weather was so bitterly cold that the session had begun before she and a good many of the members arrived in Frankfort. The bill had already been brought up and laid on the table until June. A less determined lady would have quit for the time being and gone home to look after her boarders, and she felt like doing just that. Then she learned from some sympathetic senators with whom she conversed at the hotel and elsewhere that it was possible to obtain a vote for reconsideration. She decided to stay on in Frankfort.

She had her way. The Texas Resolutions passed, with a few cautious amendments, thanks to the eloquence of several senators to whom she supplied facts and arguments. She sat during the debates with the other ladies, participating in their chatter about mutual friends and current fashions, but missing no move in the strategy on the floor of the Senate. She knew now how much she could accomplish for Texas, not only with her pen but by her personal exertions and influence.

The Sunday after she returned home—by now it was the fourteenth day of January—she reported her achievements to Stephen in a long, gay letter.[70] She was in high spirits, and lightly suggested that she should go to Washington City at once to work for the interests of Texas among the political leaders of the North and East, so many of whom she knew personally. Some of her colleagues during this matter of the Kentucky Resolutions were urging her to do so, and she was willing even if she had to sell a league of land to get money for the trip. Probably, she added, she would take her niece Henrietta with her—she had a pretty good idea that Henrietta was Stephen's favorite of Henry's children. She went on and on about her personal plans and the recent news of the family. Never had she let herself go so freely in a letter to him, not even in the romantic aftermath of the visit to Bolivar House.

She felt very close to him as she sat at her desk there in the parlor where they had talked, not much about themselves, but about what they could accomplish together. Other leaders in Texas had now taken over much of the burden of petty detail which he had carried for so many years alone. He was free at last to deal with national and international affairs. She knew that he needed her help, and when she came to the end of the paper, she impulsively signed it "Ever yours—M.A.H."

She was in earnest about proceeding to Washington. Within a fortnight she once more ran the newspaper advertisement of her Dickson's Creek land for sale. She wished to be ready if he wanted her to go.

❀ ❀ ❀

Stephen Austin never saw this message from Mary. When it was delivered into the hands of his sister at Peach Point Plantation, he was dead, and Emily faithfully put it away with the thousands of personal and state papers that were piled up in her brother's room.

He had suffered with malaria all fall and winter, only occasionally feeling strong enough to do more than attend to his pressing correspondence as secretary of state. He worked out a few plans for a cotton plantation adjoining the Perrys, and made his peace with his former secretary about their bungled land deals. He bought a mule to ride from San Felipe over to Columbia, the present seat of government, but in bad weather he was compelled to take lodgings in the town most of the time. Careless of his own comfort he worked in an unheated room of the barn-like building that served as the capitol, and contracted a severe cold that developed into pneumonia.[71]

He remained in his cheerless, rented room, stupefied by heavy doses of medicine, until Henry Austin and George Hammeken, a friend whom he had known in Mexico City, discovered him there a few days before Christmas. He was too ill to be taken to Peach Point, but they called the doctor and sent for the family, nursing him as best they could. He recognized James Perry and one of the nephews when they arrived. Sometimes he sat up to aid in breathing, resting his head on his arms. In a day or two—it was December 27, 1836—he seemed to struggle less and spoke of going to sleep. About noon he said to the little group in the room, "*Texas recognized . . . Did you see it in the papers?*" Those were his last words, and may well have been his last thoughts.

The funeral was as impressive as the impoverished frontier Republic could accord its "Patriarch," as President Houston called Austin in the official proclamation of his death. The body was buried in the Perry family graveyard, located in a live-oak glade a few hundred yards from the residence. They dug Stephen's grave near the little mounds belonging to two of Emily's children who had died since their coming to Texas.

After a proper interval the family of the late General, including Henry Austin, read his will. It was essentially the one he had written in the spring of 1833 on the eve of his departure for Mexico City, except for a codicil made about a year before his death. The bequest to "my cousin Mary Austin Holley" of a league of land on Bayou Flores was clearly stated, but there was no mention of the two hundred acres of his Peach Point premium land which he had promised to her.[72]

* * *

Mary Holley did not know that Stephen was dead during those proud weeks when she was invoking his name to impress Santa Anna, and lobbying for Texas in Frankfort, and scribbling long pages of intimate news for his eye alone. In all likelihood the report of his death reached Lexington first in the papers received at the *Intelligencer* office and was reflected in a short, inaccurate notice in its columns that appeared on the last day of January. She very surely did not compose the item. She could possibly have been mistaken as to the correct date of his death, but she would never have failed to give him his ultimate rank as General Austin:

DIED—At Columbia, Texas, on the 26th ult. Col. Stephen F. Austin, Secretary of State of Texas. We mourn the loss of Colonel Austin, of society generally, but long should his memory be embalmed with the affections of Texas.[73]

Similar brief items appeared in the other Lexington papers, and that was all. Kentucky editors were in no mood to eulogize Austin since the return of the disgruntled volunteers.

Ere long Mary received a long letter from Henry about Stephen's last illness and the will. He had himself been a beneficiary under it in that certain land fees had been relinquished to him, but he was not in agreement with James Perry in regard to other aspects of it, notably the omission of mention of her premium land. From the other news in Henry's letter it appeared that the Republic had paused only briefly to honor its founder before entering a new era. Sam Houston was moving the capital away from the Brazos to a new town named for him over on Buffalo Bayou, near the site of his victory at San Jacinto.

Stephen's death ended, with a numbing finality, all Mary Holley's dreams of participating in international diplomacy. In spite of his defeat at the polls by Houston she had believed that he was the leader destined to shape the future of the new nation, and that he would seek her aid as he had done before. A career in Washington or any capital city suited her better than life on an arcadian farm, and the sort of mutually uplifting relationship which they enjoyed briefly in Lexington was what she desired and needed to inspire her as a woman and as a writer. Romantic hero-worship was for her the heartbeat of both love and creative power, but now once more she was bereft of the companionship of the man of genius around whom her life centered. Once more she was alone. This second romance of her life left to her a packet of Stephen's letters, a portrait of him, and the two books he had encouraged and helped her to write. Besides these she had her Texas land, which now seemed the only security the future offered.

Gradually she accepted her loss, and the healing words flowed from her pen as she composed a solemn poem for him, beholding him now from afar, as if she were gazing upon a marble statue:

> . . . We have lost him; he is gone;
> We know him now; all narrow jealousies
> Are silent, and we see him as he moved;
> How modest, kindly, all-accomplished, wise;
> With what sublime repression of himself,
> And in what limits, and how tenderly;
> No swaying to this faction or to that;
> Not making his high place the lawless perch

Of wing'd ambitions, nor vantage ground
For pleasure; but thro' all this tract of years
Wearing the white flower of a blameless life,
Before a thousand peering littlenesses,
. . . for where is he
Who dares foreshadow for an only son
A lovelier life, a more unstained, than his?[74]

She laid the verses away with his letters, and as she thumbed through the pages he had written to her she found the one where he had declared his belief in "the self-existing, consistent, and bountiful Father of Worlds, of Time, and of Eternity."

Alas, her heart cried, if only he had not sacrificed himself so completely to duty, Stephen Austin might have been a poet, and a lover.

17. ON THE WING
1837-1840

During the long, late Kentucky winter the house on Constitution Street became a prison to Mary Holley. Planning the meals for her household, listening to the endless talk about the Brand nursery, and exchanging the small gossip of the town began to pall on her. Her brother's children were getting threadbare but he sent no money for new coats and shoes. Advertisements of her Texas land in the local papers brought no inquiries from interested parties.[1] The reviews of her book continued to be favorable, but in order to dispose of all those copies stacked up in the storeroom at J. Clarke, Printers, arrangements must be made soon with agents in Louisville and in the towns of the deep South. Then, too, in the back of her mind was a gnawing anxiety about her son in Guatemala.

Suddenly she could stand it no longer. In mid-March she announced that she must make a brief business trip to New Orleans at once, and urged her daughter to accompany her. William Brand dismissed that idea as impractical, and so Mary took Henrietta, the livelier of the Austin girls. Emily, the other niece, was a favorite in the Brand household and could stay there if she got lonely; the boys were in boarding school. The Negro woman Amy went along to "do for the ladies," since the boardinghouse could get along with old black Patty in charge.[2]

Before Mary could fully realize her freedom she found herself stepping down the gangplank at Vicksburg one soft spring evening for a hasty visit ashore with the Smedes family from Kentucky. The captain of the steamboat allowed her only an hour to rush up the levee, escorted by a nice young gentleman passenger, but that was time enough to say hello and goodbye, and to leave a package of the new books for distribution.

The Smedes gentlemen were all attending a bachelors' ball at the hotel just across the street, and for a little while the visitors joined the ladies of the household in listening to the music and trying to see through the brilliantly lighted hotel windows what was going on. They agreed that they had never beheld the likes of the young female creature with three birds of paradise on her head who flitted across their line of vision occasionally.

"How good it seems to get into the busy world," sighed Mrs. Holley to her niece when they had returned to their comfortable stateroom, "back where everybody is alive and prosperous and good-natured."

On the last day of their journey, in the misty sunshine of what Mary called "a glorious morning," the boat moved swiftly down the bank-full river with wide green fields and clustered houses on both sides slipping past like the scenes of the popular painted panoramas. At the levee in New Orleans a porter was waiting with letters from her business agent. It was good to be expected and welcomed. There was no word from Horace, whereupon she had Mr. Erwin forward a letter to him bidding him to come to New Orleans by the first steamer and then placed a credit for him in both Havana and Guatemala. That was all she could do except wait for developments.

The three weeks she intended to stay in Louisiana stretched out to several months, for the best and most necessary reasons. Soon after arriving she had the good fortune, through Stephen's friend George Hammeken,[3] to meet the wife of General Mexia,[4] a liberal Mexican patriot, now an exile from his own land. The Mexias were soon to sail in a chartered vessel for Guatemala and were happy to accept letters to young Holley and his companion, Mr. Savage, on the chance that they could be found there. During her stay, also, she advised with Colonel James Love,[5] a Kentucky lawyer who was dealing extensively in Texas lands, and on his recommendation sold half a league of her own holdings for fifty cents an acre in United States notes. She recklessly let the purchaser have his pick of locations because she needed funds badly and times were hard. The money Henry had recently sent her was in Texas currency, which could not be discounted at the time.

Before going to stay with Melazie and Donatien in the St. Peter Street house, which they now owned, she and her niece visited with several hospitable friends; and it seemed like coming home when she settled down in her old room with the Augustins. She was always a personage here, and likely to be included in the civic events in which Donatien participated as well as in all their social entertaining.

One morning the ladies were invited to come aboard the Texas schooner of war *Independence* as guests of Captain Wheelwright, who escorted them on a tour to show them where Santa Anna, when a prisoner on the ship, had nailed a silver piece to the head of the rudder, remarking that he had thus "signed the Independence of Texas." They were served a collation of cake and wine and fruit on the quarterdeck, with music, and Mrs. Holley formally presented the Captain with a copy of her new book and the *Texan Song of Liberty*. Everyone was talking hopefully of early annexation to the United States.[6]

That expedition made a nice bit of conversation the next time she called on some old friends from Roxbury who were residing in a suite in the unfinished but magnificent St. Charles Hotel. Her hostess received her in the private parlor, attended by impeccable Scottish servants; and the two New Englanders were moved to enthusiasm as they gazed out of the windows upon the granite columns and marble porticos and balustrades that lay about in elegant confusion, waiting to add to the impressive style of the building.

"It must be admitted, dear Mrs. Thwing,"[7] declared Mary, "that this city is beginning to look like some ancient capital of the Old World, like Rome itself."

She had never seen a foreign city, but New Orleans came close to fulfilling her dreams, and she was always reluctant to bring her stay there to an end. She and her niece paid a short visit to the German Coast for the christening of Melazie's two small children, and were fondly received by the Labranches and Trepagniers and Fortiers. This was the last time that Mary saw Mr. Jean Baptiste Labranche. He died that summer, and his extensive lands and slaves and the handsome mansion at St. Peter and Royal Streets were divided according to the French custom and law.[8] His death left Mr. Hermogene the head of the family.

At last Mr. Savage and Horace got back from Guatemala, sunburned and foreign-looking in their faded cotton clothes. The lad was grown now, standing a full head taller than his mother; and he was more amiable and alert than since his early childhood. He had learned a Spanish dialect, and spoke familiarly of strange places like Omoa and Lake Yzabal. He wanted to go back to Guatemala at once to start a cochineal plantation, but no one paid any attention to his talk but Mr. Savage. Mary Holley paid no attention to either of them about such an investment. She had long overstayed her visit and she engaged their passage for Kentucky on the first boat after her son's arrival.

Her goodbye present to Melazie was a neat little poem for her album, signed "M. A. H." and dated "New Orleans, May 1837":

> Fare thee well, for I wander where duty now calls me,
> To the land of fair flowers and fond friends bid adieu!

We live amidst dangers, but whatever befalls me,
This page, pretty maiden, will bring me to you.[9]

Back again once more on Constitution Street she lodged Horace upstairs with the Austin boys, and provided him with a new suit and starched shirts in the hope that he could be persuaded to attend the Medical Lectures at the University in the fall and discover a leaning in that direction. During the summer Mrs. Perry spent a month in Lexington on her way to Ohio to place three of her children in good Episcopal schools there. She was a devout churchwoman and found Harriette and the Brands especially congenial in this regard. Edward, oldest of the Austin boys, went with Mrs. Perry to enter Kenyon College along with young Guy Bryan. Guy was Mrs. Holley's favorite of Emily's children, and she corresponded with him while he was in Ohio, sending him Lexington papers whenever they carried any Texas news.[10] Stephen had been very fond of all Emily's children and they were devoted to his memory.

The Brands' piety as members of Christ Church drew Mary into its circle. William was the earnest and efficient Secretary of the Vestry, the children were all properly baptized, and Harriette had been confirmed.[11] So it came about that Mrs. Holley was an active worker for a fair which the ladies of the church held to raise funds, and that is how she happened to be engaged in conversation with Bishop Benjamin Bosworth Smith when he declared himself to be in favor of such fairs. Indeed, he wished the ladies would hold another one to raise money for his newly founded Episcopal Theological Seminary. There were certain members of the congregation, as it happened, who were at odds with the Bishop, including William Brand; and Mrs. Holley was persuaded to make a sworn deposition of just what the Right Reverend Smith had said about fairs.[12] She did it to be accommodating, but, even after the Bishop resigned as rector she knew the controversy to be an unprofitable one. She was increasingly critical of what she privately called the town's prejudices and narrow ways.

She wanted to disentangle herself from the trying situation in which she found herself as the year 1837 drew to a close. Financial hard times over the nation had increased. The United States Congress seemed likely to refuse the offer of Texas to be annexed, thus making conditions there uncertain. Her household debts could wait no longer, and she felt that Henry ought to take his children back home and become responsible for them. If she could rid herself of the burden of this large establishment, she could do something about her son's education and future career. There was no reason for her to be poor, not when she owned thousands of acres of land. If she understood Henry's confusing accounts of "cahoots" deals and the rest of his hasty explanations, there must be more than thirty thousand acres to which she held title. Her restlessness was intensified when she had an optimistic letter from George Hammeken, written in the East, saying that he would soon be en route to Texas in order to promote some large operations near her land, which ought to sell for a good price if she would go there at once. That settled the matter. If Henry could not or would not manage her property to enable her to live respectably, she must go to Texas herself and do so.

The first day of December found her on the wing again. She left Horace and the boardinghouse in the care of faithful Amy and Patty, with instructions to see that he attended the Medical Lectures faithfully. In Louisville, where she took the steamboat, she placed the two younger Austin boys in a school run by a Mr. Smith which was well spoken of, and she took both nieces to Texas with her.

By good luck and perhaps a certain amount of planning, Mr. Hammeken was a passenger on the same steamboat with them, and he raised her spirits at once with encouraging news. The four thousand acres of land on Dickson's Creek ought to bring two dollars an acre now, or more. He could easily act as her agent since he owned much land in that area near the holdings of Henry Austin and the Perrys.[13]

George Hammeken was a well-educated New Yorker, who travelled widely and spoke fluent Spanish. During the long days steaming down the river he talked a good deal about Stephen, whom he had known for years, and at crucial times. He had lent the Empresario two hundred dollars when he landed in New Orleans penniless after two years in a Mexican prison, and had gone with him to a book dealer's to buy histories and poetry to line the shelves in that log house at San Felipe. Hammeken had been with Stephen during the week of his last illness, and he described graphically the cold, bare room and the words of the dying man. As he talked, Mary shed a few tears, but it calmed her nerves and renewed her courage to be with someone who had known her cousin so well. They both thought Stephen Austin a great man.

Nineteen days after their departure from Lexington Mrs. Holley and her nieces reached Galveston, to find the Island still showing the effects of the battering by a great storm during the previous October. The fine pair of China trees, almost the only trees on the Island, were broken off near the ground, and the new customhouse was so wrecked that Collector Gail Borden's office was now in the cabin of the brig *Perseverance,* beached nearby on the sand. Borden had sold his newspaper and was now combining this political job in the customs office with the breeding of Durham cattle.

Numerous important persons were waiting in the town to take smaller boats around through the bay and up the bayou to the town of Houston. Since everybody else seemed to be gathering in the new capital nowadays, Mary decided that a good way to proceed to Brazoria and Bolivar would be to take the boat for Houston, too. What could be more delightful than a few more days on this glittering cerulean sea under a cerulean sky![14]

The passengers on the *Comanche* were sociable, conversing and singing popular songs as they feasted on oysters and oranges. As they rounded the Island some fellow passenger pointed out the general location of Dickson's Creek to Mrs. Holley, and she saw for the first time the flat tangle of lush green beyond which, not many miles away, was the league of land that Stephen Austin had allotted to Mary Austin *viuda* Holley. When they passed the San Jacinto Battlefield she was standing on the deck with Dr. Jack Shackelford,[15] who identified the landmarks and told her anecdotes of the men who fought there. The Doctor was a famous soldier himself, being one of the few volunteers who escaped the massacre at Goliad, where so many young men from Kentucky died. They wound their way on into the bayou, and at last tied up at the landing of President Houston's new capital.

An item in the *Telegraph and Texas Register*, now published in the town of Houston, promptly noted the arrival of this distinguished party of newcomers to the community, and Mrs. Holley was undoubtedly pleased to be the only lady passenger singled out for mention along with Dr. Shackelford, General Albert Sidney Johnston of the Texan Army, Colonel Hockley, one of the officers who had escorted Santa Anna to the States, and other equally well-known personages.[16]

At once people began coming to pay their respects to her, first on the boat and later at the commodious home of the Allens,[17] the promoters of the new town, who hospitably entertained prominent travellers as their guests in view of the lack of public accommodations. Several members of Congress were among her visitors, and later President Houston called in person—he had been out of the city the day they landed. On Sunday he dined with them on board the *Comanche* and "gallanted" the ladies to the capitol, where they viewed the portrait gallery and then listened to a long sermon which at least one hearer thought rather poor.[18]

As always Mary Holley made notes when she travelled. Although she had no immediate prospect of writing for publication, she had laid in a supply of good blue notebooks before leaving Lexington and she jotted down important items. Among observations noted at this time were these: "Two large two-story hotels with galleries—and the capitol 70 feet front, 140 rear—painted peach blossom, about ¼ miles from the landing." She included many of these facts in letters to her daughter, knowing that Harriette would preserve them.

Christmas Day was unforgettable. On the Eve came an express at full gallop to strengthen the rumor that Mexican troops were about to cross the border. From the Allen gallery Mary and her nieces watched the "whole town in motion like bees swarming . . . Nobody was afraid but everybody was busy." She felt secure. In the unlikely event that the Mexicans attacked and were, of course, repulsed, she had a promise of protection from Mr. Alcee Labranche, the United States chargé d'affaires to Texas.[19] He was the son of old Uncle Alexandre, and Mr. Hermogene's cousin, whom she had known since his youth. In spite of the alarms there was plenty of eggnog at the homes of the Allens and the Labranches and others. That in spite of the fact that eggs were selling for fifty cents apiece.

On this trip she had the feeling that destiny was driving her on to some good end, and events seemed to prove it. The rumors of invasion turned out to be groundless, and she soon made satisfactory arrangements to traverse the sixty miles across country to Brazoria. An ox cart that was already hauling corn in that direction could take the baggage, and a barouche was hired for the ladies. Some young military gentlemen riding that way would act as escorts. At Brazoria there were war scares, too, but real estate prices were booming and new houses were being built. Mary and the girls promptly joined their hostess, a Mrs. Blandin, and some other ladies who were indulging in rifle practice, followed by a sip of wine and small cakes. Mary's shots hit a clothes line instead of the mark, but *n'importe!* The next day she rode horseback over the prairies west of town with Mr. Perry and Mr. Hammeken, both of whom had come up from Peach Point to inspect developments.

While she waited in Brazoria for her brother's coming, she had an interesting caller in the person of Vice-President Mirabeau Buonaparte Lamar.[20] She and the General had not met before, he having arrived in Texas from Georgia just in time to become one of the heroes of San Jacinto, recognized on the field for bravery by Houston himself. She knew that he had been an admirer and friend of Stephen Austin, and was still a frequent visitor at the Perry home. He was a poet of some note, and as president of the newly organized Philosophical Society of Texas he was the spokesman of culture in the new nation.

She found him an agreeable and romantic gentleman. Rather short of stature, with long black hair and poetic gray eyes, he looked as French as his name. The only provincial thing about him was his clothes, which were old-fashioned and baggy. In other respects he seemed as polite and correct in speech as if he had grown up in Boston instead of on a Georgia plantation. It was generally understood that he was not on friendly terms with President Houston. Lamar favored establishing Texas as an independent nation with the assistance of England and France; and he was, like everybody else, uncertain as to what Houston's ideas were on the subject.

General Lamar, now a widower, was currently residing at Mrs. Jane Long's boardinghouse in Brazoria. Many political gentlemen lodged with that famous pioneer lady, at whose table the best stories and liveliest speculations were circulated. He undoubtedly shared with Mrs. Holley what news seemed proper for her to hear, including the fact that his friends were running him to succeed Houston, whose conduct was considered by many to be increasingly undignified. Fancy permitting the floors of the Presidential Mansion to be used for firewood! And had Mrs. Holley heard that David Burnet, himself the President of the *ad interim* government of Texas, had written of Houston in the newspapers as a "Big Drunk" and declared him to be half-Indian?

What interested her most during Lamar's call was his statement to her that he was too busy to carry forward the biography of Stephen Austin which he had engaged to write with the consent of the family. The Perrys had given him the run of all the records piled in the study at Peach Point, and he had done a considerable amount of preparatory study and issued a rhetorical "Call," asking old settlers for historical reminiscences.[21] The short life of Moses Austin which he had completed was promised to some Brazoria editors for use in a new paper they proposed to launch in the spring. Much as he wished to be known as the friend and admirer of Stephen Austin, Lamar felt that he could not complete the memoir and at the same time pursue his own political career. He suggested that she, Mrs. Holley, was the logical person to write the life story of the Founder of Texas, since she was already twice identified as the historian of that nation. If she undertook the task, he, Lamar, proposed to turn over to her the materials he had collected, whenever he could locate and arrange them.

She had come to Texas this time primarily to straighten out her financial affairs. Money she must obtain somewhere, somehow—and soon. Nevertheless, she welcomed Lamar's proposal, feeling that his offer carried weight and authority. He seemed to suggest that while he devoted his efforts to carrying forward Stephen's dreams of schools and culture in Texas, she should see that the Founder was not forgotten by future generations. Once more, at least in her own mind, she was committed to take up her pen in a noble cause.

"We all have excellent health," she wrote her daughter the next day after Lamar's call, "good appetites—good digestion—and of course, good spirits. I never felt better." Lamar called on her again while she was in Brazoria, perhaps to tell her more about the letters and manuscripts.

Henry joined them for the New Year, and they and their friends spent a happy day feasting and singing and planning for a future that looked prosperous. He was sure that he was just on the verge of disposing of a number of his Bolivar lots at a handsome profit. Then early one morning not long afterward he and his sister and his daughters set out on horseback down the river for Peach Point Plantation, following a road that was hardly more than a path through the wild peach and holly, with vistas leading off into dense woodlands. It was sundown when they reached the Perry home, a large double cabin built in the shadow of a live oak, just like the plan Stephen had drawn.

Raw, cold weather made everyone glad to stay indoors in comfort. Emily Perry had seen to it that her house was well-chinked and warm, that the cistern and the smokehouse were ample. She had even demanded that proper outhouses be put up, in the style of the large Southern plantations. Much of her furniture was of good, old-fashioned pieces brought from Missouri; and she treasured the engraved Austin silver spoons which her father had purchased in Lexington when she was a child. She had many family heirlooms, the most prized being a splendid pair of shoe buckles her mother had worn at one of President Washington's receptions. All of Stephen's possessions were carefully preserved— his tomahawk and powder horn, his special branding iron, and the little dress sword and the elegant Mexican colonel's uniform that John Phelps Austin had procured for him. Most revealing of the man were his books; histories of America and Scotland, a Spanish grammar, his father's old copy of Doctor Johnson's *Dictionary*, and a long row of others.[22]

Several of Emily Perry's sons were at home but it was young Moses Austin Bryan who squired his young lady cousins about the plantation. They went walking in the woods, and one day each of them picked a leaf of bay to keep for remembrance. Whatever Moses did with his, the girls put their souvenirs away carefully in their writing cases.[23]

While her nieces joined in the household cheer with their many cousins and numerous guests, Mary spent her daylight hours in the room that had been built for Stephen, turning over and reading family letters and official papers. She filled three blue notebooks with extracts from the record he kept while in prison in Mexico City, working as fast as she could, with little chance to sort or check her sources.[24] Just as Lamar had warned her, these masses of documents contained the story of the early American colonization of Texas, and whoever undertook to tell it must study them. She could well understand why he had put aside the idea of writing the Austin memoirs when he announced for the presidency of the Republic.

The first Sunday after her coming Mrs. Perry took her for a walk over the plantation. They ended by trudging together through the mud to the burying ground to see Stephen's tomb. It was a well-built brick sarcophagus, covered over with a flat marble slab, which Emily said was somewhat like the one they had erected for Moses Austin at the old home in Missouri. The inscription was heartbreakingly brief and modest, just as the late Empresario would have wanted it: GEN'L STEPHEN F. AUSTIN—*Departed this life on the 27th of Dec. A. D. 1836— Aged 43 Years 1 month and 24 days.*

Emily had erected a dignified memorial to her brother, and Mary praised it.

"My poor cousin sleeps in peace," she said quietly.

Under the leaden skies the high brown weeds were weeping in solitude over the wet stone; and both women shivered in the cold wind as they stood there together for a little while.

Not long afterward the two ladies, escorted by young Joel Bryan, made a trip of several days down to Quintana, the thriving settlement at the mouth of the river, which had prospered mightily since the hot day when Mary made the sketch of the warehouse there. They went on horseback, with the guest mounted on Stephen's favorite horse, and as they rode along, Emily pointed out where her brother had said he meant to build a home for himself. The tract now belonged to Joel.[25]

This was the only time Mary ever saw the spot where she and Stephen were to have had their paradise. It was a tract of woodland and open glade where shy deer flitted among the shadows, as befitted an arcadia. But as the little cavalcade ambled on past it with the proud young owner expounding his plans for farming and pasturing, she realized that their dream had been as transient as it was beautiful. All that remained of it was a handful of his letters and her memories.

They were handsomely entertained in Quintana by Emily's friends, who plied them with native oysters and imported champagne. Upon returning to the plantation they found Henry Austin and Mr. Hammeken, come to talk business with James Perry and to have a social visit. Mrs. Holley undoubtedly talked over her historical research with George, who was engaged himself in translating an important Mexican document of the period and who offered to set down some of his recollections of Stephen. Probably during this family gathering Henry brought up the question of the two hundred acres of premium land that Stephen had promised to Mrs. Holley. He felt strongly that she was entitled to it, but James Perry still refused to recognize the claim because it was not mentioned in the will. The matter seems to have been settled when Emily deeded her cousin two excellent town lots in Quintana, in due form as witnessed then and there by Henry and Mr. Hammeken.[26] The two women closest to Stephen Austin did not let a misunderstanding about his property come between them.

For all her brother's real concern about her affairs, Mary sometimes grew impatient with him when his glowing promises to obtain money from her land holdings failed again and again to materialize. He always had excellent reasons for the delay—threats of war that kept settlers away, or the low value of Texas currency, or the new real estate boom over near Houston. She grew anxious because she needed cash to repay William Brand for the advances he had already made on her household expenses and was continuing to make for Horace.

Mary lingered a while at Peach Point after her brother and his daughters had gone on to Bolivar, and then followed them to settle down there and wait for the sale of the lots. To her son-in-law she wrote apologetic letters, explaining the circumstances and suggesting that he have himself appointed Horace's legal guardian so that he could draw on the lad's Boston trust fund. She even agreed that he could sell her furniture and Amy to pay her Lexington debts.[27] She was reasonably sure that William would not dispose of her property while she was away, but the offer restored her dignity somewhat.

Life at Bolivar was not uneventful, remote as it was from any settlement. Her nieces did the housework and waited on their father, who often became physically ill whenever he was worried. Mary, as always, preferred out-of-door tasks such as supervising the garden and tending the roses. One great multiflora needed only proper pruning to make it rival anything in the Brand yard. It took her several days of patient, painful work, but it was worth doing. She had planted the rose on a previous visit and she did not like to see it neglected.

There was a raging flood, too, during which the ferry boat and the yawl both broke their moorings and were lost. A neighbor unceremoniously borrowed the canoe the very day a distressed young man needed it to cross the river for Dr. Phelps to come and save his dying father. Then while waiting for the canoe the youth accidentally shot himself in the hand, and the whole family must needs turn nurse to save him. This glimpse of frontier life was so exhilarating to Mary that when the doctor finally arrived to take charge of the situation, she withdrew to her room and composed a little piece titled "A Day in Texas."[28] Danger and discomfort and even disappointment had their compensations if they struck the creative spark within her mind.

Henry's luck did turn at last, and he sold enough land, his own and hers, to supply her with funds to go back to Kentucky. She had to take her nieces with her, since their father declared flatly that he was turning his house into a tavern for the ferry trade and would have no suitable home for young ladies. Therefore in June of 1838 Mary Holley found herself once more in Lexington with enough money to satisfy her creditors for a while but with the rest of her problems unsolved.[29] She still had her brother's family on her hands and must maintain a household. More depressing yet, her son at the age of twenty was idle and immature and unhappy. He had not applied himself to the Medical Lectures, and in the town was considered to be "no count." That harsh news she had got straight from William Brand, who was entitled to an opinion since he had done his best, as the lad's guardian, to give his brother-in-law some sound Scottish training during her absence. Mary was naturally inclined to take her son's side in the matter. Although she knew well enough that Horace was difficult and odd, her pride would not let her admit it, especially to William. Instead, she fortified her defense by telling herself that the Brands were too serious and Lexington too dull.

She had felt a resurgence of creative energy when Lamar virtually handed over his literary project to her, but it waned as she resumed once more the narrow routine of Constitution Street. Not even when Mr. Iucho called to present her with a newly published copy of her *Brazos Boat Glee* which he had arranged and recently performed at a benefit concert for the Lexington Female Benevolent and Provident Society with notable success, she was not as happy as she should have been.[30]

The money that she fancied could set her free from all her difficulties seemed always to be just beyond her reach. Her leagues of Texas land reminded her constantly that she should make Henry sell or develop them, and she wrote him rather sharply about having kept his children for four years. She corresponded with various friends—Mr. Hammeken and Colonel James Love and even Mr. Savage, who was still dreaming of a plan of his own to negotiate a million-dollar loan to the Texan government. They all advised her to do something about her land. She chose to interpret that advice as meaning that she should go to Texas.

She broke up housekeeping on Constitution Street in January, 1839, and on the last Thursday of the month sold all her household goods and kitchen furniture at public auction, even her "piano of superior quality."[31] William Brand bought Amy and Patty, her faithful, excellent house servants.

The Brands helped out the situation greatly by inviting Emily and Harriette Austin to live at Elmwood until their father made provision for them. The Austin girls, as people called them, seemed rather sad and embarrassed about living with Aunt Mary's daughter, or so they sounded in the many letters they wrote to their relatives. However, Harriette let them be useful in the household and took them with her to church and teas and concerts so that they elected to stay on in Lexington instead of going to any of the other kinfolks who asked them. They were very homesick, but clearly their father had no plans for them in Texas now. Meanwhile the sprigs of bay leaf so carefully pressed between the pages of their diaries grew dry and brittle.

In mid-February Aunt Mary set out for Louisiana. This time she took Horace with her. He was always welcome at Good Hope Plantation, and she could leave him there while she went on to the City. There she found her brother Archibald with his family, come at last to try their fortunes in southwestern country. Too, she received an invitation for Horace to pay his Aunt Dall in Baltimore a long visit, and she got him off ere long on a sailing vessel. He was delighted at the prospect of a long voyage around the eastern coastline.[32]

Everybody was in town for the season, including her wealthy friends from Lexington, the Richard Henry Chinns, who now lived in New Orleans and entertained all their Kentucky acquaintances lavishly. Archibald escorted her to the theatre to see the now famous Edwin Forrest in *Metamora*—how horrible to behold him and pretty Mrs. Duff decked out as Indians! She and George Hammeken dined with Mrs. Mexia, whose distinguished husband was away on a military expedition to Tampico. Fortunately, as she thought, Mr. Savage went off in the wild Red River country on some mission, as full of crazy plans as ever. She did not find Mr. S. interesting any more, and went a little out of her way to avoid him. She preferred more sophisticated society nowadays. How good it was to see fashionable clothes again, in the Parisian mode, with the bonnets a trifle smaller, and black net shawls all the rage, and everyone wearing little gold crosses like her own suspended around the neck with a ribbon of black velvet. She hoped to purchase a spring dress and collar and gloves for each of the girls if there was money enough for such indulgences.

Henry was annoyed when he received her sharp letter and replied while he was still angry. Why, he wrote, should his children be considered a burden on anybody when he had sent her more than he had promised? Who had supported her and her son? Let the Boston money be used for Horace. And now that he himself had got "rid of the burthen of Bolivar, furniture, servants, and all," he was not expecting her to come to Texas at this time. He intended to go East in the summer "if I live so long," to raise money for a large-scale operation. Having thus indulged his temper he sent her a modest check, all he could spare, and signed the letter "Affectionately, your Brother."[33]

When she read this letter she could see Henry as clearly as if he were stalking up and down the room before her eyes, shouting and pointing an accusing finger at her. Perhaps the funds he provided would have been sufficient for herself and six hungry young people if she had scrimped and hoarded them; but that humiliation she had no intention of enduring, certainly not in Lexington. Besides, she had never been sure whether the money he sent was from the sale of his land or hers —he was utterly unbusinesslike. And he always sent it in Texas currency that was hard to negotiate. She forgave him his fit of temper, pocketed the check, and proceeded with plans of her own.

She had in mind to go East herself that summer.[34] If Henry refused to see her in Texas, she would meet him in Baltimore. There she could perhaps promote her own interests in other ways, too, since George Hammeken was to be in New York, where he thought he knew of prospective buyers for the Dickson's Creek acreage. Another reason for her being in the East was that she could arrange for her son to go up to Boston to claim the trust fund held there in his name. He would be twenty-one on July 19, 1839.

She stopped only briefly in Lexington on her way to Baltimore, and decided to take Henrietta with her to consult a famous Dr. Martin at Blue Springs about the painful trouble she sometimes had with her hip. Emily Austin elected to stay with the Brands and help Harriette when her baby came in the fall. She was a shy, serious girl, who was eager to be confirmed at Christ Church the next time the Bishop held such services there, and much preferred reading and practising on the pianoforte at Elmwood to gallivanting with her aunt. Mrs. Holley always saw to it that young ladies under her care had plenty of "attention," and Emily vowed that she was not interested in the opposite sex.

It was Henrietta, then, who made the trip to Baltimore and had plenty of beaus all the way. They travelled by a new southern route through Virginia, which Mary Holley found as interesting as if it had been her first long journey. She was in her mid-fifties and had made this trip back and forth across the mountains at least half a dozen times, but there was no flagging in her eagerness for new experiences.

The Dalls' home on the Reisterstown Road at the edge of Baltimore was even more comfortable than Mary remembered it of old, with newly painted white columns and green blinds, and the garden and yard profusely planted. It was a happy household where any late afternoon James Dall would be out on the lawn practising on his clarinet and beaming indulgently upon his smallest daughter as she played with the miniature furniture and dolls in her "babyhouse."

The calm of the establishment was sadly disrupted that summer and fall as Aunt Dall's harried relatives came and went with a succession of problems and catastrophes. Henry arrived suddenly and then, leaving all his shirts in the wash, as his sisters noted with distress, rushed off to New York in order to secure funds, he hoped, from his brother John. In New York he was met by the news that John Phelps Austin had failed in a speculative operation in cement, leaving only his wife's patrimony for present family needs. Furthermore, rumors of the invasion of Texas by Mexico served to halt all flow of money in that direction.[35] Horace made the trip up to Boston hoping to obtain possession of his trust money and visited among the parishioners of Hollis Street, but found he could not be paid until his mother joined him there to complete the transaction.

Mary made the necessary journey to Boston to enable her son to secure his money, which turned out to be less than they expected because of previous withdrawals. This visit, which proved to be the last she ever made to see her old friends there, was not a happy one. Horace talked constantly of his wish to go back to Guatemala, and both of them developed deep colds that lasted even after they went on down to be with John and his family in Brooklyn. Her brother's family there were comfortable despite his losses, with a pleasant house and a barouche; but he could do nothing to help his kinspeople in their financial stress. After getting over her cold Mary wanted nothing so much as to return to the cheerful haven of her sister's home in Baltimore.

Her zest as an indefatigable traveller, no matter the handicaps, was proved when she stopped en route for a day in Philadelphia to drive out for a view of Girard College and to pay a call on Rebecca Gratz. The Gratzes now lived modestly in an unpretentious home since their business failure in the last panic, but Rebecca was more than ever devoting her life to good works. As she told Mrs. Holley about teaching the small children in her synagogue, the two found a new mutual interest and on parting they planned to meet again in Lexington.

Back in the peaceful autumn setting of the Reisterstown Road Mary rested and "put on her considering cap," as she phrased it. On a large sheet she jotted down first the receipt of $1448.61, precisely, from Mr. May in Boston. Disbursals were as follows: $200.00 to Horace at once and then $60.00 more for his stay in New York; $500.00 lent to Henry Austin, who had been literally without funds to take him back to Baltimore, let alone to Texas; $80.00 paid to Mr. Smith in Lexington for rent at Constitution Street; and so, after her own recent travelling expenses, a balance of about $400.00. At the end of the little calculation she scribbled: "Query—what shall I do next?"

She answered that question at her writing desk, where she always worked out her solutions. She notified George Hammeken in New York of her whereabouts, asking him to push the sale of her Dickson's Creek land in connection with his operations at the west end of Galveston Island. She also considered asking him to take Horace on to Texas with him when he went, but did not do so. She wrote to Edward Holley up in Connecticut, offering to give him a farm out of her Texas holdings if he and his family would settle there and help Horace to get established nearby. For the time being she could think of nothing else to do.

Most days she would knit silently while the two Henriettas—her gentle sister who was so much like their mother, and her favorite niece

—would sew and chatter softly about the remarkably fine potatoes that Mr. Dall raised by treading down the tops in order to stunt their growth in the rich soil of his garden. Or about Brother Charles, who had brought his wife and children over to see them lately from nearby Garrison Forest Church, where they lived. One of his little girls was named Mary Holley. They all thought highly of his wife, Sister Nancy, and her family, the Bucklers. Dear Nancy was a careful manager and a wonderful cook, who seemed content on her husband's modest salary that had to be supplemented by keeping a boys' school. Proof of her skill was her famous recipe for "fried oysters," that turned out to be just grated green corn, dipped in egg and fried in butter, but was a delicacy fit to serve to guests at the rectory when the larder was low. In a back room Horace daubed away at a canvas with his new oil paints and made remarkable progress as long as he stuck to his task.

In such surroundings Mary found it easy and pleasant to stay on for the entire autumn. News from elsewhere was sometimes good and sometimes discouraging, but at least the events it chronicled were far away. Harriette Brand's baby came in early October, a little girl called after Emily Austin,[36] who was deeply pleased to have a namesake and devoted herself to its care. Edward Holley wrote to decline the offer of the farm in Texas, saying that he and his wife were too old to make such a move. In December, at her brother Charles' insistence, Mary and her son went to stay with his family at Garrison Forest, twelve miles out from town in lovely Green Spring Valley. Despite its being winter Horace would often go to town in the carriage with his uncle and then walk back, stopping along the road to visit with new-made friends. On Wednesdays Mary usually went in, too, to get books or music, and walk about the town.

No city outside New York had more shops than Baltimore, and she found it lively to make the rounds, stopping in sometimes to chat with Messrs. Andrews and Plaskitt, who had published her book. She stopped also to see Mr. Dubois, the music publisher who had a store here as well as in New York. He sent his compliments by her to Wilhelm Iucho when she next wrote to Lexington. She conveyed the message via her daughter, along with a word of praise for Mr. Iucho's new Kentucky march that was on display in Mr. Dubois' stock.[37]

The Garrison Forest Church, or St. Thomas' Church, to give it the proper name, was a well-established country parish, founded a century earlier by some of the gentry of Baltimore County as a chapel of ease.[38] Its handsome silver altar service dated from 1773. Charles Austin had been ordained as its eleventh rector about twenty years earlier,[39] and he had never wanted to leave. His sermons were not exciting—he had published only one of them—but his services to his people as he baptized and married and buried them were, in a phrase he often used, "laden with love." He was a faithful and beloved pastor, and a good master to the eighteen or twenty small boys in the school which he conducted near the church. He got along well with Horace, too, and might have done a good deal for his maladjusted nephew if he had had him in charge when the boy was very young.

Charles Austin loved his venerable church. He proudly showed his sister the worn pews where stern men had sat with their guns beside them during the French and Indian Wars, and the blackened gravestones in the old God's Acre with inscriptions as quaint as those in the Boston Common burying ground. Nearby was a patch of Scotch broom he had planted in memory of their own great-grandmother, a bit of sentiment that was wholly in character for him. He was a man of deep feeling, and the only one of Mary's brothers who shared her aesthetic tastes. It was a joy to watch his face as they sat together through the splendid performance of Beethoven's Grand Mass at Christmas time in the great Roman Catholic cathedral in the city.

Mary was so comfortable at Garrison Forest that several months went by before she roused herself to do anything more about her own life. In spite of her lethargy some inner urge drove her to find a way to get rid of the responsibility of her young wards—to reap some benefits from her land now—to fit Horace into some safe niche somewhere—and to do these things before old age caught up with her and left her no opportunity to use those notes and manuscripts in her files. She *would not* be lazy and warm and poor in the corner by the fire of her relatives' homes!

In the spring she boarded the car of the Baltimore and Ohio Railroad's new "Grasshopper" locomotive train, and hurtled along at twenty miles an hour to Washington City. Modestly lodged there in a genteel boardinghouse on Fifteenth Street, she tried to re-establish her connections in the capital, but the society of the city had changed so greatly during the present Van Buren administration that she knew few prominent persons. General Dunlap, the minister from Texas, received her politely and seemed interested in acquiring some of her land, but only in the unlikely event that the government of the Republic paid him what it owed him.[40] She heard that Senator Edward Everett and his wife were planning a grand tour of Europe, and on the spur of the moment wrote him to offer her services as companion and interpreter in return for including her and her son in the party. It was rather beneath her dignity to ask such a favor, and Everett's reply was a cool and diplomatic refusal.[41] She did not mention the matter to her daughter, hoping that her letter had been tossed away by the great man. Instead, he filed it among his papers, maybe out of custom and maybe remembering his young brother John's youthful infatuation for her.

Finally Hammeken's optimistic predictions about the value of her Coast land were justified. A prospective buyer appeared in the person of Captain James Grant Tod of the Texas Navy, who had been dispatched to Baltimore by President Lamar to supervise the building and outfitting in the shipyards there of six Texas naval vessels.[42] He had been born and reared in Lexington, and was the youngest brother of a prominent Presbyterian preacher of the day. At seventeen he had gone down the rivers on a flatboat, enlisted on a Mexican vessel, and then transferred to the United States Navy through the influence of Henry Clay. Somewhere along the way he had dropped the final "d" from his name, but a member of that family from Kentucky needed no recommendations for Mrs. Holley to trust his offer. He also knew well who she was.

Captain Tod had about a thousand dollars in cash and prospects of more when he collected his back pay, and he wanted to buy as much of her Dickson's Creek league as he could. She was ready to start back to Kentucky when he opened up negotiations, but she waited in order to close the deal. She asked a dollar an acre; he dickered for a lower price; she ended by signing an agreement on May 21, 1840, to let him have fifteen hundred acres of his own choosing, provided he took it in a body, for one thousand dollars. She made a rather poor bargain, but, at that, the Captain took less advantage of her unbusinesslike eagerness to sell her land than many another buyer might have done. He paid four hundred dollars in advance with an agreement to settle the rest with a kinsman of the Dalls, Mr. Whitridge, at Bowley's Wharf in Baltimore. The Whitridges lived neighbor to the Dalls on Reisterstown Road in a handsome home where the hospitality included apricots and soft-shelled crabs and elaborate puddings. Mrs. Holley felt sure her interests were safe with Thomas Whitridge, as indeed they proved to be. Furthermore, Captain Tod agreed to consult George Hammeken at San Luis Island, which was near the land, about having it properly surveyed.

She liked doing business with a captain in the Texas Navy, and sealed her letters to him with a uniform button she had acquired somewhere that bore the lone star and an anchor. She hoped he would notice this diplomatic touch. She would probably conclude her affairs with him in person, because she now intended to be in Galveston by the end of the summer. This sale replenished her funds, and she could count on the trip.

She arranged with Charles and his wife for both of Henry's daughters to live with them until they could rejoin their father. She left Horace at Garrison Forest, too, but only until she could send for him to come directly by boat to Galveston. Then she returned to Lexington to see that Emily got off to Baltimore and to gather up her brother's younger sons to take them to Texas with her.

By fall Mrs. Holley was on her way down the rivers again, accompanied by James Austin, now a strapping fellow of sixteen, and Henry, Jr., who was a couple of years younger.[43] The oldest nephew had already made his own way back to Texas from a school in the East. James was so glad to be going home to rejoin his father and brother Edward and to see Bolivar again that she did not grieve too much because his schooling was ending at an early age. He was restless and adventurous—a true Austin—and Texas was the place for him.

She hoped Texas would be the place for her own son, too. There were said to be many opportunities for young men in the new settlements on the coast and farther up the rivers in the broad prairie lands. Perhaps this fabulous development on the Island of San Luis would solve the problem of her son's future. She knew that she would never share an arcadia on the Brazos, but the great empire of Texas envisioned in the plans of Lamar and Hammeken was an exciting prospect.

18. SUNNY ISLAND
1840-1841

Few women of her day travelled more often and more widely than Mary Austin Holley, and always she did so with an eye to availing herself of the most up-to-date mode of transportation. She patronized the steam cars before they were deemed wholly safe, and she chose the newest sea-going vessels to enjoy their modern conveniences. By good fortune she booked passage on the steamer *New York* out of New Orleans to Galveston in the fall of 1840, and waxed lyrical in describing the voyage to her daughter:

We left the levee at ½ past 10 Sunday A.M. & came down the "Shining River" between shores of waving cane (it is of a soft pea-green color like young corn) glistening in the sunshine, then came the moon. It was glorious. . . .
The boat is so beautiful I could think of nothing but Cleopatra as I lay in my luxurious couch of the finest and whitest. . . .
The cabin of the *New York* is on the upper deck like the river boats, the whole of it of mahogany and maple polished like the finest pianos. Drapery of blue satin damask & dimity. The windows of painted glass representing the Texas arms. The table china white, with a blue device in the center of each plate representing the *New York* at sea with the Texas eagle hovering over her. . . .
The chamber maid is a pretty white girl, all the time asking what she shall do for you. . . . The waiters are curly-headed, rosy-cheeked Irish boys with white linen roundabouts.[1]

At the Galveston wharf Colonel Love met her to escort her to Mrs. Crittenden's good boardinghouse, while her nephews gathered up their baggage and started directly for Bolivar House up the river. Their father was postmaster there and still counted it his home.

Galveston had grown rapidly in the past two years, so much so that Mary got lost one day when she went out a different door of the fashionable Tremont House onto an unfamiliar street. All sorts of people brushed past her on the downtown avenues; planters in wide hats, long-haired Creoles, Irish immigrants with an unmistakable brogue, well-fed colored persons, and a few conspicuous travellers from foreign parts in their well-cut clothes.[2] She spent much time as a welcome guest in the large frame residences, with white columns and windows to the floor, set amidst trees and gardens still green in early November. She was often entertained in the home of Colonel and Mrs. Love, where another frequent visitor was General Albert Sidney Johnston, now Secretary of War in Lamar's Cabinet. They recalled his student days at Transylvania, and he must have told her that he was in the audience in Louisville to which Stephen Austin delivered the famous address. It had persuaded him to come to Texas. He was now going back to the States on business in the *New York*, and since he was the most eligible young widower in Texas or in Kentucky, for that matter, Mrs. Holley privately hoped that his business would take him to Lexington to fetch back Mr. Robert Wickliffe's pretty daughter Mary as his bride. She may have artfully asked Johnston's opinion of Sam Houston's new wife, a lady from Alabama who was reputed to be very religious.

In all such social gatherings she heard discussions of the new capital city which Lamar had established up the Colorado River on a fine hill-ringed site, located in what Stephen Austin had called his "little colony." The town of about a thousand inhabitants was named Austin in his honor, and the broad main avenue leading to the one-story frame capitol was laid out with an eye to future greatness even if an eight-foot stockade now surrounded the building to protect it from the Indians. The chargé d'affaires from the French government, Count Alphonse de Saligny, was planning to erect a suitable embassy in the new town.[3] Lamar had built his capital and inaugurated an ambitious educational program for the Republic, but his administration was in debt and his enemies were rallying around Houston to get back in power at the next election. General Johnston was a Lamar man, with no love for Houston and his Indian policies. He may well have expressed himself freely about political matters to Mrs. Holley. He was utterly fearless.

George Hammeken was frequently in and out of Galveston at this time, since San Luis Island, the scene of some of his real estate and commercial operations, was located just off the western end of larger Galveston Island.[4] Acting as Mrs. Holley's agent, he had attended in July to the matter of having Captain Tod's fifteen hundred acres properly surveyed, all in one piece, with a fair proportion of post oak and pine and cedar. Now he proposed that she go at once to San Luis without waiting for the uncertain date of her son's arrival from Baltimore, to see the exciting progress being made there in developing a seaport to compete with Galveston. The development company proposed to connect it with the Brazos River towns first by road and then by a railroad. Mary could not resist such an opportunity to combine business and pleasure.

George Hammeken, a bachelor in his early forties, was almost as enamored of the Texas Gulf Coast and the possibilities for its future development as Stephen Austin had been; and he had persuaded the Austin heirs to join with him in his grandiose plans. When he described to Mary how the commerce of all the world would come into the harbor of his town, she, too, was carried away by his enthusiasm and revived her dream of Texas as an El Dorado. She must have regretted that George was a little too old for one of Henry's girls, who both bid fair to be spinsters if their father had his wishes. Inevitably some intelligent young lady, maybe pretty Señorita Mexia, who had rolled her great dark eyes in Hammeken's direction at dinner that evening in New Orleans, would set her cap for him and catch him. In the meantime, Mrs. Holley found his attentions helpful and entertaining. He was, as she wrote her daughter a little deprecatingly, "the same obliging creature as ever."

Hammeken took her to San Luis the next Sunday in a buggy lent him by a friend.[5] It was a delightful drive of about twenty miles for the length, east to west, of Galveston Island along a white beach as hard and smooth as a floor. The borrowed horse was not fleet, and they jogged along in silence—the horse's hoofs made no sound at all—shivering a little in the damp wind until the mounting sun warmed them. They saw gulls and snipe and curlew on the beach, and George pointed out green turtles that laid their eggs in the sand, and alligators and snakes that slithered away as the buggy approached. Trees and logs, some of them very large, were strewn along the shore, and far down the beach a boat with a tall mast lay on its side, half-buried in sand and beaten by the surf, but still unshattered.

"Whence came it?" Mary mused with a touch of romantic melancholy, and Hammeken cheerfully reminded her that it could well be some unlucky victim of Jean Laffite's pirates who once had their headquarters in these waters. He liked to make their little trip seem adventurous, and when they came to the small bayous which cut across their way along the beach he turned out into the surf to splash across over the sandbars that always washed out from them.

When they got to the "stopping place" they both chatted in friendly wise with the woman in a clean white wrapper who was in charge of the improvised building. She had come with her husband and son four weeks earlier to this spot, where they "calculated" to make a living by keeping an accommodation for travellers. Mary listened as attentively as if she had been collecting material for a volume to rival Mrs. Trollope's *Domestic Manners.*[6] She was too good a journalist to neglect any opportunity to store away authentic information.

The sun was a red ball just above the tree tops as they reached the west end of the island, where they must cross the mile-and-a-half channel to the smaller island of San Luis. Hammeken hoisted the signal, which was a flag with one star at the top of a tall pole, and the ferryman was soon there to take them over.

In spite of all that Hammeken had told her Mary could hardly believe her eyes when she saw the wharf of San Luis—it was a thousand feet long, and there were six or eight vessels tied up there. They drove off the ferry into the main street of a town where lights gleamed along the fronts of stores and houses that were very new and mostly unpainted as yet. The hotel to which they went was run by Mr. and Mrs. Charles Bennett. It also was hardly completed and smelled of freshly sawed wood; but Mrs. Holley was shown to a spotless room on the second floor that had been plastered and whitewashed and furnished with good mahogany pieces. Hammeken likewise lived in the hotel when he was in San Luis. Both of them were ravenous when the supper bell clanged and they sat down to a damask-covered table piled high with tender venison steaks and roast wild duck and great dishes of sweet potatoes dripping in their own syrup. Tomorrow there would be fish, George assured her, since everybody went fishing on the Island.

The next day he took her around town to see the warehouses in which he was financially interested, and an extraordinary cotton compress, first of its kind in Texas, equipped with a huge wooden screw and operated by mule power. Piers were being set on the mainland side for a bridge and a causeway to connect with a proposed road in the direction of Brazoria and Columbia. The town of San Luis boasted two general stores, a portrait painter, and the *San Luis Advocate*, a thriving weekly issued approximately every Tuesday from its office at the corner of Market and Liberty Streets.[7] It had been established the previous September by two enterprising young men named Robinson and Hopkins. It was Tod Robinson whose buggy Hammeken had borrowed to drive over from Galveston. The editors welcomed to the Island and to their columns so well-known a literary figure as the author of two histories of Texas. Mrs. Holley promised to send a contribution to the *Advocate* when she had settled herself in her lodgings.

She could hardly remember feeling so well and being so much in harmony with the world and with herself as during this stay at San Luis. Left to her own devices most of the day, she could retire to her room, open the windows—they all gave upon the sea—and sit for hours with the soft air blowing gently on her cheek, looking out past the points of land to deep blue water beyond. She could see half the little island from where she sat, since it was only three miles in circumference. Oftentimes she watched four or five vessels looming simultaneously out of the distance to navigate the breakers and thread their narrow course through the Pass and into West Bay, which opened into the waters of Galveston Bay itself. The Island of San Luis had been part of Stephen's original grant, and people were saying that Emily Perry was likely to get rich from this new development of it. Mary wished that Stephen had lived to see the channel cleared and the railway built. Someday, she felt sure, all the cotton of the Brazos would pour through here to be cargo for ships from the seven seas, and his dreams would come true.

She took long walks on the smooth, gleaming beach, gathering shells as eagerly as a child and fetching them back to her room in a small basket. When her eyes tired of the sunlight she would draw the curtains at her windows and read at leisure. She had with her *Don Quixote* and *Gil Blas* in the original, to keep up her Spanish; and Irving's *Conquest of Florida* and a handsome edition of the *British Poets,* enough in all to keep her mind active if she applied herself.

She was thoroughly bored with knitting and feminine talk about household remedies and recipes. Here once more she could burnish her mind and use her wits again. Since the editors of the *Advocate* wanted something from her pen, she would start by letting them republish the verses to her husband's miniature. This was a poem of which she thought highly, and it would be interesting to see if it appealed to these young editors who knew nothing of its personal connotations. They evidently liked it. It appeared in the *Advocate* early in December,[8] and for the rest of her stay on the Island she was a regular contributor to the paper.

Soon after her arrival George Hammeken had his pianoforte brought down from his own room to the parlor on the first floor, and from that time forward the evening concerts in the Bennett House were extraordinarily pleasant. With practice she and George managed to play simple duets passably, and on one occasion she performed with the assistance of a Methodist preacher from Virginia, who sang as well as he had preached in the long dining room on the previous Sunday.

Local society was greatly enlivened during the few weeks that two

British brigs rode at anchor in the bay, the *Ironside* and the *Milton*. Their officers were gallant and well-bred, and returned the town's hospitality with promptness. One mild, sunshiny afternoon the captain of the *Ironside* invited a party, including Mrs. Holley, to go on a rowing excursion in his official gig. They landed over on the mainland, disturbing clouds of birds as the boat was beached, and then they rambled a little distance along the shore. Afterward, the gig circumnavigated San Luis Island and got back to the wharf just as the brilliant sunset faded.

Mary wrote a lively account of the excursion for the *Advocate*, embellishing it with a few verses and a colorful description of the scenery around the Island. Other contributions from her pen followed from time to time:[9] a jolly song called "The Invitation" to the tune of a popular quickstep that the musicians in the Bennett parlor must have rendered lustily; a poetic farewell to the British brigs when they weighed anchor in February; a reprint of the little verses she had done for Melazie's album. Occasionally she sent the editors more serious pieces.

In the quiet of her own chamber and during long walks on the beach, she found tranquillity. She was not rid of all her troubles or free yet from the petty ambitions and jealousies that had burdened her life for the past several years, but she found once more the source from which she had always drawn strength and courage. Sea and sky and sand spoke to her of Heaven and Majesty Divine. Nature was an image of the joys she had known and a solace for life's trials and sorrows.

One poem published at San Luis was the credo of her religious faith, the same faith that her husband attained in his maturity, the one that Stephen Austin declared in his letter to her. When she sent the verses to the *Advocate*, she gave them no title, but she might well have called them "Rhapsody to the Sea":

> Oh how I love the sea—the dark blue sea—
> The pale, the gray, the white, the foaming seas—
> The calm, the placid or the bellowing sea!
> By turns it roars, it thunders, or it moans.
> In every change I love it still. And with it
> Daily I converse . . .
> I love thee, sea; I could embrace thee, and
> My cares forget. In thy wide bosom there is
> Room for miseries like mine. Alone
> I should not be, for in thy depths is one,
> To whom my faith was pledged. Oh, what a world

Of trials have been mine. What swells of anguish,
What billowy cares were left for me, widowed,
To buffet and to stem, since the blue waters
Closed on him so mourned, so loved;
So honored, so impressed with nature's signet
Of nobility—of mental grandeur! . . . .
    What wealth is treasured in the sea! What loves
Within the mermaids' coral caverns sleep!
What mysteries lie hid from mortal ken or aim!
Rapt thought, bewildered, lost, in mazy wanderings
'Mongst the infinity of waters—peopled all,
And filled with untold wonders,—soars above
To lighter elements; and, rushing through
Illimitable space, hung with night's starry lamps—
Guides to the mariner through trackless, devious ways:
Worlds upon worlds—seeks the creating and
Sustaining cause—The Hand Divine.[10]

Even in San Luis there was business to look after, with Hammeken's help, in connection with her land. In due time Horace arrived at the port in Galveston,[11] and visited on the mainland with his uncle and cousins to get his first view of Texas. James Austin, four or five years younger than he, was already nagging his father to be allowed to join the army, and the notion came to Mary's mind that her son would be expected to serve as a soldier if they settled here. It might be a good thing for him, she thought. However, he showed no inclination to become a soldier or a farmer or anything else that required him to assume responsibility. He liked to fish and hunt and go on expeditions in the new country, if someone else showed the way.

Her son's lack of purpose served to crystallize Mary's own resolve not to fall into inertia and laziness. All her life she had found pleasure in intellectual occupation. When beset by misfortune and disappointment she had roused herself to activity. Here on San Luis she felt the excitement of creative inspiration—Madame de Staël called it enthusiasm—and her ideas flowed freely. With editors at hand who were asking to publish her work, she set down her philosophy of the "active life" in a small essay. This was a literary form that suited her admirably, and one that she might have undertaken earlier save that she had no precedent in her day for a woman's writing personal essays:

That *occupation* is a source of content, if not of happiness, is a trite remark that nobody disputes. But few are aware of the great pleasure flowing from mental activity—*intellectual occupation.* . . .

Idleness is no less the mother of misery than of vice—"I cannot study," says one; "I cannot write," says another, "I have nothing to do, the day is long, the night still longer; it is cold, it is stormy, it is hot." "I am wretched," Satan said—

"Which way I fly is hell, myself am hell."

Child of idleness, you do not try; you have not learned that there is pleasure in effort; that from a first effort springs a second, a third, with increasing power until the whole mind is roused into action, and lighted with happiness; and the long train of blue devils fly, like apparitions before the dawning of reason—"the clear day spring from on high."[12]

She had meant to spend only ten days or so on San Luis but it was several months before she left. She realized at length that her practical affairs would be better attended to in Galveston and that Horace needed her presence there. The happy interlude on the little island had been like a brief return to the days of her youth, and her goodbye in the *Advocate* to her friends was in the familiar romantic pattern:

Adieu To San Luis
Adieu! sunny island; adieu! verdant glade;
Adieu! sea-girt shore, where so long I have strayed;

. . . .

Adieu! idle scribblings, that many a day,
Beguiled of its ennui, by innocent play;
Which ambling, or trotting, lame-footed or blind,
In mad prose or dull verse, would an *Advocate* find;
Thanks, thanks for indulgence, though poorly deserved,
In memory's casket 'twill long be preserved.

. . . .

San Luis, March 25, 1841   M.[13]

Back in Galveston she sold more land to Captain Tod, who was now in command of the Naval Station there, accepting his notes and crediting him in the deal with the cash he had advanced to her son for his passage from Baltimore. She completed this transaction over the protest of Henry Austin, who had controlled her Texas property up to now. He disapproved of the terms of the sale, and declared Hammeken to be "as visionary as a girl." Whether or not it was good business for her to sell out to Tod at the time, the money was necessary for her needs.

Life in Galveston was very unlike the quiet society of San Luis. Everywhere she found turmoil and talk of change. People were gossiping about the difficulties of Count Saligny, the French chargé d'affaires, who took refuge here after being "outraged," as he declared, in Austin. He had built his dignified legation on one of the hills overlooking the town and entertained the citizens lavishly. But, alas, his charming premises were invaded by the pigs of a neighboring innkeeper, one Richard Bullock; and the quarrel which ensued was reported through proper diplomatic channels all the way to the King of France himself. Saligny's brother-in-law, as it happened, was the French Minister of Finance; and the matter took on an international significance that made it a serious threat to the new Republic.[14] The Texans, some of whom had caught the Count in some sharp money deals, laughed behind his back at the "Pig War," and merely listened politely to his threats and speeches on the subject.

Much more important was the military expedition which President Lamar was organizing to send troops and traders westward to the town of Santa Fé on the Upper Rio Grande to invite its residents, still citizens of Mexico, to become Texans. By the acquisition of Santa Fé Texas would extend its borders to the mountains and also control the valuable trade from the United States, which was now beginning to move westward from Missouri on the Santa Fé Trail. Volunteers who joined the expedition anticipated a profitable trip, enlivened by hunting and exploration. Its organizers were confident that the New Mexicans would welcome a chance to be annexed.

Already in May, 1841, every vessel entering the port of Galveston brought recruits for the Lamar project. Men seeking to enlist were camping near the town of Austin while they waited. An enterprising young New Englander who had recently established the New Orleans *Picayune* arrived expecting that the tour would furnish him with material to emulate Washington Irving's literary chronicle of the prairies to the north. His name was George W. Kendall,[15] and since he was a frequent guest of the Chinns in New Orleans, he and Mrs. Holley may well have been acquainted. One of Kendall's fellow volunteers was the son of General Leslie Combs of Lexington. Young Franklin Combs was seeking not only adventure but a cure for defective hearing.[16]

Mrs. Holley envied these young men on their way to begin the long journey to Santa Fé, especially George Kendall, who could easily fill a score of notebooks with interesting observations. Her own hopes for travel to distant lands had faded. She knew now that she would never be privileged to record her impressions of Scotland or London or Rome. Nevertheless, she still had plans for writing which she felt she must complete—the memoir of Stephen that Lamar had abandoned—and she was resolved to push forward with it as soon as she got her son settled in life. When she was in honest mood she had to admit to herself that she did not know how or when she would be able to accomplish the latter task.

19. THE NEW TEXAS
1841-1844

When Mrs. Holley and her son arrived at the Brand home in Lexington the last of June to occupy their old rooms they found that Elmwood, spacious as it was, seemed a trifle crowded. The birth of a son early in the spring[1] gave William and his wife seven children, the oldest of them being seventeen. They were all healthy and well behaved and biddable, and their Grandmother Holley was proud of them, discerning in each one a unique personality. She had always advocated new ideas about child training, especially in music and drawing and languages; and during this extended stay with her grandchildren she had the leisure to try out some of her theories on them.

Quite naturally she was out of touch with the life of the community after her long absence, and in some regards out of step as well. Transylvania was once more strait-laced and orthodox under the control of President Robert Davidson, who was known to be laboriously compiling a history of the Presbyterian Church in Kentucky.[2] She winced at the certainty that he would show no mercy to the late Horace Holley in his book. The relationship of the Brands with the University was friendly, however, and William H., as the oldest son was called to distinguish him from his father, was enrolled as a freshman along with other lads from the town's best families. Mrs. Holley did not enter her own son in the University again. At his age there was no use trying any longer to make him attend classes. Out of friendship to her some of the doctors of the Medical College took an interest in the youth's nervous symptoms and prescribed for his various ailments, real and imaginary.

Upon her return she talked freely about Texas to General McCalla and others who had been her colleagues in supporting the fight for its liberation from Mexico, but she now found them interested only in whether it could be annexed and so increase the number of senators from the cotton kingdom. The Brands and the Gratzes and the other Clay followers gladly avoided any mention of Texas. Their Whig Party was endeavoring to effect a compromise between the North and the

South on the issue of slavery, and they counted Texas well lost if a conflict could be averted. Nobody seemed to comprehend what a vast territory would be added to the nation if Texas were admitted. Nobody displayed any interest in the Santa Fé Expedition until it turned out to be a tragic failure, its members marched as prisoners all the way to Mexico City. Then people wagged their heads and said they had not thought much of Texas since the Kentucky volunteers were badly treated down there. Mrs. Holley learned to maintain a diplomatic silence on the subject, and turned her attention to the activities of her daughter's world.

A happy hour in the round of each succeeding week was morning prayer at Christ Church when the household, including all the children old enough to sit still, occupied two full pews. Beloved Mr. Berkeley read the service in a fine tenor voice, and if Wilhelm Iucho happened not to be there to play the organ, or the bellows boy failed to show up, the rector would raise the tune himself. Mrs. Holley would willingly have done so if it had been proper for a woman to be that forward in church.

Mr. Iucho was now a great asset to the community. He not only gave music lessons to a large class of young pupils, including Lizzie and Mary Brand, but also ran a popular music store cluttered with the newest sheet music. He carried a stock of fine-toned pianofortes, sometimes at reduced prices. He frequently accompanied visiting artists in approved professional manner.

The cheerful Iucho home on Market Street near the College Lot was a favorite stopping place for Mrs. Holley on her customary afternoon walks. Gentle Julia Iucho, with several round-faced, blue-eyed children clinging to her skirts, served steaming coffee in her good china cups while Wilhelm played a set of his own quadrilles titled *Heatherflowers* or maybe one of his polkas.[3]

A few doors from the Iuchos lived Dr. Robert Peter, an English-born professor of chemistry and pharmacy in the Medical College, who had married into one of the aristrocratic Fayette County families—his wife's great-uncle was the orator Patrick Henry—and soon became an enthusiastic Kentuckian. He was a dedicated scientist and teacher, and a collector of learned books and instruments. Mrs. Holley found him congenial because, more than any of the present faculty, he cherished her husband's dream of true academic distinction for the University.[4] In the Peter library was a copy of the *Discourse* inscribed by Dr. Caldwell to his younger colleague.[5] She could very properly have asked to be allowed to add her own name as coauthor to the inscription on the fly-leaf, and she might have done so had she foreseen that Robert Peter would be the first historian of Transylvania to defend President Holley's liberal views against the continuing maledictions of Davidson and other orthodox theologians.

For more than a year and a half she and her son stayed as guests at the Brand home, neither of them very contented. Drastic remedies did little for Horace's bad health and the doctor's diagnosis was usually that he was well enough to do whatever he wanted to do. What he wanted to do was to get away from Lexington, and since Mary was making no progress with her own plans, literary or financial, she decided to go once more to Texas, not at Henry's invitation this time, but independently.

She stayed on through the end of December, 1842, however, to be with her daughter when another baby arrived.[6] She did not approve of the heavy responsibilities that her daughter was undertaking or of William's masculine assumption that their large family was a blessing in which all the relatives should have a part. He expected his own mother and sisters to help out with the care of his children from time to time, and, of course, thought that his wife's mother, living there in the house, should do so. She found such duties confining, and managed her plans so that the Galveston newspapers noted the arrival of Mrs. Holley and her son February 5, 1843, aboard the *New York* from New Orleans, along with a score or more of other passengers.[7]

Fortunately for her, this ship's list included several influential persons and in conversing with them during the voyage she was quick to recognize the rapidly changing currents in Texas affairs. One of the passengers was William Kennedy, recently appointed British consul at Galveston,[8] who was on his way to that place with two servants to establish a residence for the coming of his wife and family. He had recently published a handsome, two-volume work titled *The Rise, Progress, and Prospect of Texas*, based upon his extensive travels in the area soon after the battle of San Jacinto and upon much research and intelligent use of the previous writers on the subject. He had noted and quoted "Mrs. Holley" as an early authority in a flattering number of instances, and reproduced the poetic description of a Texas prairie in spring from her 1836 volume. In contrast with the unfriendly attitude of some other recent commentators on the Republic, he was as pro-Texas as she was.

After an exchange of literary compliments, the two historians had an opportunity during the voyage to discuss his government's policy toward Texas. He was being sent as consul to promote the relations of the

Southern cotton planters with British interests. His country opposed the annexation of Texas to the United States, desiring rather that it should become an independent nation. When he talked of that vexatious problem he did so in guarded terms, because another of the prominent passengers was William Sumter Murphy, chargé d'affaires from the United States to Texas, who was, as everyone knew, being sent to promote President Tyler's plans for early annexation. Mrs. Holley listened carefully to Mr. Murphy, too, finding him likewise an agreeable and friendly gentleman.

Most probably the general conversation among the passengers pacing the deck or politely gathering in the dining saloon was carried on by outspoken Texas citizens like Robert Mills,[9] a merchant of Brazoria, whose counting rooms were reputedly stacked high with bars of Mexican silver, and George M. Collinsworth,[10] famous fighter at the battle of Velasco in 1832 and now port collector at Matagorda. Both gentlemen were acquainted with Henry Austin, and could inform Mrs. Holley that her brother's son James had enlisted during the previous autumn in the Brazoria company to march against the Mexicans. When the Texas troops reached the border the lad had been one of three hundred impetuous soldiers who refused to obey the order to turn back from Laredo, and had crossed the Rio Grande to engage a large force of the enemy drawn up for battle at a village called Mier. Outnumbered and outmaneuvered, they had surrendered and, like the Santa Fé adventurers, had been marched away as prisoners. Nobody could say for sure who was dead and who was living, if being a Mexican prisoner could be called living. Sam Houston, now serving a second term as President, disclaimed responsibility for the plight of the prisoners because they had gone against orders, and was making only diplomatic efforts in their behalf. His political enemies blamed him bitterly for the tragic muddle.

Mary Holley was grief-stricken at the thought of her young nephew marching under the lash across the mountain trails toward a Mexican dungeon, and her son listened to the news with wide eyes and pale lips, shaken at last out of his indifference toward public events. He was beginning to think that he did not want to live in Texas. Within a few weeks the newspapers announced that James Austin was officially listed among those killed at the Battle of Mier. Survivors of the expedition told later how he had died on Christmas Day in a gallant, foolhardy skirmish when a handful of Texans tried to halt the advance of a troop of Mexican cavalry that outnumbered them twenty-five to one.[11] Mary's annoyance with her brother over money matters was softened by their grieving together over young James, dead before he had a chance to live.

For some months she was too involved in the problems of her own personal world to share as much as she would have liked in the exciting public events that were taking place around her. At one time there were rumors of invasion and the President ordered the state papers removed for safety from the new capital on the Colorado to the village of Washington-on-the-Brazos. The irate citizens of Austin resisted the removal with cannon fire, and actually succeeded in keeping possession of the documents. Houston let the matter pass. He had enough troubles without getting involved in an archives war with his own people.

One of his most vexing problems was the Texas Navy. It was reduced now to just two seaworthy vessels under the command of Commodore Edwin Moore, a Lamar appointee, who was carrying out the terms of an old contract made under the Lamar administration to assist the state of Yucatán in its attacks on Mexican ships. President Houston pronounced Moore and his men to be pirates; but the Texas Navy continued to carry on its maneuvers at sea.

There the matter stood in the summer of 1843, and the town was rocked with excitement as rumors and counterrumors blew in on every wind from the Gulf. Would Old Sam clap the Commodore in irons and courtmartial him and his men when they came into port? Would the fleet be sold at auction as Congress had ordered? How would all this affect the troubling question of annexation?[12]

In such exciting times Mary lived a divided life. Before her very eyes the drama of the Republic, of the Austin Colony and all that had resulted from it, was being enacted. Behind the scenes great nations were using Texas as a pawn in a world-wide chess game; in the foreground politicians and commodores quarrelled for power, and offstage on the dusty banks of the Rio Grande incompetent officers blundered into Mexican traps and surrendered their men to be imprisoned or shot. She pored over the local newspapers, doubly interested because she was acquainted with the editors. *The Civilian and Galveston Gazette,* loyal at all cost to Houston, was the mouthpiece of Hamilton Stuart, who had learned his undeviating Democratic Party politics in Georgetown, Kentucky.[13] The other journals were anti-Houston, one being the continuation of the *San Luis Advocate,* now run by Ferdinand Pinckard, brother of Dr. Thomas B. Pinckard of the Transylvania Medical School and the Christ Church Vestry. There was no longer a pro-Lamar paper, but his influence was strongly felt wherever there was opposition to Houston.

Mary proceeded cautiously when she conversed with these influential editors in order to draw them out and discover what the leaders were planning. She did not wish to be anti-anyone; she wanted to be known only as pro-Stephen F. Austin. She wondered what policies he would have advocated in these later crises, and as she made up her own mind she thought always of his ideals and ambitions.

The other half of her divided life was given over to the old, familiar wrestling with money matters and land deals and to making some sort of satisfactory settlement with Henry about their joint holdings. She seems to have lived quietly, maybe with her brother, who was then residing in the town, and to have turned Horace over to his uncle's companionship or to his own devices on the beach, where he could ride horseback and hunt for wild fowl and fish along the shore.

In March after her arrival the will of Stephen F. Austin, which James Perry had presented for probate six years earlier, was filed in court and Perry legally appointed executor.[14] That made available to her the league of land on Bayou Flores which had been bequeathed to her. Henry Austin was up to his ears in debt, not only to her but to various other persons, but by the end of June he figured out an arrangement that acknowledged his obligation to her of thirty-six hundred dollars. The best he could do by way of settlement was to make a small cash payment and to execute a chattel mortgage on four of his slaves until he could repay her in full with legal interest. Archibald Austin, who was one of the witnesses, may have come from New Orleans to help arrange this matter. Along in the fall, on somebody's shrewd advice, Mary Holley had this legal instrument sworn to before the County Clerk of Galveston County by the other witness.[15] She was resolved to get what she believed was due her from Henry, both in settlement of his various investments for her as agent and in payment for her years of caring for his children. She had at times lent him money outright. Henry also owed William Brand a sizable sum of money, but she concluded that William and the other creditors would have to look out for themselves.

George Hammeken was not in the Galveston area during her first months there. His ambitious project on San Luis Island had been destroyed in a tropical storm the previous summer. Tides and gales had filled the harbor and closed it to navigation. Residents of the battered and still unpainted houses and stores had left them standing vacant while they settled elsewhere, and letters addressed to Hammeken were advertised as uncalled for by the Galveston post office.[16] Mary found it sad to know that the "sunny island" was a ghost of its former self, and all the plans for the railroad abandoned. She missed George's solicitude and helpful attentions. However visionary his plans were, he had been diligent in her behalf, and she found it harder to make business arrangements without his aid.

The storm that ruined San Luis had spared Galveston, which now boasted three hundred buildings besides four churches.[17] Well-to-do families dined on Westphalia ham and Holland cheese and imported wines if they chose to do so. At Mr. Pix's store opposite the court house the ladies could obtain silk parasols, much needed in the summer sunshine, or embroidered black hose and tooth powder and lavender water; and at Mr. Jonse's bookshop they could purchase either a new Lever novel or the *Ladies Self-Instructor in Millinery*. At the end of a round of morning shopping it was quite proper for Mrs. Holley and the other ladies to sit a while in the rocking chairs on the Tremont House veranda to look over the newly arrived newspapers. One always met a few friends there or, better still, strangers from the States with news of the kind that was not to be found in the papers.

In mid-July Commodore Moore brought his fleet into the harbor, the sloop of war *Austin* and the brig *Wharton*. On board was Texas Commissioner James Morgan, whom Houston had ordered to meet the ships at New Orleans and sell them forthwith. Colonel Morgan had, however, been converted by the Commodore to the wisdom of preserving the vessels and had accompanied them as a sympathetic observer while they engaged the Mexican ships in battle. He and Commodore Moore published long justifications of their actions in the anti-Houston *Telegraph*.

Most Galvestonians supported the Navy against the President, including Mary, who liked Colonel Morgan as a long-time friend and fellow admirer of Austin. At a Ladies Meeting the Texan seamen were openly declared to be heroes, and a poem in their praise written "By a Lady of Galveston" appeared in the newspaper—an anti-Houston one, naturally.[18] The anonymous author may have been Mrs. Holley, although the town boasted other literary ladies who appeared in the press from time to time. At all events, she approved when the Commodore and his gallant men were cleared of the charge of piracy by the Texan Congress. She relished being once more in the main stream of politics. She was at her best, her mind most active and fruitful, when she was engaged with the world beyond the four walls of a house.

Life in Galveston became highly diverting. Along in the winter a crowd of prominent citizens was invited to an elegant party given by the officers of the United States schooner *Flirt*, which lay in the harbor. Dancing began at eight with a promenade, and the brilliantly lighted deck was crowded with ladies in their best silks and gentlemen in multicolored uniforms and official decorations, including Mr. Murphy and Consul Kennedy. At eleven-thirty the curtain of flags that hung across the afterdeck was raised to reveal a supper table that, according to the account in the Galveston *Gazette*, "groaned beneath the weight and variety of rich viands." Afterward dancing was "resumed and kept up until a late hour."[19]

In March Mrs. Holley drove over with a party of friends to spend a week at the extensive plantation home of Colonel and Mrs. Morgan, located at the mouth of the San Jacinto River, only a few miles from the town of Houston.[20] As a settler in the Austin Colony, James Morgan had become rich in mercantile and real estate operations. Here at Orange Grove he bred fine cattle and conducted agricultural experiments, both of which he proudly exhibited to his numerous guests, telling them as he did so how the naturalist Audubon had found some of his rarest birds during a stay on the plantation.[21] The fortunate visitors feasted on oranges and were served all manner of delicately prepared oysters and shrimp and wild game.

Mrs. Holley almost persuaded the house party of which she was a member to go on with her for a similar visit at Peach Point Plantation, and was genuinely disappointed when they "backed out." She had no conveyance at her personal disposal, and this had seemed an excellent chance to drive over to see the Perrys and confer with Emily about making use of the family papers for the biography of Stephen. Now she would have to resort to correspondence with her cousin.

Another entertainment in the bay proved as enjoyable as the ball on the *Flirt* and more rewarding, because it furnished her with a valuable bit of unrecorded history. Captain Taylor of the United States clipper *Vigilant* entertained a party of townspeople by showing them a collection of "piratical trophies" which adorned his cabin. There were scimitars, daggers, pistols, a suit of hammered steel armor with a helmet covered by a scarf, *à la Turc*, and, in particular, a bright brass fourpounder, inscribed as of 1640 and surmounted with the crown of England. This last prize the Captain had captured from one of Laffite's privateers.

Mary made notes in her journal about these excursions. Extravagant as she was with money, she carefully hoarded the interesting things she saw and heard as useful material for her writing. The attentiveness with which she listened in her youth to Uncle Nathan Beers or Luther Holley remained hers through the years. While she was in the cabin of the *Vigilant* she made a hasty drawing of the inscription and the crown on Captain Taylor's brass four-pounder. It might prove useful some time or other.[22]

At last, after about a year in Galveston, she turned her attention to collecting material about Stephen Austin and the Texas of his day. First, she arranged to send Horace to visit his relatives in the East, and then she moved into an excellent boardinghouse presided over by the wife of the Reverend Mr. John Newland Maffitt, a cheerful, Irish-born Methodist preacher, who had conducted mighty revivals in Lexington and other towns in the South some eight or ten years previously. He was also known as a poet whose lines appeared in many newspapers.[23] His three young-lady daughters further enlivened the social life of the establishment, which was frequented by many prominent persons, notably Captain Elliott, chargé d'affaires from Great Britain, and other public men who favored England as an ally of Texas. When the Captain heard of Mrs. Holley's proposed literary project he urged her to pursue it. So did Lamar, who was on friendly terms with the Maffitt family and often at the house. And when President Houston occasionally joined them for one of Mrs. M.'s excellent dinners, he also encouraged her to memorialize Stephen Austin at the earliest practicable season.

Such requests were heartening, but the immediate cause for bestirring herself about this long-contemplated task was the news that Stephen's relatives at Peach Point were actively gathering information about his life. Young Guy Bryan began to push the matter.[24] George Hammeken, now back in Texas, was asked for the detailed story of Stephen's death, which he had faithfully set down and sent to Guy. A similar request was made of Gail Borden when he visited the plantation in February, probably in connection with buying cattle from James Perry; and he obligingly furnished a firsthand account of Austin's return to the Colony in September, 1833, all the more valuable because at the time he was serving the Empresario as surveyor, clerk, editor, and friend.

Mrs. Holley met and talked with Gail Borden during her stay in Galveston.[25] They were on the best of terms, but neither seems to have made a strong impression on the other. Borden was a tall, shabbily dressed man in his forties who was always in a hurry. He was currently engaged in a protracted legal battle with President Houston to keep from being dismissed from the office of port collector on account of some minor infractions of rules. Meanwhile, he was the busiest man in the town, forever promoting good causes and experimenting with ingenious inventions. The authorities had discouraged his "Locomotive Bath House for Both Sexes," thus depriving the ladies of Galveston of the pleasure of the beach, but he had in mind other equally beneficial ideas, such as pulverized meat biscuits, and milk so treated that it would be safe for babies. He was oblivious of other people, but Mary should have discerned in him another eccentric genius like Rafinesque and cultivated his acquaintance more assiduously for the sake of his invaluable knowledge of Stephen Austin's Colony. However, Borden was not a gallant man, and he answered her inquiries about the Austin records by advising her to go to Peach Point and settle down to copy her materials for herself. He was absorbed in his own intellectual adventures, and at the time he conversed with her he may well have been on his way home to see if his long-suffering wife Penelope was stirring a fruit mixture he was boiling in a huge iron kettle. He believed that it could be put up as preserves by using hydraulic pressure. Or Mrs. Holley may have talked with him while his five-year-old son, Stephen F. Austin Borden, was coming down with a fatal fever.

The letter to Emily Perry about the family papers was a difficult one to write, and Mary spent a sleepless night or two before she arose early one spring morning to get the task done:

Dear Cousin:
I have tried in vain ever since I've been in Texas to get to see you. Every attempt has been futile. I'm about to leave in the *New York* in a few days, having passed more than a year in Texas without seeing you, much to my regret.

She knew that the relatives at Peach Point had been aware of her proximity, through Henry or Hammeken or numerous other persons, and they might have wondered that she had not come to see them. Let them wonder. She could not bring herself to set down that she had been too poor to afford a carriage, nor would she tell them that as long as her son was with her she had not been free to go on extended visits. The rest of the letter was easier once she had got past the beginning:

In the retirement of Lexington I shall have leisure to undertake a work which has been much urged upon me—a memoir of our lamented Stephen. Not an elaborate work, but a neat & concise history of him, that will bring out his name from the rubbish that surrounds it, in bright relief before the Country and the world. Strange as it may seem, it has become necessary to rescue his name from comparative oblivion even before the generation in which it shone has passed away. Gen. Lamar and Capt. Elliott urge me to the work & even Houston is always preaching to me of Stephen.

For this object I want such papers in your possession as may best elucidate the subject. Whatever relates to the early settlement & your father's plans & efforts, especially, which will form the introduction. Correspondence with Baron de Bastrop—& others—Hawkins—etc. Mr. Hammeken or Major Austin, no doubt, will make copies for me. I want copies of his letters of instructions & other papers while Stephen was Secy. of State & everything else that will illustrate his character & shed light on his name. I have copies of the journals.

If, dear Cousin, you will send these papers to Edward Hall, Texas Consulate, N.O., I will do my best to produce a work that you will not be ashamed of & that will be welcomed by everybody. It shall bring out the Austin name. The Harpers will be glad to send out such a volume & I feel that it is my province to be its author. The men are too much involved in party politics, & have too many selfish aims to subserve.[26]

After she had finished out the sheet with a little news of the town and many kind remembrances to Mr. Perry, Eliza, Guy, Henry, and "one and all," she felt much better. This was all she could do about the Peach Point manuscripts, and she must now use her remaining time at Galveston interviewing people who could furnish fresh material for her story. She did not intend to leave town for several weeks but communication with the interior was so uncertain that it had seemed best to urge haste upon her cousin.

She had an opportunity to talk at length with General Lamar during the first week in April when he was staying with the Maffitts. The friendly air of the place and the pretty misses seemed to help him forget his grief at the recent loss of his own sixteen-year-old daughter. He was probably not aware that one of the Maffitt girls, about that same age, was deeply enamored of him. He spent his time in the parlor talking about politics and books with Mrs. Holley, who busily noted down what he was telling her.

Assuming a dramatic pose, he assured her that the biography of Austin was a task for which she was uniquely suited, and then began to talk about himself.[27]

"I never write anymore if I can help it," he said. "If I have a letter to perpetrate, I get some one to do it for me. I will tell you the following anecdotes and you can write them down."

He recalled vividly the sights and sounds of the fighting at San Jacinto—how a beautiful young man named Lane had saved him from certain death by a Mexican lance, and about the broken scabbard and blade of Santa Anna's sword, picked up on the field, which were among his souvenirs in Georgia. Always in his rambling remarks he came back to Houston. He recalled Houston's feverish colloquy with Santa Anna the night after the battle as the two commanders, the captor and the conquered, lay in adjacent tents; and he spoke of that famous lost document which some of the Texas officers drew up the next day to prove that Sam was a coward, a document that he, Lamar, had heard read aloud by a man who secreted the paper, and was now dead. Lamar still distrusted the President, accusing him of "blowing hot and cold" about union with the United States. He himself had given up his dream of making Texas an independent nation. He was now openly for annexation, and he criticized Houston for vacillating about this all-important question.

Lamar talked of Stephen, too, always with admiration and respect. He resented the treatment the founder of the Colony had received at the end of his career and mourned the circumstances of his death.

"Austin took the humble and onorous place of Secretary of State against his wishes and his sense of justice," he commented bitterly, "and only from pure patriotism. Newcomers who could not understand his pure motives called it love of office—better have called it love of work! He had the brunt of the labor, all the thinking and writing and instruction. . . . it killed him."

Mary copied down his words as nearly *verbatim* as she could, reassured by the way in which Lamar's opinions about Stephen coincided with her own. His unfavorable estimate of Houston was no part of her story but she recorded the derogatory anecdotes with a certain satisfaction. She bore a literary grudge against Sam Houston, who, according to a Texas newspaper, had frequently and publicly accused her of not reporting the truth in her history of Texas in order to benefit her cousin's Colony.[28] Nevertheless, she proposed to get help from him for her biography of Stephen.

The next Sunday while people were at church, President Houston arrived at the Galveston wharf, receiving a salute of welcome from the volunteer company that startled the worshippers. When Mrs. Holley and the other guests got back to the Maffit House they were told that the President was closeted with Captain Elliott on business that must surely pertain to diplomatic relations with Great Britain.

At the dinner table there was a parade of dignitaries. Seated with the President were not only Captain Elliott but also three German ships' captains and the consul from Bremen, all bursting with pride at the honor of dining with a great man who ranked, they declared, with the

King of Prussia and the Emperor of Russia. Afterward Houston asked how to get to the home of a friend and Mrs. Holley offered to conduct him there. This was as good a chance as she was likely to get for asking his views on Stephen. As they proceeded slowly on their way he willingly gave his opinions.[29]

"I always liked General Austin, the Father and Foundation of the country," he began. "There would have been nothing here but for him." Mary concentrated on his words so she could record them the moment she got back to her notebooks:

I am peace man—followed Austin policy—he was forced into war measures by demagogues—I pledged myself to him not to take civil office—Conflicting circumstances forced me to do so, in order to reconcile discordant elements—had I not run, Smith would—enemies of Austin filled the public with base slanders —charging him with speculations—subscribing to Mexico acting for his own interests &c., &c. We always agreed—I followed him to his grave—Was one of those rare spirits that come but seldom—a real patriot—not a mere politician, few would appreciate his rare qualities—he knew the Mexican character—act slow—must be approached quietly—slowly.

Mary asked a good many questions that required answers. Houston defended his much discussed orders regarding the Alamo, and denied that he had commanded San Felipe to be burned in the retreat before San Jacinto, but merely brushed aside the matter of liberating Santa Anna. They parted with mutual protestations of gratitude for favors done, and she went home to weigh his words carefully against what others had told her.

Another dignitary was in town, Chargé d'Affaires Murphy of the United States, with whom she also had an interview.[30] In fact, he called upon her formally for the express purpose of warning her that the Maffitt House was a hotbed of foreign intrigue. Immediately after that Sunday dinner he had heard alarming news of what went on. On unimpeachable authority he had been informed that Houston had said to the foreigners, "There will be no annexation," and he had then rushed to demand an explanation.

"Is it true, Mr. President?" he had asked. "Am I deceived after all?"

"Oh, my dear sir," Sam had replied lightly, "I must talk to suit my company. I didn't mean anything. Spare me! I am dogged—I am obliged to say anything, do anything."

Murphy went on to pour out an indictment of Houston for shifting back and forth on the question of annexation, thereby greatly embarrassing him officially in the eyes of the authorities in Washington. To such an extent that he was being recalled. He was going home gladly, he vowed, "to see my children, my wife, whom I love better than anything in the world, though very ugly—and be governor of my state."

Mary jotted down amusing little sidelights like Mr. Murphy's ambitions, knowing that they might give color in some way to her writing. Most of her interviews proved to be about the present political situation and added little to the story of Stephen.

She had made up her own mind about annexation and decided independently that Texas ought to be a part of the United States. She had been loyal in her two earlier books to Stephen's political policies advocating first allegiance to Mexico and then patriotism for the new Republic; but there was every reason to believe that if he were living he would now favor admission to the Union. In her heart she had always looked upon Texas as an extension of her native country. When she saw how eager Captain Elliott and Consul Kennedy and other foreign representatives were to bring Texas under the sphere of their influence, she knew that she wanted to see it a part of the United States.

The most colorful of all her interviews with early Texans that spring was a series of visits with Mrs. Angelina Belle Eberly, a tavern keeper of the town, who had come out from Tennessee as a bride with some of the first settlers of Austin's Colony in 1822.[31] She had lived a hard, rugged life, and Mary thought of her now as an old woman, although Angelina was in reality fifteen or sixteen years the younger of the two. She and her first husband had run a hostelry at San Felipe which was well patronized up to the time of its being burned when Houston's army retreated before the advance of Santa Anna in 1836. She was a gold mine of information about the early days of the Austin Colony, including the mistakes and misfortunes and scandals of a good many respected citizens. She remembered Stephen Austin with affection. She had knit a pair of socks for him once when he had no money to pay her for them.

Never had Mrs. Holley taken such copious and rapid notes. This was the very stuff of pioneer life, and she encouraged Angelina to continue.

"All looked up to Austin—he seemed like the father of a happy family. He entered into our sport," Angelina recalled in telling of the very early days at San Felipe. "All young and gay people—never were people happier. We used to hunt and fish and dance in little parties. Only one priest came all this time—he christened my son, and Austin was godfather."

Mrs. Eberly remembered many rough and vulgar incidents. She saw a man tarred and feathered in her own yard with feathers from one of her pillows, and a little girl prisoner in San Antonio whom the Comanche Indians sold for money. She told a terrible story of Governor Joseph Desha's son Isaac, pardoned by his father for one murder in Kentucky and convicted for another afterward in Texas.[32] Memories must have crowded around Mary Holley as she wrote down this last sordid tale, remembering that Governor Desha, more than any other man, had destroyed her husband's career at Transylvania.

Liveliest of Mrs. Eberly's reminiscences were those of the perilous times before and during the battle of San Jacinto. As a civilian caught in the tangle of confusion and destruction, she had seen or heard first hand a thousand things that the military reports omitted, and she had not forgotten any of them. She had told some of her stories to Lamar and others before she met Mrs. Holley, but no one else took such copious notes of her remarks. When Angelina had finished relating the realistic background of Houston's glorious victory, she got around to telling about the Archives War in Austin, in which she had fired the cannon at the wagons that were taking away the documents from the Capitol. Unfortunately she did not make a long story of that lively episode, maybe because her time ran out on one of their visits. Moreover, Mary was trying to keep the garrulous pioneer lady close to the subject of Stephen Austin.

Having received no reply from Emily Perry at the end of several weeks, Mary wrote her again in somewhat more detail about the memoir of Stephen, and about another matter which seemed to call for correspondence:

I met the other day with Mr. Baldwin, who told me that Austin and Guy were coming to go to the U.S.—thought with some view to getting Mr. Bancroft, or some other to write a life of Stephen. I know that gentleman well. He is an excellent writer & no doubt could do it well . . . according to rule. But would a person indifferent to the subject, knowing nothing about the country, & full of *prejudices* against it, be apt to do it *con amore* as I should? I think not. I am an Austin—& a Texan. With him it would be a speculation . . . and a work to sell.

She went on at some length to argue her case, and expressed a hope that Emily's sons would make the trip back to the States on the same vessel with her. She ended with an item of news that was going the rounds in Galveston: "They say Annexation is near in the U.S., but my doubts rest with Sam Houston . . ."[33]

On the same day she wrote a long, formal letter to Judge David G.

Burnet, who had served both as Provisional President and Vice-President of the Texas government.[34] He was a brusque, honest man, who was always on the conservative side, always an Austin-Lamar man, and always an implacable foe of Houston. She asked for his "ideas . . . in relation to S. F. Austin, causes of his not being elected—state of parties then, &c., &c., not forgetting Foreign Relations at this present momentous crisis." She addressed him at his plantation near Houston, where he was engaged in experimental farming until such time as he could once more enter the political arena. She was discovering that she must turn to men of her own generation to find anyone who still thought of himself as a follower of Stephen Austin, and she was finding it difficult to avoid current political issues in her book, which she wished to center on the life and character of the Founder. She told Judge Burnet that she planned not "an elaborate work . . . but a concise, exact, truthful volume of reference."

At the end of April she still had not heard from Peach Point, but she could wait no longer. As she had expressed it to the Judge, circumstances compelled her to return to Lexington for "retirement and leisure to begin her labors." She could have added that she must stay there until the question of annexation was settled and Texas land could once more be sold at a reasonable figure. She sent a third, even longer appeal for help to Emily, still using the most intimate style. After she had closed it with an affectionate "Yours, dear Cousin," she added a postscript: "If Guy would come to Lexington we might put our heads together on this business. Harriette has a large house, plenty of room."[35] She sent this letter by one of the Perry's neighbors, a Mr. Hawkins, thus insuring its arrival.

She recalled Guy as an intelligent lad, with a real interest in his uncle's fame and in the family history. Maybe he could be persuaded to read and copy those documents in the study at Peach Point for her. It would be helpful to have a young assistant and critic. Guy might turn out to be as helpful as Julius Clarke.

Just before she left Galveston a reply written on April 29 came from Emily, prompted by that last letter sent in Hawkins' care. "Yes, dear Cousin," it read, "come on over to Peach Point and examine Stephen's papers. Take copies of any you want, but I cannot part with the originals . . . Stay with us and my Eliza will help you copy. I am anxious that my Brother's life be written and I am willing that you should write it . . . but I cannot help you with the Expenses. It was signed "Sincerely and affectionately, your friend and Cousin."[36]

When this affectionate, noncommittal message arrived, Mary was packing her trunks to leave, but she paused to consider carefully what it said and what it did not say. Emily agreed for her to write a life of Stephen but carefully did not refer to it as a history, and did not intend to lend her any of the family records. Perhaps the Perry family really did propose to authorize someone else to use them for a full-scale book on Texas. Since Mary had not asked for financial assistance in publishing her biography Emily's flat refusal to share the expense seemed a little unnecessary. Maybe James Perry had advised with his wife on that point and also urged her not to agree to the suggestion that Guy collaborate on the biography. Nevertheless, Mary resolved not to drop the matter entirely. She would write her cousin again from New Orleans.

Whenever Mary undertook a prose work she sought assistance and ideas from others, but her poetry was entirely her own. She was wholeheartedly in favor of annexation, and about the time she left Galveston she wrote a ringing poem to urge that the United States should welcome Texas into the Union. It appeared in the New Orleans *Republican* in the early summer of 1844, while she visited in Louisiana prior to proceeding to Kentucky. Several Texas newspapers reprinted it during the next few months while the issue of annexation still hung in the balance:

The Plea of Texas

Admit us—we would deem it shame,
Of other lands such boon to claim,
　For we are free and proud.
But we a mother's love may seek,
And feel no blush upon our cheek,
　Before her to have bowed.

We are thy children; doubt it not—
We've proved our birth on many a spot
　Where cannon thunder pealed.
'Twas Saxon heart that dared the fight,
'Twas blood of yours that gave us might
　Upon Jacinto's field.

. . . .

We love your flag, your laws, your land—
Wishing to worship, see we stand
　At Freedom's Temple door.
Admit us now for it may be,
That tos't on Time's tempestuous sea,
　We part, to meet no more.

H——37

Her support of annexation stemmed from the deepest loyalties of her whole life. As a child she had listened to stories of patriots who fought against the British for freedom, and she believed the Texans to be Americans on another frontier defying the tyranny of the Centralist Mexican dictator. She felt, as did most of the Texans themselves, that the new Republic was a natural and inevitable part of the Union.

Mary knew that by taking a public stand for annexation she was severing the ties that bound her to her old associates in New England. She was also parting company, at least politically, with many of her friends and her husband's supporters in Kentucky. Most regrettable of all, she was setting herself at odds with her son-in-law and his family. On the thirtieth day of the next October she would be sixty, and past the time for being reckless, but she published "The Plea of Texas" as boldly as if her whole life still stretched out before her.

20. MADAME HOLLEY
1844-1846

As Mary Holley started back to Kentucky that summer of 1844[1] she found it bitterer than ever to be poor. Her cash money was almost exhausted, and her prospects in Texas were not favorable enough to justify her staying longer. Everything was distressingly high. Seven dollars for a week's board; seventy-five cents for having a colored woman wash out a few pieces; fifty cents just for carting her trunk to the wharf. By the time she paid four dollars for passage to New Orleans her purse was flat. Somehow she would have to borrow twenty dollars in the City for her fare up the rivers.

In New Orleans she was a welcome guest in the handsome new residence that Donatien Augustin had built for his wife on the northwest edge of the French Quarter at Esplanade and St. Claude Streets.[2] The old home on St. Peter had been sold to one of the Labranche cousins. Melazie had planned her house to resemble those on the German Coast, especially her Aunt Felicite Fortier's charming mansion on the Right Bank just across from Good Hope Plantation. A large central hall, opening directly onto the dining room, was flanked by parlors on either side. The ample rooms were furnished with sideboard and chairs of hand-rubbed rosewood, and with marble-topped tables and damask sofas, all executed by the excellent cabinetmakers of the town. Books were everywhere, spilling out of three or four armoires devoted to them; and set high on a carved mahogany pedestal was Donatien's cherished plaster bust of General Washington.

Attorney Augustin was busy and prosperous. Since he belonged to the younger generation of Louisianians who had been reared under the American flag, he felt as much at home in the lobby of the St. Charles Hotel as on Royal Street, and spoke English as often as French. It was true that in his earlier days he had fought a few duels—one blood-letting affair with the eminent Alexandre Graihle, after which the two lawyers became friends and served together on the City Council— but of late Donatien had concurred with the Association against Duelling, composed chiefly of French-speaking citizens, which advocated abolishing affairs of honor as far as possible and at least keeping them out of the newspapers.[3] For several years he had been secretary of the City Council, no small honor in a community of more than one hundred thousand population.

Mary liked life in the Augustin town house rather better than the placid routine of the river plantations.[4] It was extremely pleasant to reside again in a city, especially one that boasted gas works and water works and nineteen fire companies, not to mention eight newspapers. The new residence was about a mile away, across Canal Street, from the St. Charles Hotel and most of the larger Protestant churches, but that distance consituted no handicap when she could call a convenient public hack if Melazie's carriage was in use. It was even considered proper and safe for a lady to go on foot to the Quarter and Canal Street if she walked along Esplanade and so avoided following St. Claude Street over toward Congo Square, where the Negroes danced and sang at all hours and were sometimes strangely violent.

She had scant opportunity to work on her manuscript during this visit with the sociable Augustins. While she was there, however, she received a packet of Austin family records and documents from Mrs. Perry, who had evidently reconsidered her earlier refusal to send them.[5] Mary replied promptly, to express her thanks and to ask for still more information.[6] She did not know why Emily had changed her mind, and probably did not care greatly so long as help for the biography was forthcoming from Peach Point.

In point of fact, Emily's conscience had given her a bad time after the flat refusal in her letter of April 29. She was a good and kind person, who wanted everybody in her small world to be happy, and so she made up a package of a few of the documents, tied it and sealed it, and forwarded it to Mrs. Holley in New Orleans, care the Texas Consulate, as requested. Then she began to compose a letter to her cousin, one in which she had to explain a rather delicate matter. She was not a ready writer, since neither of the genteel schools which she attended in her youth had expected the young ladies to say much of anything if their compositions displayed beautiful penmanship. Painfully she began a first draft, using the back of Mary's latest letter.

"Dear Cousin," she began, and explained first that she had meant all during Mary's stay in Texas to send her son Guy to Galveston to bring her to Peach Point for a visit, but had been too poor to furnish his expenses to any place until just recently when the payment of a land note had permitted him to proceed to the States for much needed medical care. Thus she excused herself for having perhaps seemed inhospitable, an unforgivable lapse in an Austin.

The real point of her message was to say that the family had decided it wanted Judge Burnet to do a "history of the Austins and of Texas," but not to publish it until some of Stephen's enemies, about whom it would reveal the harsh truth, were dead and gone. Meanwhile, Emily hastened to add, Mrs. Holley was welcome to write and publish a biography of Stephen. She noted that "Mr. Hamican thinks you might glean much information from Mr. Blanco of Mexico respecting the time of Stephen's imprisonment there." That was as far as she got with the draft, and apparently she never completed and copied it to post to her cousin.

It is clear that during one of George Hammeken's frequent visits in her household she talked over Mary's letter with him and that he helped the Perrys to formulate the complicated plan outlined in her letter for preserving the fame of Stephen Fuller Austin. They wanted someone experienced in law and public affairs to examine the family papers as the basis for writing a history that would portray Stephen Austin as the true hero of Texas. Then, they hoped, the author would "lay it aside to be published in after years" lest some living person be "mortified" by it. In the meantime, there was no objection to Mrs. Holley's biography, since her romantic personal portrait would offend no one.

From Emily Perry's point of view this extraordinary proposal had its merits, and her idea proved prophetic. Long after everyone was dead who could be "mortified" by the truth, a learned scholar did actually spend a lifetime poring over the documents preserved at Peach Point and wherever else the Austins made their mark on the American frontier in order to publish the "full and correct history of my brother and Texas" of which she dreamed.[7] But in 1844 her proposal offered no inducements to undertake such a work. Burnet was more concerned with politics than with research; and in any event he would hardly have felt inclined to read a thousand documents preserved by Stephen Austin in order to write the true story of events in which he himself had played an important role. Like Mirabeau Lamar, who also declined the privilege of being biographer to the Austins, the Judge was too busy making history to write it.

Nor would Mary Austin Holley, widely known as author of the first history of Texas in English, have been tempted by Emily's offer of the Austin papers for a history that could not be published for a generation. She was intent upon writing a popular biography, enlivened with personal recollections, to appear at the earliest possible date. If she had ever received Emily's communication with its suggestion that she take great pains to obtain minor reminiscences about Stephen's imprisonment when she already had in her possession a copy she had made of his journal covering that period, she would have dismissed the proposal as "visionary" with a shrewd suspicion that Hammeken had meddled in it.

Mary stayed on in New Orleans during the early summer because for a short time she was ill.[8] Not very seriously, thanks to careful nursing and attention from the whole household on St. Claude Street; and for a few weeks she found it pleasant to permit herself to be inert and without responsibility for anything or anybody, even herself. If she could have foreseen that this was the last time in her life that she would be wholly carefree, she might have found it even more difficult to rouse herself and start the long journey up the rivers.

When she reached Lexington along in July the temper of the town was as torrid as the weather, with the citizenry at odds about half a dozen issues. Kentuckians were usually divided among themselves, it seemed to her, so much so that the motto of the Commonwealth warned against the danger of fraternal strife. If in Boston or New Orleans or Texas a controversy arose, one could eventually find solid ground on which to stand along with most of the community. But here in the Ohio Valley members of the same family took opposite sides on all sorts of questions—salvation, slavery, sound money, or card playing. Kinsmen became enemies over whether churchgoers ought to attend Miss Clarendon's benefit performance in *The Wife*, during which she danced "La Cachucha."

New tensions had mounted during Mrs. Holley's absence. Alexander Campbell, the celebrated evangelical preacher and cofounder of a new religious denomination, held public disputations with other clergymen on the fundamentals of baptism and grace and ecclesiastical government. The Campbell-Rice Debate lasted for days, and pamphlets containing the arguments were for sale in the book stores.[9]

Another long-standing debate concerning the so-called "Negro Law" was being carried on in the columns of the *Observer and Reporter* between proslavery Robert Wickliffe—they called him "the Old Duke" nowadays—and the Reverend Dr. Robert J. Breckinridge, who back in 1833 had been chiefly responsible for the passage of this law forbidding the importation of slaves into Kentucky for purposes of sale. Breckinridge, who as yet advocated only the gradual emancipation of Negroes, was getting some support from the Whigs, most of whom were men of means and owners of a few families of blacks but opposed to any extension of the slave traffic. Such moderate citizens remembered with regret a scene on Cheapside in Lexington the previous year when the girl Eliza, only one sixty-fourth Negro, had been sold at auction for $1485 to an agent of certain prominent abolitionists who immediately set her free. They recalled with even more distress the dreadful murder this very summer of a sadistic white woman by her own house slave whom she had tortured and goaded.[10]

Many Kentuckians were unhappy about slavery, and it seemed to them that Mr. Clay had the best solution—a compromise under the Constitution, with reasonable hope for gradual and peaceful emancipation. This policy was one of the planks in his present platform of "Union and Liberty" as for the third time he was a candidate for the presidency.[11] His Democratic opponent in November would be James K. Polk of Tennessee, known as "Young Hickory," whose slogan was "Oregon and Texas."

Mrs. Holley knew most of these men who were struggling to control the destiny of Kentucky and the nation. Old Mr. Wickliffe had inducted Horace Holley into office as president of Transylvania. Robert Breckinridge, one of her husband's favorite students, had often taken part in the University's oratorical exercises. It would be very pleasant for her to have Henry Clay and the gracious Lucretia in the White House, and to be able to call on them there. As for Mr. Polk of Tennessee, he was another of Jackson's protégés, like Sam Houston; and it was said that he got the place Sam might have claimed if he had not gone to Texas. Polk was wholeheartedly for annexation, which Clay had at first opposed lest it bring on war with Mexico, but was gradually accepting on the advice of his political friends.

The issue of annexation determined Mary's choice of candidates in the election of 1844. She favored Polk, whatever the stand might cost her in Lexington. She made her personal position clear, but it became judicious and all but necessary to remain an observer as the campaign rose to fever pitch. The newspapers revealed how the wind was blowing. Almost everybody in her circle was pouring money and enthusiasm into Clay's campaign. The reception committee for the great Whig mass meeting included nearly all the men who had supported the Holley Administration two decades earlier: John Brand, Benjamin Gratz, Dr.

Dudley, William Brand, Robert Todd, Mr. Bodley, and many others. It also listed newer citizens like Edwin Bryant and Dr. Pinckard, who had worked with her for Texas in '36.[12] Only lifelong Democrats were pro-Texas now, men like General McCalla, who was circulating a petition for annexation and rallying votes for Polk.

The lines were clearly drawn, and she felt almost like a stranger as she watched the ceremonies in front of Morrison College when flags were awarded to both the Whig Clay Club and the Ashland Artillery by the Ladies of Lexington.[13] Chairman Edwin Bryant called attention especially to the inspiring strains of Mr. Ratel's original *Ashland Quick Step*, performed by the Lexington Amateur Brass Band. It seemed a very long time since she had composed the speech for Henrietta Austin to recite in presenting the lovely silk flag to the Ladies' Legion bound for Texas. Those arrangements, she recalled, had been in the hands of Edwin Bryant and Julius Clarke. Julius had long since returned to New England, and Edwin was now a loyal Clay man in all respects, including a lukewarm attitude toward the annexation of Texas.

In Lexington and the rich surrounding bluegrass counties of Kentucky, the larger issues of this campaign, or any other in which Henry Clay was a candidate, were obscured by the fabulous presence of the man himself in his panelled study at Ashland. While devoted followers fought his political battles for him he remained in seclusion, entertaining famous visitors as his house guests and granting audiences to emissaries from all over the country. He had need of staunch adherents because few national leaders were ever more bitterly attacked in their own homelands.

Mr. Wickliffe, who was an arch-Democrat, swore on oath that Clay was in the habit of playing cards for money "at watering places, on steamboats, and at private houses." The Old Duke, however, made the tactical error of specifying that he had done so on a Sunday at Blue Licks Springs; and that brought forth a public statement signed by John Brand and others that they had personally accompanied the statesman in a carriage to the Springs on that Sunday and were prepared to swear that he did not gamble on that day.[14] Thus the great battle became a succession of skirmishes. When Clay's opponents brought up the several duels in which he had participated, and asked him if he would fight one now, the sixty-seven-year-old Kentuckian declined to say yea or nay, thus leaving both his enemies and friends convinced that he would protect his honor if it were impugned. As a rule, however, he wisely left these petty accusations to be dealt with in the speeches of such loyal henchmen as State Senator Robert Todd of Kentucky or the young Illinois Whig named Lincoln, who would soon be Todd's son-in-law. Actually, it was well known over the nation that Mr. Clay now lived a sober and reasonably godly life. He sat with his wife in her pew at Christ Church on Sunday mornings when he was in town, and permitted his campaign managers to make political capital of the frugal domesticity of Ashland. Lucretia Hart Clay's excellent butter and fresh eggs, sold at times by the lady herself to the local taverns, were valuable Whig assets.

Keeping to her decision to stay out of politics upon her return to Lexington, Mrs. Holley nevertheless managed to make her customary homecoming bow in the newspaper. She reverted to her husband's custom of contributing historical items to the press, and sent the *Observer and Reporter* a neat little article about the brass four-pounder she had inspected on Captain Taylor's clipper in Galveston Bay. She signed it plainly "M. A. Holley," lest people should have forgotten her old initialled signature.[15]

Then she settled down to getting reacquainted with her numerous grandchildren. The line of young heads around the great dining table, reverently bowed while their father pronounced a longish grace, was an impressive sight, even for a grandmother who did not propose to be overawed by her descendants. Sometimes when she had important guests she would summon the children to the parlor and introduce them in order: William Holley Brand, due to graduate from Transylvania within a year; Lizzie and Mary, both making nice progress in music under Mr. Iucho; Horace, aged twelve, and Harrietta, eight; Emily Austin, five, and John Watt, three, all of them old enough to say how-do-you-do. Small Katherine, not yet two, and the newest baby, George Charlton,[16] born early this summer, were in the care of nursemaids, of course.

With such a large family it was well that William Brand had lately bought furniture on a grand scale from a firm in Philadelphia, including eighteen mahogany dining chairs, a pair of Gothic mahogany divans, a pier pedestal, some occasional tables, and a massive bedstead.[17] He could well afford the money; and now Elmwood began to take on the air of a representative Lexington mansion. Mary Holley devoutly hoped that Baby Charlton would be her daughter's last child, and that from now on Mrs. William Brand would have time to entertain suitably and often. Harriette's health was good, under the circumstances, and it was high time that she took her place in the town's society.

Her husband, on the contrary, was not well. Business cares fatigued him, and he was easily annoyed by household confusion. He even lost interest in his thoroughbred mare, Lady Adams, and her fleet sons and daughters by Medoc and Eclipse and Gray Eagle. He was stern and unyielding in his opinions, and increasingly spartan in the régime he demanded of his family. According to Mrs. Holley, who was not fond of oatmeal porridge and boiled meat and plain puddings, they lived "too low" in her daughter's household, and to this shortcoming she promptly attributed any ailments they developed.

William's bad health deprived him of a well-earned honor at this season. In a flattering letter signed "Many Voters" that appeared in the *Observer and Reporter* he was asked to consent to run for the Legislature as the candidate of both the Whig and the Democratic Parties. He felt compelled to decline on account of "the state of his health," to the deep disappointment of his still vigorous and active father and to his own regret as well.[18]

In November Clay was defeated by Polk for the presidency in a very close race. The Whigs carried Tennessee but lost New York and with it the election. Lexington gossip had it that Mr. Clay received the final verdict when the New York mail was reported to him in the midst of a family wedding party. Mrs. Robert Todd, who was present, told her step-daughter, Mary Lincoln, all about it in a letter soon afterward. As Mr. Clay opened the paper, she wrote, his face turned blue; and then, after a long pause, he raised his glass and proposed a toast to the health and happiness of all present. Nothing further, apparently, was said about the election during the rest of the evening.[19]

For Henry Clay, and for his state as well, this election was the end of forty years of political good fortune and power. He would live to frame one last great compromise between the opposing sections before the inevitable conflict rent the nation; but his own homeland was already a region of divided loyalties and brilliant partisans beyond all reconciliation. In the struggle to come both Presidents, North and South, would be Kentuckians, born within the borders of the Commonwealth.

After the election of Polk the advocates of annexation in the United States believed the admission of Texas could be accomplished at once if they moved swiftly. Three Presidents—John Tyler, of Virginia, outgoing executive, and President-elect Polk, and the aged Jackson, already on his deathbed at the Hermitage—combined to overcome the opposition of New Englanders and abolitionists and to achieve their goal. The United States Congress offered statehood to Texas on March 1,

1845, and then, together with the other interested nations, waited anxiously for the vote of the people of the Republic on the question. Newspapers in the States believed that the decision would be determined chiefly by Sam Houston in spite of the fact that his term as President of Texas had expired and the office was now held by Anson Jones, a little-known physician and politician. Even in Texas there seemed to be uncertainty as to the attitude of Houston and Jones regarding the entry of Texas into the Union. There was no doubt that both England and France were trying to prevent it.

Mrs. Holley's satisfaction at the offer of statehood to Texas was clouded by the oblivion into which Stephen Austin's name was falling. Already people were forgetting that he had pledged his personal fortune to the interim government, and literally given his life for the young Republic as its Secretary of State. A new set of actors was on the stage and Houston seemed likely to get all the credit for annexation if such were the ultimate outcome of the diplomatic chess game. She must counteract such unfair judgments before it was too late. Although neither the time nor the place was auspicious she worked hard on the biography of Austin during the winter months in Lexington.[20]

As long as her son was content to remain in the East with his relatives she could spend long, quiet days in her room, organizing her material and composing sections of the narrative. She meant to enliven this account of the Austins in Texas with personal details, more in the style of the 1833 volume than her statistical second book on Texas, and to risk offending a few persons in order to make the story colorful and original.

She began with the Austins in Connecticut, paying a tribute to her father and her brother Henry for their exploits before she discussed the career of Moses, frontiersman and colonist. She interwove her childhood recollections and family records with the materials she had copied at Peach Point, thankful now for all the hours she had shivered in that lonely study. She sketched Stephen's youth, with a glimpse of his boyhood on the frontier and his school days in Connecticut and Kentucky. The first two chapters done, she stitched the foolscap sheets together in neat sections; and then began Chapter Three with the public career of Stephen Fuller Austin, "to whom we shall now give our undivided attention." The rest of the biography would deal with him as leader of the colony he founded.

She had ample material, old and new. Thus, to an excerpt from her *Texas* (1836) describing the first colonists she could add Mrs. Eberly's homespun account of the landing of the sloop *Good Intent*. Mary found the reminiscences of this "intelligent lady who was amongst the pioneers" to be very useful, although she polished the style and left out some of the scandals, such as the arrival in the Austin Colony of a prominent gentleman accompanied by his mistress. But she did not expurgate all the racy anecdotes. She took the risk of including Mrs. E.'s backstairs account of General Houston at San Jacinto and her story of the self-confessed murderer in Texas who admitted to being the son of Kentucky Governor Desha. The public would find such items lively reading, Mary hoped.

She pushed on with her task, filling the long pages with neat script, until seven chapters were completed. She endeavored to be objective in dealing with Stephen's career but at times it was difficult to be wholly impersonal. For example, a number of years before his meeting with her at Bolivar House he had written to his sister, discussing plans for his own future. Mary had copied the letter when she was at Peach Point. It read, in part:

My prospects for making a fortune are bad. I shall be but poorly compensated for years of toil and anxiety though I expect to pay my debts and make a comfortable support for old age. . . . I shall settle down on a stock-farm; and perhaps follow the example of Mr. Perry and hunt up some jolly widow to comfort me in my old age.[21]

As a conscientious biographer, she must decide whether or not to omit this statement because it made her own relationship with him seem less romantic. She included it, but explained it in the light of his character:

Neither the plan of the Stock Farm, the jolly widow marriage, or any other plan of comfort and happiness was ever carried into execution by Stephen Austin. He was, to the day of his death, too much the slave of the public ever to provide for himself, or for those dear to him. He was one of the few purely disinterested men who have ever lived, not for themselves, but to benefit their race. To such should be awarded the Crown of Martyrdom.[22]

These sentiments were similar to the verses she had written about him just after his death, and she was reminded that her poem ought to be used in this biography, perhaps in the last chapter.

She was already encountering the problem of how to include herself as one of the figures in Stephen's life. In the memoir of her husband she had felt it wise to minimize her share in his career, but she did not intend to leave herself out of the story of the Austin Colony. Therefore she wrote a lively account of her first visit to Bolivar House and included Stephen's letters to her, letting him "speak for himself," as she expressed it. It was a good chapter but that was as far as she proceeded. She laid aside her pen, maybe because of the stiffness in her fingers or the slight ache in her shoulders that always afflicted her in the winter. Also her son was growing unhappy and demanding that he be furnished means to come to Kentucky. She could never write when he was on her mind.

By springtime other troubles also prevented her from working on her book. William's severe rheumatism kept him at home most of the time, fretting over neglected business and growing irritable at enforced inactivity. To aggravate his ills he developed a painful water brash that was too embarrassing to permit him to enjoy outside company. When he began to suffer occasional spasms John Brand announced that he was taking his son to Edinburgh to consult medical authorities there. If William's health improved sufficiently they would make a short tour of the Continent.

Their plan was to set out in early May, proceeding via Philadelphia, where arrangements would be made somehow to send Horace back to Kentucky. Before departing William instructed his eldest son in the management of the hemp factory and farms. At last the day came when he clasped his beloved Harriette in his arms with an unwonted display of affection and tenderly kissed her goodbye. They had not been parted for longer than a fortnight during the twenty years of their happy married life, and they were both frightened at this illness which separated them.[23]

Mary Holley was shaken, too, by the events of the spring. Her son would be more than ever a misfit in this house full of young children, and an added expense to her; and William's collapse deprived her of the only masculine support on which she could rely for unfailing and ready help. Yet she forced herself to seek diversion outside the family circle, and tried to distract Harriette by lively accounts of local happenings.

Who could fail to be lifted above the mundane realm when listening to Ole Bull's inspired renditions on his violin at the concert he gave in Lexington a few weeks after the departure of the travellers? Such richness of tone, such wildly romantic improvisations on the simple melodies from his mountain homeland—no wonder that Mrs. Holley was impelled to compliment the artist in person afterward. He responded by presenting her with an engraved likeness of himself, flatteringly inscribed and autographed: "Most respectfully presented to Mrs. Holley from her most devoted servant, Ole B. Bull. Lexington, the 24th May, 1845."[24]

There were numerous other concerts in the city that summer, encouraged doubtless by Mr. Iucho, who was currently the chief musical authority in the community. He helped to persuade his fellow parishioners of Christ Church to order a new organ from a famous factory in the East. It was to be built with twenty stops, two sets of keys and pedals, and more than eight hundred pipes.[25]

Some of the news in the papers was sad. In faraway Vermont Editor Julius Clarke was dead, his prestige as faded as that of the middle-of-the-road Whig Party to which he had remained unswervingly loyal.[26] Other news was alarming. In Lexington the citizens who favored compromise, while not yet powerless, were caught between fires. During the summer many of the most prominent of them assembled to protest publicly against a band of ruffians called "Black Indians" who were abusing free Negroes. On the other hand, a few weeks later some of the same men felt it their duty to invoke legal means to compel Cassius M. Clay, kinsman of Henry, to remove from the city and the state a printing press on which he had for two months been issuing his weekly anti-slavery newspaper, *The True American.* Peace-loving men hardly knew which way to turn.[27]

Southward at the Hermitage in Tennessee old Andrew Jackson died a few days too soon to know that on July 4 the Texan Congress had eagerly accepted annexation to the Union. Rumor had it that Sam Houston was spending the summer in Nashville building his political fences for his election to the United States Senate from the new state.[28] Mary Holley contemplated with no joy in her heart the almost certain prospect of Sam Houston's going to Washington as the spokesman for Texas, a position she had dreamed that Stephen would fill, with her aid and support. This aspect of the shifting political scene made it harder than ever to resume work on her book.

Horace reached Lexington in early June in the company of a traveller with whom William Brand had made the arrangements to look after him en route. He was as restless a hypochondriac as ever, and by now given to excessive use of all kinds of remedies; but he could be good company when he chose. So long as the house had no master at home he could occupy a small upstairs room without upsetting the routine very greatly.[29]

Late in August nineteen-year-old William Holley Brand was graduated from Transylvania, and delivered a commencement oration address titled "The Course of Empire."[30] The handsome lad did credit to a long row of proud relatives who sat through the ceremonies that hot summer day. His father and grandfather probably arrived in time for the occasion, since their trip was not as extended as they had hoped. The invalid's health had not permitted even a brief excursion over into France.

William was exceedingly weary, and it was obvious that the trip had done him no good at all. Buoyed up by the joy of getting home, however, he rallied enough to tell the family about the visit with his father's brother William, who took them to Montrose to view the ancestral burying ground and read the faint epitaphs on tombs of numerous Brands and their wives, long since dead and gone. His uncle had made him a farewell present of sterling silver—twelve table spoons and twelve tea spoons and other pieces, including a toddy lifter, which he specified was to be used first when Mr. and Mrs. John Brand, Sr., should come for apple toddy at their son's home.[31]

William handed the heirlooms into Harriette's keeping, and everybody laughed at the canny foresight displayed by the donor. It took a bit of courage for them to be merry because more than likely the old gentleman in Scotland would outlive his namesake.

William grew worse until, racked by pain and weakness, he lost all the forebearance and patience he had exercised for so many years toward his wife's difficult brother, and sternly forbade him to remain longer in the household. He reminded his wife that just before boarding the ship for Europe he had written her a letter to that effect, telling her also that he intended having a talk with Mrs. Holley on the subject as soon as he returned. Very probably Harriette had not mentioned the matter at the time his letter came. She knew that William was still fond of his mother-in-law, and that when he got home he might change his mind and let things work out as they had done so often in the past. But he did not change his mind, and his final decision included the demand that now his wife must tell her mother.

It was the most heartbreaking situation that gentle Harriette had ever faced, but she had no choice.[32] This was William's house; and he had surely been long-suffering and kind beyond the call of duty in permitting her to make it a haven for her relatives throughout their married life. Blinded by tears she slowly climbed the long stairs to her mother's room and for a moment stood in the doorway, almost unable to utter the harsh ultimatum that while Mrs. Holley was welcome, always, at Elmwood, Horace must leave at once.

When she had spoken, she saw her mother staring at her coldly, and she wrung her hands.

"How can I help it?" she sobbed. "What else can I do?"

It was the first time she had ever opposed her untried will to her mother's stronger one, and she was so inwardly torn that she hardly heard the sharp reply accusing her of driving her brother from the house with no care for what would become of him.

At that moment Mary Holley and her daughter could have quarrelled irrevocably and parted in bitterness, but they did not. Instead, they were drawn to look silently into each other's eyes, and then they wept in each other's arms. Their shining love guided them out of the fog of sorrow and disappointment that was engulfing them both, and each was moved to grieve for the other's misfortunes. Mary remembered that William seemed mortally ill in spite of the doctor's insistence that his latest trouble was only dyspepsia. Harriette sorrowed anew over the disappointment that Horace had always been to her mother—"the child of misfortune ever," she called him once in a letter. Thus the two women made their peace with each other, and faced what they must inevitably do.

Harriette returned to her duties in the sickroom and household. Mary broke the news to her son, who was surprisingly calm about it all. He even made allowances for William's sternness, declaring that the poor man had a right to scold and order people around when he was nervous, a feeling which he himself understood perfectly. Pleased at Horace's magnanimity, she saw to it that all the Brand family heard how handsomely he was behaving in the crisis. He was really not in the least sorry to leave Lexington. When his mother's correspondence with the Labranches resulted in an invitation for her to resume her duties as governess at Good Hope Plantation whenever she wished and to bring her son with her, his disposition improved and his various ailments began to mend.

In early November mother and son bade farewell to their Lexington friends and to the assembled Brand connection. They parted amicably with William in spite of the circumstances of their leaving. Whatever their feelings were toward him, it was all too apparent that this was a last farewell. In the great west parlor the children gathered around their grandmother, sobered by this most solemn of all her leavetakings, and dimly aware that their whole world was rocking with change. Three-year-old Kate wailed for "Grandmamá," who took the child on her lap and promised "to come back some time or other, *ma chère*."[33] This smallest granddaughter, so like herself, was admittedly her favorite. Leaving Harriette was hardest of all, but at last it was over and the travellers were rattling along in the railway car toward Louisville and the river landing at Shipping Port.

This was the ninth time she had made the long journey down the rivers, thought Mary, as she sat on the deck of the steamboat day after lazy day, watching the low gray-green banks slide past her view. Ere long they were out of the Ohio and into the Mighty River; and after a while she caught the last glimpses of the Kentucky shore at the great bend in the Mississippi where a devastating earthquake a few years before she came West had changed the shape and course of the stream for all future time. Once they got past this point, she recalled, it would grow wider and ever more awesome as its muddy current swept toward the blue Gulf and the endless oceans beyond. The river's course reminded her of her own life. After this sudden shock, so unexpected and irrevocable, her days would no doubt flow on inexorably toward the river's end.

Not the least disturbing aspect of her hasty removal from Harriette's home was its effect on her plans for completing the biography of Stephen Austin. Even were her nerves and mind not so shaken, she knew she could not do much writing in Louisiana under the double responsibility of teaching and looking after Horace. She had left her precious manuscript and papers in a great trunk in the back room at Elmwood. The family portraits and some treasured keepsakes were left with Harriette, too, for safekeeping. She could send for them if she ever got well enough established, and the important thing was for them to be preserved. If anything happened to her perhaps Guy Bryan would finish the biography or see that it was done. She was glad that she had mentioned to Emily Perry that she would like to have him as a collaborator.[34] *Quién sabe,* she sighed.

One might become melancholy on a river journey were it not for the gay spirits of the passengers and the endless *divertissements*. One day the boat picked up some stranded travellers from off a steamer stuck on a sandbar, and later on rescued another group from a vessel sinking on snags where its luckless pilot had veered out of the channel. Everybody rose early to rush to the dining saloon at the sound of the gong to spear the best buckwheat cakes from the great stacks of them set out on the long tables. Horace was up at dawn to get his share, and seemed quite another person from the gloomy semi-invalid huddled by the fire at Elmwood. Of evenings a troupe of travelling musicians gave concerts on deck in which everybody joined lustily. Mary found herself improving daily, in body and mind.[35]

As they approached the German Coast it seemed a month instead of only a little more than a week since she had spoken softly with William Brand in the shadowed room that reeked of drugs and fever, and eons since the unforgettable day that Harriette had come weeping to her door. On that day she had been near to desperation, even after she and her daughter had embraced in loving sorrow. Left alone she had been tempted to fall on the bed with her face to the wall and give up the struggle for independence. Why not spend her own last years in comfort here and let her son get along in life as best he could? He was a man grown, already in his twenty-eighth year, and she was past the age for strenuous effort and responsibility. But from the depths of her being had come a surge of strength and pride, as in the days of her youth. Horace was her son, and she would somehow find a place for him to be contented and useful. Throughout this journey her mind had been coining romantic phrases or remembering them from the past. Once they fell into a kind of rhythm: ". . . all the swan's feathers have been plucked from the fan of my early fancy and only the eagle feathers remain, but here is courage and to spare for the long journey."

Being more than a little histrionic, Mrs. Holley had convinced herself that she was going back to teaching solely for her son's sake. She had been haughty with Harriette on the subject of her sacrifices, but her reason for going lay deeper, of course. Her own independence and pride were affected by William's decision. She knew it would have been better had she assumed the full responsibility for her son much earlier. At all events, now that the matter was decided, she was not frightened by the precarious prospect that lay before her. She turned her back on her last chance for a secure and placid old age with great dignity and resourcefulness for a gently reared lady already in her sixties.

On Sunday morning, the eighteenth of November, she arose betimes to dress, pack, and take a seat on deck with her son to watch for the Good Hope landing. As they moved swiftly downstream with the current, the fields of cane on either side glistened in the soft sunshine, and soon through the mist appeared the distant point of the Red Church steeple. Shortly after noonday dinner the pilot swung over to the Left Bank and the gangplank was swiftly lowered to deposit them, bag and baggage, on the wooden stand at the top of the levee. They rang the bell and a bright young Negro came to take charge of their belongings. Then they entered the trellised gateway and proceeded along the garden alley of blooming roses and myrtles and jasmine to the spacious new residence which Mr. Hermogene had just built on a slight rise well back from the river.

At the open door of the *salle à manger* Mary paused to throw aside the curtains, and remained for a moment a *tableau vivant* in full view of the assembled Labranche family and their guests, who were lingering at table over wine.

"*Madame Holley!*" they exclaimed, as with one voice. "*Bienvenue, chère Madame Holley!*"

It was perhaps the proudest moment of her life.

Everyone rose, even Mr. Hermogene, who was crippled by rheumatism; and everyone embraced her, and her son, too. In a matter of moments all were seated, the *maitre d'hotel* filled their glasses, and she was beginning to relate her adventures on the boat coming down.

"... and so I dropped suddenly into your Paradise!"

Good Hope Plantation was a veritable paradise in those days. The new mansion had long galleries that overlooked the landscaped terraces and afforded a magnificent view both up and down the river. Gorgeous roses bloomed everywhere—Luxumbourgs and Pride of France and Marechal Soulet, and the grounds, supervised by an English gardener, were considered the finest along the Coast. They were the pride of Nemese, a kind, sensible young man, who had married his cousin from a nearby plantation and settled down to carry out his boyhood wish to be a Louisiana planter all his life.[36] He expected to ship four hundred and fifty hogsheads of sugar from Good Hope this year.

Nemese's oldest child had lessons each morning with Mrs. Holley, and in the evenings before supper his young wife received instruction in English. It was good to have this rich young planter remember gratefully all Mrs. Holley's kindnesses to him as a lonely boy in her home long ago. He even gave her credit for his handwriting, which was unusually legible and firm.

"*Chère Madame Holley,*" he said seriously to her one evening in the hearing of the whole family, "*nous serons trop contents si vous resterez ici pour toute votre vie.*"[37] He was telling her that this serene household, if she chose, could be her home in the future. The offer did a great deal to heal her wounded ego and even more for her peace of mind.

Evidence of Nemese's sincerity was his providing bachelor quarters for Horace with the plantation carpenters and coopers, where he could hammer away on benches and stools, and even rig up an arrangement for taking cold showers. The two young men had played together happily as children and they seemed as fond of each other now as if they were kinsmen. Orders were given that "Mr. Holey," as the plantation people called him, was to occupy these quarters for as long as he liked.

Life settled into a comfortable routine, all in a matter of five or six weeks. Melazie wrote from the City urging her beloved governess to come for a visit ere long, just as soon as the new Augustin baby was born. Plantation neighbors up and down the Coast invited Mrs. Holley out for dinings at which the tables were loaded with tureens of spicy soup and platters of freshly caught fish and bowls of rare fruits. The conversation at these gatherings was lively, and the gossip ranged from faraway New York and Baltimore to Natchez under the Hill. She was an honored mourner, almost a member of the family, at the sad and elaborate obsequies of her former pupil Eusebe, son of Madame Jean Baptiste Labranche across the river. And when the sugar was made, Nemese asked if she would like to have him send a barrel of "syrop" to her daughter's family the next time he made a shipment up the river. She wrote to Lexington about the syrop, with explicit instructions that the grandchildren were to have all they wanted. She did not wish her gifts—she somehow considered that it was she who sent them the syrop —to be doled out sparingly. "Tell Kate I sent it," she added at the end of the letter.

Mary's spirits rose as she felt a sense of security and dignity. She had been right in acting promptly on her resolve to be independent, and she summoned up her courage once more and wrote her brother Henry a firm letter to remind him that he still owed her a sizable amount of money. She let him know that he could now send it to her safely and conveniently in care of Mr. D. Augustin, Attorney, New Orleans.

She was shocked, even if not surprised, when her daughter's letter with the news of William's death reached her the week before Christmas. He had died peacefully, surrounded by his loved ones, on the twenty-second day of November, after weeks of suffering that made his going seem a blessed release. The funeral was attended by "a large concourse of sorrowing friends," as the newspaper obituary expressed it.[38] The local editors paid high tribute to the deceased as a "perfectly exemplary man," and listed his many civic services. All agreed that Lexington had lost one of its most valuable citizens in the prime of his manhood.

In view of their recent break in relations, Mary did not pretend to be grief stricken about her son-in-law's death; but she was shaken and concerned. He had been a good son to her for more than twenty years, and now that he was dead it seemed almost as if he had never come back from Scotland to turn Horace out of the house. Her deepest concern was for her daughter, who had always seemed young and inexperienced in spite of her many responsibilities. Now she was a widow, swathed in black veils, driving daily out to the cemetery to place flowers or wreaths on her husband's grave. Mary herself disliked widow's weeds and had laid them aside as soon as she could do so with propriety, but she knew full well that Harriette would carry out the letter as well as the spirit of Lexington's austere code of mourning.

The Widow Brand was a wealthy woman. In his last illness her husband dictated a will leaving her the home and all the personal property around it—which included, of course, the Philadelphia furniture and the silver and six or seven slaves, together with much else of value—for her lifetime or widowhood. She was to be amply provided with money out of the remaining holdings; and, in the event she did marry again, she was to have a one-third share of everything, even ahead of the children's portions.[39] William provided for her more generously than was the custom of the day, and, best of all, he named their eldest son as one of the executors along with his own father and one of his brothers, this in spite of the lad's not yet having attained his majority. Young William H. could be relied upon to see that his mother was well treated.

In all likelihood the family would go on living at Elmwood, Mary mused as she considered the various items in her daughter's long letter, and she hoped that they would not dispose of old Amy. The house servants belonged now to Harriette, who must immediately acquaint herself with the business of the estate and assert her rights. Widowhood was hard enough at best, and full of unforeseen difficulties—how well she herself knew that to be true.

For days she could not bear to sit down at her desk and compose a suitable reply to Harriette's letter, and in the meantime she was called to the City to stay with Melazie, who was not recuperating promptly from childbirth. Mr. and Mrs. Hermogene, both ailing, were worn out with running the household, and their nervous solicitude made everybody uncomfortable. Melazie wrote that "the old people" would be glad to come back to the plantation and let Madame Holley take charge of the situation at the Augustin home. According to the calendar

Madame Hermogene was two years younger than Mrs. Holley, who nevertheless joined Melazie in speaking of her as a "poor old lady full of trouble and infirmity," and conjecturing that neither of the elder Labranches "would last a great while longer." She enjoyed the lively companionship of Melazie and her sociable husband, and was more than glad to live in the City with them for as long as she was needed. Horace could remain on the Plantation. Some of the people there thought he got along better without her.

For once the City's yuletide gaiety and the multicolored shop windows failed to charm her, so haunted was she by the sadness in Harriette's letter. The bells of L'Eglise de Saint Augustin around the corner from the house sounded more mournful than happy, and the wretched weather made it seem hardly worth while to post a letter to Kentucky. Finally, however, for her own peace of mind, she wrote to her daughter. She began by offering consolation—"God's will be done"—and stoic advice that "only time, with the aid of religious reflection, together with the occupation which new cares and responsibilities involve, can soften such griefs." Then, to make it clear that she understood the sorrows of widowhood, she enumerated her own similar misfortunes, long endured and surely more cruel than her daughter's "less unfortunate condition . . . with home, children, friends, all the comforts of life about you."

Whether or not she intended it to be so, her letter was formal and cold in spite of the expressions of sympathy for the Brand family and the closing "God direct & protect & keep us all, prays your Mother." It was colored with self-pity and self-justification, as if by outliving William Brand she had somehow proved him wrong about her son. Yet Mary's message was not wholly unworthy of her. She remained proudly independent, and did not mention the possibility of bringing Horace back to Elmwood now that William was gone. Her admonition to her daughter was meant for herself, too—"No words—not anything can avail in the bitterness of grief. *There is nothing left but duty.*"

In spite of wintry delays, the letter eventually reached Harriette, who put it away carefully with the many others from her mother which she was saving. Of them all only this one had ever been cold or heartless: and she may have been so glad to see the familiar script and seal that she did not notice the tone of the message. She understood instinctively that William's action had wounded her mother's pride and put an end to the long pretending about Horace's future prospects. More galling still, it had destroyed Mary's cherished image of herself as an important personage in Lexington. But Harriette must have thought that her husband's death cancelled out the grievances which he and her mother had against each other; and she herself had no heart for holding grudges as she faced the problems of the future with her fatherless children. She poured out her sorrow and loneliness in the letters which went to Louisiana just as she had always confided in her mother, and when she began to compose sad little verses to enshrine William in her poetic words, she sent those, too. Her generous nature showed her to be Horace Holley's spiritual daughter as well as the child of his heart.

Once her relations with her daughter were firmly re-established, Mary settled down to a calm and well-ordered life on St. Claude Street. This was surprising in view of the fact that the household was anything but restful with its mistress half sick and the older children getting out of hand. Melazie improved gradually on a diet of weak chicken broth, and the baby, who was christened Marie Emma in a hurried ceremony one day when it was feared she might not live, finally took to a bottle. Seven-year-old John Alcee[40] and his sister were summoned to lessons each morning right after breakfast by their governess, who rewarded them for good behavior with stories of their mother when she, too, was Madame Holley's pupil. Sometimes she recited poetry to them or sang little French folk rhymes, and then John, who had been considered an unmanageable child before her coming, listened wide-eyed and begged for more. Piano and drawing lessons came later in the day, with instruction in needlework for the little girl, who promptly began to work a sampler to send little Harrietta Brand in Kentucky, since they were about the same age. No definite agreement was made about a salary for the teacher, but every week Mr. Augustin put a sizable gold piece in her hand.

Her airy little chamber was located up in the tower, with its own balcony overlooking a flat roof which was used by the family in pleasant weather as a terrace. The room was large enough for a narrow bed, a table, and three chairs—a rocker for the teacher and a straight one for each small pupil. It was private and cool, and convenient for reading or writing in her leisure hours. She managed to have considerable time of her own, but writing had become an effort, even letters. When she tried to produce some lines for her daughter in her hour of sorrow, she discarded them as "hard and dry."[41]

She found satisfaction, instead, in the original verses which Harriette sent her. She showed some of them—the poems about the children, not the melancholy ones about William—to Melazie, who was reminded of her own baby; and to a distinguished clergyman, who recalled a lovely daughter he had lost; and finally to a discriminating lady upon whom she was calling at the St. Charles.

"She thinks them beautiful, as I do," Mary wrote her daughter, "or I should not have been proud to show them. Your mind has awakened a new resource—a healthful one." Then as if to explain her own poetic silence, she added, "I do not love to record my thoughts when I have any—they vanish in talk."

It was very good talk into which her thoughts "vanished" that season in New Orleans, as good as any she had ever shared. Mr. Augustin, now a brigadier in the Louisiana militia, was very active in the Democratic Party, riding with his staff at the head of the Jackson Day Parade, and running, with but moderate success, for various public offices. The City was humming with preparations for hostilities against Mexico, certain to break out on the border by spring. Generals in dress swords and brilliant uniforms, heavy with gold braid, were fêted in the parlors of the St. Charles by the local *beau monde*; and hundreds of volunteers embarked at the levee to join General Zachary Taylor's army on the Rio Grande. Donatien Augustin was pulling political wires to get a commission in a unit going to the front, and he welcomed every opportunity to call upon or to entertain influential visitors. Mrs. Holley obliged him by introducing him to Commodore and Mrs. Stuart[42] of the United States Naval contingent in the City and to others of her friends. She and Donatien combined social connections to their great mutual advantage.

It was through the Augustins that she extended her already wide acquaintance in the American-French society of the City. Charles Gayarre, former United States senator and now *secretaire d'état* of Louisiana, brought her the proof sheets of his new history of Louisiana to get the benefit of her comments on it as it went through the press.[43] It was written in French, naturally, but he proposed to do a version of it in English shortly. She found the learned historian somewhat too dignified for so young a man—he was forty at the time; and, thinking that he needed a wife, she tried without success to see that he met Mary Wickliffe, who was spending the winter in the City. This was the same spinster daughter of the Old Duke in whose behalf she had exercised her vain hopes regarding Albert Sidney Johnston. However, being an inveterate matchmaker, she never gave up romantic scheming for her unmarried female friends. In particular she was concerned about Henry's two shy daughters. They were living now in Baltimore with the Dalls and were not even engaged so far as she could learn, but she always inquired hopefully about their prospects when Marylanders like Mr. Whitridge showed up in the City.

She brought her friends to dinner at the Augustin home, among them the Reverend Mr. Theodore Clapp,[44] pastor for thirty-five years of the handsome Gothic-style Congregational Church on St. Charles, who in his New England youth had been an ardent admirer of Mr. Holley in Hollis Street, Boston. Mary found his theological views so like her husband's, both men having proceeded from Yale orthodoxy to rational Unitarianism, that she preferred his "masterly" sermons on Sunday mornings to the less dramatic services of the Episcopal church over on Canal Street. At the "Clapp Church," moreover, she was promptly invited to share the pew of Judge Carleton,[45] well-known jurist and savant, and a long-time widower. He had been at Yale in Horace Holley's day there, and habitually read his New Testament in Greek, it was said. His daughter was the wife of Dr. Thomas Hunt, of the Lexington family of Hunts, who was Mrs. Holley's personal physician.

In the midst of such congenial society, in which she occupied a special position as a well-known authoress, she abandoned an ambition that had goaded her ever since her childhood days in Uncle Timothy Phelps' lavish home. She accepted the fact that she was never going to be rich, that she must get along on what the Augustins or Labranches allowed her plus an occasional remittance from Henry; and she no longer let herself be irked by poverty. In a letter to her daughter explaining her financial arrangements with the Augustins, she said: "Should I get nothing, I should stay. . . . when they get money they will give it to me, for they are generous. I am as necessary to them as they to me."

By shopping carefully and being her own dressmaker she stretched her meager funds. Shopping in the French Quarter one day she found a white book-muslin bonnet imported from Paris—it was "seized goods" —for only a dollar. She purchased the material for a black and white bombazine dress, and also a black lace mantilla, paying three dollars for each item, and thus devised a handsome costume. For several days she spent her leisure time up in her small room, cutting and stitching and fitting, to make sure that the blouse sloped properly to the front and fit her well on the shoulders. She had discovered this to be the secret of keeping a blouse from sagging under the arm, the sign of a badly made garment. She had always been fastidious about the fit of her clothes. As a result of this venture in mantua-making she made what she termed a "pretty decent appearance" when she joined the generals and their wives and other local dignitaries in the hotel drawing room on special occasions.

Another cause for her new peace of mind was her acceptance of the inevitable for her son. It seemed likely that he would be, at most, no more than a plantation carpenter for the rest of his days, and at last she stopped inventing elaborate plans for his future career in an attempt to deceive other people about him. To her daughter, who could be counted upon to pass the word on to the family and friends in Lexington, she wrote: "In the carpenter shop he is as happy as he can be, so I will be satisfied." She knew that he would never fulfill her own, and his father's, ambitions for him.

Now that she no longer tried to make Horace study, the two of them got on well together. There was one morning, just at sunrise, as she sat before her desk, pen in hand, recollecting the very brilliant wedding she had attended the night before in the St. Louis Cathedral in order to write Harriette about it, when the curtain of her door was drawn aside and in burst Horace, laughing at the surprise he was giving her. Of his own volition he had come down the river to consult the doctor in the City about some special treatments, and had got up early to walk out to St. Claude Street before going back to the plantation. He lounged on one of his own handmade benches out on the balcony and brought her up to date on news from the Coast. He was a great gossip, and his eyes twinkled as he made sly remarks about this person or that. In his own way he was a keen observer.

He looked handsome in his new frock coat of black alpaca, with a neat cap and well-brushed shoes. The coat had cost thirty-six dollars and the cap five bits, but no matter for that, thought his mother, as she listened to him rattling on cheerfully. His new shower was fine for cold baths in the early morning, he said, and the plantation coopersmith, an accommodating fellow, was teaching him how to do more with a hammer and saw than just make benches. He was in fine spirits as he ate a huge breakfast with his mother and Mr. Augustin and then hurried off to catch the ten o'clock boat for "home," as he called the Good Hope Plantation.

Mary's own health was good. She was plump and sun-tanned enough to be accused of being a "Creole," as the French Louisianians were sometimes called. She had not suffered even one of her depressing headaches since returning to the South, and her lameness was gone—well, almost gone, except for the times when she walked all the way to the St. Charles Hotel and back. On soft spring evenings she and Melazie joined Judge Carleton and his daughter for strolls along Esplanade Street, and on one such occasion visited a beautiful private courtyard to see a century plant about to bloom. Another time the Judge gave Mrs. Holley his arm and the two of them went to the levee to see the embarkation of several companies of volunteers for the war against Mexico. They were bound for a port in Texas. It was thrilling to hear the band play "Yankee Doodle" and the "Marseilles Hymn," but sad, too, and sadder by far than when she had waved at the boatloads of soldiers on the Hudson going to fight the British. But she was young then, and romantic about war. Now she kept thinking of James Austin, shot down in the dust of the barren borderland where these youths were going.

In spite of such occasional melancholy reflections, she felt once again a *joie de vivre* that made life seem good and worth the living. Not wishing to miss any part of the excitement of the time and place, she went everywhere she got the chance. She saw Ellen Tree as Lady Macbeth, and was introduced to the great actress afterward at the hotel. She heard De Meyer—the wonderful De Meyer, she called him enthusiastically—in piano concert, and thought he looked more than a little like Wilhelm Iucho, especially around the eyes. Donatien escorted her to sit in the Augustin box to hear Calve in *The Martyrs*, and again offered her a seat for the very last performance of the season. It was on a Sunday and it was not her custom to attend theatrical performances on that day; but opera was, after all, the most respectable kind of theatre, and she might not ever again get to hear that particular score. Who was there now to be hurt by her example? A few days later Mr. Whitridge from Baltimore took her to see Hackett as Falstaff in *Merry Wives*, which by chance she had never before seen. She was entranced with the boisterous comedy, and felt fully repaid for the walk home of half a mile when Mr. Whitridge could not secure a hack at midnight.

These many social activities made her feel satisfyingly young, but she realized her age when Horace came to town next and presented her with the caricature which he had done of her. It was so appallingly unflattering that she promptly destroyed it. Yet the sketch was clever and showed real talent. She took pleasure of a wry sort in reporting the episode to the family in a long letter to her oldest granddaughter, Lizzy.[46] If it had been any other subject than herself she would have sent the caricature along to prove Horace's talent as an artist.

The memory of her last days in Lexington was more deeply embedded in her consciousness than she realized. One night, after she had been away for several months, she had a strange dream about William Brand.

It was not an unpleasant experience, yet it disturbed her a little. In her dream she saw him coming toward her with a smile on his face. Then he held out his hand and asked her to go with him because he wanted to talk with her. She was about to do so when she awoke.[47] Dreams always impressed her greatly, and this one seemed at the time like a reconciliation with William's spirit. Next day the thought struck her that it might also be a fatal prognostication. "So be it," she murmured as she shrugged off the gloomy premonition. Life was pleasant in this friendly haven, and almost every day turned out to be interesting in some way or another. She must not permit herself to be superstitious.

Oftentimes, when she had completed the children's afternoon classes, she put on her good black silk and walked in leisurely fashion to the hotel to take dinner with friends, stopping along the way to make a call or two. She would slip her last letter to Lexington in her pocket on the chance of meeting someone who was leaving on the next boat up the river. It was safer, and much cheaper, to send letters in the care of friends.

The St. Charles was a world in itself—everybody was there. Many of the visitors came to try out the hotel's new-fangled style of serving the four-o'clock dinner, and the Robert Wickliffes from Lexington invited her on one occasion to dine with them. They were all seated promptly at a long, crowded table on which there was nothing at all to eat, and each guest was handed a very large bill-of-fare. That proved awkward for those who could not read without their spectacles and had been too vain to wear them! Then capable Mary Wickliffe announced all the items on the card in her bad French so that they could make their choices. Now, what in the world was *chou de la crème*? And all those other odd names? The *chou* turned out to be merely custard cakes done in the form of cabbage heads, but as the ladies nibbled daintily on them, they pronounced them to be very, very nice. Mr. Wickliffe called loudly for a large order of Kentucky bacon.

After dinner there was dancing, with all the younger ladies and gentlemen demonstrating how well they had been taught to do the polka by the Polish dancing master who conducted a studio in the hotel. When asked to join them Mrs. Holley protested that her dancing days were over, but she occupied a prominent chair among those watching along the wall, and spent a lively evening chatting with old friends and meeting new people.

General Gaines[48] made her acquainted with Mrs. Le Vert,[49] the daring and fascinating lady who, according to gossip, was often seen at the opera with Mr. Clay.

"Oh," said Mrs. Le Vert, when they were introduced, "I have long wished to meet you, Mrs. Holley. We have so many mutual friends." To this Mary replied in kind, and at once they were engaged in the most cordial conversation.

"You must stay and see me dressed," the lady urged. "There is a *soirée* at ten in the drawing room and I am going as a Dancing Baya-dère. My dress is of white satin and glass tissue."

It was getting late for a lady to be out unattended, and Mary was about to decline the tempting invitation and arrange for a cab when the room resounded with the entrance of General Augustin and his staff of twelve militia officers, resplendent in full dress uniform. That solved Mrs. Holley's problem.

"*Mon Général*," she cried gaily, as he bowed to greet her, "I want an escort!"

So she remained to see Mrs. Le Vert arrayed in the shining dress and to watch the opening sets of the soirée. In due time she walked home with Donatien, her heels tapping on the sidewalk and his dress sword knocking against the lamp posts, all the way to St. Claude Street.

The satisfactions that brightened her days were modest ones, but she counted them over just as Melazie did the beads on her rosary. Then she recounted them when she wrote to her daughter. She reported that her brother had sent her two hundred dollars from Texas; at least, it amounted to nearly that sum after she had settled a small debt he owed in New Orleans. Poor, dear Henry, he did well to scrape to-gether this much out of the confusion of their joint holdings, and doubt-less it was his industrious son Edward who managed to do it. Colonel Love had written recently that her nephew was a really fine young man and "would do right" about her claims. Through all their difficulties she and her brother were still fond of each other.[50]

She was rewarded each day in teaching the Augustin children, espe-cially John Alcee. When he recited his lesson well or proved his sums, she taught him to recite little poems. Here was a boy in whom her cherished pedagogical methods awakened the spark of enthusiasm that was the object of all good teaching. She still believed in the romantic theories of education which her husband had put into practice when he instructed the children of Greenfield Hill and when he lectured to spell-bound lads at Transylvania who never forgot the sound of his voice.

Mary wrote her daughter, too, about a touching tribute which she received one afternoon in early summer when the maid requested her to come downstairs to the parlor to receive a gentleman caller. As she entered the room she was met by a man in his early thirties, handsome in spite of being a trifle portly, who rose and bowed low to kiss her hand, murmuring, "How do you do, Mother?" It was Adelard Evalture Charbonnet, one of the pupils of the old Preparatory School, now a dignified business man, who had just learned that she was residing in the City.[51] Harriette would understand what an exalted honor Charbonnet was bestowing upon her! He had been a proud, pompous little boy when he lived in the Holley household.

Bad luck befell Donatien's public ambitions that year of 1846. He was not commissioned by the army, and he was overlooked for the political offices of judge and of sheriff. Pressed for ready money, he decided to rent out his Coast plantation near Pass Christian instead of taking his family there as usual during the unhealthy season. That was why the Augustins remained in their comfortable house on the edge of town during the hot weather. They were well situated, and after the heat of the day had abated they often sat out on the terrace to enjoy a languid breeze that always came up from the Gulf at dusk, and to watch the lines of small, twinkling lights leading down toward the French Quarter. When the streets grew dark, they gazed up in silence at the orderly procession of stars moving across the summer sky.

As the days grew sultry Mary rose earlier than her wont, often by three o'clock, to go out on her little balcony and watch Jupiter and Venus burning brightly. The morning air was fresh and delicious. When it became light enough she would sew or read or write until the call for breakfast at eight. In spite of the heat she decided to remain in the City because Melazie and the children needed her. Perhaps the next time the Labranches came down the river she would go back with them to the plantation for a while. All the news from Horace was encouraging. Madame Hermogene had said of him on her last visit, "*Il va superiorment, ma chère.*"

Along in July Mary had a convenient opportunity to send a parcel of gifts to Lexington by Mr. James Erwin, who was taking his children north for the summer to be near their Grandmother Clay. The gifts were only some quilt patches and various clever small things contrived out of paper and feathers, with a piece of fancy cake saved from an elegant wedding for the girls to put under their pillows and dream on. She toyed with the idea of sending a cornet of sugar plums for Kate, but thought better of it because she might be thought partial. The sampler which Aline Augustin had worked went into the parcel; for her own daughter there was a pretty brooch that Mary had purchased for herself. She winced at parting with it, but she knew that without some nudging from her mother Harriette would never begin to get out of mourning. She could think of nothing to contrive for the boys, and so she sent affectionate messages to them.

"Tell them I love them all," she said in the letter that accompanied the parcel. "My love to friends—& to you, dear, dear Harriette."

The Erwins were leaving before the middle of the month, and she busied herself to get the parcel ready and wrapped by the evening of the tenth, which was a Friday and the end of a hard week of classes in the hot weather. Early next morning she rose, feeling reluctant to close the letter without one more word. As she sat on the balcony in the brilliant moonlight she added a postscript at the bottom of the page.

"Good morning, dear Harriette!" she scribbled gaily.

Soon the gifts and the folded sheet, duly sealed, were on their way. They were the last messages that Mary Holley ever sent to her daughter.

Already the yellow fever was increasingly prevalent in the City, and soon the newspapers were issuing warnings to all residents to leave town or at least take proper precautions. Mrs. Holley was confined to her bed on the twenty-fifth; and from the start Dr. Hunt knew that she was gravely ill. Melazie nursed her as she would have done her own mother, and the servants, too, were devoted in spite of the risk to themselves. Friends called and did what they could to be of assistance.

As Mary Holley lay in her small tower room, with the summer sun beating on the drawn shutters, she must have remembered other times when she had been stricken by the fever, and thought of all its ravages upon those she loved. It was the scourge of her family, claiming her father and his namesake son, then Horace Holley, and likewise Henry's wife and daughter. Now it was to be her mortal enemy, too. But she was not terrified, and her spirit remained unbroken.

Those who watched at the bedside said she talked about the vast sky and beautiful stars which they had watched from the terrace. Long years later Melazie repeated reverently to her children the very words that Madame Holley spoke as she was dying.

"I see worlds upon worlds rolling in space," she cried. "Oh, it is wonderful!"[52]

No doubt she was delirious, but her fevered words were a declaration of her conviction about the Eternity into which she was entering. She had always believed that in life the human mind transcends

Illimitable space, hung with night's starry lamps,

and that in death the human soul reaches out to

Worlds upon worlds—seeks the creating and
Sustaining cause—*The Hand Divine.*

She died on Sunday morning, August 2, 1846, at eleven o'clock; and as was the custom in times of the fever, the interment took place that same day. In the afternoon a *cortège* escorted the *bière* on the short journey to St. Louis Cemetery, where it was laid in the handsome tomb belonging to Donatien Augustin's family.[53] The Reverend Mr. Clapp conducted the funeral services in "thrilling tones of eloquence," which, according to a local newspaper, "went deep into the hearts of the friends who escorted the deceased to her last abode." If they sent for her son during his mother's last illness, he attended her funeral and walked with the procession through the pillared gates of the old cemetery, wearing his black alpaca coat and his good cap and the new shoes that by now were not well brushed.

Dr. Clapp wrote an unusually long and complimentary obituary for the next day's *Courier*. After a short biography of his subject he listed her literary achievements, adding a discriminating description of her personal character that would have pleased her greatly.

Mrs. Holley was no less gifted in person than in mind. Her form was slight and graceful, and her finely turned features glowed with animation, when aroused by her subject. She was sought after in every society where she appeared; admired for the justness of her sentiments, her benevolence of heart and cheerfulness of temper that sustained her under the multiplied ills of which she had her share.[54]

Judge Carleton also published a eulogistic tribute which appeared in the *Jeffersonian* of August 4.[55] It was only half as long as the notice in the *Courier* but it, too, praised her as the "pride and ornament of society." Since Dr. Clapp's account had said that she was sixty, the Judge thoughtfully omitted to mention the matter of her age. He had examined the post-mortem certificate signed by Dr. Hunt and knew her to be somewhat older than Dr. Clapp had stated. Mrs. Holley would have appreciated the Judge's chivalrous omission fully as much as the clergyman's tactful guess as to how old she was.

Someone, probably the Augustins, wrote the sad news to Harriette

Brand and sent her the newspaper clippings. It took her a while, of course, to notify the Dalls in Baltimore and the brothers in New York and Henry Austin in Texas. For several weeks the *Picayune* advertised that there were unclaimed letters in the New Orleans post office for Mrs. Mary A. Holley.[56]

Horace stayed on at Good Hope, just as Nemese Labranche had promised he could do if he wished. He eventually became the plantation wheelwright, and seemed so much at home on the place that when the next census count was taken somebody wrote it down that "Horace Holey" was a native of Louisiana.[57]

It seems wholly fitting that Mary Austin Holley should have found a last resting place in the vibrant, somnolent city in the crescent of the Great River, with its tall-masted ships bound for Texas or heading out past the Tortugas toward the Long Wharf at New Haven and Boston Harbour and all the distant seas that the enterprising Austins charted in their dreams. Her small, frail body crumbled to dust in the borrowed tomb on which her name was never added; but she has not been unknown or forgotten during the century and more since her death.[58] Her two books on Texas and perhaps some others of her published pieces bid fair to last longer than marble, however carved or inscribed; and her cherished papers and unfinished manuscripts have served the needs of a long succession of scholars and writers, who have diligently sought them out to continue her appointed tasks.

ACKNOWLEDGMENTS—PEOPLE AND PLACES

All her life Mary Austin Holley preserved her personal papers and family records, thus accumulating a mass of letters, documents, clippings, and pamphlets. Her only daughter, Harriette Holley Brand, to whom the collection was entrusted, kept it reverently and added to it, bequeathing it to various ones of her numerous descendants. A valuable portion of these "family papers" came into the possession of Harriette's granddaughter, the late Mrs. Benjamin Gratz Crosby, of Spring Station, Kentucky, who died in 1961. She graciously permitted me to study and quote from them in the preparation of this biography, and in various interviews told me charming family anecdotes and showed me the family heirlooms. Mrs. Crosby had in times past allowed researchers to examine, quote, and sometimes publish items from her collection, and had let a number of copies be placed in the libraries of Transylvania College, the University of Texas, and the University of Kentucky, where they can be conveniently consulted. Other portions of the "family papers" have been preserved by descendants of Horace and Mary Austin Holley, particularly the Aldrich and Dall families, who have likewise generously made materials available to scholars and libraries. The Barker Texas History Center Archives of the University of Texas has in its possession a valuable collection consisting of original papers and also copies of materials relating to Mary Austin Holley.

Since the career of Mary Austin Holley is inextricably involved with those of two eminent men, her husband, Horace Holley, and her cousin, Stephen F. Austin, much of the investigation of her life must be made in the records which concern them. Source material about Horace Holley's personal life is widely scattered but focuses in his wife's "family papers," in the Horace and Mary Austin Holley Collection of the Transylvania College Library, and in the official records of early Transylvania University (now Transylvania College). His letters are preserved in many libraries, often in collections devoted to his correspondents rather than to him. Mary Austin Holley's contacts with Stephen F. Austin are documented in the three volumes of the *Austin Papers* and the unpublished Austin papers in the Barker Texas History Center Archives as well as in the collections devoted primarily to her.

For permission to examine and sometimes to quote from these and many other sources I wish to acknowledge my indebtedness and gratitude to the following: the American Historical Association; the Barker Texas History Center Archives and Library, the University of Texas; the Boston Public Library; the Grosvenor Reference Division, Buffalo and Erie County (New York) Public Library; Christ Church, Lexington, Kentucky; the Connecticut Historical Society; Duke University Library; the Historical and Philosophical Society of Ohio; the Lexington (Kentucky) Public Library; J. B. Lippincott Company; the Manuscripts and Music Divisions of the Library of Congress; the Margaret I. King Library, University of Kentucky; the Massachusetts Historical Society; the National Archives; the New Haven Colony Historical Society; the New Orleans Public Library; the New York Public Library; the Rosenberg Library, Galveston, Texas; the Texas State Library, Austin; the Transylvania College Library; Trinity Church, New Haven, Connecticut; the University of North Carolina Press; the University of Texas Press; the Yale University Library.

I am deeply indebted to Mrs. Richard French Spencer, of San Antonio, Texas, for her generous interest in this biography of Mary Austin Holley and for her approval of it as the second title in the Elma Dill Russell Spencer Foundation Series.

For their cooperation and personal courtesies I am grateful to many members of the Austin family, especially to Mr. and Mrs. W. Joel Bryan, the late Mrs. Benjamin Gratz Crosby, Mrs. John P. Crosby, Mrs. Collister Johnson, Mrs. Kelly Muir, the late Mrs. Hallie Bryan Perry, and Mr. and Mrs. Stephen S. Perry. In Kentucky I owe much to the interest and assistance of Dr. Jacqueline Bull, Dr. J. Winston Coleman, Jr., Dr. and Mrs. Davis Buckner, Miss Virginia Hayes, Miss Roemel Henry, Owen S. Lee, Miss Mary O'Connell, Mrs. Julia Sherer, and Dr. and Mrs. Lawrence Thompson. My obligations in Texas are equally great and my especial thanks go to Miss Winnie Allen, Dr. Llerena Friend, Miss Mabel Major, Jack H. Meeks, Miss Marion Day Mullins, and Dr. Walter Prescott Webb.

Research in libraries and manuscript collections, even with the gracious assistance of professional staff members and friends, was not sufficient, however, to recapture the story of Mrs. Holley, who, in contrast to most ladies of her time, led an active and public life. I found it necessary to follow her career with the help of contemporary maps and newspapers, and to set it against the diverse backgrounds of ten or a dozen cities and communities in which she resided at various times. My attempt to record her day-by-day activities in these many localities kept me "on the wing," because I found out early in my research that her words and actions came to life only when I followed her faithfully on her travels. Happily, because of excellent local historians and dedicated preservers of historic houses, it was not difficult to reconstruct in my own mind and, I hope, in the pages of this biography most of the settings in which she lived.

Were she to return to her birthplace today she would readily recognize the New Haven Green and the pattern of the old town leading down to the Harbour. Greenfield Hill has changed so little that she could find there the familiar landmarks of church and school and home even if she came again by night as she did the last time she was there. In metropolitan Boston, on the other hand, the Hollis Street Church has long since been demolished and the only reminder that the location, now occupied by a parking lot, was once famous is a small sign reading "Holley Square." Orange Street, a part of the present Washington Street, is a thoroughfare roaring with downtown city traffic.

Much of early nineteenth-century Lexington still remains. Mrs. Holley's first home on Limestone Street houses a large private school; the residence on Constitution Street is editorial headquarters for a magazine; John Brand's Rose Hill and William Brand's Elmwood are occupied by descendants of families she knew well; and classic Morrison College crowns the old College Lot, now Gratz Park. In Christ Church her descendants in the fifth generation occupy a pew near that of the Clays.

The Texas that Mary Austin Holley knew is also remarkably intact. At Peach Point Plantation the present-day Perrys and Bryans welcome strangers as if they were invited guests and permit them to go on private pilgrimages to the empty tomb of the Empresario in the family burying ground. His ashes now rest in an honored spot in the state capital. The leagues of land on the Gulf that Mary sold from time to time are part of that vast South Texas industrial complex which is surpassing all the dreams of wealth and power that she and Stephen F. Austin and even the visionary Hammeken once had.

Good Hope Plantation on the Louisiana German Coast is the property of an oil company, and its mansion, like the other Labranche homes along the river, is gone; but the Edmond Fortier house, in which she surely was a frequent guest, remains over on the Right Bank to delight countless visitors. One quaint Trepagnier cottage still hugs the embankment of the great Bonnet Carré Spillway built in recent years to divert the flood waters of the Mississippi into nearby Lake Pontchartrain.

In New Orleans so much of the past remains as part of the present that one almost expects to encounter Madame Holley at the corner of Royal and St. Peter Streets or in the lobby of the venerable St. Charles Hotel. The tomb of the Augustin family is still in use and admirably preserved. The handsome gravestone which Harriette Brand caused to be erected over her brother Horace's resting place in the Red Church cemetery when he died on the German Coast in 1853 is gone, either washed away by the river in one of its recurrent floods or misplaced when the new levee was built and a highway run across the corner where members of the Labranche family were buried.

In acknowledging my obligations to the many persons who have helped and guided me in this undertaking and to the places which have given me understanding and inspiration, I must end by admitting that no biographer was ever more indebted to the subject of the work. As the reader of this book has doubtless discovered, the liveliest and most revealing parts of it draw heavily upon Mary Austin Holley's own words and follow the clues which she provides about herself. She is, one might well say, its "onlie begetter."

NOTES

Key to Abbreviations

Holley Coll.-Trans.—Horace and Mary Austin Holley Collection, Transylvania College Library

MAH Papers—Mary Austin Holley Papers, Barker Texas History Center Archives, University of Texas

CHAPTER 1

[1] New Haven in Mary Austin Holley's youth has been reconstructed chiefly from the Dana Collection, "New Haven, Old and New," Vols. 35–36: Meadow Street; maps of New Haven by Ezra Stiles (1775) and Amos Doolittle (1812), in the New Haven Map Collection of the New Haven Colony Historical Society; Timothy Dwight, *A Statistical Account of the City of New Haven, passim;* and Edward E. Atwater (ed.), *The History of the City of New Haven to the Present Time, passim.*

[2] "History of Elias Austin . . . prepared from records in Durham, Connecticut, by Mildred Scranton, 1924," and "Genealogy of Elijah Austin," by Mrs. Harry Jensen, both in the Austin Genealogical Papers; *The Record of Service of Connecticut Men in the Revolution,* p. 18; L. F. Middlebrook, *The History of Maritime Connecticut during the American Revolution, 1775–1783,* II, 244–245; K. S. Latourette, *The History of Early Relationships between the United States and China, 1784–1844,* p. 39. See Mary Austin Holley's Family Relationships, Chart I, in this volume.

[3] Dana Collection, "New Haven, Old and New," Vol. 35: "Meadow Street." Whiting Street was earlier known as Allen's Lane.

[4] *The Phelps Family of America and their English Ancestors,* compiled by Oliver Seymour Phelps and Andrew T. Servin, is the standard reference for Mary Austin Holley's maternal relatives. For Judge John Phelps see Charles J. Hoadly (ed.), *Public Papers of the State of Connecticut,* I, 22, 244, 472; II, 6, 224; III, 461. See also Mary Austin Holley's Family Relationships, Chart II, in this volume.

[5] Mary Austin Holley, Notes for a History of Texas, Section No. 37, Mary Austin Holley Papers (hereinafter cited as MAH Papers).

[6] Franklin B. Dexter, *Biographical Sketches of the Graduates of Yale College,* IV, 159–160.

[7] Trinity Church Records, New Haven, Connecticut.

[8] The Austin family's traditional version of Elijah Austin's death is corroborated in a sketch of the clerk, Henry Hubbard (1774–1794) in Dexter, *Biographical Sketches of the Graduates of Yale College,* V, 20.

[9] Administration and Inventory of Elijah Austin's Estate, New Haven, Connecticut, District Court, Probate Records, Vol. 17, pp. 17, 139.

[10] Mary Austin Holley, "Notes for a History of Texas," Section No. 37, MAH Papers; William R. Hogan, "Henry Austin," *Southwestern Historical Quarterly*, XXXVII (1933–1934), 185–214.

CHAPTER 2

[1] Rollin G. Osterweis, *Three Centuries of New Haven, 1638–1938*, pp. 157–160. The mercantile house of Broome and Platt flourished in New Haven *ca.* 1784–1800.

[2] *Phi Beta Kappa Directory, 1776–1941*, p. 1183.

[3] Accounts of Lady Abigail Richardson and considerable Beers family history are in the Crosby Papers.

[4] Charles E. Perry (ed.), *Founders and Leaders of Connnecticut, 1633–1788*, pp. 258–261. From 1793 to 1798 Peleg Sanford (*ca.* 1744–1802) was a business partner of Daniel Wadsworth, later founder of the Wadsworth Atheneum, Hartford, Connecticut.

[5] For the children of Timothy Phelps see Mary Austin Holley's Family Relationships, Chart II, in this volume. His first wife's name is variously spelled in the records as "Janet," "Jennett," and "Jennette."

[6] Timothy Dwight (1752–1817) was pastor at Greenfield Hill, Connecticut, from 1783 to 1795. Vernon Parrington deplores Dwight's dominant influence as upholder of Federalist and Calvinist conservatism (*The Connecticut Wits*, pp. xxxix–xliii). Van Wyck Brooks holds Dwight largely responsible for "the narrow Connecticut mind" (*The World of Washington Irving*, pp. 45–65).

[7] Elijah Phelps Austin [from Hartford, Connecticut,] to Henry Austin, ["on board the ship *Neptune*, Captain Daniel Green, Canton,"], March 15, 1798, Crosby Papers.

[8] "M. A." to "My dearest C——a," December 13, 1799, and other related letters, Crosby Papers.

[9] Minutes of the Brothers in Unity, April 30, 1800, December 30, 1801, Yale College, Brothers in Unity Records, 1783–1802; Dexter, *Biographical Sketches of the Graduates of Yale College*, V, 588–589; Charles Caldwell, *A Discourse on the Genius and Character of the Rev. Horace Holley, LL.D. . . .*, pp. 121–133 (hereinafter cited as Caldwell, *Discourse*).

[10] "M. A." to "My dearest C—a," December 13, 1799, Crosby Papers; Atwater (ed.), *The History of the City of New Haven*, p. 157.

[11] Timothy Phelps to Oliver Wolcott, July 15, 1800, September 18, 1800, in George Gibbs (ed.), *Administrations of Washington and Adams*, II, 360, 418–419.

[12] "An Extract from a College Exercise, written in 1802," *Western Review*, II (1820), 190–191. As will appear later in this biography Horace Holley and his wife contributed many of their early literary compositions to the *Western*

Review, published in Lexington, Kentucky, while he was President of Transylvania University there. This "Extract" is signed "P. P.," one of his several signatures as a contributor. Mary Austin Holley is undoubtedly referring to this piece in her published account of his college career: "Some of the exercises of this time remain. . . . Among them, the product of the Junior Year, is a poem of some length. They embrace, however, many popular sentiments of the day, which are now obsolete" (Caldwell, *Discourse,* p. 127.)

[13] Horace Holley, "The Late Timothy Dexter of Newburyport, Massachusetts," *Western Review,* III (1820), 278–285; Myron Holley to Horace Holley, October 12, 1804, Crosby Papers.

[14] Certificate signed by Dr. Timothy Dwight, Yale College, January 7, 1804, Crosby Papers.

[15] Horace Holley to Mrs. Luther Holley, October 27, 1801, June 30, 1802, Crosby Papers.

[16] Phelps and Servin (comps.), *The Phelps Family, No.* 990: Timothy Phelps.

[17] Caldwell, *Discourse,* pp. 127–128; Malcolm D. Rudd, "Men of Worth of Salisbury Birth," No. 45: Horace Holley, *Lakeville Journal,* December, 6, 1934.

[18] Luther Holley to Horace Holley, March 21, 1802, July 13, 1803, Crosby Papers. Excerpts of undated letters from Luther Holley to Horace Holley in Caldwell, *Discourse,* pp. 124, 129.

[19] Luther Holley to Horace Holley, December 25, 1803, Crosby Papers.

[20] Caldwell, *Discourse,* p. 128.

[21] Luther Holley to Horace Holley in 1804, excerpts in Caldwell, *Discourse,* p. 133.

[22] This courtship episode is based on "Music. A letter from a lady to a gentleman who was thought not to be pleased with Music . . . dated March 30th, 1804," *Western Review,* IV (1821), 314–318.

[23] "Lines addressed to a beautiful young lady by a gentleman . . .," *Western Review,* I (1819), 314–315.

[24] Elijah Phelps Austin to Henry Austin, March 15, 1798, Crosby Papers; Biographical Notes on Elisha Lewis, Crosby Papers.

[25] Moses Austin to Stephen F. Austin, December 16, 1804, *Austin Papers,* I, 93–95; Eugene C. Barker, *The Life of Stephen F. Austin: Founder of Texas, 1793–1836,* pp. 17–20.

[26] Family Records of Mary Austin Aldrich, typescript, MAH Papers.

[27] Horace Holley, "The Late Timothy Dexter of Newburyport, Massachusetts," *Western Review,* III (1820), 278–285.

[28] License, dated December 19, 1804, Crosby Papers.

[29] "This is to certify that Mary Austin is a regular communicant of Trinity Church, New Haven. Bela Hubbard, Rector"—a folded sheet addressed to "Miss Mary Austin, New Haven," in the Crosby Papers. On the outside of

the sheet is written: "December 31, 1804, Rev. B. Hubbard, D.D., inclosing a certificate of my church membership."

30 Trinity Church Records, New Haven, Connecticut.

31 Interview, Rebecca Smith Lee with Mrs. Benjamin Gratz Crosby, August 24, 1952.

CHAPTER 3

1 Caldwell, *Discourse*, the engraving, "Lake Wanscopomac," facing p. 103, pp. 106–133. See also Horace Holley to Mrs. Luther Holley, October 27, 1801, June 20, 1802; Luther Holley to Horace Holley, March 21, 1802; Crosby Papers.

2 Rudd, "Men of Worth of Salisbury Birth," *Lakeville Journal*, December 6, 1934.

3 For Luther Holley's immediate family see Mary Austin Holley's Family Relationships, Chart III, in this volume.

4 About a year before his death Luther Holley wrote an autobiographical sketch, which Mary Austin Holley adapted for the excellent account of him in Caldwell, *Discourse*, pp. 110–113 and *passim*.

5 The most authentic account of Horace Holley's youthful theological orthodoxy is offered by Mary Austin Holley: "The doctrines of the old divines were thought too lax, and the system of Hopkins was engrafted upon that of Calvin. . . . It must in justice be said of the distinguished head of Yale, that he did not go the full length of that austere system. It often happens, however, that the pupil exceeds the master in zeal, just in proportion as he lacks knowledge" (Caldwell, *Discourse*, p. 131).

6 Myron Holley became an Erie Canal contractor, a horticulturalist, and an early abolitionist. See two pamphlets about him: Elizur Wright, *Myron Holley. What he did for liberty and true religion;* and *The History of the Erection of the Monument on the Grave of Myron Holley;* also James Parton, *Captains of Industry*, pp. 163–169.

7 Luther Holley to Horace Holley, August 20, 1812, Crosby Papers.

CHAPTER 4

1 For Holley see George H. Merwin, *Ye Church and Parish of Greenfield . . . 1725–1913*, pp. 63–69 and *passim*.

2 Caldwell, *Discourse*, pp. 134–136.

3 The Holleys' house in Greenfield Hill from 1805 to 1808 is described as "Colonial No. 8" by Duane Hamilton Hurd, *The History of Fairfield County, Connecticut . . .* , pp. 332–333.

4 Henry Austin was appointed about 1805 as guardian for his younger brothers, John Phelps and Charles (New Haven, Connecticut, District Court, Probate Records, Vol. 23, pp. 421, 444).

5 Caldwell, *Discourse*, pp. 134–135.

[6] Mary Austin Holley to Stephen F. Austin, January 21, 1831, and June 8, 1832, *Austin Papers,* II, 570–571, 778–779.

[7] See Hurd, *History of Fairfield County, Connecticut,* pp. 331–332, for "Colonial No. 7," the Bronson home.

[8] "Mr. Holly [*sic*] brought with him the first piano ever seen in Greenfield," according to Hurd, *History of Fairfield County, Connecticut,* p. 333. Holley probably obtained it between 1806 and 1808 from Timothy Phelps, who left New Haven in 1806, according to Dexter, *Biographical Sketches of the Graduates of Yale College,* IV, 159.

[9] *Western Review,* II (1820), 186–188. Signed "U," one of the signatures of Horace Holley. The opening lines are: "When first to my fair mistress' hand I came, Inscrib'd and honour'd with Bronsonia's name . . ."

[10] Isaac Lewis, for the Committee of the Congregation, signed the certificate on May 12, 1807, at West Greenwich, Connecticut (Crosby Papers).

[11] "An Investigation of the Facts relative to a descent of Stones from the Atmosphere to the Earth, on the 14th of December, 1807, in the Towns of Fairfield, Weston, and Huntington, Connecticut, and to the Meteor whence these earthy bodies proceeded. In a Memoir addressed to Samuel L. Mitchell, by the Rev. Horace Holley, and Isaac Bronson, Esq., of Fairfield, dated December 23, 1807," *The Medical Repository, comprehending Original Essays and Intelligence relative to Medicine, Chemistry, Natural History, Agriculture, Geography, and the Arts* . . ., V (1808), 418–421. Also Samuel L. Mitchell to Horace Holley and Isaac Bronson, December 29, 1807, in the Horace and Mary Austin Holley Collection (hereinafter cited as Holley Coll.-Trans.).

[12] Horace Austin to Moses Austin, August 20, 1807, *Austin Papers,* I, 134–135; Timothy Phelps to Moses Austin, August 17, 1807, and November 28, 1807, *ibid.,* I, 133–134, 142–143. For Timothy Phelps in Ste. Genevieve see *Territorial Papers of the United States,* Vol. XIV: *The Territory of Louisiana-Missouri, 1806–1814,* pp. 171, 176, 180.

[13] Caldwell, *Discourse,* p. 134.

CHAPTER 5

[1] Horace Holley to Mary Austin Holley, October 9, 1808, Crosby Papers.

[2] Mary Austin Holley to Horace Holley, October 13, 1808, MAH Papers.

[3] Caldwell, *Discourse,* pp. 135–136; Dismissal Papers, September 13, 1808, Crosby Papers.

[4] Henry Austin to John C. Stephens, March 19, 1840: "You may possibly remember me from the circumstance of my being the roommate of Robert Fulton, at No. 13 Broadway, whilst he was building the first steamboat battery, *Fulton,* when you called often to see him" (photostat in Henry Austin Papers).

[5] Horace Holley to Mary Austin Holley, October 3, 1808, October 9, 1808, October 16, 1808, and fragment of letter dated in November, 1808, Crosby Papers.

6 Mary Austin Holley to Horace Holley, October 9, 1808, October 13, 1808, October 20, 1808, MAH Papers.

7 Harriette Williman Holley was born in New Haven, December 13, 1808 (*The Phelps Family*, No. 5228).

8 Caldwell, *Discourse*, p. 137.

9 Harriette Williman, the friend for whom Mary Austin Holley named her daughter, was in 1831 a "Mrs. De Jon of New York City" (Mary Austin Holley to Harriette Brand, March 11, 1831, MAH Papers).

10 See George Leonard Chaney. *The Hollis Street Church from Mather Byles to Thomas Storr King, 1732–1861*, for pictures of the two church buildings in which Holley preached, lists of members, and other data.

11 Horace Holley to Mary Austin Holley, January 23, 1809, Crosby Papers.

CHAPTER 6

1 *The Boston Directory, containing the names of the inhabitants, their occupation, places of business, and dwelling houses . . . for 1809* and subsequent directories for 1810, 1813, and 1818. About twenty families in the Hollis Street Church lived between No. 3 and No. 136 on Orange Street.

2 See William Ellery Channing (1780–1842) in *Dictionary of American Biography*, IV, 4–7; William Emerson (1769–1811) in *ibid.*, VI, 141–142; Joseph Buckminster (1774–1812) in *ibid.*, III, 233–234 (hereinafter cited as *DAB*).

3 Joseph Eckley, D.D., *Sermon delivered at the Installation of the Rev. Horace Holley to the Pastoral Care of the Church and Society in Hollis Street*, pp. 3–36.

4 Lathrop's Charge, *ibid.*, pp. 37–46; Kirkland's Welcome, *ibid.*, pp. 47–53. See John Thornton Kirkland (1770–1840) in *DAB*, X, 431.

5 James S. Loring, *The Hundred Boston Orators Appointed by the Municipal Authorities and other Public Bodies, from 1770 to 1852 . . .*, pp. 368–375.

6 Caldwell, *Discourse*, p. 144.

7 Horace Holley to Benjamin Goddard, November 9, 1809, Benjamin Goddard Papers.

8 Mary Austin Holley to William Brand, February 21, 1838, MAH Papers.

9 Van Wyck Brooks, *The Flowering of New England, 1815–1865*, p. 8.

10 *Centennial Celebration of the Wednesday Evening Club, 1777–1877*, pp. 26–33.

11 Chaney's *The Hollis Street Church* gives details of the sale of the old building, erection of the new one, and the sojourn with the First Church.

12 The Reverend William Emerson was "one of the ministers who, before the break occurred with Congregationalism, had already shown a lack of sympathy for Calvinism" (Arthur Cushman McGiffert, Jr., [ed.], *Young Emerson Speaks*, p. xii).

13 Caldwell, *Discourse*, pp. 146–147. This account of the disagreement

between Holley and the Braintree committee, written substantially by Mary Austin Holley, reveals the extent of his theological liberalism by 1810.

[14] See James Freeman (1759–1835) in *DAB*, VII, 10.

[15] George C. D. Odell, *Annals of the New York Stage*, II, 486.

[16] Edward Warren, *The Life of John Collins Warren, M.D.*, I, 78–79, 115, 159.

[17] Mary Austin Holley to Mrs. Luther Holley, September 23, 1812, MAH Papers.

[18] Horace Holley to Mary Austin Holley, August 6, 1811, Crosby Papers.

[19] *Program of the Fiftieth Anniversary of the Dedication of the Meeting House in Hollis Street, Thursday, January 31, 1861*. The program of the original dedication is reprinted in this folder.

[20] Caldwell, *Discourse*, pp. 180–185.

CHAPTER 7

[1] Henrietta Austin was married to James Dall in Boston, February 9, 1812 (Crosby Papers).

[2] *The Boston Directory for 1813* lists the Reverend Horace Holley "at Mr. Haskell's, Boylston St." John Haskell, Schoolmaster, listed in the Boston directories for 1809 and 1810, is listed in Chaney's roll of pewholders at Hollis Street Church in 1811. References to the Haskells appear in the Holley letters from 1812 to 1818, for example, Mary Austin Holley to Horace Holley, September 28, 1812, and October 5, 1812 (MAH Papers).

[3] Mary Austin Holley's travels to Ballston Springs, New York City, and New Haven are described in her letters to Horace Holley of September 21, 1812, September 23, 1812, September 30, 1812, and October 3, 1812 (MAH Papers).

[4] Maria Brown Austin to Moses Austin, August 18, 1811, and October 25, 1812, Austin Papers. Also Barker, *The Life of Stephen F. Austin*, pp. 21–22.

[5] Timothy Phelps "died on November 20, 1812, aged 55 years, while on passage from La Guira, Venezuela, to the Island of St. Thomas" (Dexter, *Biographical Sketches of the Graduates of Yale College*, IV, 160).

[6] "From a Husband to a Wife, on seeing their daughter, a little girl, at play," *Western Review*, III (1820), 255. This poem is acknowledged by Horace Holley as his composition in a letter to Orville Holley, December 19, 1820 (Crosby Papers).

[7] *Phi Beta Kappa Directory, 1776–1941*, p. 711.

[8] Horace Holley's principal addresses in Boston were: Ancient and Benevolent Artillery Company, 1811; Discourse on the Death of the Rev. Joseph Buckminster, 1812; Washington Benevolent Society, 1815; Female Asylum, 1816; Discourse on the Death of President Dwight, 1817; Sermon at Plymouth on the Anniversary of the Landing of the Pilgrims, 1817; and the Farewell Sermon on Leaving for Kentucky, 1818 (Dexter, *Biographical Sketches of the Graduates of Yale College*, V, 588).

[9] *A General Repositary and Review*, III (1813), 377. See Niels Henry Sonne, *Liberal Kentucky, 1760–1828*, pp. 162–165, for Holley's development from Hopkinsian theology toward Unitarianism.

[10] See John Louis Ann Magdalen Lefebre Cheverus (1768–1836) in *DAB*, IV, 61–62. Bishop Cheverus wrote a flattering letter of introduction for Horace and Mary Austin Holley in 1815 (Crosby Papers).

[11] Charles Francis Adams (ed.), *The Works of John Adams, Second President of the United States*, X, 312. John Adams disliked Timothy Dwight, which fact may have influenced his approval of Holley's escape from Dwight's influence.

[12] Horace Holley to Mary Austin Holley, October 3, 1814, Holley Coll.-Trans.

[13] The travels of the Holleys are recounted in: Horace Holley to Mary Austin Holley, September 20, 1814, and October 3, 1814, Holley Coll.-Trans.; Horace Holley to Mary Austin Holley, October 5, 1815, Crosby Papers; Mary Austin Holley to Horace Holley, September 15, 1814, September 23, 1814, and October 3, 1814, MAH Papers.

[14] Mary Austin Holley to Horace Holley, September 25, 1814, MAH Papers. See also Anne Louise Germaine (Necker), Baronne de Staël-Holstein, *Germany*, reprint of the Murray translation of 1814, p. 374; and Richard Lawrin Hawkins, *Madame de Staël and the United States*, pp. 2–6, 21–45.

[15] Harriette Holley Burwell to Harriette Brand, November 11, 1842, Crosby Papers.

[16] "The Swan and the Eagle," *Western Review*, I (1819), 125–128, signed "U," one of Horace Holley's signatures. The date of composition of this translation is suggested in Mary Austin Holley to Horace Holley, October 3, 1814 (Holley Coll.-Trans.).

[17] *Western Review*, I (1819), 319–320. This untitled poem of thirty-six lines, signed "M," beginning "Of that sweet Spot," is prefaced by the editor as follows: "The following lines accompanied by a drawing of a beautiful lake in India ink, which was presented by a lady to a friend, who was born on its shore, and whose childhood was spent in the place of his birth . . ."

[18] See Benjamin Bussey (1757–1842) in *Appleton's Cyclopedia of American Biography*, I, 475; and John Ritto Penniman (1783–?) in *The New York Historical Society's Dictionary of Artists in America, 1564–1860*, compiled by George C. Groce and David H. Wallace, p. 498.

[19] Loring, *The Hundred Boston Orators*, p. 368.

[20] Luther Holley to Horace Holley, December 4, 1814, Crosby Papers.

[21] *North American Review*, Vol. 2 (1815), pp. 59–67. See Willard Phillips (1784–1873) in *DAB*, XIV, 547; and Walter Channing (1786–1876) in *ibid.*, IV, 3–4.

[22] Caldwell, *Discourse*, pp. 149–151.

[23] "Lines written immediately on first beholding Niagara Falls, July, 1815, *Western Review*, I (1819), 127–128.

[24] Minutes of the Trustees of Transylvania University, November 11, 1814; James Prentiss to L. Baldwin, Esq., November 19, 1814, both in Transylvania University Official Records.

[25] Romie D. Judd, *The Educational Contributions of Horace Holley*, pp. 17–23.

[26] Loring, *The Hundred Boston Orators*, pp. 407–410. Also John Everett, *An Oration delivered July 5, 1824*, p. 25, footnote crediting Horace Holley with revising an earlier essay by Everett on Byron. See Edward Everett (1794–1865) in *DAB*, VI, 223–226.

[27] The certificate is preserved in the Crosby Papers.

[28] Ernest Henry Wilson, *America's Greatest Garden, the Arnold Arboretum*, p. 5 and *passim*, especially the map; Francis Samuel Drake, *The Town of Roxbury: Its Memorable Persons and Places . . .*, pp. 439–441.

[29] Horace Holley to Mary Austin Holley, *ca.* May 23, 1816, Crosby Papers. These verses, slightly revised, appeared as a forty-eight-line poem beginning "While away to the country, dear Mary," in *Western Review*, I (1819), 316–318.

[30] Drake, *The Town of Roxbury*, pp. 359, 371.

[31] "The Landing of the Pilgrim Fathers at Plymouth, New England, December 22nd., 1620," *Western Review*, III (1820), 285–301.

CHAPTER 8

[1] John Pope, W. T. Barry, James Prentiss, and J. Cabell Breckinridge for the Board of Trustees of Transylvania University to Horace Holley, November 18, 1817, Transylvania University Official Records.

[2] Horace Holley to Messrs. Pope, Barry, Prentiss, and Breckinridge, December 26, 1817, Crosby Papers (a copy in Holley's handwriting).

[3] Horace Holley, "A Journey from Boston in Massachusetts to Lexington in Kentucky," Crosby Papers. This manuscript is referred to by some writers about Holley as his "Journal."

[4] John Adams to Thomas Jefferson, January 28, 1818, in Lester J. Cappon (ed.), *The Adams-Jefferson Letters*, II, 522–523.

[5] Letters included in Horace Holley, "A Journey from Boston in Massachusetts to Lexington in Kentucky," Crosby Papers.

[6] For Horace Holley's travels in the spring of 1818 see: Horace Holley to Harriette Holley, February 23, 1818, April 2, 1818, Crosby Papers; Horace Holley to John C. Warren, March 5, 1818, and April 1, 1818, John Collins Warren Papers; Horace Holley to James Freeman, April 2, 1818, and Horace Holley to Mary Austin Holley, April 9, 1818, Holley Coll.-Trans. Also Caldwell, *Discourse*, pp. 151–163, 198–199.

[7] See Joseph Desha (1768–1842) in *DAB*, V, 254; and Edna Talbott Whitley, *Kentucky Ante-Bellum Portraiture*, p. 126.

[8] Thomas Jefferson to John Adams, May 17, 1818, in Cappon (ed.), *The Adams-Jefferson Letters*, II, 523–525.

[9] Bernard Mayo, *Henry Clay: Spokesman of the New West,* pp. 1–125; Elizabeth M. Simpson, *Bluegrass Houses and Their Traditions,* pp. 399–408.

[10] Simpson, "Chaumiere du Prairie," *Bluegrass Houses,* pp. 93–98; "Rose Hill," *ibid.* pp. 201–226. For John Brand see William H. Perrin, *The History of Fayette County, Kentucky,* pp. 566–567.

[11] Caldwell, *Discourse,* pp. 159–160, 162.

[12] *Ibid.,* p. 163.

[13] Horace Holley to Robert Wickliffe, June 25, 1818, Transylvania University Official Records.

[14] "Horace Austin Holley, born Boston, July 19, 1818; died La., August 8, 1853, unmarried" (*The Phelps Family,* No. 5229).

[15] Dr. Walter Channing was professor of obstetrics at Harvard, 1815–1864.

[16] The Hollis Street Society to Horace Holley, August 30, 1818, signed by Benjamin West. Samuel May, William Brown, Joseph Richards, W. A. P. Davis, Barzillai Homes, and William Dall; Resolutions from the Boston School Committee, n.d.; Resolutions from the Congregational Ministers of Boston, October 3, 1818; Resolutions from the Town Clerk of Boston, March, 1819; all in the Crosby Papers.

[17] Caldwell, *Discourse,* pp. 160–161.

[18] Henry Clay to Horace Holley, September 8, 1818; Horace Holley to Henry Clay, September 15, 1818 (copy), Holley Coll.-Trans.

[19] Caldwell, *Discourse,* pp. 164–165, 198–199.

[20] Lawrence Park to Mrs. Charles Norton, August 13, 1919, Holley Coll.-Trans. Also Loring, *The Hundred Boston Orators,* p. 373; Drake, *The Town of Roxbury,* pp. 305–306.

[21] John Adams to Thomas Jefferson, May 29, 1818, in Cappon (ed.), *The Adams-Jefferson Letters,* II, 525–526.

[22] "Academic Appointments. The Rev. Mr. Holley, of Boston, who has proceeded to Kentucky to assume the government of Transylvania, is accompanied by Mr. Charles Walker, Jr., as Assistant Instructor in Ethics, and Mr. John Everett, as Tutor in the Latin and Greek languages" (*The American Monthly and Critical Review,* IV [1818], 65).

[23] Mary Austin Holley to Willard Phillips, October 24, 1819, Willard Phillips Papers.

[24] Caldwell, *Discourse,* p. 155.

[25] Mary Austin Holley to Willard Phillips, March 20, 1819, Willard Phillips Papers. See John Trumbull (1756–1843) in *The National Cyclopedia of American Biography,* III, 334–335. The painting that Mrs. Holley viewed was probably Trumbull's *Resignation by General Washington of his Commission to Congress.*

[26] Committee of Trustees to James Dall [of Baltimore, Maryland], September 22, 1818, Crosby Papers, asking that the Reverend Horace Holley preach at the dedication of their new church on October 15.

[27] Caldwell, *Discourse,* pp. 161, 163.

CHAPTER 9

1 James Taylor to James Madison, November 7, 1818, in James A. Padgett (ed.), "Letters of James Taylor to the Presidents of the United States," *Register of the Kentucky State Historical Society*. Vol. 34 (1936), pp. 328–329. Also *Kentucky Reporter*, November 25, 1818.

2 For the early months of Holley's administration see: Caldwell, *Discourse*, pp. 199–201; Transylvania University Unbound Documents, 1820-U-383. Also Joseph Story to Horace Holley, October 2, 1818; Henry Clay to Horace Holley, December 9, 1818; John Adams to Horace Holley, December 25, 1818; Holley Coll.-Trans.

3 *Kentucky Gazette*, December 25, 1818.

4 President Holley leased the residence on Mulberry Street (already beginning to be called Limestone Street) from the estate of Thomas Hart, Jr. Built in 1797 by Colonel George Nicholas, officer in the Revolution, the house was rebuilt in 1846 by the architect, Thomas Lewinsky, retaining some of the "central part," and is now occupied by the Sayre School. Asa Blanchard, well-known silversmith, billed Transylvania University for four different orders of engraved silver spoons between November 10, 1818, and January 28, 1819 (Transylvania University Unbound Documents, 1818-U-173).

5 Mary Austin Holley to Willard Phillips, March 20, 1819, Willard Phillips Papers.

6 Mary Austin Holley to Willard Phillips, October 24, 1819, Willard Phillips Papers.

7 "Miss Hunt must be accomplished indeed to extract poetry from the Greek and Latin" (Rebecca Gratz to Maria Gist Gratz, May 10, 1820, *The Letters of Rebecca Gratz*, edited by David Philipson, p. 31). Theodosia Hunt was the daughter of John W. Hunt, of New Jersey, who built Hopemont in 1811 for his large family, which included another daughter, Henrietta, mother of the Confederate General, John Hunt Morgan (Simpson, *Bluegrass Houses and Their Traditions*, pp. 149–158).

8 For the Holley's hospitality as viewed by their friends see Caldwell, *Discourse*, pp. 218–220, 240; and William Leavy, "Memoir of Lexington and its Vicinity, with Some Notice of Many Prominent Citizens and its Institutions of Religion and Learning . . .," *Register of the Kentucky State Historical Society*, Vol. 41 (1943), p. 121.

9 See William Gibbes Hunt (1791–1833) in *DAB*, IX, 396. Also Algernon Smith Dickson, "*The Western Review and Miscellaneous Magazine*," pp. 19–31; and Christ Church Records, Communicants, July 1, 1820.

10 See William H. Venable, *Beginnings of Literary Culture in the Ohio Valley. Historical and Biographical Sketches*, pp. 62–66; Frank Luther Mott, *A History of American Magazines, 1741–1850*, I, 311–312.

11 "On Education in the Western States," *Western Review*, I (1819), 53–59. Included in Caldwell, *Discourse*, pp. 256–265, as one of Holley's writings.

12 "It is near to the Hour," *Western Review*, I (1819), 63–64; "Madame de

Staël," *ibid.*, p. 124; "Lines written immediately on first beholding Niagara Falls, July, 1815," *ibid.*, pp. 127–128; "The Swan and the Eagle," *ibid.*, pp. 125–127; and the review of the *Second Annual Report of the American Society for Colonizing the Free People of Colour in the United States, ibid.*, pp. 142–164.

Horace Holley owned slaves as early as 1819 (Fayette County, Kentucky, Tax Rolls for 1820); but he favored colonization (Horace Holley to Orville Holley, December 19, 1820, in Holley Coll.-Trans.).

[13] Mary Austin Holley to Willard Phillips, March 20, 1819, Willard Phillips Papers; Horace Holley to Orville Holley, December 19, 1820, Crosby Papers.

[14] See *Western Monitor*, July 6, 1819 (account of Monroe's visit); July 27, 1819 (reprint of Holley's welcome speech); August 10, 1819 (criticism of speech and also an editorial defense by "Common Sense"); August 17, 1819 (defense of Holley's speech by "Fair Play"); August 31, 1819 (defense of Holley by "Fair Play").

[15] *Ibid.*, August 24, 1819.

[16] Sonne, *Liberal Kentucky*, p. 188.

[17] Robert Peter, *The History of the Medical Department of Transylvania University*, pp. 24–25.

[18] C. S. Rafinesque. "A Life of Travels," *Chronica Botanica*, Vol. 8 (1944), pp. 321–341. Also Harry B. Weiss, *Rafinesque's Kentucky Friends*, pp. 7–20; and Huntley Dupre, *Rafinesque in Lexington, 1819–1826*, pp. 69–74, 80–81.

[19] Mayo, *Henry Clay: Spokesman of the New West*, pp. 89–125; Whitley, *Kentucky Ante-Bellum Portraiture*, pp. 122–123. A portrait of Lucretia Hart Clay by Oliver Frazer hangs in the dining room at Ashland, now open to the public as a museum.

[20] *Western Review*, I (1819), 124.

[21] *The Western Minerva, or American Annals of Knowledge and Literature*, I (1821), No. 1.

[22] Christ Church Records, 1820–1830 (compiled and inscribed by the Reverend George Chapman). Also Elizabeth King Smith and Mary LeGrand Didlake, *Christ Church, 1796–1946*, pp. 10–15; and Transylvania University Unbound Documents, 1829-U-233.

[23] A list of Transylvania tutors includes: "Accessus 1818, *Johannes Everett, A.M., Greek, exitus 1820" (*Catalogue of Transylvania University, 1826*).

[24] Moses Austin to James Elijah Brown Austin, February 8, 1820, *Austin Papers*, I, 354–355.

[25] Mary Austin Holley to Orville Holley, August 20, 1820, Crosby Papers; *Kentucky Reporter*, October 4, 1820. Horace Holley's St. Louis sermon is included in his Sermon Notes, Crosby Papers.

[26] Judd, *Educational Contributions of Horace Holley*, pp. 34–36.

[27] The removal of the Holleys to the Seminary Building is proved by numerous references: *Kentucky Reporter*, August 2–October 11, 1820, advertis-

ing the Hart dwelling "lately occupied by Mr. Holley" as for rent; Mary Austin Holley to Orville Holley, December 5, 1820 (Crosby Papers); Leavy, "Memoir of Lexington," *Register of the Kentucky State Historical Society*, Vol. 41 (1943), pp. 45–46; *Kentucky Reporter*, March 15, 1825; and J. M. Roach to Mrs. Benjamin Gratz Crosby, September 23, 1933 (Crosby Papers). Repairs of the Seminary Building made for the Holleys appear in Transylvania University Unbound Documents, 1820-U-349, 1820-U-374, 1820-U-377, 1820-U-381, 1820-U-383, 1820-U-384, and 1820-U-386.

[28] Mary Austin Holley to Orville Holley, December 5, 1820, Crosby Papers.

[29] John Carl Parish, *George Wallace Jones*, p. 260. Jones, from Ste. Genevieve, Missouri, was a student at Transylvania from 1821 to 1825.

[30] See Matthew Jouett (1787–1827) in *DAB*, X, 222; and George W. Ranck, *The History of Lexington, Kentucky*, pp. 146–147. Also Matthew Jouett to [Robert Wickliffe], June –, 1821, Transylvania University Official Records. The Jouett portrait of Horace Holley is in the possession of Transylvania College. A miniature of Mary Austin Holley attributed to Jouett is in the possession of the family of Mrs. Harriette Holley Aldrich, and a copy of it painted in color on wood is owned by Mrs. Eleanor Muir Johnson, of Far Hills, New Jersey (Mrs. Kelly Muir to Rebecca Smith Lee, January 23, 1953; Mrs. Eleanor Muir Johnson to Rebecca Smith Lee, February 3, 1953). This likeness of Mary Austin Holley is reproduced as the frontispiece in Hatcher, *Letters of an Early American Traveller: Mary Austin Holley, Her Life and Works, 1784–1846*.

CHAPTER 10

[1] For Mary Austin Holley's trip East in 1821–1822 see Mary Austin Holley to Horace Holley, June 27, 1821, July 7, 1821, August 6, 1821, August 13, 1821, August 28, 1821, September 16, 1821 (MAH Papers). See Rebecca Gratz (1781–1869), in *DAB*, VII, 505–506. For Benjamin Gratz see Perrin, *History of Fayette County, Kentucky*, pp. 612–613.

[2] Dexter, *Biographical Sketches of the Graduates of Yale College*, VI, 441–442.

[3] Horace Holley's activities in 1821–1822 are indicated in Horace Holley to Josiah Kingsley, July 14, 1821 (Horace Holley Papers-Yale); and Josiah Quincy to Transylvania University, July 21, 1821 (Holley Coll.-Trans.).

[4] Mary Austin Holley to Horace Holley, August 13, 1821, MAH Papers.

[5] Mary Austin Holley to Orville Holley, August 7, 1821, MAH Papers.

[6] See John Everett to Mary Austin Holley, "20 days at Sea—Midsummer, 1821," September 12, 1821, October 25, 1821, Holley Coll.-Trans.

[7] Mary Austin Holley to Horace Holley, September 16, 1821, MAH Papers.

[8] Horace Holley to Harriette Holley, August 17, 1821, Crosby Papers.

[9] Mary Austin Holley's long stay in the East in 1821–1822 is scantily documented, since her letters after September, 1821, are not in collections known to the present writer. Light is shed on her plans in Mary Austin Holley to

Horace Holley, September 16, 1821 (MAH Papers). Horace Holley owed taxes on two horses and one carriage on January 1, 1822 (Fayette County, Kentucky, Tax Rolls for 1822).

[10] Horace Holley to John W. Hunt, February 3, 1822, John W. Hunt Papers; Dr. John C. Warren to Horace Holley, June 10, 1822, Holley Coll.-Trans.

[11] Maria Brown Austin to James Elijah Brown Austin, August 3, 1821, *Austin Papers*, I, 404–405.

[12] Horace Holley to Benjamin Bussey, December 28, 1821, quoted in Judd, *Educational Contributions of Horace Holley*, pp. 45, 47.

[13] Margaret Newnan Wagers, *The Education of a Gentlemen; Jefferson Davis at Transylvania, 1821–1824*, pp. 4–5, 23–24.

[14] Transylvania University Unbound Documents, 1822-U-77, 1822-U-99, 1822-U-267.

[15] Dr. John C. Warren to Horace Holley, June 10, 1822, Holley Coll.-Trans.

[16] Transylvania University Unbound Documents, 1822-U-199. In 1823 an unfriendly writer in the *Literary Pamphleteer* asserted that the University Trustees gave Dr. Holley one thousand dollars to bring out his family at first; and then when they had all returned to Boston, another large allowance was made to bring them out a second time (quoted in Sonne, *Liberal Kentucky*, p. 210).

[17] Horace Holley preached in Boston on "The Nature of Man," August 18, 1822, and on "The Nature and Sources of Human Happiness," August 31, 1822 (Sermon Notes, Crosby Papers).

[18] Horace Holley to John Knapp, November 20, 1822, G. E. Ellis Papers. Also *Kentucky Reporter*, October 7, 1822.

CHAPTER 11

[1] *School Exercises of the Lafayette Female Academy, including Triumphs of Genius, a Poem by Caroline Clifford Nephew, of Darien Georgia* [1826]. This pamphlet is advertised in the *Kentucky Reporter*, May 29, 1826, for fifty cents.

[2] Toasts of Horace Holley, manuscript in the Crosby Papers.

[3] Ranck, *History of Lexington, Kentucky*, p. 204; Parish, *George Wallace Jones*, p. 257; *Kentucky Reporter*, January 27, 1823, February 10, 1823, February 17, 1823. Also Richard Moody to Rebecca Smith Lee, April 26, 1955, regarding Edwin Forrest in Lexington.

[4] William H. Allen to John A. Trimble, March 19, 1823, John A. Trimble Papers.

[5] Transylvania University Unbound Documents, 1823-U-88, 1823-U-89.

[6] Elijah Slack to Horace Holley, October 3, 1823, Crosby Papers.

[7] For the Holleys' journey to Nashville in 1823 see: Horace Holley to Luther Holley, August 14, 1823, August 16, 1823, August 31, 1823, September 7, 1823, Crosby Papers. Also Mary Austin Holley to John C. Warren,

August 26, 1823, John Collins Warren Papers; and John C. Warren to Mary Austin Holley, July 31, 1824, Holley Coll.-Trans. In the Crosby Papers are letters inviting President Holley to preach in Hopkinsville, Russellville, and Bowling Green, Kentucky, and in Nashville, Tennessee; also Holley's notes for the sermons at Bowling Green, Hopkinsville, and Nashville.

[8] *The Catalogue of the Officers and Students of Transylvania University, January, 1823* lists Andrew Jackson Donelson, Nashville, Tennessee, in the Law Class, and William Harris Wharton and John Overton Wharton, both of Nashville, as students.

[9] Horace Holley to Jeremiah Day, May 13, 1823, Horace Holley Papers-Yale; Jeremiah Day to Horace Holley, May 28, 1823, Crosby Papers.

[10] See Isaac Shelby (1750–1826) in *DAB*, XVII, 60.

[11] Marquis James, *Andrew Jackson: Portrait of a President*, pp. 20–21; Ralph Earl, Portrait of Andrew Jackson, *American Heritage*, XII (1960), front cover and p. 3. The Earl portrait of Horace Holley is in the possession of the Tennessee Historical Society, Nashville.

[12] Marquis James, *Andrew Jackson: The Border Captain*, pp. 327–329.

[13] Lewis Collins, *Historical Sketches of Kentucky . . . revised by Richard Collins*, pp. 253–261.

[14] *The Story of St. Joseph's Proto-Cathedral and its Paintings*, p. 5. See Rexford Newcomb, *Architecture in Old Kentucky*, pp. 77–79.

[15] Marquis James, *Andrew Jackson: Portrait of a President*, pp. 95–97.

[16] *Western Monitor*, December 2, 1823.

[17] Sonne, *Liberal Kentucky*, pp. 202, 222–225.

[18] Judd, *Educational Contributions of Horace Holley*, pp. 50–51.

[19] Sonne, *Liberal Kentucky*, pp. 229–231.

[20] Ida V. Harrison, "The Transylvania Botanical Gardens," *Journal of American History*, VII (1913), 43–44.

[21] *School Exercises of the Lafayette Female Academy*, pp. 65–67.

[22] *Biographical Directory of the American Congress, 1774–1927*, p. 1617.

[23] William Moses Brand (1804–1845), son of John and Elizabeth Hay Brand.

[24] Horace Holley to Harriette Holley, July 24, 1824, Crosby Papers.

[25] For Horace Holley's trip East in 1824 see: Horace Holley to Mary Austin Holley, July —, 1824, August 2, 1824, August 22, 1824, September 6, 1824, Crosby Papers; Horace Holley to Luther Holley, July 27, 1824, Crosby Papers; Horace Holley to Mary Austin Holley, August 28, 1824, Holley Coll.-Trans.

[26] For Mary Austin Holley's trip to Cincinnati in 1824 see Mary Austin Holley to Horace Holley, August 7, 1824, and August 14, 1824, MAH Papers.

[27] "Ode Salutaria ad Rev. Dom. Horatium Holleium . . .," *Cincinnati Literary Gazette*, II (1824), 16; and "America" by Caroline Clifford Nephew, *ibid.*, II (1824), 74.

[28] "Lines by a Lexington Lady on leaving Cincinnati," *Cincinnati Literary*

Gazette, II (1824), 80. The piece is unsigned, but Mary Austin Holley is listed as a contributor to the magazine (Venable, *Beginnings of Literary Culture in the Ohio Valley,* p. 67).

[29] Horace Holley describes his visit with Thomas Jefferson in a letter to Mary Austin Holley, September 6, 1824 (Crosby Papers). See also Horace Holley to Thomas Jefferson, October 10, 1824, Holley Papers, Massachusetts Historical Society; and Thomas Jefferson to Horace Holley, April 5, 1825, copy in Holley Coll.-Trans.

[30] Manuscript of lecture, November 8, 1824, Crosby Papers.

[31] Archibald Austin to Stephen F. Austin, January 30, 1825, *Austin Papers,* I, 1027–1029.

[32] Fayette County, Kentucky, Marriage Bonds for 1825–1828, Documents File No. 2. Christ Church Records, Marriages by the Reverend George Chapman, 1820–1830: "Lexington—Jan. 8, 1825—Mr. William Moses Brand to Miss Harriette Williman Holley, both of Lexington."

[33] Toasts of Horace Holley, No. 26, Crosby Papers.

[34] Rafinesque's manuscript consisting of seventy-seven lines of poetry is preserved in the Crosby Papers. See Hartley Dupre, "Transylvania and Rafinesque," *Filson Club History Quarterly,* Vol. 35 (1961), p. 117, for a similar signature of "Constantine of Byzantium" used by Rafinesque.

[35] For Lafayette's visit to Lexington see *Kentucky Reporter,* May 23, 1825. Also two pamphlets titled *The Order of Exercises in the Chapel of Transylvania University, a Collection of Original Pieces in Honour of the arrival of General Lafayette . . .* and *The Visit of General Lafayette to the Lafayette Female Academy. . . .* Modern accounts of Lafayette's visit to Lexington are Edgar Erskine Hume, *Lafayette in Kentucky,* pp. 60–99 and J. Winston Coleman, Jr., *Masonry in the Bluegrass,* pp. 105–110.

[36] Mrs. Holley's Scrapbook, Holley Coll.-Trans.

CHAPTER 12

[1] "An Anniversary Discourse before the Kentucky Institute in the Chapel of Transylvania University, January 29th, 1825," Sermon and Lecture Notes, Crosby Papers.

[2] Horace Holley to Henry Clay, April 18, 1825, Henry Clay Papers, Library of Congress.

[3] Outline of Holley's Report to the Board of Trustees of Transylvania University, November 22, 1825, itemizing salaries, fees, etc., Crosby Papers.

[4] Caldwell, *Discourse,* pp. 237–238.

[5] Littleberry Hawkins to Stephen F. Austin, October 7, 1824, *Austin Papers,* I, 917–922.

[6] Caldwell, *Discourse,* p. 269.

[7] C. S. Rafinesque, "A Life of Travels," *Chronica Botanica,* Vol. 8 (1944), pp. 326–327. The traditional account of Rafinesque's friendship with Mary Austin Holley, based on statements by Johanna Peter, is recorded in Richard

Ellsworth Call, *Life and Writings of Rafinesque*, pp. 43, 63.

[8] Weiss, *Rafinesque's Kentucky Friends*, pp. 7–16, 40–41. The original drawings are now in the possession of Transylvania College Library.

[9] Horace Holley to John Bradford, December 23, 1825, Transylvania University Official Records. See John Bradford (1749–1830) in *DAB*, II, 555–556.

[10] Caldwell, *Discourse*, pp. 178–179.

[11] John Everett to Mary Austin Holley, December 21, 1825, Holley Coll.-Trans.

[12] *The Catalogue of Transylvania University, January, 1826*, lists a total of twenty-three students from Louisiana, including in the Preparatory Department the names of Cyprien, Eusebe, Drausin, Nemese, and Romuald Labranche, of the German Coast.

[13] Caldwell, *Discourse*, pp. 269–271.

[14] Horace Holley to John Bradford, June 5, 1826, Transylvania University Official Records.

[15] See Horace Holley's comment on his father's death (Caldwell, *Discourse*, pp. 114–116); and notice of Caroline Holley's marriage (*Kentucky Reporter*, January 6, 1827).

[16] "Report of the Trustees of Transylvania University, 1828," newspaper clipping in Mrs. Holley's Scrapbook, Holley Coll.-Trans.

[17] Horace Holley to John Bradford, January 10, 1827, Transylvania University Official Records.

[18] Horace Holley to the Honorable Board of Trustees of Transylvania University, March 24, 1827, in Caldwell, *Discourse*, pp. 207–215. A twenty-four page folder in Horace Holley's handwriting titled "Extracts from the Records of Transylvania University from 1815 to 1827" summarizes the facts of his elections to the presidency and his resignations from it (Crosby Papers).

[19] Transylvania University Unbound Documents, 1827-U-3; and Horace Holley's bill against the University, March 16, 1827, Transylvania University Official Records. Also discussions of Horace's personal affairs in Horace Holley to Orville Holley, October 23, 1826, February 4, 1827, Crosby Papers.

[20] *Kentucky Reporter*, March 3, 7, 10, 1827.

[21] United States Passport No. 1147, signed by Henry Clay, Secretary of State, for "The Rev. Horace Holly [*sic*], D.D., and Mrs. Mary Holly [*sic*], and their son Horace Austin" (Crosby Papers). Horace Holley's letters of introduction include: William Lee to Mr. Beasley, Consul, Havre, March 13, 1827; Joseph Ficklin to Nat. Cox, Esquire, New Orleans, May 27, 1827; and Mr. Needsletter, Minister to the United States from Prussia, to Mr. Sliffert, Berlin, March 25, 1827 (Crosby Papers). Also James Madison to Horace Holley, February 20, 1827, enclosing "a few lines to Mr. Gallatin in Paris"; James Monroe to Horace Holley, March 21, 1827, enclosing a letter to Mr. Gallatin "in compliance with the object expressed in yours of last month"; Edward Everett to Benjamin Constant, April 18, 1827; Edward Everett to

Sir Walter Scott, Edinburgh, both in care of Mr. Holley; and Mrs. Ann F. Humphreys to Mrs. Parr Bulkley in Paris, February 29, 1827 (Holley Coll.-Trans.).

22 "On the Death of Miss Susannah Agnes Tibbatts," *Kentucky Reporter,* January 31, 1827. Horace Holley says this poem is by Mary Austin Holley (Horace Holley to Orville Holley, February 4, 1827, Crosby Papers).

23 "On Leaving Kentucky," *Kentucky Reporter,* March 10, 1827. Broadsheets of this poem were given by the Holleys to friends; one is pasted in Mrs. Holley's Scrapbook (Holley Coll.-Trans.). See also Horace Holley to Orville Holley, April 3, 1827, Crosby Papers.

24 William A. Leavy to Robert Peter, September 7, 1875, Robert Peter Papers. The silhouettes of Horace and Mary Austin Holley and of William A. Leavy were bequeathed to Transylvania College by the late Miss Elsie Leavy, of Austin, Texas, granddaughter of William A. Leavy.

25 Transylvania University Unbound Documents, 1827-U-83. For the Holleys' departure from Lexington see Caldwell, *Discourse,* pp. 215–216; and *Kentucky Reporter,* February 17, 1827, March 14, 1827, March 21, 1827.

26 *Kentucky Reporter,* March 24, 1827, March 31, 1827; and Caldwell, *Discourse,* pp. 272–273.

27 Christ Church Records, Account of Baptisms: "March 19, 1827—William Holley Brand—born May 28, 1826."

28 Horace Holley to Orville Holley, April 3, 1827, Crosby Papers.

20 Mary Austin Holley to Harriette Brand, April 8, [1827], MAH Papers.

30 New Orleans *Courier,* April 11, 1827, April 12, 1827.

31 The most precise information available about Hermogene and Jean Baptiste Labranche is to be found in legal documents related to the settlement of their estates, particularly in Acte departage entre la veuve en las Héretiers de feu Sieur H. Labranche, April 6, 1847, St. Charles Parish, Louisiana; Acts, Francois Choix, 1840–1847, pp. 713–720; and Estate of Jean Baptiste Labranche, Orleans Parish, Louisiana, Civil District Court, Settlements of Estates, Document 19,714.

32 The plantation residences of Hermogene and Jean Baptiste Labranche are no longer in existence. They were probably like the "Plantation House and Works" in Benjamin Moore Norman, *Norman's New Orleans and Environs,* p. 29.

33 Roger Baudier, *The Catholic Church in Louisiana,* pp. 302–308; Stanley Clisby Arthur, *Louisiana Tours,* p. 39.

34 Mary Austin Holley explained her husband's abandonment of his European tour as his "yielding to the beauty of utility" by planning a school near New Orleans (Caldwell, *Discourse,* pp. 274–276). The general opinion over the nation was that his career ended in a series of failures. John Quincy Adams wrote a long comment in his Diary to that effect after reading in the New York papers of Holley's death. See Charles Francis Adams (ed.), *Memoirs of John Quincy Adams,* VII, 323.

[35] Advertisement of auction of Jean Ayme house, New Orleans *Argus,* April 17, 1827. Advertisement in English, dated April 25, 1827, of proposed school in the New Orleans *Argus,* May 11, 1827; continuing in French and English versions, *ibid.,* May 14, 15, 19, 1827, and appearing intermittently until July 9, 1827. A statement in the original advertisement particularly indicates Holley as the author: "The proprietor, having a certain number of pupils, is willing to make himself more extensively useful to the community." Holley brought eight Louisiana pupils with him from Transylvania. It should be pointed out that Mary Austin Holley makes no mention in her memoir in Caldwell, *Discourse,* of such a plan at Bonnet Carré.

[36] *Prospectus d'un College à Etablir auprès de la Nouvelle Orleans,* printed copy in Mrs. Holley's Scrapbook, Holley Coll.-Trans. English version in Caldwell, *Discourse,* pp. 276–279.

[37] "Charbonnet, A., merchant, negociant, 56 Toulouse; dwelling 64 St. Ann" (*The New Orleans Directory and Register, 1827*). *The Catalogue of Transylvania University for 1826* lists Adelard Evalture Charbonnet of the German Coast in the Preparatory Department.

[38] Horace Holley to John Bradford, May 25, 1827, Holley Coll.-Trans. Also Horace Holley to Harriette and William Brand, June 1, 1827, Crosby Papers; and Horace Holley to "My Dear Children," July 19, 1827, in Caldwell, *Discourse,* pp. 282–283.

[39] For Mary Austin Holley's account of her husband's illness and death see Caldwell, *Discourse,* pp. 279–294.

[40] 18 Juillet 1827. Vente d'esclave par Horace Holley à Diego Guady, New Orleans, July 18, 1827, in Orleans Parish, Louisiana, Record of Conveyances, I, 397. The slave sold on July 18, 1827, was Susanna, one of two slaves Holley brought to Louisiana from Kentucky (Horace Holley to Orville Holley, April 3, 1827, Crosby Papers). The other undoubtedly was Ben, the coachman, who somehow obtained his freedom and later called to see Mary Austin Holley in New Orleans (Mary Austin Holley to Harriette Brand, March 7, 1830, MAH Papers).

[41] John Pierpont, *A Discourse in Hollis Street Church, Boston, September 2, 1827; Occasioned by the death of Horace Holley, LL.D., late President of Transylvania University,* p. 30. Pierpont closes his tribute with these nine lines of verse, terming them "the wail of the sick and solitary widow." Timothy Flint's review of Pierpont's pamphlet in *The Western Monthly Review,* I (1827), 430–434, does not recognize the poem's authorship but praises it as beautiful.

CHAPTER 13

[1] *New England Galaxy* (Boston), August 17, 1827; *Niles Weekly Register* (Baltimore), August 25, 1827; New Orleans *Courier,* September 4, 1827.

[2] Charles Francis Adams (ed.), *Memoirs of John Quincy Adams,* VII, 323.

[3] Caldwell, *Discourse,* pp. iii–v.

[4] See John Pierpont (1785–1866) in *DAB*, XIV, 586; and Brooks, *The Flowering of New England*, pp. 59, 157, 158, 159. Pierpont's esteem for the Holley family is evidenced by his "Tribute to the Holley Family. Poem Delivered at the Centennial Celebration in Litchfield, 1821" (copy in the Crosby Papers).

[5] Boston *Evening Gazette*, November 10, 1827. This clipping in the Crosby Papers has a handwritten notation that "the author is known to be Gerry Fairbanks," who was "formerly intimately acquainted with Mr. Holley."

[6] "We feel ourselves not only prompted by our hearts, but required by our duty to the Church and Society of Hollis Street, to say that, while you are in the neighborhood, the people of your husband's former care will feel a pleasure . . . in contributing what they may to your consolation . . . in knowing how we may best contribute to your comfort while you are among us, or lighten the heavy load of your affliction" (The Hollis Street Church and Society to Mrs. Mary A. Holley, September 21, 1827, signed by John Pierpont, Samuel May, William Brown, and Henry Bass, in the Crosby Papers).

[7] "The Swan and the Eagle," *Western Review*, I (1819), 127.

[8] Mary Austin Holley to Orville Holley, September 29, 1827, MAH Papers.

[9] John Milton Holley to Orville Holley, January 27, 1828; John Milton Holley to Myron Holley, January 27, 1828; Myron Holley to Orville Holley, April 5, 1828, June 21, 1828, Crosby Papers.

[10] Mary Austin Holley to Henry Clay, November 8, 1827, Henry Clay Papers.

[11] Caldwell, *Discourse*, pp. v–viii.

[12] Fayette County, Kentucky, Administrators Bonds, Vol. 2 (1823–1838), p. 176.

[13] The frontispiece of Caldwell, *Discourse*, is a portrait titled "The Rev. Horace Holley, LL.D. Engraved by T. Kelly from the Portrait by Stuart."

[14] The title page reads: *A Discourse on the Genius and Character of the Rev. Horace Holley, LL.D., Late President of Transylvania University, by Charles Caldwell, M.D., Professor of the Institutes of Medicine and Clinical Practice in said University; with an Appendix, containing Copious Notes, Biographical and Illustrative.* Boston: Hilliard, Gray, Little, and Wilkins. Sold by Cottons and Barnard, and O. C. Greenleaf, Boston; Carey, Lea, and Carey, Towar and Hogan, and J. Grigg, Philadelphia; E. H. Coale, Baltimore, and J. Flint, Cincinnati. 1828.

[15] Mary Austin Holley to Orville Holley, March 15, 1828, Crosby Papers.

[16] Caldwell, *Discourse*, p. 294.

[17] Mary Austin Holley to Harriette Brand, April 27, 1828, MAH Papers.

[18] Edward Everett to Mary Austin Holley, "At Mr. Clay's, F. St., Tuesday," Crosby Papers.

[19] (Mrs.) Margaret Bayard Smith, *The First Forty Years of Washington Society . . .*, pp. 85, 253–260.

[20] "Proposals to publish, by subscription, a Discourse on the genius and

character of the Reverend Horace Holley, LL.D., Late President of Transylvania University, by Charles Caldwell, Professor of the Institutes of Medicine and Clinical Practice in said University: with copious Notes. Biographical and illustrative. . . . for the benefit of the infant son of the deceased . . . Terms: To be elegantly printed, on paper of the first quality; to contain 200 pages Octavo; to be ready for delivery in July or August next. To be ornamented by an engraved likeness of Doctor Holley, executed by a distinguished artist from a painting by Stuart. Price to subscribers two dollars in boards. [Signed] Isaac Phillips, George F. Weld, N. F. Williams, Henry P. Sumner, C. A. Pearce, E. D. Williams, John C. Moab, Alexander Holley, George Williams" (manuscript, Crosby Papers).

21 Mary Austin Holley to Harriette Brand, April 25, 1829, MAH Papers.

22 Henry Austin to Stephen F. Austin, October 20, 1826, *Austin Papers*, I, 1478–1479. For Henry Austin's introduction of the date palm into the United States, see "A Letter to Hon. Josiah Meigs from Sam'l Mitchell, of New York, September 26, 1818," *American Monthly and Critical Review*, IV (1818–1819), 47.

23 Henry Austin to Stephen F. Austin, August 3, 1829, *Austin Papers*, II, 244.

24 Edward Everett, review of Caldwell's *Discourse, North American Review*, Vol. 27 (1828), pp. 403–415.

25 Mary Austin Holley to Orville Holley, January 3, 1828 [1829?], Crosby Papers. The date of "1828" must be an error since there is a reference to Orville's having received copies of Caldwell's *Discourse*, published in 1828.

26 "S.," "Letter to the Editor," *The Transylvanian, or Lexington Literary Journal*, I (1829), 27–28.

27 *Ibid.*, I (1829), 121–131; and Mary Austin Holley to Harriette Brand, November 13, 1830, MAH Papers. See Benjamin Orr Peers (1800–1842) in *DAB*, XIV, 389.

28 Mary Austin Holley to Harriette Brand, April 25, 1829, May 1, 1829, May 10, 1829, MAH Papers.

29 Christ Church Records, Account of Baptisms, 1820–1830: "Lexington, May 3, 1830—Mary Austin Brand—born May 20, 1829."

30 See Cassius Marcellus Clay (1810–1903) in *DAB*, IV, 169–170. For the traditional account of the fire see J. Winston Coleman, Jr., "Historic Kentucky. Transylvania University," Lexington *Herald-Leader*, July 31, 1960.

31 Mrs. Holley's Scrapbook (Holley Coll.-Trans.) is a twelve-by-eight-inch gray blank book of eighty-eight pages. According to a memorandum by Dr. Robert Peter, dated August 10, 1878, which is pasted on the flyleaf, the scrapbook turned up at an auction in Cincinnati and was acquired by Lyman Draper, the historian, who returned it to the Transylvania University Library.

32 Christ Church Records, Communicants, 1820–1830; Confirmations by Bishop John Stark Ravenscroft, of North Carolina, July 26, 1829.

33 "February 3, 1829: Elisha Lewis, aged 61, died of bladder trouble (Epis-

copalian) . . . "August 10, 1829, widow E. Lewis, aged 79, Dysenteria (Episcopalian)" in *Vital Statistics of New Haven, 1649–1850*, II, 635, 638.

³⁴ For Mrs. Holley's journey to the German Coast in 1829 see Mary Austin Holley to Harriette Brand, November 14, 1829, November 20, 1829, November 29, 1829, December 20, 1829, January 1, 1830, MAH Papers.

CHAPTER 14
¹ For Mary Austin Holley's stay in Louisiana during early 1830 see Mary Austin Holley to Harriette Brand, January 17, 1830, January 24, 1830, February 2, 1830, February 20, 1830, March 3, 1830, and March 30, 1830, MAH Papers.

² Orleans Parish, Louisiana, Record of Conveyances, Vol. 22, p. 415: Certification on March 11, 1837, of Vente de terrain Joseph Olbat à Jean B. La-Branche et Hermogene La Branche, dated August 21, 1829.

³ Stanley Clisby Arthur, *Old New Orleans*, pp. 27–28.

⁴ Among Mary Austin Holley's callers were C. Shamburgh and Jefferson Wells, former Transylvania students (Mary Austin Holley to Harriette Brand, January 24, 1830, MAH Papers).

⁵ Mary Austin Holley to Harriette Brand, January 17, 1830, MAH Papers.

⁶ For Mary Carroll see *The New Orleans Directory and Register for 1827*; also Frances Trollope, *Domestic Manners of the Americans*, pp. 9–10.

⁷ Mary Austin Holley to Harriette Brand, March 11, 1831 [*sic*], MAH Papers.

⁸ Mary Austin Holley to Harriette Brand, March 30, 1830, MAH Papers.

⁹ For Mary Austin Holley's visit in 1830 to Cincinnati see Mary Austin Holley to Harriette Brand, May 10, 1830, May 15, 1830, MAH Papers.

¹⁰ Timothy Flint, *Recollections of the Last Ten Years . . . in the Valley of the Mississippi*, pp. 67–68; Timothy Flint, Review of Caldwell's *Discourse, Western Monthly Review*, II (1828–1829), 212–227; Timothy Flint to Stephen F. Austin, November 29, 1824, *Austin Papers*, I, 979–980. See Timothy Flint (1780–1835) in *DAB*, VI, 474.

¹¹ See Alexander Campbell (1788–1866) in *DAB*, III, 446–448.

¹² Mary Austin Holley to Harriette Brand, May 17, 1830, MAH Papers.

¹³ Mary Austin Holley to Orville Holley, September 29, 1831, MAH Papers. She recapitulates their meeting of the previous summer, and hints of her "*real* chateau d'Espagne," by which she probably means land in Texas.

¹⁴ The many contacts between the Austins in Texas and those in New York appear in a series of letters in the *Austin Papers*: John Phelps Austin to Stephen F. Austin, January 1, 1830, II, 313–315; [Stephen F. Austin] to Archibald Austin, February 24, 1830, (which appeared in the New York *Journal*), II, 336–337; Henry Austin to Stephen F. Austin, May 27, 1830, II, 395–396; Henry Austin to Stephen F. Austin, June 3, 1830, II, 407; Archibald Austin to Stephen F. Austin, May 31, 1830, II, 401–403; Stephen F. Austin

to Henry Austin, June 1, 1830, II, 404–405; Stephen F. Austin to James F. Perry, July 11, 1830, II, 445–447; Archibald Austin to Stephen F. Austin, July 14, 1830, II, 453–454; Archibald Austin to Stephen F. Austin, October 10, 1830, II, 506–510; Henry Austin to Stephen F. Austin, October 20, 1830, II, 517–519; James F. Perry to Stephen F. Austin, October 27, 1830, II, 522–524; Archibald Austin to Stephen F. Austin, November 11, 1830, II, 531–532. Mary Austin Holley saw some of these letters when she was in New York in 1830 (Mary Austin Holley to Stephen F. Austin, January 21, 1831, *Austin Papers*, II, 570–571).

[15] [Stephen F. Austin] to Archibald Austin, February 24, 1830, *Austin Papers*, II, 336–337.

[16] Mary Austin Holley to Harriette Brand, November 9, 1830, MAH Papers.

[17] "Stranger, you ask," a fifty-eight-line poem signed "Lexington, Kentucky, October, 1830. M. A. H." in the Crosby Papers. For a slightly revised version see Lexington *Observer and Reporter*, June 4, 1834.

[18] Newcomb, *Architecture in Old Kentucky*, pp. 114–115.

[19] For Mary Austin Holley's visit in Louisville in 1830 see Mary Austin Holley to Harriette Brand, November 9, 1830, November 31, 1830, MAH Papers.

[20] Hyder E. Rollins, *Keats' Reputation in America to 1848*, pp. 1–43.

[21] For Judge Fortunatus Cosby see Josiah S. Johnston (ed.), *The Memorial History of Louisville*, II, 5.

[22] Thomas Leaming Caldwell had been a tutor at Transylvania University in 1820 (*Catalogue of Transylvania University, January, 1826*).

[23] W. W. Worsley published the *Daily Focus*, Louisville, Kentucky, in the 1830's.

[24] For Alexander Graihle see Arthur, *Old New Orleans*, pp. 56, 96.

[25] Mary Austin Holley to Harriette Brand, November 13, 1830, MAH Papers.

[26] Harnett Kane, *Plantation Parade*, pp. 126–139.

[27] Mary Austin Holley to Stephen F. Austin, January 21, 1831, *Austin Papers*, II, 570–571.

[28] Mary Austin Holley to Harriette Brand, March 11, 1831, MAH Papers.

[29] The pamphlet which Henry Austin gave to Mary Austin Holley was apparently *Translation of the Laws, Orders, and Contracts on Colonization, from January, 1821, up to 1829; by virtue of which Col. Stephen F. Austin introduced and settled foreign emigrants in Texas, with an explanatory introduction.* . . . Gordon B. Cotten, San Felipe de Austin, Texas, 1829. Stephen F. Austin's 1830 map of Texas is included in Carlos E. Castañeda and Early Martin, Jr. (comps.), *Three Manuscript Maps of Texas by Stephen F. Austin*. For the changes in the regulation of emigration to Texas see Barker, *The Life of Stephen F. Austin*, pp. 296–328.

[30] Henry Austin to Stephen F. Austin, March 15, 1831, *Austin Papers*, II, 613–616, and March 20, 1831, *ibid.*, II, 617–621.

[31] Henry Austin to Mary Austin Holley, May 7, 1831, May 16, 1831, Henry Austin Papers.

[32] Stephen F. Austin to Mary Austin Holley, July 19, 1831, *Austin Papers*, II, 674–677.

[33] Barker, *The Life of Stephen F. Austin*, pp. 32–33.

[34] Stephen F. Austin to Samuel Williams, April 2, 1831, *Austin Papers*, II, 636–639. Also Petition of Mary Austin *viuda* Holley; Title of Possession of League No. 14, June 13, 1831; and English Field Notes, VI, 153; all in the Spanish Archives VIII, 531–534. General Land Office, State of Texas.

[35] Henry Austin to Mary Austin Holley, July 22, 1831, Henry Austin Papers.

CHAPTER 15

[1] For indications that before Mary Austin Holley left Louisiana in 1831 she was planning to write a book on Texas see: Mary Austin Holley to Orville Holley, September 19, 1831, MAH Papers; and Henry Austin to Stephen F. Austin, November 15, 1831, *Austin Papers*, II, 702–703.

[2] The first five chapters of Mary Austin Holley's book about Texas that she composed on this trip are a journal of her voyage from New Orleans to Bolivar, Texas. See Mary Austin Holley, *Texas. Observations, Historical, Geographical and Descriptive, in a Series of Letters, Written during a Visit to Austin's Colony, with a view to a permanent settlement in that country, in the Autumn of 1831*, pp. 17–51 (hereinafter cited as Holley, *Texas* [1833]).

[3] Mary Austin Holley's biographical notice of John Austin (1801–1833), of Brazoria, Texas, in her *Texas* (1836), pp. 248–250, has been much quoted by later historians.

[4] Mary Austin Holley's letter to Stephen F. Austin, written *ca.* November 2, 1831, can be reconstructed from Stephen F. Austin to Mary Austin Holley, November 14, 1831 (*Austin Papers*, II, 701–702).

[5] Mary Austin Holley left several accounts of her visit with her brother Henry in 1831 and her meeting at that time with Stephen F. Austin: Mary Austin Holley to Orville Holley, December 24, 1831; Mary Austin Holley to Harriette Brand, January 6, 1832; and Mary Austin Holley, Notes for a History of Texas, Section No. 24 (MAH Papers); also Holley, *Texas* (1833), *passim.*

[6] The family of Mary Tailer, wife of Henry Austin, were in business in New York City with John Phelps Austin. Henry apparently invested money for his wife in Texas land, as shown by their daughter's property holdings (Will of Emily Austin, probated March 2, 1860, Galveston County, Texas, Will Book No. 2, p. 133).

[7] Stephen F. Austin to Mary Austin Holley, November 14, 1831, *Austin Papers*, II, 701–702.

[8] Henry Austin [from Bolivar] to Stephen F. Austin, November 15, 1831,

Austin Papers, II, 702–703; Henry Austin [from Brazoria] to Stephen F. Austin, November 28, 1831, *ibid.*, II, 713–714.

[9] The only version of this song found by the present writer is *The Brazos Boat Glee, written by Mrs. Holley. Composed, arranged, & Dedicated to Henry Austen* [sic], *Esq., by Wilhelm Iucho (1838)*. Mrs. Holley mentions in a letter to her daughter dated January 6, 1832, "a Brazos Boat Song which I have composed and set to music" (MAH Papers). It seems likely that she wrote the lyric originally to some familiar air as she did later with another Texas song.

[10] Stephen F. Austin to Mary Austin Holley, November 17, 1831, *Austin Papers*, II, 704–706.

[11] Stephen F. Austin to James F. Perry, November 17, 1831, *Austin Papers*, II, 706–707. See also Jack H. Meeks, "Memorandum Relating to the Heirship of Stephen F. Austin and his sister Emily Margaret Bryan Perry, April 8, 1940."

[12] John Phelps Austin to Stephen F. Austin, October 10, 1831, *Austin Papers*, II, 696–697.

[13] Stephen F. Austin to Emily Perry, December 23, 1831, *Austin Papers*, II, 725.

[14] John McCalla to Stephen F. Austin, October 6, 1829, *Austin Papers*, II, 261–263.

[15] For evidence that Stephen F. Austin furnished Mary Austin Holley with the "Answers" and other help for her book see Stephen F. Austin to Mary Austin Holley, November 14, 1831, *Austin Papers*, II, 701–702; and November 17, 1831, *ibid.*, II, 704–706. She wrote Orville Holley concerning her manuscript: "The article not in my hand is by Col. Austin . . ." (Mary Austin Holley to Orville Holley, December 24, 1831, MAH Papers).

[16] "Descriptions of Texas by Stephen F. Austin, contributed by Eugene C. Barker," *Southwestern Historical Quarterly*, XXVIII (1924–1925), 98–121. Barker thinks that one of these "descriptions" ("Emigration from Europe to Texas") was "intended for publication in pamphlet form to be circulated in Europe." Comparison of "Emigration from Europe to Texas" with Mary Austin Holley's *Texas* (1833), pp. 51–78, indicates that she drew freely upon Austin's "description."

[17] Holley, *Texas* (1833), p. 127.

[18] Barker, *The Life of Stephen F. Austin*, pp. 230–231, 258–262.

[19] Mary Austin Holley to Orville Holley, December 24, 1831, MAH Papers.

[20] Mary Austin Holley's Spanish Certificate of Citizenship was inscribed on "the last page of Austin's address to emigrants from Europe, Dec. –, 1831" (*Austin Papers*, II, 724–725, footnote).

[21] Holley, *Texas* (1833), p. [3].

[22] Thomas F. Leaming to Stephen F. Austin, April 7, 1832, Austin Papers, File for 1832.

[23] Mary Austin Holley to Orville Holley, December 24, 1831, MAH Papers.

[24] For the relationship of Mary Austin Holley and Stephen F. Austin after their meeting in Bolivar see Stephen F. Austin to Mary Austin Holley, December 25, 1831, *Austin Papers*, II, 727–730; December 29, 1831, *ibid.*, II, 730–731; January 4, 1832, *ibid.*, II, 732–733; January 14, 1832, *ibid.*, II, 736–738; January 30, 1832, *ibid.*, II, 745.

[25] Mary Austin Holley, Notes for a History of Texas, Section No. 24, MAH Papers.

[26] Stephen F. Austin to James F. Perry, December 27, 1831, *Austin Papers*, II, 726.

[27] Stephen F. Austin to Mary Austin Holley, December 29, 1831, *Austin Papers*, II, 730–731.

[28] Mary Austin Holley to Harriette Brand, January 6, 1832, MAH Papers.

[29] John Phelps Austin to Stephen F. Austin, January 27, 1832, *Austin Papers*, II, 741–742.

[30] Mary Austin Holley to Orville Holley, February 26, 1832, MAH Papers.

[31] Stephen F. Austin to Mary Austin Holley, February 19, 1832, *Austin Papers*, II, 753–754.

[32] For the news from New York see Mary Austin Holley to Harriette Brand, April 3, 1832, MAH Papers.

[33] The letter from James Drake to Mary Austin Holley, June 12, 1832 (Holley Coll.-Trans.) is evidently part of a "literary correspondence."

[34] Mary Austin Holley to Stephen F. Austin, June 8, 1832, *Austin Papers*, II, 778–779.

[35] Christ Church Records, Register of Baptisms: "July 28, 1842—Horace Holley Brand—born April 4, 1832—by Rev. Edward F. Berkley."

[36] The rest of the events during 1832 in the life of Mrs. Holley are chiefly drawn from: Mary Austin Holley to Harriette Brand, October 3, 1832, October 10, 1832, October 19, 1832, November 2, 1832, November 10, 1832, November 16–18, 1832, November 25, 1832, and December 23, 1832, MAH Papers.

[37] These news items reached Mrs. Holley in a letter from Archibald, quoted in Mary Austin Holley to Harriette Brand, November 10, 1832 (MAH Papers).

[38] Stephen F. Austin suggested that Mary Austin Holley include in her book on Texas the "Colonization Law and Translation side by side" (Stephen F. Austin to Mary Austin Holley, December 25, 1831, *Austin Papers*, II, 725–726). Eventually she omitted the Colonization Law, substituting for it the "Communication from San Felipe de Austin relative to late Events in Texas, 1832," possibly at the suggestion of her brother Charles. See Holley, *Texas* (1833), pp. 141–167.

[39] Evidence is scanty regarding the circumstances of the publication in Baltimore of Mary Austin Holley's *Texas* (1833). A "Texas Prospectus" about it was being circulated in New Orleans by the spring of 1833; it was off the

press by midsummer and receiving notices in the Baltimore papers. See Mary Austin Holley to Harriette Brand, April 22, 1833, July 21, 1833, August 19, 1833, MAH Papers.

[40] Mary Austin Holley to Harriette Brand, December 23, 1832, MAH Papers.

[41] Mary Austin Holley to Harriette Brand, March 24, 1833, MAH Papers. "Mr. Savage" may well have been "John E. Savage. Coffee house, 142 Chartres, & also boarding & coffee house, 153 Old Levee, and bath & coffee house at light house, Bayou St. John" (*New Orleans Commercial Register,* 1835); and likewise "J. E. Savage, residing at a boarding house, 117 Old Levee St., in New Orleans" (*Gibson's Guide and Directory of Louisiana, New Orleans, and Lafayette,* 1838). He was probably the writer of J. E. Savage to Hon. W. H. Wharton, Gen'l Austin, and Hon. B. S. Archer: from opposite Port 96 Level, Free Ports, New Orleans, January 18, 1836 (Austin Papers, File for 1836), a proposal to bring in emigrants from England to Texas via New Orleans. He operated at one time in the Red River region (Mary Austin Holley to Harriette Brand, April 5, 1839, MAH Papers).

[42] Stephen F. Austin to Mary Austin Holley, April 20, 1833, *Austin Papers,* II, 954–956.

[43] Will of Stephen F. Austin, Brazoria County, Texas, Will Book A, p. 8.

[44] Stephen F. Austin to James F. Perry, April 20, 1833, *Austin Papers,* II, 954–956.

[45] Mary Austin Holley to Harriette Brand, August 19, 1833, December 19, 1833, MAH Papers.

[46] The copy of Holley, *Texas* (1833) described in the text is owned by the present writer. Another copy, once the property of Emily Bryan Perry, is bound in tan cloth, with no label on the spine and marked in ink "Mrs. Holley's Texas" (Austin-Bryan Books, in the Barker Texas History Center Library).

[47] Mary Austin Holley to Harriette Brand, August 19, 1833, MAH Papers.

[48] "Donatien Augustin, attorney at law, avocat, 80 Toulouse" appears in the *New Orleans Directory and Register, 1827.* Augustin's address is 89 St. Peter Street, next door to J. B. Labranche, planter, 93 St. Peter Street, in *Michel's New Orleans Annual and Commercial Register, December, 1833.*

[49] "Stranger, you ask," Lexington *Observer and Reporter,* June 4, 1834. "To Melazie on Parting," Lexington *Intelligencer,* April 4, 1834. See also, *Intelligencer,* April 11, 1834, for Melazie's reply.

[50] Simpson, *Bluegrass Houses and Their Traditions,* pp. 93–98.

[51] Wilhelm Iucho, *The Lexington Grand Waltz, ca.* 1834. Iucho was born in Germany *ca.* 1803 (United States Census Returns, Seventh Census, 1850, Fayette County, Kentucky). He came to Lexington in the summer of 1834 (Christ Church Records for baptism of his daughter, Lucilla, November 5, 1834).

[52] "The Invitation," Lexington *Intelligencer,* November 14, 1834. A broad-

sheet of this poem with the notation "By Mrs. Holley, 1834, for Ladies Fair" is in the Crosby Papers.

CHAPTER 16

1 Mary Austin Holley had reached Texas by early May, 1835 (Henry Austin to Gail Borden, May 9, 1835, Austin Papers, File for 1835).

2 Abigail Curlee, "History of a Texas Slave Plantation," *Southwestern Historical Quarterly,* XXVI (1922–1923), 79–127; Abner J. Strobel, *The Old Plantations and their Owners of Brazoria County, Texas,* p. 8. Interview Rebecca Smith Lee with Mr. and Mrs. Stephen S. Perry, and Mr. and Mrs. W. Joel Bryan at Peach Point Plantation, February 8, 1953.

3 Holley, *Texas* (1836), pp. 91–94.

4 See James Aeneas E. Phelps (–1847) in *The Handbook of Texas,* edited by Walter P. Webb, H. Bailey Carroll, and others, II, 371–372; Strobel, *The Old Plantations and their Owners of Brazoria County, Texas,* p. 21.

5 Stephen F. Austin to James F. Perry, March 10, 1835, *Austin Papers,* III, 46–48; James F. Perry to Stephen F. Austin, May 5, 1835, *ibid.,* III, 71–72.

6 See John A. Wharton (1806–1838) in *The Handbook of Texas,* II, 888–889; and William Harris Wharton (1802–1839), *ibid.,* II, 889–890.

7 Joe B. Frantz, *Gail Borden: Dairyman to a Nation,* pp. 69–81.

8 "For Lease or for Sale—The estate called Bolivar, 1500 acres of first rate peach and cane land, 60 acres cleared; a frame dwelling house and out buildings . . . Henry Austin" (*Texas Republican,* February 4, 1835, March 21, 1835).

9 Prospectus for the *Telegraph and Texas Planter* by Joseph Baker, Gail Borden, and John P. Borden (*Texas Republican,* February 14, 1835). The name was changed to the *Telegraph and Texas Register* in the first issue, October 10, 1835.

10 Groce and Wallace (comps.), *New York Historical Society Dictionary of Artists in America, 1564–1860,* p. 40. George Beck, early Kentucky artist, and his wife conducted in Lexington a female boarding school which Emily Austin, daughter of Moses Austin, attended from October, 1804, to December, 1808 (*Austin Papers,* I, 2).

11 C. Frank Dunn, "Notes on the Matthew Kennedy (Frame) House, East Second Street, Built 1814." The present East Second Street in Lexington was called Constitution Street in 1835.

12 Lexington *Observer and Reporter,* August 6, 1846.

13 Peter, *The History of the Medical Department of Transylvania University,* p. 83.

14 See Julius P. B. McCabe (comp.), *Directory of the City of Lexington and County of Fayette, for 1838 & '39;* Christ Church Records, Minutes of the Vestry, April 4, 1836; Lexington *Observer and Reporter,* June 28, 1845.

15 See Ranck, *The History of Lexington, Kentucky,* pp. 234–235; Johnston (ed), *The Memorial History of Louisville,* II, 68; *Appleton's Cyclopedia*

of American Biography, I, 421. See also Edwin Bryant (Late Alcalde of San Francisco), *What I Saw in California,* a travel book for emigrants.

[16] Lexington *Intelligencer,* April 3, 1835.

[17] Rebecca Gratz to Maria Gist Gratz, January 20, 1835, in Philipson (ed.), *The Letters of Rebecca Gratz,* p. 69.

[18] *Oh Lady, Do Not Bid Me Sing. A Song Written, Composed & Dedicated to Mrs. Holley by Wilhelm Iucho, ca.* 1835.

[19] John Phelps Austin to Stephen F. Austin, November 8, 1835, *Austin Papers, III,* 244–247.

[20] *Kentucky Gazette,* September 5, 1835–December 12, 1835.

[21] Lexington *Intelligencer,* August 21, 1835.

[22] H[enry] Meigs to Stephen F. Austin, May 2, 1835, *Austin Papers,* III, 69; John Phelps Austin to Stephen F. Austin, November 8, 1835, *ibid.,* III, 244–247; and July 29, 1836, *ibid.,* III, 407–409.

[23] Stephen F. Austin to Mary Austin Holley, August 21, 1835, *Austin Papers,* III, 101–103.

[24] Lexington *Intelligencer,* August 28, 1835.

[25] Henry Austin to Mary Austin Holley, September 10, 1835, *Austin Papers,* III, 119–120. An extract from this letter appeared in the Lexington *Intelligencer,* October 16, 1835.

[26] "Speech of Colonel Austin, delivered on the 8th of September, 1835, at a public dinner in Brazoria . . .," *Austin Papers,* III, 116–119.

[27] Stephen F. Austin to Columbia Committee, September 19, 1835, *Austin Papers,* III, 128–129.

[28] Moses Austin Bryan to James F. Perry, November 7, 1835, *Austin Papers,* III, 243–244.

[29] "By the newspapers, both of which have been ordered to be sent to you as a subscriber, you will get all the public news that I get" (Henry Austin to Mary Austin Holley, November 27, 1835, Henry Austin Papers). A few numbers of the *Telegraph and Texas Register* and the *Texas Republican* of 1835 and 1836 in the University of Texas Library newspaper collection are inscribed "Mrs. Mary A. Holley, Lexington, Kentucky."

[30] See Holley, "Description of a Nopalade, or, Estate for Cultivating the Cochineal," *Texas* (1836), pp. 81–86; and Rezin P. Bowie's narrative, *ibid.,* pp. 161–173. J. Frank Dobie states that this Bowie story is "said to have been printed first in a Philadelphia periodical" (*Coronado's Children,* p. 344, n. 8).

[31] Marquis James, *The Raven: A Biography of Sam Houston,* pp. 50–51; 77–85.

[32] Holley, *Texas* (1836), p. 289.

[33] "The circling year has closed around," *Kentucky Gazette,* January 16, 1836. The verses here attributed to Mary Austin Holley contain a footnote about the Dust family, descendants of Daniel Boone. The story of the Dust family, almost in the same words, appears in Holley, *Texas* (1836), p. 134, footnote.

[34] Lexington *Intelligencer*, January 15, 1836.

[35] Lexington *Intelligencer*, January 26, 1836; January 29, 1836.

[36] Christ Church Records, Account of Baptisms: "Baptized July 28, 1842—Harriette Holley Brand—born January 27, 1836."

[37] Stephen F. Austin to Mary Austin Holley, January 7, 1836, *Austin Papers*, III, 300–301.

[38] Lexington *Intelligencer*, February 19, 1836.

[39] "Texas. The following letter from Col. S. F. Austin to a female relation in this city has been politely furnished us for publication . . ." (Lexington *Observer and Reporter*, March 2, 1836). There follows the full letter from Stephen F. Austin to Mary Austin Holley, February 16, 1836. Extracts from it had already appeared in the Lexington *Intelligencer*, February 26, 1836, and the *Kentucky Gazette*, February 27, 1836. The version of this letter in the *Austin Papers*, III, 316, is credited to the *Northwestern Gazette and Galena Advertiser* (Galena, Illinois), April 2, 1836.

[40] See Lexington *Intelligencer*, March 1, 1836, March 12, 1836, and March 15, 1836.

[41] Holley, *Texas* (1836), p. 297, footnote.

[42] Stephen F. Austin's "Address delivered in Louisville, Kentucky, March 7, 1836," appeared in the Lexington *Intelligencer*, April 8 and April 12, 1836; *Kentucky Gazette*, April 9 and April 16, 1836; and in Holley, *Texas* (1836), pp. 253–280.

[43] Stephen F. Austin designed the flag for the Lexington Company (Lexington *Observer and Reporter*, June 8, 1836). For his proposed Texas flag see Stephen F. Austin to Gail Borden, January 18, 1826, Austin Papers, File for 1836; and Austin Papers, Docs. No. 147, No. 148.

[44] Manuscript note and sketch signed "H. B. P." [Mrs. Hallie Bryan Perry], Hally Bryan Perry Collection.

[45] The contacts Stephen F. Austin made in Lexington in March, 1836, are indicated in a series of letters to him from citizens there: John M. McCalla to Stephen F. Austin, June 1, 1836; Joseph Ficklin to Stephen F. Austin, June 2, 1836, and June 4, 1836; Edwin Bryant to Stephen F. Austin, June 5, 1836; Austin Papers, File for 1836. Listed in *Austin Papers*, III, xxviii, calendar.

[46] William H. Townsend, *Lincoln and the Bluegrass: Slavery and the Civil War in Kentucky*, pp. 25–29.

[47] *The Handbook of Texas*, I, 22–23.

[48] Lexington *Intelligencer*, March 25, 1836, March 29, 1836, March 31, 1836, April 15, 1836.

[49] Lexington *Intelligencer*, April 8, 1836, and April 15–26, 1836.

[50] Mary Austin Holley to Stephen F. Austin, April 21, 1836, *Austin Papers*, III, 335–336.

[51] *Kentucky Gazette*, April 16, 1836.

[52] *Kentucky Gazette*, April 30, 1836. Similar notices appeared in the Lexington *Intelligencer*, April 26, 1836, May 3, 1836, May 6, 1836. Mrs. Holley's

report to the Texas Executive Committee about clothes made for the Volunteers was printed in the Lexington *Intelligencer*, June 10, 1836. See also James E. Winston, "Kentucky and the Independence of Texas," *Southwestern Historical Quarterly*, XV (1912), 40–41.

[53] Mary Austin Holley to Stephen F. Austin, June 1, 1826, *Austin Papers*, III, 361–363.

[54] Holley, *Texas* (1836), p. vii. The identity of the "distinguished young gentleman" who assisted Mary Austin Holley with her second book on Texas rests upon circumstantial evidence. Also, the orderly arrangement of this book points to a collaborator with editorial experience.

[55] Holley, *Texas* (1836), pp. vii–viii.

[56] "The Texan Song of Liberty," *Kentucky Gazette*, May 19, 1836; and Lexington *Intelligencer*, May 20, 1836. The version in the *Kentucky Gazette* includes a notation: "Air—Bruce's Address."

[57] Mary Austin Holley to Stephen F. Austin, June 1, 1836, *Austin Papers*, III, 361–363; Lexington *Intelligencer*, June 3, 1836..

[58] Lexington *Observer and Reporter*, June 8, 1836; *Kentucky Gazette*, June 6, 1836, June 17, 1836.

[59] Joseph Ficklin or John McCalla to Stephen F. Austin, July 3, 1836, *Austin Papers*, III, 377–378; and Henry Austin to Mary Austin Holley, July 25, 1836, Henry Austin Papers.

[60] Lexington *Intelligencer*, August 9, 1836, quoting a review in the Louisville *Journal*. The publication date of Holley, *Texas* (1836) is established by an editorial announcement in the Lexington *Intelligencer*, July 15, 1836.

[61] Christ Church Records, Funerals: "August 6, 1836—John Samuel, infant son of Wm. M. Brand, by Rev. B. B. Smith."

[62] For the Lexington Volunteers' view of their experience in Texas see Lexington *Intelligencer*, August 30, 1836, September 13, 1836, October 11, 1836. For a Texan reply see *Telegraph and Texas Register*, November 12, 1836.

[63] Stephen F. Austin to Mary Austin Holley, November 7, 1836, *Austin Papers*, III, 452.

[64] Stephen F. Austin to Joseph Ficklin, October 30, 1836, *Austin Papers*, III, 441–444.

[65] Henry Austin to Mary Austin Holley, November 8, 1836, December 9, 1836, Henry Austin Papers.

[66] *The Texan Song of Liberty. Written by Mrs. M. A. Holley. Composed &Dedicated to General Houston, by Wilhelm Iucho, ca.* 1836.

[67] "The blandness of a gentler clime," Lexington *Intelligencer*, December 20, 1836.

[68] Printed invitation to the funeral of Charlton Hunt, Esq., December 29, 1836, Crosby Papers.

[69] For Santa Anna's stay in Lexington see *Kentucky Gazette*, January 5, 1837. Also Mary Austin Holley to Stephen F. Austin, January 14, 1837, *Aus-*

tin Papers, III, 480–482; Barnard E. Bee to Stephen F. Austin, January 1, 1837, *ibid.,* III, 480.

[70] Mary Austin Holley to Stephen F. Austin, January 14, 1837, *Austin Papers,* III, 480–482.

[71] *Telegraph and Texas Register,* December 30, 1836. Also George L. Hammeken, "Recollections of Stephen F. Austin," *Southwestern Historical Quarterly,* XX (1916–1917), 369–380.

[72] Henry Austin to Mary Austin Holley, February 27, 1837, Crosby Papers.

[73] Lexington *Intelligencer,* January 31, 1837. A shorter notice appeared in the *Kentucky Gazette,* February 2, 1837.

[74] "We have lost him; he is gone," a fifteen-line poem included in "Stephen F. Austin. Biography of the Great Empresario, Prepared from the most Authentic Materials by Hon. Guy M. Bryan of Galveston. . . . For the *Encyclopedia of the New West.* . . . Contributed exclusively to the *News* by Professor William S. Spear . . .," The version of Bryan's biography of Austin in *The Encyclopedia of the New West* (1878) does not include these lines. Clippings of Bryan's biography of Austin are preserved in the Crosby Papers and the MAH Papers.

CHAPTER 17

[1] *Kentucky Gazette,* January 26, 1837.

[2] For Mrs. Holley's trip down the river in early 1837 see Mary Austin Holley to Harriette Brand, March 19, 1837, March 24, 1837; and for her stay in New Orleans, Mary Austin Holley to Harriette Brand, March 31, 1837, April 3, 1837, April 10, 1837, April 26, 1837, May 1, 1837, MAH Papers.

[3] See George Louis Hammeken in *The Handbook of Texas,* I, 762; Andrew Forest Muir (ed.), *Texas in 1837: An Anonymous Contemporary Narrative,* pp. 202, 211; George L. Hammeken to Stephen F. Austin, July 18, 1836, *Austin Papers,* III, 398. Also Brazoria County, Texas, Deed Book A, p. 124.

[4] See José Antonio Mexia (*ca.* 1800–1839) in *The Handbook of Texas,* II, 182.

[5] See James Love (1795–1874), in *The Handbook of Texas,* II, 85.

[6] Mary Austin Holley to Harriette Brand, April 3, 1837, MAH Papers. See George Washington Wheelwright in *The Handbook of Texas,* II, 893.

[7] A copy of Holley, *Texas* (1833), in the Austin-Bryan Books once belonged to Supply C. Thwing, Roxbury, Massachusetts.

[8] Orleans Parish, Lousiana, Civil District Court, Settlement of Estates, Doc. No. 19, 714, Estate of Jean Baptiste Labranche.

[9] "From My Portfolio," *San Luis Advocate,* March 9, 1841.

[10] Emily Austin to Moses Austin Bryan, April 18, 1839, Austin Papers; Guy M. Bryan to James F. Perry, October 31, 1837, Guy Morrison Bryan Papers.

[11] Christ Church Records, Confirmations: On July 26, 1829, Bishop John Stark Ravenscroft, of North Carolina, confirmed seventy-one persons, includ-

ing Mrs. Harriette Williman Brand. Also Christ Church Records, Minutes of the Vestry, April 3–December 26, 1837.

[12] Deposition of Mrs. M. A. Holley, October 10, 1837, Henry Hobart Papers.

[13] For Mrs. Holley's journey to Texas in December, 1837, see John Dexter to Dear M. [his sister], December 9, 1837, John Dexter Papers; Mary Austin Holley to Harriette Brand, December 1, 1837, MAH Papers.

[14] Mary Austin Holley to Harriette Brand, December 19, 1837, MAH Papers.

[15] See John Shackelford (1790–1857) in *The Handbook of Texas*, II, 594.

[16] *Telegraph and Texas Register*, December 22, 1837. See Albert Sidney Johnston (1803–1862) in *The Handbook of Texas*, I, 919–920; and George Washington Hockley (1802–1854), *ibid.*, I, 820.

[17] See Augustus Chapman Allen (1806–1864) in *The Handbook of Texas*, I, 29–30.

[18] For Mrs. Holley's visit to Texas in 1837–1838 see Mary Austin Holley to Harriette Brand, February 8, 1838, March 6, 1838, March 21, 1838, April 4, 1838, May 13, 1838, MAH Papers.

[19] See Alcee Labranche (1806–1861) in *Biographical Directory of the American Congress, 1774–1927*, p. 1197.

[20] Herbert P. Gambrell, *Mirabeau Buonaparte Lamar: Troubadour and Crusader*, pp. 183–187.

[21] Mirabeau B. Lamar to Gail Borden, January 20, 1837, *Austin Papers*, III, 282–284; James F. Perry to the Public, *ca.* 1844 (according to editorial footnote), *ibid.*, III, 484–487. Examination of the original manuscript of Perry's notice to the public indicates that the notice was written by Lamar "when he commenced writing the life of Stephen F. Austin, 1837" (Austin Papers, File for 1837).

[22] Interview, Rebecca Smith Lee with Stephen S. Perry, February 8, 1953, at Peach Point Plantation, at which time he graciously showed the family heirlooms there. In 1807 Alexander Frazer, silversmith of Lexington, Kentucky, billed Moses Austin for engraved silver spoons(*Austin Papers*, I, 151).

[23] Emily Austin to Moses Austin Bryan [care Texan Minister, Washington, D.C.], April 18, 1839, Austin Papers.

[24] Mary Austin Holley, Notes for a History of Texas, Section No. 35, MAH Papers. The blue cardboard notebooks in which she copied Stephen F. Austin's experiences in Mexico bear small labels titled "Made and sold by A. J. Skillman, Main St., Lexington, Ky."

[25] Strobel, *Old Plantations and their Owners of Brazoria County, Texas*, p. 8, Durazno Plantation. See William Joel Bryan (1815–1903) in *The Handbook of Texas*, I, 234.

[26] For Mrs. Holley's claim to the "two hundred acres of premium land," see Henry Austin to Mary Austin Holley, February 27, 1837, and August 4, 1837,

Crosby Papers. For Emily Perry's gift to Mrs. Holley see Brazoria County, Texas, Deed Book D, p. 353, dated March 1, 1838, witnessed by Henry Austin and George L. Hammeken, filed April 25, 1847, by Henry Austin.

27 Mary Austin Holley to William M. Brand, February 21, 1837, MAH Papers.

28 "A Day in Texas," one-page manuscript, MAH Papers.

29 Mary Austin Holley to Harriette Brand, May 13, 1838, MAH Papers.

30 Lexington *Intelligencer*, October 12, 1838. See Chapter 15, Note 9, *supra*, regarding the *Brazos Boat Glee*.

31 Advertisement of auction at the residence of Mrs. Mary A. Holley on Constitution Street of "all of her Household and Kitchen Furniture," mentioning "One Piano, of superior quality, good tone, and of a handsome style; Also, Two Negro Women, said to be first rate house servants" (Lexington *Observer and Reporter*, January 19, 1839). A slave named Amy is named in William Brand's estate inventory (Fayette County, Kentucky, Will Book R, pp. 202–204). See also Emily Austin to Moses Austin Bryan, February 12, 1839, Austin Papers.

32 For Mrs. Holley's trip to New Orleans in the spring of 1839 see: Emily Austin to Moses Austin Bryan, April 18, 1839, Austin Papers; Mary Austin Holley to Harriette Brand, February 26, 1839, March 30, 1839, and April 5, 1839, MAH Papers.

33 Henry Austin to Mary Austin Holley, April 8, 1839, Henry Austin Papers.

34 For Mrs. Holley's trip East in 1839 see: Mary Austin Holley [from Baltimore] to Harriette Brand, July 11, 1839, and July 26, 1839; [from Brooklyn], September 5, 1839; [from Baltimore] September 16, 1839, and October 21, 1839; [from Forest, Maryland] December 8, 1839; MAH Papers.

35 Henry Austin to Mary Austin Holley, July 25, 1839, and September 28, 1839, Henry Austin Papers.

36 Christ Church Records, Baptisms: "Baptized July 28, 1842—Emily Austin Brand—born October 9, 1839."

37 Mary Austin Holley to Harriette Brand, September 16, 1839, MAH Papers. Mrs. Holley is undoubtedly referring to Iucho's *The Transylvania March* (1839).

38 Helen West Ridgely, *Old Brick Churches of Maryland*, pp. 113–127; John Thomas Scharf, *The History of Baltimore, City and County* . . ., pp. 857–865.

39 Dexter, *Biographical Sketches of the Graduates of Yale College*, V, 441–442.

40 Mary Austin Holley [from Washington, D.C.] to John G. Tod, John G. Tod Papers.

41 Paul R. Frothingham, *Edward Everett, Orator and Statesman*, p. 157.

42 Mary Austin Holley's sale of land to John G. Tod appears in a series of letters: Mary Austin Holley to John G. Tod, March 15, 1840, March 18,

1840, March 19, 1840, March 20, 1840, March 21, 1840, March 24, 1840, April 6, 1840, July 2, 1841 [*sic*]; and John G. Tod to Mary Austin Holley, *ca.* March 3, 1840; John G. Tod to George L. Hammeken, June 18, 1840; George L. Hammeken to O. Rowley, Surveyor, July 8, 1840; (John G. Tod Papers). Also Galveston County, Texas, Deed Book 2, p. 38: Mary A. Holley to John G. Tod, League No. 14 on Dickson Creek, April 7, 1841; filed October 19, 1841.

[43] Mary Austin Holley to Harriette Brand, November 12, 1840, MAH Papers.

CHAPTER 18

[1] Mary Austin Holley to Harriette Brand, November 12, 1840, MAH Papers.

[2] For another view of Galveston at the time of Mrs. Holley's visit in 1841–1842 see W. Eugene Hollon and Ruth Lapham Butler (eds.) *William Bollaert's Texas*, pp. 17–20.

[3] See Alphonse de Saligny in *The Handbook of Texas*, II, 533.

[4] *Texas Sentinel* (Austin), July 25, 1840.

[5] Mary Austin Holley to Harriette Brand, November 27, 1840, MAH Papers.

[6] Mary Austin Holley read Mrs. Trollope's *Domestic Manners of the Americans*, and criticized her for not seeing the "grand and glorious in our institutions and history because individuals would chew and spit" (Mary Austin Holley to Harriette Brand, November 16–18, 1832, MAH Papers).

[7] The *San Luis Advocate*, a weekly newspaper edited by Tod Robinson and Matthew Hopkins, ran intermittently from *ca.* September 1, 1840, to October, 1842, when it was removed to Galveston as the *Texas Times*. For San Luis Island see Dick King, *Ghost Towns of Texas*, pp. 92–94.

[8] "To My Husband's Miniature. On New Year's Day, 1836," *San Luis Advocate*, December 3, 1840. It is signed "Lexington, Kentucky—Mary."

[9] Letter to the Editor, *San Luis Advocate*, January 22, 1841; "The Invitation," *ibid.*, January 29, 1841; "To the *Milton* and the *Ironside*," *ibid.*, February 16, 1841; "From My Portfolio," *ibid.*, March 9, 1841.

[10] "Oh, how I love the sea," *San Luis Advocate*, March 2, 1841.

[11] Horace's arrival in Texas was prior to a receipt he gave to John G. Tod, May 9, 1841, at Galveston, for $150.00 plus "the receipt of my passage from Baltimore" (John G. Tod Papers).

[12] Essay (appended to "To the *Milton* and the *Ironside*"), *San Luis Advocate*, February 16, 1841.

[13] "Adieu! To San Luis," *San Luis Advocate*, April 13, 1841.

[14] For a contemporary view of Saligny see Hollon and Butler (eds.), *William Bollaert's Texas*, pp. 102, 106, 108.

[15] George Wilkins Kendall, *Narrative of the Texan Santa Fé Expedition*, pp. 3–27. Kendall is mentioned in Eliza Chinn's memoirs (Eliza [Chinn]

Ripley, *Social Life in Old New Orleans, being Recollections of My Girlhood,* pp. 105, 170).

[16] General Leslie Combs was a hero of the War of 1812 and a prominent attorney in Lexington (Ranck, *History of Lexington, Kentucky,* pp. 290–291). His son Franklin is buried in the old Episcopal Cemetery in Lexington. Captured on the Texan Santa Fé Expedition, young Combs was released by Santa Anna, and later assassinated in Louisiana. On his tombstone we read: "The sod of grass on which his head reposed when he died is now growing at the head of his grave" (Copy from files of J. Winston Coleman, Jr., Lexington, Kentucky).

CHAPTER 19

[1] Christ Church Records, Baptisms: "Baptized July 28, 1842—John Watt Brand—born April 27, 1841."

[2] For a harsh condemnation of Holley as an atheist see Robert Davidson, *The History of the Presbyterian Church in the State of Kentucky,* pp. 298–318.

[3] Wilhelm Iucho, *Heatherflowers, or Recollections of Scotland.* ca. 1840.

[4] See Robert Peter (1805–1894) in *DAB,* XIV, 499–500; and Robert and Johanna Peter, *Transylvania University: Its Origin, Rise, Decline, and Fall* (1896), the first full-scale history of the institution. Johanna was Robert Peter's daughter.

[5] Now in the possession of Catherine Peter Evans (Mrs. Howard), of Winton, Fayette County, Kentucky, ancestral home of the Meredith and Peter families.

[6] Christ Church Records, Baptisms: "Baptized, August 25, 1844—Catherine McAlester Brand—born December 22, 1842." The name should be spelled Katherine Macalester Brand.

[7] *Civilian and Galveston Gazette,* February 8, 1843.

[8] See William Kennedy (1799–1871) in *The Handbook of Texas,* I, 948. For his references to Mrs. Holley see William Kennedy, *The Rise, Progress, and Prospects of the Republic of Texas,* I, 89, 112–113; II, 7, 270.

[9] See Robert Mills (1809–1888) in *The Handbook of Texas,* II, 200.

[10] See George Morse Collinsworth (1810–post 1857) in *The Handbook of Texas,* I, 376–377.

[11] Texan casualties at the Battle of Mier, including James Austin, killed, are listed in the *Civilian and Galveston Gazette,* February 25, 1843. For the death of James Austin see Thomas Jefferson Green, *Journal of the Texian Expedition against Mier,* pp. 91–92, 437.

[12] Jim Dan Hill, *The Texas Navy in Forgotten Battles and Shirtsleeve Diplomacy,* pp. 181–194; *Telegraph and Texas Register,* April 29, 1843, November 22, 1843.

[13] Paul Tyler McCaleb, "Moore and Stuart: Rival Editors in Early Texas (1837–1862)."

[14] Brazoria County, Texas, Will Book A, p. 8.

[15] Galveston County, Texas, Deed Book "I," pp. 92–93: Mortgage Henry Austin to Mary Austin Holley, November 3, 1843; filed September 3, 1850.

[16] *Civilian and Galveston Gazette,* December 30, 1843, January 6, 1844, January 24, 1844.

[17] Hollon and Butler (eds.), *William Bollaert's Texas,* pp. 3–37, 126–178.

[18] Houston *Telegraph,* July 20, 1843. In the same issue appear articles by Colonel James Morgan and Commodore Edwin Ward.

[19] *Civilian and Galveston Gazette,* January 31, 1844. Mrs. Holley's presence on the *Flirt* is a conjecture based upon her proven presence aboard the *Vigilante* for a similar party in early 1844.

[20] Mary Austin Holley to Emily Perry, March 23, 1844, MAH Papers.

[21] See James Morgan (1786–1866) in *The Handbook of Texas,* II, 234. A rumor was current that a guest of Colonel Morgan's died of eating too much (Hollon and Butler [eds.], *William Bollaert's Texas,* p. 135).

[22] See Lexington *Observer and Reporter,* August 17, 1844, for account of this visit.

[23] For the Reverend John Maffitt (or Maffit or Moffitt) see Ranck, *History of Lexington,* Kentucky, p. 154; *Louisville Literary Messenger,* February 23, 1839, March 23, 1839; *Brazos Courier,* June 16, 1839. Eliza Chinn Ripley calls him "a jolly, itinerant Irish preacher" who was "the father of John L. Moffitt of Confederate fame and his daughter married Lamar" (Ripley, *Social Life in Old New Orleans,* p. 48).

[24] George L. Hammeken, "Recollections of Stephen F. Austin," *Southwestern Historical Quarterly,* XX (1916–1917), 369–380. This article is a letter from Hammeken to Guy M. Bryan, dated February 28, 1844, beginning "In answer to yours of the 8th instant, respecting what I know of your uncle . . ." See also three "Notes" by Gail Borden, signed at Peach Point, February 6–7, 1844 (*Austin Papers,* III, 113–114, 115).

[25] Mary Austin Holley to Emily Perry, April 12, 1844, MAH Papers. See also Joe B. Frantz, *Gail Borden: Dairyman to a Nation,* pp. 169–172.

[26] Mary Austin Holley to Emily Perry, March 23, 1844, MAH Papers.

[27] Mary Austin Holley, Notes for a History of Texas, Section No. 15: "Conversation with General Lamar, Galveston, April 4, 1844," MAH Papers.

[28] Article signed "A Western Man," *Texas Sentinel,* May 30, 1840.

[29] Mary Austin Holley, Notes for a History of Texas, Section No. 14: "Conversation with General Houston, Galveston, April 7, 1844," MAH Papers.

[30] *Ibid.,* Section No. 14: "Conversation with General Murphy, April 8, 1844." See William Sumter Murphy (1796–1844) in *The Handbook of Texas,* II, 251.

[31] Mary Austin Holley, Notes for a History of Texas, Section No. 14: "Conversations with Mrs. Eberly," MAH Papers. Mrs. Eberly is listed as delinquent for taxes in Travis County, Texas (*Texas Sentinel,* August 19, 1841), indicating that she had moved to Galveston about that time. See L. W. Kemp, "Mrs.

Angelina B. Eberly," *Southwestern Historical Quarterly*, XXXVI (1932–1933), 193–199.

32 See Andrew Forest Muir, "Isaac B. Desha, Fact and Fancy," *Filson Club History Quarterly*, Vol. 30 (1956), pp. 319–323.

33 Mary Austin Holley to Emily Perry, April 12, 1844, MAH Papers.

34 Mary Austin Holley to David G. Burnet, April 12, 1844, David G. Burnet Papers. See David Gouverneur Burnet (1788–1870) in *The Handbook of Texas*, I, 252–253.

35 Mary Austin Holley to Emily Perry, April 25, 1844, MAH Papers.

36 Emily Perry to Mary Austin Holley, April 29, 1844, Crosby Papers.

37 *The Red-Lander*, August 17, 1844; *Telegraph and Texas Register*, August 21, 1844.

CHAPTER 20

1 Mary Austin Holley was in New Orleans at least until May 19, 1844 (Mary Austin Holley, Notes for a History of Texas, Section No. 6, MAH Papers); and she arrived in Lexington before the middle of August (Lexington *Observer and Reporter*, August 17, 1844).

2 *The New Orleans Directory for 1841* lists D. Augustin, Attorney, residing at St. Claude and Esplanade Avenues. For this house in which Mrs. Holley spent her last years see Orleans Parish, Louisiana, Civil District Court, Settlement of Estates, Doc. No. 38,886, Inventory of Estate of J. B. Donatien Augustin, deceased, July 25, 1876.

3 John Alcee Augustin, "The Oaks: The Old Duelling Grounds of New Orleans," *Arts and Letters*, I (1887), 123–134. General Augustin appears in various political activities (New Orleans *Jeffersonian*, December 15, 1845, January 10, 1846).

4 For the precise scenes of Mary Austin Holley's last years see Benjamin Norman, *Norman's New Orleans and Environs, passim*.

5 Emily Perry to Mary Austin Holley—1844. MAH Papers. This letter was written on the back of one of Mrs. Holley's letters to Emily, and was annotated by Mrs. Hally Bryan Perry as follows: "Mrs. Holley to Mrs. J. F. Perry, March 23, 1844—on same sheet Mrs. Perry answers but perhaps never sent the letter about biography of Stephen F. Austin."

6 Mary Austin Holley, Notes for a History of Texas, Section No. 6: "New Orleans, May 1844. Mrs. Holley to her cousin—makes inquiry relative to paper concerning Stephen F. Austin and Texas."

7 Eugene C. Baker, editor of *The Austin Papers* (1924–1927) and author of *The Life of Stephen F. Austin* (1925), made accessible the materials preserved by Emily Perry and her descendants. Of them he writes: "The Austin papers were accumulated by Moses and Stephen F. Austin. For more than sixty years they were reverently preserved by Colonel Guy M. Bryan, grandson of Moses Austin, and after his death were given by his children to the

University of Texas. . . . In mass this collection probably totals four thousand printed pages" (*The Life of Stephen F. Austin*, p. 525).

[8] Mattie Austin Hatcher, *Letters of an Early American Traveller: Mary Austin Holley, Her Life and Works, 1784–1846*, p. 82. Mrs. Hatcher obtained information from Melazie Labranche Augustin's descendants regarding Mrs. Holley's last years.

[9] Lexington *Observer and Reporter*, May–December, 1844, especially May 4, 1844 (Clay's view of annexation), May 22, 1844 (Campbell-Rice Debate), August 17, 1844 (benefit for Miss Clarendon).

[10] Townsend, *Lincoln and the Bluegrass*, pp. 88–94.

[11] Clement Eaton, *Henry Clay and the Art of American Politics*, pp. 170–179.

[12] Lexington *Observer and Reporter*, June 29, 1844.

[13] *Ibid.*, November 9, 1844.

[14] *Ibid.*, August 31, 1844.

[15] *Ibid.*, August 17, 1844.

[16] Christ Church Records, Baptisms: "Baptized August 25, 1844—George Charlton Brand—born June 8, 1844."

[17] Crawford Readell [of Philadelphia] to William M. Brand, December —, 1843, Crosby Papers.

[18] Lexington *Observer and Reporter*, April 9, 1845, April 12, 1845.

[19] Townsend, *Lincoln and the Bluegrass*, pp. 97–98.

[20] A substantial portion of the manuscript about Texas on which Mrs. Holley was writing during 1843–1844 is preserved in her Notes for a History of Texas (MAH Papers). This collection, as now preserved, includes a small tan notebook labelled "Contents of Subject Matter for Writing History of Texas Compiled by Col. Guy M. Bryan and Mrs. Mary Holly [*sic*]," which outlines thirty-eight sections for arranging the material. The material came to the University of Texas with the Austin family papers given by the children of Guy M. Bryan. Not all thirty-eight sections appear in the collection filed as Mrs. Holley's Notes for a History of Texas. Some of her material is dispersed among the unpublished Austin Papers. Some of it may well have been lost. There remain in the Notes several sections of her proposed third book on Texas. Most important of these are: No. 24, "Notes on General Austin," and No. 37, "Seven Complete Chapters on Texas History."

[21] Stephen F. Austin to Emily Bryan [Perry], August 21, 1826, *Austin Papers*, I, 1427–1428.

[22] Mary Austin Holley, Notes for a History of Texas, Section No. 37, MAH Papers.

[23] For John and William Brand's trip to Scotland see William Brand to Harriette Brand, May 21, 1845, June 17, 1845, and John Brand to Elizabeth Brand [his wife], July 1, 1845, Crosby Papers.

[24] Inscription on an engraved picture of Ole B. Bull, Holley Coll.-Trans.

[25] Lexington *Observer and Reporter*, October 18, 1845.

26 *Ibid.*, June 28, 1845.

27 *Ibid.*, August 20, 1845, August 23, 1845. Also Townsend, *Lincoln and the Bluegrass*, pp. 110–117.

28 Llerena Friend, *Sam Houston: The Great Designer*, pp. 162–167.

29 Elmwood, the well preserved William Brand home, has several rooms on the third floor, which Mrs. Holley and her son probably occupied during their long sojourns there. She complained about "my cold, smoky room, so far off, so poorly attended" (Mary Austin Holley to Harriette Brand, December 23, 1845, MAH Papers).

30 Lexington *Observer and Reporter*, August 23, 1845. William Holley Brand (1826–1866) became an attorney and served in the Confederate Army. Some of his letters are in the Crosby Papers.

31 Interview, Rebecca Smith Lee with Mrs. Benjamin Gratz Crosby, August 24, 1952, at her home, Spring Station, Kentucky, at which time she exhibited the William Brand heirlooms and related the family traditions about them.

32 For references to this scene see Mary Austin Holley to Harriette Brand, December 23, 1845, MAH Papers.

33 "Kate" was Katherine Macalester Brand. See Mary Austin Holley's Family Relationships, Chart I, in this volume. Kate's daughter, Eliza Pitman (1875–1961), became Mrs. Benjamin Gratz Crosby, preserver of the Crosby Papers.

34 The following facts suggest how Mary Austin Holley's Notes for a History of Texas (MAH Papers), came into the possession of Guy M. Bryan (see Chapter 20, Note 20, *supra*): (1) Mary Austin Holley wanted Guy Bryan to collaborate with her on her third book about Texas (Mary Austin Holley to Emily Perry, April 12, 1844, April 25, 1844, MAH Papers). (2) In the Austin-Bryan Books Collection is a copy of Caldwell's *Discourse* inscribed: "Mrs. H. Brand to her cousin, Guy M. Bryan, Lexington, Ky., June 18, 1856." (3) About 1867 Harriette Brand rearranged her store of family papers (her poem, "Old Letters, Old Letters," in the Crosby Papers). (4) Bryde Neill Taylor in "Women Writers of Texas" for the Galveston *Daily News*, June 18, 1893, states that Mrs. Holley at the time of her death "was engaged on a life of Stephen F. Austin. Mr. Guy M. Bryan has the manuscript now in his possession." She also states that Harriette Holley Brand furnished information for this article. Therefore it seems reasonable to the present writer to conclude that Harriette Brand gave the Notes to Guy M. Bryan in the late 1860's with the understanding that he would complete Mary Austin Holley's project as coauthor.

35 Facts concerning the closing years of Mrs. Holley's life are drawn chiefly from a series of letters to her daughter: Mary Austin Holley to Harriette Brand, November 17–18, 1845, December 7, 1845, December 23, 1845, January 28, 1846, February 19, 1846, March 31, 1846, April 20, 1846, May

10, 1846, June 7, 1846, June 24, 1846, June 30, 1846, July 10, 1846, MAH Papers.

[36] "No. 158, N. H. Labranche—aged 35—planter—[worth] $150,000. — [born] Louisiana" and "Widow H. Labranche—aged 64—[born] Louisiana" (United States Census Returns, Seventh Census for 1850, St. Charles Parish, Louisiana).

[37] Mary Austin Holley to Harriette Brand, December 7, 1845, MAH Papers.

[38] Lexington *Observer and Reporter*, November 26, 1845. William Brand was buried in the Episcopal Cemetery on the north edge of town. His remains were removed in January, 1850, to the new Lexington Cemetery, opened in 1849, and interred on the Brand lot, No. 120, where Harriette Brand's remains were placed, August 12, 1900 (Lexington, Kentucky, Cemetery, Record of Burials).

[39] See William Brand's original will, signed in a feeble hand on November 10, 1845 (Fayette County, Kentucky, Wills and Settlements, File for 1845–1846). The inventory of his estate, filed December 23, 1845, by William H. Brand, estimates the estate at $59,917.45 (Fayette County, Kentucky, Will Book R., pp. 202–205).

[40] John Alcee Augustin, *War Flowers, Reminiscenses of Four Years Campaigning. Respectfully Dedicated to the Ladies of New Orleans.*

[41] Mary Austin Holley to Harriette Brand, March 31, 1846, MAH Papers.

[42] Mrs. Holley kept her daughter informed of these social activities: "Mrs. Gaines dined with us Sunday—as did Mrs. Stuart. . . . She is a talented woman, notwithstanding their talk of dotage." (Mary Austin Holley to Harriette Brand, June 24, 1846, MAH Papers). Mrs. Gaines was the former Mrs. Myra Clarke Whitney, whose inheritance from her father was so long in litigation.

[43] Charles Etienne Arthur Gayarre, *Histoire de la Louisiane* (1846–1847). See Grace King, *Creole Families of New Orleans*, pp. 269–290.

[44] Theodore Clapp (1792–1866), author of *Autobiographical Sketches and Recollections during a Thirty-five Years' Residence in New Orleans* (1857), came to New Orleans in 1821 from Louisville, Kentucky. See Theodore Clapp to Horace Holley, June 9, 1825, Holley Coll.-Trans. Also Ripley, *Social Life in Old New Orleans*, pp. 120–124.

[45] Henry Carleton (1785–1863), graduate from Yale, Class of 1806, was appointed Judge of the Supreme Court of Louisiana (New Orleans *Bee*, April 3, 1837). See Dexter, *Biographical Sketches of the Graduates of Yale College*, VI, 12–14.

[46] Mary Austin Holley to Elizabeth Brand [her granddaughter], February 5, 1846, MAH Letters.

[47] *Ibid.*

[48] See Edmund Pendleton Gaines (1777–1849) in *DAB*, VII, 92–93.

[49] Ripley, *Social Life in Old New Orleans*, pp. 85–86.

[50] Light is shed on the complicated financial relations between Mary Austin Holley and her brother Henry by his will, dated July 27, 1851, and pro-

bated April 20, 1852 (Galveston County, Texas, Will Book 2, pp. 55–56). He estimates his real estate at about sixty thousand acres of land; but the inventory of the estate reports less than half that acreage, some of it listed as "common property" (Galveston County, Texas, Inventories, I, pp. 85–88). Some of the "common property" may have been owned with Mary Austin Holley.

[51] Mary Austin Holley to Harriette Brand, July 10, 1846, MAH Papers.

[52] Hatcher, *Letters of an Early American Traveller*, p. 92.

[53] *Ibid.*, p. 93. The Augustin family tradition recorded by Mrs. Hatcher establishes beyond reasonable doubt that the body of Mary Austin Holley was placed in the Augustin family tomb in the St. Louis Cemetery in New Orleans, although there is no carving on it to indicate her interment. The St. Louis Cemetery Record of Burials (Cemetery No. 2, Square No. 2, Tomb 13, Range F, St. Philomen's Aisle No. 1) examined by the present writer in 1954 did not include Mrs. Holley's name. Among those buried in the Augustin tomb are: Widow H. Labranche, 85 years, January 12, 1871; Melazie Augustin, 46 years, February 26, 1863; D. Augustin, 74 years, July 27, 1876; John Augustin, 50 years, February 5, 1888.

[54] New Orleans *Courier*, August 3, 1846 (unsigned). A reprint of this obituary appeared in the Lexington *Observer and Reporter*, August 22, 1846. A clipping of the Lexington obituary preserved in the Crosby Papers is attributed in Harriette Brand's writing to "Mr. Clapp."

[55] New Orleans *Jeffersonian*, August 4, 1846 (unsigned). A clipping of this obituary in the Crosby Papers is attributed in Harriette Brand's writing to "Judge Carlton."

[56] An obituary of Mary Austin Holley appeared in the *Telegraph and Texas Register*, August 26, 1846. Unclaimed letters for her were advertised in the New Orleans *Picayune*, August 28, 1846, September 4, 1846, September 11, 1846.

[57] In the vicinage of the Labranche plantations the 1850 census taker noted: "No. 160—Horace Holey [*sic*]—30—wheelwright—Louisiana" (United States Census Returns, Seventh Census, 1850, St. Charles Parish, Louisiana).

[58] Many histories of Texas specifically acknowledge indebtedness to Mary Austin Holley's writings, and others apparently borrow from her work without acknowledgment. Examples of acknowledged indebtedness are: David Woodman, *Guide to Texas Emigrants*, pp. 85, 103, 113–123; William Kennedy, *The Rise, Progress, and Prospects of the Republic of Texas*, I, 89, 112–113; II, 7, 270; Henderson Yoakum, *The History of Texas from its First Settlement in 1685 to its Annexation to the United States in 1846*, I, 209, 213, 230, 282–290; D. W. C. Baker (comp.) *A Texas Scrapbook*, 35–37, 330; Homer S. Thrall, *A Pictorial History of Texas*, pp. 496–497; Hubert Howe Bancroft, *The History of the North Mexican States and Texas*, II, 118, 119, 120, 121, 129, 172, 179, 184, 188, 217, 278, 284, 385 (bibliographical evaluation).

Bancroft (*op. cit.*, II, 385–386) analyzes W. B. Dewees, *Letters from an Early Settler of Texas* (1852) to show by examples that a portion of the book was plagiarized from Mrs. Holley. Some of the early reviewers of David B. Edward, *The History of Texas: or, The Emigrant's, Farmer's and Politician's Guide* (1836) charged the author with plagiarizing from Holley, *Texas* (1833); see the Lexington *Intelligencer*, July 29, 1836, August 9, 1836.

BIBLIOGRAPHY

MANUSCRIPT COLLECTIONS

Austin Genealogical Papers. Rosenberg Library, Galveston, Texas.

Austin Papers. Barker Texas History Center Archives, University of Texas, Austin.

Austin, Henry. Papers. Barker Texas History Center Archives, University of Texas, Austin.

Bryan, Guy Morrison. Papers. Barker Texas History Center Archives, University of Texas, Austin.

Burnet, David G. Papers. Barker Texas History Center Archives, University of Texas, Austin.

Clay, Henry. Papers. Manuscript Division, Library of Congress, Washington, D.C.

Crosby Papers. Estate of the late Mrs. Benjamin Gratz Crosby, Spring Station, Kentucky.

Dana Collection, "New Haven, Old and New." New Haven Colony Historical Society, New Haven, Connecticut.

Dexter, John. Papers. Transylvania College Library, Lexington, Kentucky.

Ellis, G. E. Papers. Massachusetts Historical Society, Boston.

Goddard, Benjamin. Papers. Massachusetts Historical Society, Boston.

Hobart, Henry. Papers. Protestant Episcopal Church Archives, deposited with the New York Historical Society, New York City.

Holley, Horace. Papers. Massachusetts Historical Society, Boston.

———. Papers. Yale University Library, New Haven, Connecticut.

Holley, Horace, and Mary Austin Holley. Collection. Transylvania College Library, Lexington, Kentucky (Cited as Holley Coll.-Trans.).

Holley, Mary Austin. Collection (Chiefly sketches, photographs, pictures). Barker Texas History Center Library, University of Texas, Austin.

Holley, Mary Austin. Papers. Barker Texas History Center Archives, University of Texas, Austin (Cited as MAH Papers).

Hunt, John W. Papers. University of Kentucky Library, Lexington.

New Haven Map Collection. New Haven Colony Historical Society, New Haven, Connecticut.

Perry, Hally Bryan. Collection. Barker Texas History Center Library, University of Texas, Austin.

Peter, Robert. Papers. Transylvania College Library, Lexington, Kentucky.

Phillips, Willard. Papers. Massachusetts Historical Society, Boston.

Rafinesque, C. S. Collection. Transylvania College Library, Lexington, Kentucky.

Silliman, Benjamin. Papers. Yale University Library, New Haven, Connecticut.

Tod, John G. Papers. Barker Texas History Center Archives, University of Texas, Austin.

Trimble, John A. Papers. Manuscript Department, Duke University Library, Durham, North Carolina.
Warren, John Collins. Papers. Massachusetts Historical Society, Boston.

OFFICIAL RECORDS

Brazoria County, Texas (Angleton). Deed Books A, D; Will Book A.
Christ Church (Episcopal). Records. Lexington, Kentucky.
Fayette County, Kentucky (Lexington). Administrators' Bonds, Vol. 2 (1823–1838); Marriage Bonds, Doc. File (1825–1828); Tax Rolls, 1820, 1822 (Microfilm, Kentucky Historical Society, Frankfort, Kentucky); Will Book R; Wills and Settlements, File (1845–1846).
Galveston County, Texas (Galveston). Deed Books, Vols. 2; "I"; Inventories, Vol. I; Will Book, Vol. 2.
Lexington Cemetery, Lexington, Kentucky. Record of Burials.
New Haven, Connecticut, District Court. Probate Records: Vol. 17, pp. 17, 139, 302; Vol. 23, pp. 23, 421, 444 (copy, Henry Austin Papers, Barker Texas History Center Archives, University of Texas).
Orleans Parish, Louisiana (New Orleans). Civil District Court, Settlement of Estates, Docs. Nos. 19,714, 38,886; Record of Conveyances, Vols. I and 22.
St. Charles Parish, Louisiana (Hahnville). Acts, Francois Choix, 1840–1847.
St. Louis Cemetery, New Orleans, Louisiana. Record of Burials.
Texas, State of. Spanish Archives. General Land Office, Austin.
Transylvania University. Official Records. Transylvania College Library, Lexington, Kentucky.
Transylvania University. Unbound Documents. Transylvania College Library, Lexington, Kentucky.
Trinity Church (Episcopal), New Haven, Connecticut. Records. (Excerpts from the Reverend C. Lawson Millard to Rebecca Smith Lee, August 20, 1951).
United States. Census Returns (Seventh Census, 1850: Fayette County, Kentucky; St. Charles Parish, Louisiana). The National Archives, Washington, D.C.
Yale College, Brothers in Unity. Records, 1783–1802. Yale University Library, New Haven, Connecticut.

THESES AND NOTES

Dickson, Algernon Smith. *"The Western Review and Miscellaneous Magazine."* M.A. Thesis, Columbia University, 1946.
Dunn, C. Frank. "Notes on the Matthew Kennedy (Frame) House, East Second Street, Built 1814." Typescript in possession of Miss Rebecca Edwards, Lexington, Kentucky.
Jensen, Mrs. Harry. "Genealogy of Elijah Austin." Typescript, Austin Genealogical Papers, Rosenberg Library, Galveston, Texas.

McCaleb, Paul Tyler. "Moore and Stuart: Rival Editors in Early Texas (1837–1862)." M.A. Thesis, University of Texas, 1948.

Meeks, Jack H. "Memorandum relating to the Heirship of Stephen F. Austin and His sister, Emily Margaret Bryan Perry, April 8, 1940." Typescript in possession of Jack H. Meeks.

Scranton, Mildred. "History of Elias Austin . . . prepared from records in Durham, Connecticut." Typescript, Austin Genealogical Papers, Rosenberg Library, Galveston, Texas.

BOOKS AND PAMPHLETS

Adams, Charles Francis (ed.). *Memoirs of John Quincy Adams, Comprising Portions of His Diary from 1795 to 1848.* 12 vols. Philadelphia, J. B. Lippincott and Company, 1874–1877.

——. *The Works of John Adams, Second President of the United States. . . .* 10 vols. Boston, Little, Brown and Company, 1850–1856.

Appleton's Cyclopedia of American Biography. Edited by James G. Wilson and John Fiske. 6 vols. New York, D. Appleton and Company, 1887–1900.

Arthur, Stanley Clisby. *Louisiana Tours.* New Orleans, Harmanson, 1950.

——. *Old New Orleans: A History of the Vieux Carré, Its Ancient and Historical Buildings.* New Orleans, Harmanson, 1952.

Arthur, Stanley Clisby, and George Campbell Huchet de Kernion. *Old Families of Louisiana.* New Orleans, Harmanson, 1931.

Atwater, Edward E. (ed.). *The History of the City of New Haven to the Present Time.* New York, W. W. Munsell and Company, 1887.

Augustin, John Alcee. *War Flowers: Reminiscences of Four Years Campaigning. Respectfully Dedicated to the Ladies of New Orleans.* New Orleans, Hinton, Printer, *ca.* 1865.

Austin-Bryan Books. (Collection). Presented in 1933 to the University of Texas Library by the Children of Guy Morrison Bryan (1821–1901). Barker Texas History Center Library, University of Texas, Austin.

Baker, D. C. W. *A Texas Scrapbook.* New York, A. S. Barnes and Company, 1875.

Bancroft, Hubert Howe. *The History of the North Mexican States and Texas.* 2 vols. San Francisco, The History Company, 1889.

Barker, Eugene C. (ed.). *The Austin Papers.* Vol. I, in two parts, published as Vol. II of the *Annual Report of the American Historical Association for the Year 1919*, Washington, D.C., 1924; Vol. II, published as the *Annual Report of the American Historical Association for the Year 1922*, Washington, D.C., 1928; Vol. III, Austin, University of Texas Press, 1927.

——. *The Life of Stephen F. Austin, Founder of Texas, 1793–1836: A Chapter in the Westward Movement of the Anglo-American People.* Nashville, Cokesbury Press, 1926.

Baudier, Roger. *The Catholic Church in Louisiana.* New Orleans, A. W. Hyatt Stationery Company, 1939.

Biographical Directory of the American Congress, 1774–1929. Washington, D.C., United States Government Printing Office, 1950.

Bollaert, William. *William Bollaert's Texas.* Edited by W. Eugene Hollon and Ruth Lapham Barker. Norman, University of Oklahoma Press, 1956.

Boston Directory, containing the names of the inhabitants, their occupations, places of business, and dwelling houses. . . . Boston, Edward Cotton, Publisher, 1809. Also for 1810, 1813, 1816, 1818.

Brooks, Van Wyck. *The Flowering of New England.* New York, E. P. Dutton and Company, 1936.

———. *The World of Washington Irving.* New York, E. P. Dutton and Company, 1944.

Bryant, Edwin (Late Alcalde of San Francisco).*What I Saw in California . . ..* 5th ed. New York, D. Appleton and Company, 1848.

Caldwell, Charles. *A Discourse on the Genius and Character of the Rev. Horace Holley, LL.D. . . . with an Appendix, containing Copious Notes, Biographical and Illustrative.* Boston, Hilliard, Gray, Little and Wilkins, 1828. (Cited as Caldwell, *Discourse*).

Call, Richard Ellsworth. *The Life and Writings of Rafinesque.* Louisville, J. P. Morton and Company, 1895.

Cappon, Lester J. (ed.). *The Adams-Jefferson Letters.* 2 vols. Chapel Hill, University of North Carolina Press, 1959.

Castañeda, Carlos Eduardo, and Early Martin, Jr. (eds.). *Three Manuscript Maps of Texas by Stephen F. Austin; with Biographical and Bibliographical Notes.* Austin, Texas, privately printed, 1930.

Chaney, George Leonard. *The Hollis Street Church from Mather Biles to Thomas Storr King, 1732–1861.* Boston, Press of G. H. Ellis, 1877.

Clapp, Theodore. *Autobiographical Sketches and Recollections during a Thirty-Five Years' Residence in New Orleans.* Boston, Phillips, Sampson, and Company, 1857.

Coleman, J. Winston, Jr. *Masonry in the Bluegrass.* Lexington, Kentucky, Transylvania Press, 1933.

Collins, Lewis. *Historical Sketches of Kentucky . . . Revised by Richard H. Collins.* Covington, Kentucky, Collins and Company, 1874.

Davidson, Robert, D. D. *The History of the Presbyterian Church in the State of Kentucky.* New York and Pittsburgh, R. Carter, 1847.

Deiler, J. Hanno. *The Settlement of the German Coast of Louisiana and the Creoles of German Descent.* Philadelphia, Americana Germanica Press, 1909.

Dexter, Franklin B. *Biographical Sketches of the Graduates of Yale College, with Annals of the College History.* 6 vols. New York, H. Holt and Company, 1885–1919.

Dictionary of American Biography. Edited by Allen Johnson. 20 vols. New York, Charles Scribner's Sons, 1928–1937. (Cited as *DAB*).

Dobie, J. Frank. *Coronado's Children: Tales of Lost Mines and Buried Treasure of the Southwest.* Dallas, Texas, Southwest Press, 1930.

Drake, Francis Samuel. *The Town of Roxbury: Its Memorable Persons and Places . . ..* Roxbury, Massachusetts, Published by the Author, 1878.

Dupre, Huntley. *Rafinesque in Lexington, 1819–1826.* Lexington, Kentucky, Bur Press, 1945.

Dwight, Timothy. *A Statistical Account of the City of New Haven.* New Haven, Connecticut, Walter and Steele, 1811.

Eaton, Clement. *Henry Clay and the Art of American Politics.* Boston, Little, Brown and Company, 1957.

Eckley, Joseph. *Sermon delivered at the Installation of the Rev. Horace Holley to the Pastoral Care of the Church and Society in Hollis Street.* Boston, J. Belcher, 1809.

Everett, John. *An Oration delivered July 5, 1824.* Boston, privately printed, 1824.

Flint, Timothy. *Recollections of the Last Ten Years . . . in the Valley of the Mississippi.* Boston, Cummings, Hilliard and Company, 1826.

Frantz, Joe B. *Gail Borden: Dairyman to a Nation.* Norman, University of Oklahoma Press, 1951.

Friend, Llerena. *Sam Houston: The Great Designer.* Austin, University of Texas Press, 1954.

Frothingham, Paul R. *Edward Everett: Orator and Statesman.* Boston, Houghton Mifflin Company, 1925.

Gambrell, Herbert P. *Mirabeau Buonaparte Lamar: Troubadour and Crusader.* Dallas, Texas, Southwest Press, 1934.

Gayarre, Charles Etienne Arthur. *Histoire de la Louisiane.* Nouvelle-Orleans, Magne & Weiss, 1846–1847.

Gibbs, George (ed.). *Administrations of Washington and Adams, edited from the Papers of Oliver Wolcott, Secretary of the Treasury.* 2 vols. New York, W. Van Norden, Printers, 1846.

Gibson's Guide and Directory of Louisiana, New Orleans, and Lafayette. New Orleans, J. Gibson, 1838.

Green, Thomas Jefferson. *Journal of the Texian Expedition against Mier.* New York, Harper & Brothers, 1845.

Groce, George C., and David H. Wallace (comps.). *The New York Historical Society's Dictionary of Artists in America, 1564–1860.* New Haven, Connecticut, Yale University Press, 1957.

Gulick, Charles A., Jr., and others (eds.). *The Papers of Mirabeau Buonaparte Lamar.* 6 vols. Austin, Texas, Von Boeckmann-Jones, 1921–1927.

Handbook of Texas, The. Edited by Walter Prescott Webb, H. Bailey Carroll, and others. 2 vols. Austin, Texas State Historical Association, 1952.

Hatcher, Mattie Austin. *Letters of an Early American Traveller: Mary Austin Holley, Her Life and Her Works, 1784–1846.* Dallas, Texas, Southwest Press, 1933.

Hawkins, Richmond Lawrin. *Madame de Staël and the United States.* Cambridge, Massachusetts, Harvard University Press, 1930.

Hill, Jim Dan. *The Texas Navy in Forgotten Battles and Shirtsleeve Diplomacy.* Chicago, University of Chicago Press, 1937.

History of the Erection of the Monument on the Grave of Myron Holley, The. Utica, New York, privately printed, 1844.

Hoadly, Charles J. (ed.). *The Public Records of the State of Connecticut. . . .* 3 vols. Hartford, Connecticut, Case, Lockwood and Brainard Company, Printers, 1894–1922.

Holley, Horace. *A Discourse Occasioned by the Death of Col. James Morrison, Delivered in the Episcopal Church, Lexington, Kentucky, May 19th, 1823, by the Rev. Horace Holley, A.M., President of the Transylvania University.* Lexington, Kentucky, J. Bradford, 1823. Printed by order of the Board of Trustees of the University.

Holley, Mary Austin. *Texas.* Lexington, Kentucky, J. Clarke and Company, 1836. (Cited as Holley, *Texas* [1836]).

———. *Texas. Observations, Historical, Geographical, and Descriptive, in a Series of Letters, Written during a Visit to Austin's Colony, with a view to a permanent settlement in that country, in the Autumn of 1831. With an Appendix, containing answers to certain questions, relative to Colonization in Texas, issued some time since by the London Geographic Society. Also some notice of the recent political events in that quarter.* Baltimore, Armstrong and Plaskitt, 1833. (Cited as Holley, *Texas* [1833]).

Hollon, W. Eugene, and Ruth Lapham (eds.). *William Bollaert's Texas.* Norman, University of Oklahoma Press, 1956.

Hume, Edgar Erskine. *Lafayette in Kentucky.* Frankfort, Kentucky, Transylvania College and the Society of the Cincinnati in Virginia, 1937.

Hurd, Duane Hamilton. *The History of Fairfield County, Connecticut . . . .* Philadelphia, J. W. Lewis and Company, 1881.

James, Marquis. *Andrew Jackson: The Border Captain.* Indianapolis, Bobbs-Merrill Company, 1933.

———. *Andrew Jackson: Portrait of a President.* Indianapolis, Bobbs-Merrill Company, 1938.

———. *The Raven: A Biography of Sam Houston.* Indianapolis, Bobbs-Merrill Company, 1929.

Johnston, Josiah S. (ed.). *The Memorial History of Louisville from Its First Settlement to the Year 1896.* 2 vols. Chicago, American Biographical Publishing Company, 1896.

Judd, Romie D. *The Educational Contributions of Horace Holley.* Nashville, George Peabody College for Teachers, 1936.

Kane, Harnett. *Plantation Parade*. New York, W. Morrow and Company, 1945.

Kendall, George Wilkins. *Narrative of the Texian Santa Fé Expedition*. Historical Introduction by Milo Milton Quaife. Chicago, Lakeside Press, R. P. Donnelly and Sons Company, 1929.

Kennedy, William. *The Rise, Progress, and Prospects of the Republic of Texas*. 2 vols. London, R. Hastings, 1841.

King, Dick. *Ghost Towns of Texas*. San Antonio, Texas, Naylor Company, 1953.

King, Grace. *Creole Families of New Orleans*. New York, Macmillan Company, 1921.

Latourette, K. S. *The History of Early Relationships between the United States and China, 1784–1844*. New Haven, Connecticut, Yale University Press, 1917.

Loring, James S. *The Hundred Boston Orators Appointed by the Municipal Authorities and other Public Bodies, from 1770 to 1852 . . . .* 4th ed. Boston, J. P. Jewett and Company, 1855.

Mayo, Bernard. *Henry Clay: Spokesman of the New West*. Boston, Houghton Mifflin Company, 1937.

McCabe, Julius P. Bolivar (comp.). *Directory of the City of Lexington and County of Fayette, for 1838 & '39*. Lexington, Kentucky, J. C. Noble, Printer, 1838.

McGiffert, Arthur Cushman, Jr., (ed.). *Young Emerson Speaks*. Boston, Houghton Mifflin Company, 1938.

Merwin, George H. *Ye Church and Parish of Greenfield . . . 1725–1913*. New Haven, Connecticut, Tuttle, Morehouse and Taylor Press, 1913.

Michel's New Orleans Annual and Commercial Register, containing the names, professions and residences of all the heads of families and persons in business . . . New Orleans, Gaux and Sollee, 1833.

Middlebrook, L. F. *The History of Maritime Connecticut during the American Revolution, 1775–1783*. 2 vols. Salem, Massachusetts, Essex Institute, 1925.

Mott, Frank Luther. *The History of American Magazines, 1741–1905*. 4 vols. Cambridge, Massachusetts, Harvard University Press, 1938–1957.

Muir, Andrew Forest (ed.). *Texas in 1837: An Anonymous Contemporary Narrative*. Austin, University of Texas Press, 1958.

The National Cyclopedia of American Biography. 35 vols. New York, J. T. White and Company, 1893–1949.

New Orleans Annual Commercial Register, containing the names, professions and residences of all heads of families and persons in business . . . . No publisher, 1835.

*The New Orleans Directory and Register . . . .*New Orleans, John A. Paxton, editor and printer, 1827.

The New Orleans Directory, for 1841, made by the United States Deputy Marshals (while taking the late census) . . ..New Orleans, Michel and Company, 1840.

Newcomb, Rexford. *Architecture in Old Kentucky*. Urbana, University of Illinois Press, 1953.

Norman, Benjamin M. *Norman's New Orleans and Environs*. New Orleans, B. M. Norman, 1845; New York, D. Appleton and Company, 1845.

Odell, George C. D. *Annals of the New York Stage*. 15 vols. New York, Columbia University Press, 1927–1949.

The Order of Exercises in the Chapel of Transylvania University: a Collection of Original Pieces in Honour of the arrival of General Lafayette . . .. Lexington, Kentucky, May, 1825.

Osterweis, Rollin G. *Three Centuries of New Haven, 1638–1938*. New Haven, Connecticut, Yale University Press, 1953.

Parish, John Carl. *George Wallace Jones*. Iowa City, State Historical Society of Iowa, 1912.

Parrington, Vernon E. (ed.). *The Connecticut Wits*. New York, Harcourt, Brace and Company, 1926.

Parton, James. *Captains of Industry*. Boston, Houghton Mifflin Company, 1884.

Perrin, William H. (ed.). *The History of Fayette County, Kentucky*. Chicago, O. L. Baskin and Company, 1882.

Perry, Charles E. (ed.). *Founders and Leaders of Connecticut, 1633–1788*. Boston, D. C. Heath and Company, 1954.

Peter, Robert. *The History of the Medical Department of Transylvania University*. Louisville, Kentucky, J. P. Morton and Company, 1905.

Peter, Robert, and Johanna Peter. *Transylvania University: Its Origin, Rise, Decline, and Fall*. Louisville, Kentucky, J. P. Morton and Company, 1896.

Phelps, Oliver Seymour, and Andrew T. Servin (comps.). *The Phelps Family of America and their English Ancestors*. Pittsfield, Massachusetts, Eagle Publishing Company, 1899.

Phi Beta Kappa Directory, 1776–1941, The. New York, United Chapters of Phi Beta Kappa, 1941.

Philipson, David (ed.). *The Letters of Rebecca Gratz*. Philadelphia, Jewish Publication Society of America, 1929.

Pierpont, John. *A Discourse delivered in Hollis Street Church, Boston, September 2, 1827; Occasioned by the death of Horace Holley, LL.D.,* . . .. Boston, Press of Christian Examiner, 1827.

Program of the Fiftieth Anniversary of the Dedication of the Meeting House in Hollis Street, January 31, 1861, The. Printed folder. No date.

Ranck, George W. *The History of Lexington, Kentucky*. Cincinnati, R. Clarke and Company, 1872.

The Record of Service of Connecticut Men in the War of the Revolution. Hartford, Adjutant General's Office of Connecticut, 1889.

Ridgely, Helen West. *The Old Brick Churches of Maryland.* New York, A. D. F. Randolph and Company, 1894.

Ripley, Eliza (Chinn). *Social Life in Old New Orleans, Being Recollections of My Girlhood . . ..* New York and London, D. Appleton and Company, 1912.

Rollins, Hyder E. *Keats' Reputation in America to 1848.* Cambridge, Massachusetts, Harvard University Press, 1946.

Scharf, John Thomas. *The History of Baltimore City and County . . ..* Philadelphia, L. H. Everts, 1881.

School Exercises of the Lafayette Female Academy, including Triumphs of Genius, a Poem by Caroline Clifford Nephew. Lexington, Kentucky, ca. 1826.

Simpson, Elizabeth M. *Bluegrass Houses and Their Traditions.* Lexington, Kentucky, Transylvania Press, 1932.

Smith, Elizabeth King, and Mary LeGrand Didlake. *Christ Church, 1796–1946.* Lexington, Kentucky, Whittet and Shepperson, Printers, 1946.

Smith, (Mrs.) Margaret Bayard. *The First Forty Years of Washington Society, portrayed by the Family Letters of Mrs. Samuel Harrison Smith . . ..* New York, Charles Scribner's Sons, 1906.

Sonne, Niels Henry. *Liberal Kentucky, 1780–1828.* New York, Columbia University Press, 1939.

Staël, de, Madame (nee Anne Louise Germaine Necker). *Germany.* Reprint of Murray translation into English, 1814. Boston and New York, Houghton Mifflin Company, 1887.

The Story of St. Joseph's Proto-Cathedral and its Paintings. Bardstown, Kentucky. No date. Pamphlet sold at the Cathedral.

Strobel, Abner J. *The Old Plantations and Their Owners of Brazoria County, Texas.* Rev. ed. Houston, Texas, Bowman and Ross, Printers, 1930.

The Territorial Papers of the United States. Compiled by Clarence E. Carter. Vol. XIV: *The Territory of Louisiana-Missouri, 1806–1814.* Washington, D.C., United States Government Printing Office, 1949.

Thrall, Homer S. *A Pictorial History of Texas.* St. Louis, N. D. Thompson and Company, 1879.

Todd, Charles Burr. *In Olde Connecticut.* New York, Grafton Press, 1906.

Townsend, William H. *Lincoln and the Bluegrass: Slavery and Civil War in Kentucky.* Lexington, Kentucky, University of Kentucky Press, 1955.

Translation of the Laws, Orders, and Contracts on Colonization from January, 1821, up to 1829; by virtue of which Col. Stephen F. Austin introduced and settled foreign emigrants in Texas, with an explanatory introduction. (Published originally by Godwin B. Cotten, San Felipe de Austin, Texas, 1829.) Houston, Texas, Borden and Moore, 1837.

Transylvania University. *The Catalogue of the Officers and Students of Transylvania University, Lexington, Kentucky, January, 1823.* No publisher, no date.

———. *The Catalogue of the Officers and Students of Transylvania University, Lexington, Kentucky, January, 1826.* No publisher, no date.

Trollope, Frances. *The Domestic Manners of the Americans.* Edited by Donald Smalley. New York, A. A. Knopf, 1949.

Venable, William Henry. *Beginnings of Literary Culture in the Ohio Valley: Historical and Biographical Sketches.* Cincinnati, R. Clarke and Company, 1891.

Visit of General Lafayette to the Lafayette Female Academy . . . together with a Catalogue of the Instructors, Visitors, and Pupils of the Academy, The. Lexington, Kentucky, May, 1825.

Vital Statistics of New Haven, 1649–1850. New Haven, Connecticut, 1850.

Wagers, Margaret Newnan. *The Education of a Gentleman: Jefferson Davis at Transylvania, 1821–1824.* Lexington, Kentucky, Buckley and Reading, 1943.

Warren, Edward. *The Life of John Collins Warren, M.D.* 2 vols. Boston, Ticknor and Fields, 1860.

Webb, Walter Prescott, H. Bailey Carroll, and others (eds.). *The Handbook of Texas.* 2 vols. Austin, Texas State Historical Association, 1952.

Wednesday Evening Club. *Centennial Celebration of the Wednesday Evening Club, 1777–1877.* Boston, privately printed, 1878.

Weiss, Harry B. *Rafinesque's Kentucky Friends.* Highland Park, New Jersey, privately printed, 1936.

Whitley, Edna Talbott. *Kentucky Ante-Bellum Portraiture.* Paris, Kentucky, from the Collection of the National Society of Colonial Dames in Kentucky, 1956.

Wilson, Ernest Henry. *America's Greatest Garden: the Arnold Arboretum.* Boston, Stratford Company, 1925.

Woodman, David, Jr. *Guide to Texas Emigrants.* Boston, M. Hawes, Printers, 1835.

Wright, Elizur. *Myron Holley. What He Did for Liberty and True Religion.* Boston, privately printed, 1882.

Yoakum, Henderson. *The History of Texas, from Its First Settlement in 1685 to Its Annexation to the United States in 1846.* 2 vols. New York, J. S. Redfield, 1855.

ARTICLES

"Academic Appointments," *American Monthly and Critical Review,* IV (1818), 65.

Augustin, John Alcee. "The Oaks, the Old Duelling Grounds in New Orleans," *Arts and Letters,* I (1887), 123–134.

Barker, Eugene C. "Descriptions of Texas by Stephen F. Austin, contributed by Eugene C. Barker," *Southwestern Historical Quarterly,* XXVIII (1924–1925), 98–121.

Curlee, Abigail. "History of a Texas Slave Plantation," *Southwestern Historical Quarterly*, XXVI (1922–1923), 79–127.

Dupre, Hartley. "Transylvania University and Rafinesque," *Filson Club History Quarterly*, Vol. 35 (1961), pp. 110–121.

Earl, Ralph. Portrait of Andrew Jackson, *American Heritage*, XII (1960), front cover and p. 3.

"1810 Census of the St. Charles Parish of Louisiana," *Genealogical Register of the Louisiana Genealogical Society*, IV (1958), 39–40.

Everett, Edward. [Review of Caldwell's *Discourse*], *North American Review*, Vol. 27 (1828), pp. 403–415.

Everett, John. "An Anecdote," *Western Review*, III (1820), 254.

———. "Enigmas," *Western Review*, II (1820), 320.

Flint, Timothy. [Review of Caldwell's *Discourse*], *Western Monthly Review*, II (1828–1829), 212–227.

———. [Review of Pierpont's *Discourse delivered in Hollis Street Church, Boston*], *Western Monthly Review*, I (1827), 430–434.

Hammeken, George L. "Recollections of Stephen F. Austin," *Southwestern Historical Quarterly*, XX (1916–1917), 369–380.

Harrison, Ida V. "The Transylvania Botanical Gardens," *Journal of American History*, VII (1913), 43–44.

Hogan, William R. "Henry Austin," *Southwestern Historical Quarterly*, XXXVII (1933–1934), 185–214.

Holley, Horace. "An Extract from a College Exercise, written in 1802," *Western Review*, II (1820), 190–191.

———. "From a Husband to a Wife, on seeing their daughter, a little girl at play," *Western Review*, III (1820), 255.

———. "The Landing of the Pilgrim Fathers at Plymouth, New England," *Western Review*, III (1820), 285–301.

———. "The Late Timothy Dexter of Newburyport, Massachusetts," *Western Review*, III (1820), 278–285.

———. "Lines addressed to a beautiful young lady by a gentleman . . .," *Western Review*, I (1819), 314–315.

———. "On Education in the Western States," *Western Review*, I (1819), 53–59.

———. "On the Pleasure Derived from Witnessing Scenes of Distress," *North American Review*, Vol. 2 (1815), pp. 59–67.

———. [Review of *A Contrast between Calvinism and Hopkinsianism*,] *General Repositary and Review*, III (1813), 377.

———. [Review of *Second Annual Report of the American Society for Colonizing the Free People of Colour in the United States*] *Western Review*, I (1819), 142–164.

———. "The Swan and the Eagle," *Western Review*, I (1819) 125–127.

———. "When first to my fair mistress' hand," *Western Review*, II (1820), 186–188.

——. "While away to the country, dear Mary," *Western Review*, I (1819), 316–318.

Holley, Horace, and Isaac Bronson. "An Investigation of the Facts relative to a Descent of Stones from the Atmosphere to the Earth, on the 14th of December, 1807, in the Towns of Fairfield, Weston, and Huntington, Connecticut, and to the Meteor whence these earthy bodies proceeded . . .," *Medical Repositary, comprehending Original Essays and Intelligence relative to Medicine, Chemistry, Natural History, Agriculture, Geography, and the Arts* . . ., V (1808), 418–421.

Holley, Mary Austin. "Adieu! To San Luis," *San Luis Advocate*, April 13, 1841.

——. "The blandness of a gentler clime," Lexington *Intelligencer*, December 20, 1836.

——. "The circling year has closed around," *Kentucky Gazette*, January 16, 1826.

——. "From My Portfolio," *San Luis Advocate*, March 9, 1841.

——. "The Invitation [to the Fair]," Lexington *Intelligencer*, November 14, 1834.

——. "The Invitation," *San Luis Advocate*, January 29, 1841.

——. "It is near to the hour," *Western Review*, I (1819), 63–64.

——. Letter to the Editor, *San Luis Advocate*, January 22, 1841.

——. Letter to the Editor, Lexington *Observer and Reporter*, August 17, 1844.

——. "Lines by a Lexington Lady on leaving Cincinnati," *Cincinnati Literary Gazette*, II (1824), 80.

——. "Lines written immediately on first beholding Niagara Falls, July, 1815," *Western Review*, I (1819), 127–128.

——. "Madame de Staël," *Western Review*, I (1819), 124.

——. "Music. A letter from a lady to a gentleman who was thought not to be pleased with Music . . . dated March 30th, 1804," *Western Review*, IV (1821), 314–318.

"O! had he lived" in Pierpont, *A Discourse* . . . (Boston, 1827), 30.

"Ode to Lafayette" in *Order of Exercises* (Lexington, Kentucky, 1825).

——. "Of that sweet spot," *Western Review*, I (1819), 319–320.

——. "Oh, how I love the sea," *San Luis Advocate*, March 2, 1841.

——. "On the Death of Miss Susannah Agnes Tibbatts," *Kentucky Reporter*, January 31, 1827.

——. "On Leaving Kentucky," *Kentucky Reporter*, March 10, 1827; *The Transylvanian, or Lexington Literary Journal*, I (1829), 27–28.

——. "The Plea of Texas," *Red-Lander*, August 17, 1844; *Telegraph and Texas Register*, August 21, 1844.

——. "Reply to Pestalozzi," *The Transylvanian, or Lexington Literary Journal*, I (1829), 121–131.

——. "Stranger, you ask," Lexington *Observer and Reporter*, June 4, 1834.

———. "The Texan Song of Liberty," *Kentucky Gazette,* May 19, 1836; Lexington *Intelligencer,* May 20, 1836.

———. "To Melazie, on Parting," Lexington *Intelligencer,* April 4, 1834.

———. "To the *Milton* and the *Ironside,*" *San Luis Advocate,* February 16, 1841.

———. "To My Husband's Miniature," Lexington *Intelligencer,* January 15, 1836; *San Luis Advocate,* December 3, 1840.

———. "We have lost him; he is gone," included in Guy M. Bryan, "Stephen F. Austin: Biography of the Great Empresario . . ." (Clipping, Crosby Papers).

———. "Welcome, Lafayette" in *Visit of Lafayette* . . . (Lexington, Kentucky, 1825).

Kemp, L. W. "Mrs. Angelina B. Eberly," *Southwestern Historical Quarterly,* XXXVI (1932–1933), 193–199.

Leavy, William A. "Memoir of Lexington and its Vicinity, with Some Notice of Many Prominent Citizens and its Institutions of Religion and Learning . . .," *Register of the Kentucky State Historical Society,* Vol. 40 (1942), pp. 107–131, 251–267, 352–375; Vol. 41 (1943), pp. 44–62, 107–137, 250–260, 310–346; Vol. 42 (1944), pp. 26–53.

Mitchell, Samuel. "A Letter to the Hon. Josiah Meigs . . .," *American Monthly and Critical Review,* IV (1818–1819), 47.

Muir, Andrew Forest. "Isaac B. Desha, Fact and Fancy," *Filson Club History Quarterly,* Vol. 30 (1956), pp. 319–323.

Nephew, Caroline Clifford. "America," *Cincinnati Literary Gazette,* II (1824), 72.

Padgett, James A. (ed.). "Letters of James Taylor to the Presidents of the United States," *Register of the Kentucky State Historical Society,* Vol. 34 (1936), pp. 103–130, 251–278, 318–346.

Rafinesque, Constantine S. "A Life of Travels," *Chronica Botanica,* Vol. 8, No. 2 (Spring, 1944). Reprint of original edition, Philadelphia, 1836.

Rudd, Malcolm D. "Men of Worth of Salisbury Birth," No. 45, *Lakeville Journal,* December 6, 1934. Typescript, Holley Coll.-Trans.

"S." Letter to the Editor, *The Transylvanian, or Lexington Literary Journal,* I (1829), 27–28.

Taylor, Bryde Neill. "Women Writers of Texas," Galveston *Daily News,* June 18, 1893.

"W." "Ode Salutaria ad Rev. Dom. Horatium Holleium . . .," *Cincinnati Literary Gazette,* II (1824), 16.

Western Minerva; or American Annals of Knowledge and Literature, Vol. I, No. 1 (January, 1820). Facsimile. New York, P. Smith, 1949.

Winston, James E. "Kentucky and the Independence of Texas," *Southwestern Historical Quarterly,* XV (1912), 27–62.

MUSIC

Holley, Mary Austin, and Wilhelm Iucho. *The Brazos Boat Glee, written by Mrs. Holley. Composed, Arranged, and Dedicated to Henry Austen [sic] Esq., by Wilhelm Iucho.* New York, Firth and Hall, 1838. (Transylvania College Library, Lexington, Kentucky).

——. *The Texan Song of Liberty. Written by Mrs. M. A. Holley. Composed and Dedicated to General Houston, by Wilhelm Iucho.* New York, Dubois and Bacon, *ca.* 1836. (Grosvenor Reference Division, Buffalo and Erie County Public Library, Buffalo, New York).

Iucho, Wilhelm. *Heatherflowers, or Recollections of Scotland. A Favorite Set of Quadrilles arranged for the Pianoforte.* New York, Firth and Hall, *ca.* 1840. (Music Division, Library of Congress, Washington, D.C.).

——. *The Lexington Grand Waltz. Composed and Dedicated to Mrs. Henry Clay, by Wilhelm Iucho.* New York, Firth and Hall, 1834. (Music Division, Library of Congress, Washington, D.C.).

——. *Oh, Lady, Do Not Bid Me Sing. A Song Written, Composed, and Dedicated to Mrs. Holley by Wilhelm Iucho.* New York, Firth and Hall, 1834. (Grosvenor Reference Division, Buffalo and Erie County Public Library, Buffalo, New York).

——. *The Transylvania March. Composed and Dedicated to Mrs. D. Sayre, of Lexington, Kentucky, by Wilhelm Iucho.* New York, W. Dubois, *ca.* 1839. (Music Division, Library of Congress, Washington, D.C.).

PERIODICALS

Boston *Evening Gazette,* 1827.
Brazos Courier (Brazoria, Texas), 1839, 1840.
Civilian and Galveston Gazette, 1843–1844.
Galveston *Daily News,* 1893.
Houston *Telegraph,* 1843.
Kentucky Gazette (Lexington), 1818, 1835–1836.
Kentucky Reporter (Lexington), 1818–1827.
Lakeville Journal (Lakeville, Connecticut), 1934.
Lexington *Herald-Leader,* 1960.
Lexington *Intelligencer,* 1834–1837.
Lexington *Observer and Reporter,* 1834–1836, 1844–1846.
Lexington *Public Advertiser,* 1821.
Louisville Literary Messenger, 1839.
New England Galaxy (Boston), 1827.
New Orleans *Argus,* 1827.
New Orleans *Bee,* 1837.
New Orleans *Courier,* 1827, 1846.

New Orleans *Jeffersonian*, 1845, 1846.
New Orleans Republican, 1844.
Niles Weekly Register (Baltimore), 1827.
Red-Lander (San Augustine, Texas), 1844.
San Luis Advocate, 1840–1841.
Telegraph and Texas Register (Columbia, Texas), 1836–1837, 1843–1844, 1846.
Texas Republican (Brazoria), 1835.
Texas Sentinel (Austin), 1840–1841.
Western Monitor (Lexington), 1819, 1823.

INDEX

Abbreviations HH–Horace Holley
MAH–Mary Austin Holley
SFA–Stephen Fuller Austin

Holley, Edward: 89, 144, 300, 301

Holley, Harriette Williman. SEE Brand, Harriette Williman Holley (Mrs. William Moses)

Holley, Harriette (daughter of John Milton): 91

Holley, Horace: youth and education of: in boyhood, 28, 47, 189; and record at Yale, 28, 67; and influence of President Dwight, 28, 35; and espousal orthodoxy, 30; and College Church, 31; and study of law, 33–35; and study of divinity, 35
—as orator and writer: college debater, 28; college exercise poem, 30; graduation oration, 32; early poems, 37, 55; contributes to scientific journal, 57; public addresses, 73, 87, 93, 98–99, 150–151, 154, 161, 164, 166, 174–175; contributes to theological journal, 88; contributes to literary journals, 94–95, 122–123, 368–369 n 12, 371 n 9, 375 n 29; contributes to newspaper, 124–125; publishes Morrison *Discourse*, 150
—courtship and marriage of: courts Mary Austin, 36–38; love poem to her, 37; letter to her from Newburyport, 40, 369 n 13; marriage to her, 40–41
—as traveller: to Newburyport, 39–40; sightseeing trip to Niagara, 95–96; to Kentucky, 101–112, 114–117; to St. Louis, 131; to East, 146–147, 158, 160–161, 380 n 16; to Nashville, Tennessee, 151–155; to Louisiana, 175–177; plans for European trip, 170–171, 173, 383–384 n 21; to New York, 182–184
—as clergyman: licensed to preach, 40; preparation of sermons, 43, 71–72; pastorate at Greenfield Hill, 49–58 *passim*; manner of preaching, 48, 51–52, 79–80; growing theological liberalism, 55–56, 76–77, 88, 90, 97, 113; preaching tour, 60–66 *passim*; sermons, 62, 64–65, 75–76, 79–80, 87–88, 103–104, 108, 113, 115, 131, 147, 153; pastorate at Hollis Street Church, 65–114 *passim*; political views, 88, 93, 108; chaplain in War of 1812, 89; chaplain of Massachusetts House of Representatives, 93–94

—as educator: skill as teacher, 53; on Harvard Board of Overseers, 73, 94; accepts presidency of Transylvania University, 96–118 *passim*; administrative policies of, 107–108, 110, 111, 116, 117–118, 126, 131, 132, 150–151; relations with faculty, 118, 126–127, 156–157, 167–168; hospitality of, 121–122, 124, 125–126, 163–164; religious and political attacks on, 124–126, 150–151, 155–156, 166–167, 168–169, 315; LL.D. from Cincinnati College, 151; exchanges views on education with Jefferson, 160–161; resignation as president, 168–169, 171–172; plans for European travel school, 170–171; plans for schools in Louisiana, 179–181, 384 n 34; death and burial at sea, 183–184; obituaries, 185–186
—personality and reputation of: appearance, 28, 31, 32, 33, 40, 79, 114; friends at Yale, 28, 33; relations with parents, 28–29, 31–32, 33, 35, 41–47 *passim*, 91, 94; attitude toward MAH, 36, 40, 41, 55, 60, 66, 84, 155; relations with daughter, 66, 87, 143, 158; attitude toward slavery, 123–124, 172, 182; and opinions held by Transylvania students, 149, 174, 380 n 4; Pierpont's *Discourse* on, 185; Caldwell's *Discourse* on, 186, 188, 193; discussion of by later historians, 315, 317; Theodore Clapp an admirer of, 355
—portraits of: by Gilbert Stuart, 113–114; by Matthew Jouett, 133, 379 n 30; by Ralph Earl, 153, 381 n 11; silhouette, 174, 384 n 24
—letters of: to MAH, 40, 60, 62, 64, 78, 87, 90, 91–92, 98, 102–107, 109–111 *passim*, 143, 145, 375 n 3; to Transylvania University, 96, 100; to Harriette Brand, 143, 158, and William Brand, 182, 385 n 38; to Benjamin Bussey, 145; to Orville Holley, 172
—writings of: "An Extract from a College Exercise," 30, 368–369 n 12; "Lines addressed to a beautiful young lady," 37; "Dedication of a Lady's Album," 55; "Investigation of the Facts . . . ," 57; "From a Husband to

239, 246–247, 291, 293, 305, 350, 352, 354, 355, 356, 359, 361; to Henry Clay, 187; to Milton Holley, 187, 188; to Myron Holley, 187; to SFA, 216–217, 226, 238, 239, 241–242, 272, 275, 281; to Thomas F. Leaming, 236; to John Phelps Austin, 240; to Henry Austin, 297, 350; to William Brand, 295; to Edward Holley, 300; to George Hammeken, 300; to Edward Everett, 303; to John G. Tod, 303; to Emily Perry, 324–325, 329, 330; to David G. Burnet, 329–330; to Elizabeth Brand, 357

—writings of: "Of that sweet spot," 93, 123; "Lines written immediately on first beholding Niagara Falls," 95, 123; "It is near to the hour," 123; "Madame de Staël," 128; "Music. A letter," 145, 369 n 22; "Lines by a Lexington Lady on Leaving Cincinnati," 159–160; "On the Death of Miss Susannah Agnes Tibbatts," 173; "On Leaving Kentucky," 173–174, 196–197; "O! had he lived," 184; Caldwell's *Discourse* (compiled by MAH), 193; "Reply to Pestalozzi," 197; "Stranger, you ask," 213, 250; *Texas* (1833), 223–237; "Brazos Boat Song," 228, 297; "Invitation to the Fair," 251; "The circling year," 265; "To My Husband's Miniature," 265–266, 309; "To ———— ————," 279; *Texas* (1836), 273–274; *Texan Song of Liberty,* 274, 279, 284; "We have lost him," 283–284, 342, 398 n 74; "To Melazie, on Parting," 287–288, 310, 393 n 49; "To the *Milton* and the *Ironside,*" 310; "The Invitation," 310; "Oh, how I love the sea," 310; Letter to the Editor, 311–312; "Adieu to San Luis," 312; "The Plea of Texas," 331; Letter to the Editor, 339

Holley, Myron: 27, 43, 46, 141, 187, 188, 370 n 6

Holley, Newman: 46

Holley, Orville: resembles HH, 44; admires MAH, 46; in Greenfield Hill, 50, 53, 59; in New Haven, 61, 63, 64; accompanies MAH to Boston, 69, 71, 78, 87; in Salisbury, 90–92; editor in New York City, 103, 124, 127; MAH's correspondence with, 132, 140; and assistance with memoir on HH, 186, 187, 190, 196; meeting with MAH, 210–211; and assistance with Texas book, 236–237, 240, 241, 243, 244; mentioned, 231, 239, 273

Holley, Sarah Dakin (Mrs. Luther): 31, 43, 45, 46, 78, 91, 187

Hollis Street Church, Boston, Massachusetts: 65–113 *passim,* 138, 142, 147, 185–186, 193, 210, 299, 355, 365

Hollis Street Society. SEE Hollis Street Church, Boston, Massachusetts

Homes, Barzillai: 69, 101

Hopemont: 377 n 7

Hopkins, Matthew: 308, 401 n 7

Hopkinsianism: 45, 56, 62, 88, 370 n 5

Hopkinsville, Kentucky: 154

Hosmer, Mr. (of Middletown, Connecticut): 62

Hot Springs, Virginia: 276

Houston, Sam: as governor of Tennessee, 246; as general of Texas armies, 264; MAH's Texas lyric dedicated to, 274; elected president of Republic of Texas, 277; appoints SFA to cabinet, 277, 278; eulogizes SFA, 382; moves capital, 283, 290; political policies of, 318–321; Lamar's views on, 292, 325–326; Murphy's opinion of, 327; MAH's interview with, 327; Mrs. Eberly's view of, 329, 342, 344; and annexation of Texas, 329, 341; Burnet's opinion of, 330; Andrew Jackson a friend of, 337; mentioned, 261, 292, 306, 325

Houston, Texas: 290, 291, 322, 330

Hubbard, Bela: 8, 9, 17, 18, 87, 369 n 29

Hubbard, Henry: 10, 367 n 8

Hubbart, Mrs. (of Albany, New York): 83

Hubbell, Gershon: 52, 54

Hull, Mrs. (of Boston): 105

Humphreys, Charles: 149

Humphreys, Dr. (of Louisiana): 248

Humphreys, Mrs. (of Kentucky): 197, 198, 245, 383–384 n 21

Hunt, Charlton: 279

MARY AUSTIN HOLLEY
A Biography
by Rebecca Smith Lee
with decorations
by Margaret Al Jumah

Has been set in ten-point Caledonia
leaded two points and printed on Chilli-
cothe, Dresden Pamphlet Adena; manufactured by the University of Texas Printing Division.